ROBERT HOLMAN

Robert Holman is a renowned and celebrated playwright in British theatre. His plays include *Mud* (Royal Court Theatre, 1974); *German Skerries* (Bush Theatre, 1977, and revived at the Orange Tree Theatre, 2016); *Rooting* (Traverse Theatre, 1979); *Other Worlds* (Royal Court Theatre, 1980); *Today* (Royal Shakespeare Company, 1984); *The Overgrown Path* (Royal Court Theatre, 1985); *Making Noise Quietly* (Bush Theatre, 1987, and revived at the Donmar Warehouse, 2012); *Across Oka* (Royal Shakespeare Company, 1988); *Rafts and Dreams* (Royal Court Theatre, 1990); *Bad Weather* (Royal Shakespeare Company, 1998); *Holes in the Skin* (Chichester Festival Theatre, 2003); *Jonah and Otto* (Royal Exchange Theatre, 2008, and revived at Park Theatre, 2014); *A Thousand Stars Explode in the Sky*, co-written with David Eldridge and Simon Stephens (Lyric Theatre, Hammersmith, 2010); and *A Breakfast of Eels* (Print Room at the Coronet, 2015). He has also written a novel, *The Amish Landscape* (1992).

Mike Bartlett
ALBION
BULL
GAME
AN INTERVENTION
KING CHARLES III
SNOWFLAKE
WILD

Howard Brenton
55 DAYS
#AIWW: THE ARREST OF AI WEIWEI
ANNE BOLEYN
BERLIN BERTIE
THE BLINDING LIGHT
CREDITORS & MISS JULIE
    after Strindberg
DANCES OF DEATH *after* Strindberg
DOCTOR SCROGGY'S WAR
DRAWING THE LINE
ETERNAL LOVE
FAUST – PARTS ONE & TWO *after* Goethe
LAWRENCE AFTER ARABIA
NEVER SO GOOD
PAUL
THE RAGGED TROUSERED
    PHILANTHROPISTS *after* Tressell
THE SHADOW FACTORY

Jez Butterworth
THE FERRYMAN
JERUSALEM
JEZ BUTTERWORTH PLAYS: ONE
JEZ BUTTERWORTH PLAYS: TWO
MOJO
THE NIGHT HERON
PARLOUR SONG
THE RIVER
THE WINTERLING

Caryl Churchill
BLUE HEART
CHURCHILL PLAYS: THREE
CHURCHILL PLAYS: FOUR
CHURCHILL PLAYS: FIVE
CHURCHILL: SHORTS
CLOUD NINE
DING DONG THE WICKED
A DREAM PLAY *after* Strindberg
DRUNK ENOUGH TO SAY I LOVE YOU?
ESCAPED ALONE
FAR AWAY
HERE WE GO
HOTEL
ICECREAM
LIGHT SHINING IN BUCKINGHAMSHIRE
LOVE AND INFORMATION
MAD FOREST
A NUMBER
PIGS AND DOGS
SEVEN JEWISH CHILDREN
THE SKRIKER
THIS IS A CHAIR
THYESTES *after* Seneca
TRAPS

Robert Holman
BAD WEATHER
A BREAKFAST OF EELS
GERMAN SKERRIES
HOLES IN THE SKIN
JONAH AND OTTO
MAKING NOISE QUIETLY

Stephen Jeffreys
THE CLINK
THE CONVICT'S OPERA *after* John Gay
A GOING CONCERN
I JUST STOPPED BY TO SEE THE MAN
THE LIBERTINE
STEPHEN JEFFREYS: PLAYS

Ayub Khan Din
AYUB KHAN DIN: PLAYS ONE
EAST IS EAST
LAST DANCE AT DUM DUM
NOTES ON FALLING LEAVES
RAFTA, RAFTA...
TO SIR, WITH LOVE *after* Braithwaite

Lucy Kirkwood
BEAUTY AND THE BEAST
    with Katie Mitchell
BLOODY WIMMIN
THE CHILDREN
CHIMERICA
HEDDA *after* Ibsen
IT FELT EMPTY WHEN THE
    HEART WENT AT FIRST BUT
    IT IS ALRIGHT NOW
LUCY KIRKWOOD PLAYS: ONE
MOSQUITOES
NSFW
TINDERBOX

Liz Lochhead
BLOOD AND ICE
DRACULA *after* Stoker
EDUCATING AGNES ('The School
    for Wives') *after* Molière
GOOD THINGS
LIZ LOCHHEAD: FIVE PLAYS
MARY QUEEN OF SCOTS GOT
    HER HEAD CHOPPED OFF
MEDEA *after* Euripides
MISERYGUTS & TARTUFFE *after* Molière
PERFECT DAYS
THEBANS
THON MAN MOLIÈRE

Conor McPherson
DUBLIN CAROL
McPHERSON PLAYS: ONE
McPHERSON PLAYS: TWO
McPHERSON PLAYS: THREE
THE NIGHT ALIVE
PORT AUTHORITY
THE SEAFARER
SHINING CITY
THE VEIL
THE WEIR

Enda Walsh
ARLINGTON
BALLYTURK
BEDBOUND & MISTERMAN
DELIRIUM
DISCO PIGS & SUCKING DUBLIN
ENDA WALSH PLAYS: ONE
ENDA WALSH PLAYS: TWO
LAZARUS *with* David Bowie
MISTERMAN
THE NEW ELECTRIC BALLROOM
ONCE
PENELOPE
THE SMALL THINGS
ROALD DAHL'S THE TWITS
THE WALWORTH FARCE

ROBERT HOLMAN

Plays: One

The Natural Cause
Mud
Other Worlds
Today
The Overgrown Path

Introduced by the author

NICK HERN BOOKS
London
www.nickhernbooks.co.uk

A Nick Hern Book

Robert Holman Plays: One first published in Great Britain as a paperback original in 2019 by Nick Hern Books Limited, The Glasshouse, 49a Goldhawk Road, London W12 8QP

Cover image: Redcar Steelworks from North Gare Sands, Hartlepool (Mike Kipling Photography/Alamy Stock Photo)

Designed and typeset by Nick Hern Books, London
Printed in the UK by Mimeo Ltd, Huntingdon, Cambridgeshire PE29 6XX

ISBN   978 1 85459 856 0

Contents

To Nathalie

Introduction
Robert Holman

Mud is the first play I wrote that had an interval. I was twenty-one.
I was used to writing plays in exercise books and would stop when I got
to the last page, so the plays were as long as the pages in the book. A
little further back in time, there had been sketches for a school review,
six and seven minutes long, done in imitation of Cambridge Footlights,
and a short play for a group of girls in Middlesbrough Youth Theatre.
I left Yorkshire when I was nineteen and stayed with a school friend in
Camden Town. I slept on an air bed. One night a bullet came through
the window, made a little hole in the glass, and passed over my head.
A prostitute lived below, but I never found out what the bullet was about.
In the kitchen in Camden Town, in a notepad and then on the portable
typewriter my parents bought me, I wrote a play which a few months
later went on in a lunchtime theatre in Edinburgh. It lasted nearly an hour
and was my first professional production. The play was a sort of fantasy
about an old man visiting a graveyard at night, and the critic of the
Scotsman newspaper said it was clearly written by a bitter old man. I was
still only nineteen. I have wondered if I might one day write about the
bullet in Camden Town, but a play has not come along.

Mud was written in Belsize Park. I had got there by way of Westbourne
Park, where I had found a room overlooking the railway to Paddington.
There were more very small spiders living around the window than
I had seen before or since, as well as untroubled mice running across
the floor. There was an old, broken wardrobe. The window was opaque
with dirt. I put down my case, sat on the bed and looked about, got
depressed, and stayed two hours. Back in Camden Town in desperation
I rang my mother, wondering if I should go home to Yorkshire, but she
had heard, from a distant relative, about a family in Belsize Park who
sometimes had a room they let out. I went to Belsize Park for a week
and stayed seven years. All the early plays were written there, in a
bright room at the top of the house overlooking the garden, with
Hampstead Heath nearby to walk across and the space to think.
Sometimes in life we are most grateful for ordinary things, if giving
someone a room to live in is ordinary. The room set the course for the
rest of my life. The rent was a few pounds a week, and very often I did
not pay it. All my life I have struggled with money, and it started then.

Mud was written in the evenings and in the early hours of the mornings, because I worked during the day on Paddington Station, selling newspapers and magazines. I was not a clever boy, but sometimes I had a good instinct about the best thing to do, and I was learning to trust myself. Intuition had told me to get an easy job, one where I did not have to think too deeply. If that sounds rude about the bookstall or the other people working there, I do not mean it to be. It's the only 'proper' job I have ever had, and to begin with I did not tell them I was also trying to write. The first draft of *Mud* was written in longhand using the fountain pen I had sat my school exams with. I made it up as I went along, with no idea of where it might end up. I put down the things I saw in my imagination and wrote what I heard people say. The dialogue was character-driven and the people in the play led me. If there were days when they said nothing it was a nuisance, and I would do my best to look at the empty page for half an hour before putting away the pen. If too many days like this came one after the other, it would be frustrating and then I would get depressed. I longed for the skills of a proper writer. My writing was in charge of me, rather than me being in charge of it.

Mud was written when writing was a hobby of mine. There were two drafts of the play written in ink, the second one bearing very little resemblance to the first, because all I was trying to do was to get a sense of who the characters were, and this was changing as I wrote them. Men were becoming women, women men, someone of nineteen was becoming sixty and vice versa. At some point a consistency emerged, as much decided by them as decided by me. It was as if I knew these people as well as I knew anybody who was actually alive. By now I was typing the play. It was still changing as I went on, still surprising me. I would sometimes look at my watch and it would be past three o'clock in the morning. One day Mrs Bradshaw, who owned the house, came up the stairs with a felt pad to put underneath the typewriter because their bedroom was below, and the clatter of the typewriter keys was keeping them awake.

The Natural Cause was the second full-length play I wrote, but it went on three months before *Mud* in the summer of 1974. On Paddington Station we used to give rude customers as many small coins in their change as we possibly could. We wore badges with our names on. One day a stranger asked to speak to me. I expected to be told off or even sacked, but it was a theatre director, who asked if I might be free to write a play for him. He had wanted Howard Brenton, but Howard Brenton was busy and had told him about me. Still standing on the

platform of the station, the director explained he had a slot. The play
would need to be written in six weeks. *Mud* had taken me over a year
to write and I was usually very slow. But who would say no to this? So,
I said yes. I would be given money for writing, which I was not used
to. When could I start? I said I could start straight away.

The Natural Cause was the play that began to turn my hobby into a
job. I had a friend at school whose younger brother had a pet rabbit,
and the family had eaten it one Sunday dinner without telling him, and
I started to write about this. A more apt description might be to say that
I messed about writing dialogue in a notepad, and sometimes this
particular boy was in my head. He did not have a room of his own but
slept downstairs on the sofa. One day he was found twenty miles from
home on the road to Whitby with no idea how he had got there or who
he was. I set the play in London not in Yorkshire, though when the
characters said something I still heard my own accent. As with *Mud*
I made it up as I went on. Some evenings I would write three or four
pages and other evenings three or four lines, and then cross out most of
it. I had to be taken in by what I was writing and get lost in it.
Sometimes it would be like bashing my head against a brick wall. At
the end of two weeks it dawned on me that there would not be a play if
I was still selling newspapers because I needed every minute of the day
to try to write. I spoke to the manager of the bookstall and told him
what I was doing. He said to come back when I was finished, and if he
had not managed to replace me, there would still be a job. I had
decided I wanted to be a writer when I was twelve years old because
I liked books but told no one about this. All I had done was write a few
dreadful poems when I was an adolescent and the first pages of short
stories for children. Now I was a writer, with no idea how I had got to
this place, and I did not feel like one.

The Natural Cause was a worrying play to write. If writing is a hobby
it matters little if there are days when you cannot do it very well. I had
four weeks left to finish a play, and a day with nothing done is a day
empty forever. I spent all one Monday walking up and down across the
Heath, all the time wondering how I was going to lie my way out of
writing the play. If I told the director I was ill that was better than
saying I could not do it. Or I could just disappear. The rain started. It
came down in heavy sheets and was soon penetrating the leaves and
branches of trees, so standing under them was pointless. On Parliament
Hill it looked as if London was drowning. As it got towards evening
and lights came on, the city was resplendent. For less than a minute, in

the hardest of the rain, London went turquoise, a colour I had not seen it go before or seen since. I stood on one of the wooden benches to get a clearer view, and decided it was better to write rubbish than to write nothing at all, and to work out the lies I would tell another time.

The Natural Cause filled the next three weeks and I wrote the best quality rubbish I could manage every morning and into the afternoon until even rubbish was difficult and my brain was numb. When there was a week to go, I bought some carbon paper, put it between sheets of Croxley Script and stated to type up the play. As had been the case with *Mud*, the play changed all the time as I typed it, and I always went with the changes even if I had no idea what they were about or whether I understood them. It was the writing itself that gave me the energy to continue. Using two sheets of carbon paper gave me three copies. The director lived an hour's walk from the top of Hampstead Heath, so I put a copy of the play in an envelope and took it to him, then walked back to King's Cross to get the train to Yorkshire for the weekend. He said to ring him on Sunday evening when I was back in London, and he would have read the play. There was a Swiss cheese plant on the landing near my room in Belsize Park, and this is where the phone was as well. On Sunday evening I sat there plucking up the courage to dial the director's number. I was still the schoolboy who expected to be told off for poor work. I was going to say some of my family had been killed in a bus crash a few weeks before because there had actually been a crash in the Yorkshire Dales, and it was on the news. The director, Ron Daniels, answered the phone. I said, 'It's Robert.' I knew I had let everyone down. He said what was I doing tomorrow, and could I come over to his place because he'd like to talk about casting. There are very few moments in life so big that they can be counted on the fingers of one hand, but this is one of them. The play did not change my life; the play being thought competent and getting a production did change it.

The Natural Cause and *Mud* are by and large set outside, where somehow the horizon, and the longing to go it, even beyond it, is important. They are plays in which at least one character is looking to escape to another world. In *The Natural Cause* when Mary and Barry are playing cricket on Brighton beach another world might be possible for them, but in the end, it is not to be, and Mary is left on her own. In *Mud*, George is looking back on his life, the door to a better world now closed, whereas for Alan and Pauline the door is open, or they think it is. Alan believes he can shape his future and the world is at his feet. In both plays the women do nothing wrong but lose their men, and for them the world is broken. *Mud* is set on the Yorkshire Moors of my childhood, *The Natural Cause* in London where I had been living for only a short time, and in both plays someone dies. It might be that in *The Natural Cause* Barry gives up on life, he no longer sees what is possible for him, or it could be he is ill. In rehearsal the actors and director talked about him being schizophrenic, which, when I wrote it, had not been in my mind, yet I could see it made sense, and I later learned the boy in Yorkshire who unknowingly ate his pet rabbit was indeed diagnosed with schizophrenia. It is odd how writing plays works. At least for me there is a lot of luck in the way all the aspects of the drama come together. I cannot explain how this works, but I am pleased that it does, because it means I can write intelligently now and again about things I know very little about. Barry does not know he is schizophrenic, and I shared this insight, or the lack of it, with him.

The Natural Cause actors went to rehearse the play along the canal near the zoo and Camden Town. It was the first time I had been in the company of actors for more than a few minutes. Natasha Pyne, who was playing Mary, had put a metal calliper on her leg and dyed her hair a mousy brown. In the following days, it was fascinating to see how she went about making Mary real. In the end an actor has to take a character away from the writer and to own it for themselves. The writer must let this happen if the production is to be good, but I was to learn it can be painful, like losing a friend. As rehearsals progressed, the play seemed to have less and less to do with me. The play belonged to the actors. At a run-through I sat gobsmacked that I had anything to do with it, let alone had written it. The scene where Mary sits on a park bench without getting up for twenty minutes and talks to her friend was riveting. In performance it would be slightly different every time the actor did it. A play is not a static thing. Together the company found a depth in the drama that I didn't know was there, and it was a revelation.

The Natural Cause went on a few weeks before Chris Parr directed *Mud* at the Royal Court. When I first went to Sloane Square, the writer Ann Jellicoe met me on the steps outside and said, 'Welcome to our theatre.' It was extraordinary to have someone waiting for me at the most important theatre in the world; at least it was in my head. We walked along a corridor and upstairs, passing posters of famous new plays. I had read these plays at school, and they had become part of my learning. I was twenty-one when I first went to the Royal Court. I knew little about life and even less about writing great plays. But here you are special. The building is damaged by the writers who have tried to

kick it down, certainly metaphorically if not also literally on occasions.
Writers are not expected to be polite or to be grateful. This theatre has
a writer's stink about it. They had had my play for a month, all had
read it, thought it was interesting, did not like the title, and would I like
a commission to write another play? It would be for £100. I said yes to
everything that was suggested, left the building, walked back to
Belsize Park to give time for my nerves and excitement to calm down,
and did not write another play for the Royal Court for nine years. This
was because, in good part, the importance of the building loomed large
in my head and I was inhibited by its history.

Other Worlds took me three years to write. By now there had also been
plays written for the Traverse in Edinburgh and the Bush in London.
Occasionally there had been kind comments from people who were
important in the theatre and the Arts Council. I was mostly living on Arts
Council money being given directly to me for two years. To these people
it must have seemed as if I was beginning to be a successful dramatist,
but it did not feel that way to me, and, rather than being flattered by their
compliments, I was inhibited by them. I was still messing about writing
in notepads with the old fountain pen and throwing most of it away. This
is not what a serious writer should do every morning, but if I tried to be
serious all I did was stare at a blank page. One day I read a newspaper
interview with David Storey, who talked about his writing being intuitive
and instinctive, and for a few hours a heavy weight lifted off my
shoulders because he was a proper writer. I was not enjoying writing
plays. The pressure of trying to write a good and proper play had become
too great. Also, I was used to being not very bright, thinking of myself as
dim because at school I had failed in most things, and it was a shock
when some people told me I was clever, and the plays were intelligent.
All sorts of mixed-up and jumbled thoughts were going through my
mind. I would go down the street feeling dismal and useless. There was
day after day when my eyes were watery with despair and I found it
difficult to focus on the world in front of me. I was happiest being
ordinary, yet wanted to write brilliant plays. I was happy being a failure,
and yet I wanted to be successful. Somehow *Other Worlds* came out of
this disorder and confusion. It is my attempt to write a 'great play',
which is why it has three acts. It is me trying to write about ideas. I did
a lot of research, and it was in the British Library that I saw a first
edition of Jethro Tull's *Horse-Hoeing Husbandry*, first published in
1731. Doing this kind of thing was new to me because I was used to
writing about people and making them up, but now I was writing a 'great
play' and research must be done. The more I learned, the more difficult it

became to write. My intuition left me. I would write three words and cross two of them out.

Other Worlds is set in Robin Hood's Bay on the North Yorkshire coast. I was in the churchyard there one morning looking at the names on gravestones and saw the name Storm on several on them. Before this I had been setting the play in Hartlepool, on the coast about twenty miles north of Robin Hood's Bay. Storm gave me the idea of moving the story these few miles south and even starting the play with a storm. I made the decision on the spot to stop researching and to make it up, because the research was inhibiting me. I told myself to fill an exercise book with dialogue without stopping, as I had very first done at school, and to stop worrying about writing a great play. I would write a great play if a great play wanted to be written by me. Out of this worry came *Other Worlds*. It is not the great play I hoped to write, but I do not care one jot. We went up to Robin Hood's Bay for a few days to rehearse it on the beach. One night we did the storm at the beginning of the play with Richard Wilson, the director, shouting instructions along the beach; but no one could hear him over the noise of the waves, so the actors made it up. The drinkers in the local pub came out to watch and then involved themselves in the scene. The theatre was funny once more. I decided not to take the company to the graveyard or show them the name Storm, which was private to me. I am mostly a private writer, which means my plays mean different things to different people, even though the theatre is a public place. My plays are not driven by a single ideology or an idea, there is no right or wrong in them, or one easy explanation. They are about what you want them to be about, and this changes. I did manage to find something private in *Other Worlds*, and yet it is the most public play I have written and will ever write.

Today was written for the Royal Shakespeare Company to stage in The Other Place in Stratford, then little more than a tin hut. I was asked to write the play for thirteen actors who were on tour with *Romeo and Juliet* and *A Midsummer Night's Dream*, and I went to meet them in Milton Keynes. As had been the case with *The Natural Cause*, there was a date for a play to begin rehearsing – it was even in the brochure – but not a word was written. If *Other Worlds* had been a marathon to write, then this was going to be a sprint. I saw the actors once or twice more as the tour went on, and then spent a month with them in Stratford as they did the two Shakespeares in the tin hut and played cricket outside in costume. A ball would sometimes land on the tin roof and clatter down during a performance. It was the first time I had worked for a big company like the RSC, so it took me a while of

feeling shy to find my feet and to understand the company just expected
me to get on with it without fuss. In taking me for granted, the RSC was
being respectful, but it took me a while to realise it. I sometimes went to
the actors' other rehearsals, saw technical run-throughs on the big stage,
had lunch in the green room, but mostly spent time with them in the pub
in the evenings and, at weekends, long into the night when the pub doors
were closed to the public. The actors would ask what I was going to
write about, and I would say that I had no idea, which was true. There is
a small zoo a short taxi-ride from Stratford, and I went there because
I had this idea of them all playing animals. I got a notepad and started to
write, giraffes, elephants, anteaters, monkeys (surely not again, I had
done that in *Other Worlds*), alligators, a heron, a hippopotamus, skunks,
a swarm of bees, zebras – and so the list went on. I had a more sensible
moment and asked the actors what they might like, if there was
something they wanted to do on stage and never had, if there was a part
they wanted to play, or a character they would like me to try to write.
I also asked them if there was anything they did not want to do. All the
while I was learning about this group of men and women and wondering
how to write a play for them. I had written for actors before, for John
Normington at the Bush and Paul Copley in *Other Worlds* amongst
others, but writing for a big group of actors was a completely different
challenge. I knew it was important they all had something to do, had at
least one moment on stage that belonged to them, and this loomed large
in my head every time I thought about the play and how to bring it all
together. Unfortunately, the animals stayed in my head, and back home
in London I tried to write them. I had many pets as a child but was not a
zoologist. It was crazy. With six weeks to go before rehearsals were to
start there was still not a play. I rang Bill Alexander, who was to direct it,
and we met in a pub by the Barbican. It was the day some of the biggest
hailstones ever to fall on north London broke windows, and the sky was
black. Inside the pub I asked if the RSC had a plan B in the event that
I did not come up with a play. If so, it was time to implement it. Bill said
not to worry, there was time yet and asked me what I was interested in,
what books I had been reading. I told him about the Spanish Civil War.
He said why not write about that. I left the pub, feeling buoyant when
I had expected to be miserable because I had failed, and got drenched to
the bone on the way home. The animals play went in the bin like so
much that I have written. It is a play I wanted to write, but it did not want
to be written by me. I was still learning this lesson.

Today is a lucky play. It is lucky that I managed to get some of it down
on paper, when at times I might have struggled, and even luckier that

we had eight weeks to rehearse it. I took the typewriter up to Stratford. In the mornings I rewrote the play scene by scene whilst the actors rehearsed the old scene. The RSC put me up in a cottage on Waterside, opposite the Royal Shakespeare Theatre, and sometimes tourists would look in through the window at me typing. When a scene was finished, I took it to the rehearsal room, and the actors put the old scene in the bin. In this way, from the first scene to the last over the course of a month, the play was written. It says much about the actors' tolerance that they went along with all this without once complaining. I would not have written a ventriloquist, a nun, or have a Guisborough man eat raw eggs, had I not been trying to find a special moment for each of the actors. Actors are brave people and *Today* owes much to the company it was written for. All plays are pieces of energy, and how they come about, the places they are written and in what circumstances, always says something about them. *Today* was written quickly. I did not have much time to think, and sometimes this is the best way to write, because thinking is inhibiting, if you are me. I still want to write a play where I do not think at all. *Today* was written in the moment, line by line, wherever the dialogue led me, rather than me leading it. It is a history play, but not one with an overarching idea or ideology. It is a play driven by the needs of its characters. I am simply not clever enough to write about history in an original way. If I might generalise for a moment, there is always at least one person somewhere in the world who is cleverer than we are. These are the people who come up with new thoughts about history – or anything else for that matter. On the other hand, our emotions, our feelings, are always slightly different and special to each of us. You might fall in love in a different way to me or be scared by very different things. Sometimes living is easy, but often it is painful. There are times when we feel alone even with friends about us. I was learning to try to write about all this and to know it is the stuff of life. If I have anything special as a writer, and you will decide if I have or not, it is writing characters who stay in the mind for an hour or two when the play is over; and they stay in the mind because the people in the plays are like you with your fears. They are my fears, too.

The Overgrown Path was commissioned by the Royal Court while *Other Worlds* was on at the theatre and playing to small audiences. A talking monkey had not been appreciated by the newspapers who came to review it. I read the notices for *Other Worlds* sitting on a hospital bed, because a few weeks before I had cut my finger and I needed to have a small operation. The nuisance of cutting my finger

turned out to be useful when I used it in the opening scenes of *Today*.
All my plays are a mixture of memory and imagination, and they have
mostly used landscapes that I know well. I was born and brought up on
a farm on the moors in north Yorkshire. Middlesbrough and the Tees
Estuary, with the chemical and steel industry close by, were twenty
miles away. All this is in the first plays I wrote, but in *The Overgrown
Path* I wanted to try to write about a different landscape. The play is
set in Greece, on an island I had been to but did not know well. The
play took me a year to write. I tried to write the Greek landscape as
best as I could, but I was also free with it in my imagination.

The Overgrown Path is a play with faults. The way my plays are
written in the moment means that they will not be perfect. They can be
strong because of the moment but also weak because of it. If I write a
scene one morning it might be slightly different if I write it the next
morning. It is down to luck, but I have learned more about the world
from writing plays in this way than I have from anything else in life.
I have surprised myself, and now and again I hope I have surprised an
audience. If an audience does not know what is coming next, it is
because I also did not know what was coming next. My writing
involves a lot of trust. I have to trust myself that something interesting
will come out of me next morning and know that I can put it down
using words. Words are everything. To trust oneself to find the right
word is sometimes a challenge. The thing that matters most to me is
the English language and how it can be used to tell a story.

The Overgrown Path begins in Japan with children performing a school
play about the dropping of the atomic bomb on Nagasaki at the end of
the Second World War. Perhaps it is a sign of madness to write such a
scene? It is certainly a difficult scene for a theatre to do because it
requires a class of Japanese children. I was not and never will be an
entirely sensible writer. The devil comes into me when I write. There is
another moment in the play when a tree is hit by lightning and kills
Sarah. It is a play about the randomness of life. It is about how choices
make us sometimes, rather than us making choices, and about how
difficult it can be to go back to the place we came from, to be the person
we used to be. It is about Daniel's guilt. It is about how knowledge
cannot be destroyed. This is what I think, but my opinion is no more
valid than your opinion, and it might also be about what you want it to
be about. I am trying to say I am not a political writer or someone who
examines the important social issues of the day, where one thing is right
and the other thing is wrong. I like to believe my plays have a moral

conscience, but that is all. In writing *The Overgrown Path* I got rid of a lot of responsibilities that I thought a writer must have to the world. A writer has no responsibilities whatsoever, other than to themselves, their integrity and intelligence. My plays are not about the world as it is, but about the world as I would like it to be and wish it was. In this way my plays are romances.

Spring 2019

THE NATURAL CAUSE

The Natural Cause was first performed at the Cockpit Theatre, London, on 27 May 1974. The cast was as follows:

MARY JACKSON	Natasha Pyne
BARRY JACKSON	Nicholas Ball
COLIN THOMPSON	George Sweeney
DAVE MILLWARD	Derek Thompson
JUNE WILSON	Maureen Sweeney
TOM WILSON	Peter Maycock

Director   Ron Daniels

Characters

A PATHOLOGIST
BARRY JACKSON
MARY JACKSON, *his wife*
COLIN THOMPSON
DAVE MILLWARD
JUNE WILSON
TOM WILSON, *her husband*
BRIAN JONES, *a passer-by*
A POLICE CONSTABLE

The voices of
LYN JACKSON, *Barry's mother*
A BOY, *Barry, aged eight*
BARRY'S FATHER
A BIOLOGY TEACHER
A MAN

The play was written to be performed by six actors.

ACT ONE

The play is an autopsy. It should take place in a mortuary on a white tiled floor.

Scene One

A mortuary.

A pair of white wellingtons by a hat stand. On the hat stand a full-length green plastic apron. A short distance away a small table. On the table; a clipboard and biro; a pair of rubber gloves; a Black and Decker drill; several scalpels. By the table a chair. The table and chair should be made of stainless steel.

The PATHOLOGIST *enters.*

PATHOLOGIST. Ladies, gentlemen.

He sits and consults the clipboard.

A pause.

The PATHOLOGIST *is in his early thirties. He wears a dark suit. He speaks slowly, matter-of-factly, clinically. Calls.*

Would you bring in the body.

TWO PORTERS *wheel on the body of* BARRY JACKSON. *It is covered by a white sheet. They exit.*

A light comes up on the body.

It is usual to consider the cause of death under three divisions. Firstly, the immediate cause, that is, why the patient died today and not tomorrow. Here a pathologist will often find incidental complications of the main disease such as broncho-pneumonia terminating a prolonged nervous illness.

The house lights dim to half.

Over speakers the voice of LYN JACKSON, BARRY'*s mother. She speaks slowly.*

The PATHOLOGIST *proceeds to follow his usual routine. That is;*
he takes off his jacket and hangs it on the stand; he takes off his
shoes and puts on the wellingtons; he rolls up his sleeves; he takes
off his tie.

LYN. I remember, he was a normal baby. Bonny. Red cheeks. A Heinz
baby, really. I entered him in a bonny baby competition once, at
Margate it was, but we never won. Couldn't control him really.
Normal upbringing. He had a pet rabbit like every other little child.

A slight pause.

We had a rabbit in our backyard. It was the last, well, last year of
his life. Well –

A slight pause.

I mean he forgot to feed his rabbit, like any other lad. Last year he
was bad. We had to put up with him.

The PATHOLOGIST *hangs his tie on the stand.*

PATHOLOGIST. Secondly, the principal cause. (*He stamps into his*
wellingtons.) That is, why the patient died now and not in ten years'
time. This is the most important in the chain of causes to get right,
for it is upon these that civilised countries base their international
statistics regarding causes of death. Certification must be accurate
or this whole elaborate structure would be unsound.

Again LYN*'s voice.*

The PATHOLOGIST *continues to prepare for the post-mortem; he*
consults the clipboard and notes something down; he stands, thinks
for a moment; he places his shoes neatly by the stand; he puts on
the apron.

LYN. He was very fond of animals, was Barry. Loved pet shops. When
he was a boy.

A slight pause.

I remember, he would be about twelve, come home from school and
tears were like flooding in his eyes. Turned out some hooligan had
gone round the biology class and stabbed all the white mice to death
with the point of a compass. Killed them, dead. Barry was all upset.
Said he'd seen all these little mice lying in a heap on this table.
Bound to be upsetting, that's what I thought. His dad told him to
grow up.

The PATHOLOGIST *puts on the rubber gloves.*

PATHOLOGIST. Thirdly, the contributory causes. Contributory causes must be looked at and examined for they help to explain deaths in which the first two findings seem inadequate.

Houselights dim to blackout.

Again LYN*'s voice.*

The PATHOLOGIST *pulls the sheet from the body; he counts* BARRY*'s teeth, measures his head circumference and the length of his body. He writes on the clipboard.*

A pause.

He goes to the table.

LYN. Don't think he got on at school, really. Never seemed to.

A slight pause.

Last year – last two years really – last three, he would, you know, know –

A slight pause.

Funny. He used to stare at himself in the mirror, just stare, for hours, looking, looking at his face. Get steamed up over things. Like a kettle. Thump the wall with his fist and leave dirty patches on the wallpaper. Throw things. Bottles. Old Ever Ready batteries. I couldn't do nothing. Mary couldn't do nothing. I liked Mary. She was a nice girl.

The PATHOLOGIST *picks up a scalpel from the table. He goes to the body.*

A slight pause.

He moves to make the first incision.

Blackout.

Scene Two

Brighton's beach.

The lights pull up to reveal MARY. *She is bending down to pick up a small cricket bat.*

MARY *is twenty. She is small and has a white round face with dull red cheeks. She limps slightly and had a metal calliper on her left leg.*

MARY *looks.*

MARY. Barry? (*She calls louder.*) Barry! You playing at silly buggers again? Barry. Where are you? Come on. You're supposed to grow out of hide and seek at infant school.

A slight pause.

Barry? I know you can hear. (*To herself.*) Silly sod.

She stares off.

Couldn' half do with a choc-ice.

BARRY *enters in shorts and shirt. He creeps up behind her.*

BARRY *is twenty-two. He is very tall and extremely thin. Lanky, bony. Long thin legs. Long arms. Long fingers. Long face with high cheekbones.*

He puts his hands over MARY's *eyes.* MARY *jumps.*

Don't tell me – Mr Universe?

BARRY. No.

MARY. Boy Wonder?

BARRY. Yes and no.

MARY. The Lone Ranger?

BARRY. Yes.

BARRY *takes his hands away.*

Right, bowl.

MARY. No.

BARRY. Bowl.

MARY. I'm used to netball.

BARRY. Netball, cricket, what's the difference?

MARY. Want me to buy you a dictionary?

BARRY (*trying to take the bat*). Come on, bowl.

MARY (*pulling the bat from him*). Oh no, if we play, I bat.

BARRY (*taking the bat*). Not for ladies.

He stands waiting for MARY *to bowl.*

At school I was always number one. Number one. Slogger Jackson. Trophies. Ribbons. Six. Respected for my upper cuts. Slip fielder. Bowl.

MARY. How about putting? You can dig a little hole and I'll putt. I'll be a proper golfer.

BARRY. No.

MARY. Putt, putt away, because I'm sick of you hitting the ball to the bloody sea.

BARRY. Hit a bloody ship one of these times.

MARY. Sick.

BARRY. Not my fault.

MARY. Fault?

BARRY. If you can't play.

MARY. Makes it sound like a musical instrument. Like, play piano. Let's just sit.

BARRY. Just once more. There's a man over there, I keep trying to hit him one on the head. Bald.

MARY. I'm sitting. (*She sits in the deckchair.*)

BARRY. Come on.

A pause.

BARRY *sits.*

What's up with you?

MARY. What's up *with* you?

BARRY. Sod, nothing.

MARY. Nothing? All this bloody running about, like an athlete sprinter, or something. It's not right, for me.

A slight pause.

Baby in my body. Stomach. Might damage it. Don't want a damaged baby.

BARRY. Alright.

MARY. Yeh?

Slight pause.

BARRY. Yeh, looked in a book. Says you can run. Run.

MARY. No more looked in a book than you have flown to the moon.

BARRY. Been up there. (*He laughs.*)

MARY. It's important not to get distressed. Leads to problems.

A slight pause.

BARRY. I was good at cricket.

MARY. Like you are at nuclear physics? Power stations, and that?

BARRY. Fuck off. (*He stands.*)

A pause.

I was.

MARY *looks at him.*

MARY. I know you were.

BARRY (*looking at her*). Yeh.

A slight pause.

BARRY *sits.*

MARY. Not talked about the baby for a long time now.

BARRY (*friendly*). What's there to bloody talk about?

MARY. Things.

BARRY. Like what things?

MARY. Just, things. Names.

BARRY. Not bothered.

MARY. Ought to be.

BARRY. What?

MARY. Bothered. Names.

BARRY. Call it what you want.

MARY. It's not an *it*; it's a person. My baby.

BARRY. Call it Shit. (*Laughs.*)

MARY. Funny eh?

BARRY. Yeh. (*He stops laughing.*)

   A slight pause.

MARY. I thought about Barbara.

   A pause.

   I want it – Barbara – now. Didn't at first. Do now.

   A slight pause.

BARRY. Yeh, I do.

MARY. True?

BARRY. Didn't have to marry you, did I. You bowl?

MARY. No but –

BARRY. Bowl.

MARY. Wouldn't have minded being called Barbara myself. You what?

BARRY. Bowl.

MARY. Long as you don't hit it to the bloody sea.

BARRY. Won't.

MARY. Yeh?

BARRY. Won't.

MARY. Right, long as you don't.

   BARRY *bats.* MARY *throws the ball underarm. The ball is mimed.*
   BARRY *hits the ball a long way. They watch.*

   It's in the sea.

BARRY. As they would say on the radio, fine stroke for six.

MARY. Piss off.

BARRY. From a lady.

MARY. Promised.

BARRY. Promised what?

MARY. You know.

BARRY. Not to hit the fuckin' ball? Well, I did. Like hitting the fuckin' ball. So bastard, you.

> MARY *walks away from him.*

Fine day this is turning out to be. About as exciting as staring at a blank bloody telly.

MARY. Whose fault's that?

BARRY. Not mine.

MARY. Not mine.

> *A slight pause.*

And that house gives me the bloody hump.

> *A slight pause.*

BARRY. I just like hitting the bloody ball, nothing wrong in that.

MARY. And I don't care?

BARRY. No, you don't.

MARY. Nice to know.

> *A pause.*

BARRY. Can't help it if I'm good at cricket.

MARY. Have to bloody prove it, don't you?

BARRY. Hope the baby drops dead from your cunt. (*He laughs.*) A half-formed baby. (*He laughs, saliva dripping down his chin.*)

MARY (*shouting*). SHUT UP!

> *Silence.*

You talk sometimes. The way you –

> *A pause.*

Go on. People hear.

A pause.

Go on about –

BARRY *turns to face her.*

BARRY. Don't feel sorry.

MARY. Didn't for half a second imagine you would.

BARRY. Cry if you want. Little tears. Like one of those dolls, that cries. Go on. My baby as well, can talk about it in the way I want to.

MARY. One month of married bliss.

BARRY. Yeh.

For a moment they stare at each other. Then BARRY *turns and exits.*

A pause.

MARY *sits.*

A pause.

BARRY *returns carrying two choc-ices.*

Bought you this.

They eat in silence.

MARY. First time we've been out since we were married. Brighton.

BARRY. Came here when I was a lad.

MARY. On your own?

BARRY. Yeh. Jumped the train. Didn't buy a ticket. Should have been at the fuckin' school. Fuckin' lessons. Learning about history, and that. Iron ages. Ape men. Tests. Came here. Sums. Didn't like it. Liked it here, only trouble was you had to run like hell after nipping through the ticket barrier. Bloody guards, shouting. (*Laughs.*)

MARY. On your own?

BARRY. Digging the sand and catching little crabs. Stamping on them. (*He laughs, saliva dripping down his chin.*) Yeh. (*He turns to face her.*) It was good. Didn't kill like, just press them into the sand and watch them struggle away. (*He laughs.*) Have to climb out of the hole.

He sits.

Liked that.

MARY. No wonder you didn't learn nothing.

BARRY. Little crabs.

They eat.

Some died of the shock. Fainted. Jump the train back.

MARY. Victoria –

BARRY. Harder there. Get some old tosser and they'd chase you. Round the station. Run into the cartoon cinema. Fuck me. Can bloody run, some of them. Station idiots. Inspectors.

MARY. Right layabout, I bet.

BARRY. Couldn't get on, not at school. Tried it at Euston, but it's harder there. Harder than Victoria.

MARY. Watch your ice cream, it's dripping down your chin.

BARRY *wipes his chin.*

BARRY. Couldn't do it.

MARY. Bet you were.

BARRY. What?

MARY. Hooligan.

BARRY. No.

MARY Being off school like that. Running around.

BARRY. No.

MARY. Wouldn't have dared, me. Did once spend a day Christmas shopping when I should have been at school. Me and this other lass, in and out of all the shops on Edgware Road.

A pause.

Didn't know you then.

BARRY. Good that.

MARY. Watch your ice cream.

BARRY *wipes his chin.*

BARRY. Didn't even cane you.

MARY. Eh?

BARRY. Being off. Didn't hit you. One teacher, he said to me, Jackson, I've given up with you. Cheeky, they hit you. Not for just not turning up.

MARY. We ought to come out more.

A slight pause.

Out that house. Your parents.

BARRY. Idiots.

MARY. Your dad?

BARRY. Both of them.

MARY. Give us a room.

BARRY. My old room. My room when my sister moved out.

MARY. Where d'you sleep before –

BARRY. Downstairs. On the sofa.

MARY. Didn't like to ask before.

BARRY. For fifteen years I slept on that bloody sofa.

MARY. Should have had a bigger house. You don't half make a mess with ice creams.

BARRY *wipes his chin.*

Get your hands sticky.

A slight pause.

Not enough, two bedrooms.

BARRY. Sleep on the sofa. (*He laughs.*) Remember one day I wasn't at school, went up Hampstead Heath, met this teacher there, told him I was on nature study and he believed me. This teacher had been off for a bit, had a heart attack. Nearly died. (*He laughs.*) Fuckin' ponce, he had this walking stick.

MARY *looks at him.*

What's up with you?

MARY. Nothing.

BARRY *throws his choc-ice paper away.*

(*Changing the subject.*) Your mam keeps telling me what it's like, having a baby. Said it's –

A slight pause.

Must hurt a lot.

BARRY. Big baby, me.

MARY. When it comes out – crude, to say that. Agony, she told me.

A pause.

Don't like her, the way she goes on about it, on and on. Like a bloody funeral, sometimes, the way she talks. Not as if she only told me once.

A pause.

Move out soon. Barry!

BARRY. Eh?

MARY. Save the pennies. In a jar.

BARRY. Buttons. (*He laughs.*)

MARY. Start working over.

BARRY. Get lost.

MARY. Have to.

BARRY. No.

MARY. Yes.

BARRY. No.

MARY. Can't live with them for ever. Not ever and ever.

A pause.

The way she talks, your mam.

A pause.

Why do you –

A slight pause.

BARRY. Eh?

MARY. Funny sometimes, you are. Talking about Brighton just now, and not going to school. Sitting here on the sand.

She looks at BARRY.

A pause.

BARRY *stands.*

BARRY. Stop fuckin' looking at me like that. Staring. Like a fucking owl.

BARRY *walks away.*

Get us somewhere to bloody live. (*Calmer.*) An igloo at the north pole, do?

MARY (*standing*). Barry? What's up with you?

BARRY (*turning to face her*). What do you think?

A pause.

Better go and find that ball. (*He moves to exit.*)

MARY. Stop.

BARRY *stops.*

Wait. Be lost now.

MARY *walks to him.*

Just the way you carry on sometimes.

BARRY *walks away.*

BARRY. When I was a lad, little kiddie, I had this dream. And that was to burn down the world. Smash it up. (*He laughs.*)

A pause.

Went all over. Not just to Brighton. (*He twists his foot on the sand.*) Smashing crabs.

MARY. Listen to me, Barry. (*She walks towards him.*) Listen.

BARRY. I'll get somewhere.

MARY. Your mam's noticed you. She blames me. Says you're get– (*Tails off, realising it is not appropriate.*) –ting worse. Not fair. Not fair on me. You listening? Barry?

BARRY. Didn't have a dream.

MARY. Eh? Listening?

A slight pause.

I've enjoyed today.

MARY *moves to comfort him.* BARRY *moves his hand away.*

BARRY. Don't touch me.

Lights change leaving a single light on them.

Over speakers the sound of a baby crying.

The light slowly fades to blackout. The sound to silence.

Scene Three

Nine months later.

A park.

DAVE MILLWARD *and* COLIN THOMPSON, *sitting on the grass. They both wear bus driver's uniforms.*

DAVE *is twenty-six and* COLIN *twenty-four.*

A pause. DAVE *studies a copy of* Exchange & Mart. COLIN *eats a meat pie.*

A pause.

DAVE *lies back.*

DAVE. Lying in the park, thinking –

COLIN. Thinking?

DAVE. Yeh.

COLIN. Want to watch that, can give you a headache.

DAVE (*laughing*). Shut up.

A pause.

Thinking wouldn't it be nice if – (*Sighs*). What's the use. If I could lie here all day.

COLIN (*pointing*). What's that, in that tree?

DAVE (*looking*). A sparrow.

COLIN. Selling your car?

DAVE. *Exchange & Mart*? Wife wants a fridge.

COLIN (*looking at his watch*). Half past twelve.

DAVE. You thought about applying to the BBC?

COLIN. Eh?

DAVE. BBC radio. Reading out the time checks. (*He laughs.*) You could pretend to be Big Ben striking midnight.

COLIN (*laughing*). Piss off.

DAVE (*laughing*). Pissed off more like, God knows what she'll want after a fridge.

COLIN (*looking at his watch*). Mine winds itself.

DAVE. Deep freezes, no end to it.

COLIN. Tick tock. Tick tock.

DAVE. Bloody fool, you are. Ticking away.

COLIN. Sell you our fridge for two hundred pounds.

DAVE. Going with the house is it? (*He laughs.*)

COLIN (*laughing*). Shut up.

DAVE. All it's worth.

COLIN (*laughing*). Worth more than your dustbin of a property.

DAVE. Our mansion? Had many an offer from a film star for it. (*He laughs.*) Wanted it for a kennel for their dogs. Serious though, you don't know anyone with a fridge, going on the cheap?

COLIN. What's cheap?

DAVE. Fifteen quid.

COLIN. No.

A pause.

DAVE. Wife wants another –

COLIN. Baby?

DAVE. Yeh.

COLIN. There I might be able to help you.

DAVE. A boy, she says. One boy, one girl. Got the girl. I told her she had to make a choice, fridge or baby. I'm no good at decisions, she says. (*He laughs.*) Can't afford to feed the other one.

A pause.

Can. Just –

A pause.

I'll make do with both, she says.

COLIN. Joker.

DAVE. Yeh. She's a comedian. She's the Charlie Chaplin of our street, except in a dress.

He sees BARRY *off.*

(*Calling.*) Oy, Barry. Barry. Come here, I want you. Barry.

BARRY (*off*). What for?

DAVE. Want you a minute.

BARRY *enters. He wears a bus conductor's uniform. He carries a Boots bag.*

COLIN. Shopping.

BARRY. Yeh. Cotton wool.

DAVE. Couldn't lend us a fag, could you, mate?

BARRY. Is that all?

DAVE. Give us two if you're feeling generous.

BARRY. I'm not.

DAVE. My stars said I wouldn't have a lucky day today.

BARRY *throws* DAVE *and* COLIN *a cigarette each. They light up.*

Remember you in my will. To Barry Jackson, one – (*He looks at the make.*) Embassy. Not Benson & Hedges? Buy you a drink sometime.

BARRY. Yeh.

COLIN. He doesn't drink now, do you, Barry? Gone teetotal.

BARRY. No.

BARRY *moves to exit. He stops and turns.*

(*Holding up the bag.*) For the baby this. Wanted to ask you something. About driving. Lessons and that.

COLIN. Oh?

BARRY. Yeh.

DAVE. Need a car.

BARRY. Buses.

DAVE. Something up with this fag, can't draw on it properly. (*He examines it.*) Must have a hole in it.

BARRY *goes to him and grabs the cigarette.*

BARRY. Not satisfied?

DAVE (*jumping up*). Only saying.

BARRY *stubs the cigarette out on the ground.*

BARRY. Making fun of me.

DAVE. Look, mate –

BARRY *walks away.* COLIN *stands.*

There was a small hole in the paper.

A slight pause.

Nothing to do with you.

BARRY *turns and throws another cigarette to* DAVE. *It lands at* DAVE*'s feet.*

Don't have to.

BARRY. Put that one in your will.

DAVE *picks up the cigarette.* COLIN *passes his cigarette and* DAVE *takes a light from it.*

COLIN. Best thing if you haven't a car, is go to a driving school. Cost you a bit, but –

DAVE. Haven't any fags of my own.

BARRY. Thanks.

BARRY *exits. They watch him go.*

A pause.

DAVE. Wants to get out. (*He sits.*) Another job.

COLIN. Him?

DAVE. Yeh.

COLIN. Huh. (*He looks at his watch.*) Twenty to. (*He sits.*) Twenty to one.

DAVE. Bloody funny.

COLIN. Yeh.

DAVE. Don't mean comic, either. Wants to buy himself a camel and find a bloody desert.

COLIN. Be lucky in England. (*He smiles.*)

DAVE (*calling*). And start walking.

COLIN. One of my cousins went funny. In the head. Took to setting himself on fire, with a petrol lighter. He died in the bath. Drowned.

DAVE (*smiling*). Don't make me laugh.

COLIN. God's truth. Like a Russian. Setting himself on fire. Once went to the toilet with all his clothes on.

DAVE *laughs.*

Doctor reckoned, among other things, he'd lost his memory. Committed suicide. Didn't leave a note, they just found him. Got back from this film and there he was, in the bath. All his clothes on. Dead. Not funny, really.

A slight pause.

Eight of them in that house. More or less living on the roof, they were. Used to walk their bloody dog at three o'clock in the morning. He did, out with it, on a lead.

A pause.

Funny, doctor advised he move out the house, but he wouldn't go.

DAVE. How old were you, when you were married?

COLIN. What's that got to do with my cousin?

DAVE. Nothing.

COLIN. Oh. Eighteen, I think – give or take a year.

DAVE. Me, nineteen. How old was your cousin?

COLIN. Year younger than me, he was.

A slight pause.

Wasn't funny. Sad.

DAVE *lies back.*

DAVE (*reflecting*). Married. A week on the coast. Look at –

A pause.

Sometimes wish I'd gone places. Somewhere. Anywhere. Done things. Sown weeds among the female flowers of England. Europe. The world – (*He sits up.*) I mean – (*He lies back, sighs.*)

COLIN. Mean what?

DAVE. Nothing.

A slight pause.

Taken to clouting our little Lucy, she isn't half getting saucy.

A pause.

I mean, what do we do? We carry on. Carry on. Carry on. (*He sighs.*) Carry on. Do, you know, this is the first time I thought about it. (*He sits up.*) First time.

COLIN. Yeh.

DAVE. Yeh, what?

COLIN. Just yeh. You think too much. (*He stands.*) What's the point of always bloody thinking? Doesn't make any difference.

COLIN *walks away.*

When it bloody comes down to it, you're lucky.

DAVE. What about you?

COLIN. Not saying I'm not.

A slight pause.

We're not idiots like some blokes.

DAVE *laughs.*

Mean that. Thick as a – (*He thinks of something.*) slab of concrete some of them. Thick as anything. If not thicker than a slab of –

DAVE (*laughing*). Shut up. Not as thick as some blokes. Who are you? Einstein? (*He laughs.*)

COLIN. Wasn't being funny.

DAVE. Sit down. Talk about me talking.

COLIN *sits*.

I mean all we do is, carry on.

COLIN. So?

DAVE. I don't know.

COLIN (*muttering*). Go on about it.

DAVE *lies back*.

A pause.

DAVE. If I had my time over again, I wouldn't have married when I did. Would have married her anyway, but –

A pause.

(*Reflecting.*) Suppose, I would do.

A pause.

Yeh, I would have done. Married her when I did, really.

A pause.

Wouldn't change. I loved her and still do some of the time.

A pause.

COLIN *looks at his watch*.

COLIN. We ought to be going.

DAVE. Yeh.

COLIN. Yeh.

DAVE. Would you?

COLIN (*standing*). Come on.

DAVE. Change?

COLIN. Come on.

DAVE (*standing*). Hold on a minute.

COLIN *exits*.

What's with this racing-car speed?

DAVE *exits*.

The sound of a bus starting.

Lights dim to blackout.

Scene Four

One month later.

A park.

A park bench and a rubbish bin.

MARY (*off*). Shall we stop here?

JUNE (*off*). Yeh.

MARY (*off*). Seems to get heavier, this pram.

JUNE (*off*). How old is she now?

MARY (*off*). Seven months.

> MARY *and* JUNE WILSON *enter*. MARY *is pushing a pram, she puts on the brake.*

Thank God for that.

JUNE. Should have told me, I'd have pushed it.

> JUNE *is twenty-two. Fairly tall. Is thin and shapely. Good looking.*

> MARY *sits.*

(*Pointing.*) See those trees over there? Remember playing under that tree when I was little. Later, this lad I was going out with, carved my initials on it. You can hardly see them now.

MARY. Long time since I've been out.

JUNE. Enjoy a walk.

MARY. Seen anybody. Busy. Don't mind, me?

JUNE. Like I say, enjoy the walk. I know what my Tom can be like sometimes.

MARY. Yes.

JUNE. Terrible. (*Offering a cigarette*.) Want one?

MARY. Please.

They light up.

His mother's been telling me about him. About when he was little, so high. Not at all like his sister, she says. Apparently, he used to piddle on their cat. When he was three. On purpose. That cat'd be asleep on their chair and he'd piss on it.

JUNE *doesn't know whether to laugh or not.*

He started doing it again when he was six. He'd be watching Lenny the Lion or something on television and then just do it.

JUNE *laughs.*

Another thing I found out the other day, he's still got his old teddy bear. In this biscuit tin on top of the wardrobe. I was just hunting around and found it. It's all horrible. Worn. Holes in it, stuffing coming out. One eye missing. Donate the bloody thing to the British Museum. Thing was, I put it in the dustbin and he went and got it back. Talk about angry, Christ.

JUNE (*smiling*). What's he want it for?

MARY. Won't say. He's hidden it. Locked it somewhere. I didn't tell his mam. He didn't say a word for the rest of the evening, just sat there. Quiet.

JUNE. Perhaps he wants it for Barbara, when she's older.

MARY. Don't know. Wouldn't want Barbara to go near it, that dirty. When he was ten, he jumped into the canal. Nearly killed himself. An old-age pensioner pulled him out. Barry couldn't swim. Did it on purpose, for a lark. Some joke. His mam reckons it was cos he must have been watching skin-divers on the telly. You know, in the Indian Ocean, films like that. Copied them. He must have known he couldn't swim. Daft.

JUNE. Was he fishing?

MARY. He didn't fall, he jumped. Old-age pensioner saw him.

JUNE *sits.*

Grabbed him with a stick. I ask you.

JUNE. Do anything when you're ten.

MARY. He did everything.

JUNE. Do you remember Kenny Flowers? We called him Tulip.

MARY. Yeh?

JUNE. White hair. He died after this operation. Gave him penicillin when they shouldn't. Strange how all those people you know at school change, different, act different even. The same and different, both at the same time.

MARY. That's where I met Barry. Two classes above me. Walk home together. Both sort of walked home by ourselves, mostly, most of the time, so we started walking together. That was it. He didn't used to be at school half the time. Used to think he was ill. Turned out he was going off for days.

MARY *stands*.

Doesn't talk about what he did. Quiet. Like a mouse. You'd think he had a lump of plasticine in his mouth half the time. (*She looks into the pram.*)

JUNE. Baby's quiet.

MARY. Barbara –

JUNE. Yes.

MARY. When I was little, I had a friend called Barbara. Barbara Evans, she had plaits. (*She looks into the pram.*) Asleep.

JUNE. It's the fresh air.

MARY. Suppose so. Barry wanted a boy, I know that. Natural I think, for a man.

MARY *walks away from the pram*.

He wants to become a bus driver. Gave some stupid reason, I forget exactly bloody what. Sick of conducting. He's bought himself a motorbike on our holiday money. A hundred and twenty pounds, we had saved. Either using the money for a holiday, or for a house, or something. Gone. Thinking of going to the Isle of Wight. Now we'll have days, he says. Days! Days in the backyard, him drinking bottled beer, looking at washing on the line. Like to go places, see things. Historical places. Lawns. Gardens. Greenhouses, foreign plants. I like looking at how religious monks lived five hundred years ago. Old ruins. Only lumps of stone to a lot of people, not to me. It's history, to me. Only lumps of old stone to Barry, don't need him to tell me that. He doesn't care. Doesn't like enjoyment. Fairs. We saw this gypsy once, both of us. An old woman, she was. Had hairs on her chin. This was just before we were married. Told us we'd be bloody contented and happy. Happy as a millionaire, her words were. Believed her for a while. She told me he didn't bring friends home.

MARY *sits*.

Barry's mother. Told me how one Easter they ate Barry's pet rabbit, for dinner.

JUNE *looks at* MARY.

Honestly true. Barry was upset. He was nine at the time. She told me she was sorry, after. Barry cried. Said they didn't think he was attached to it. Didn't tell Barry 'til after they'd eaten it, which rabbit it was. He went to its hutch and it wasn't there. They told him. He was sick. He called the rabbit Bugs after the cartoon. His dad killed it, apparently, because Barry wouldn't feed it. Banged Bugs Bunny's head against the yard wall.

A pause.

Didn't have many friends.

A slight pause.

JUNE. We're having days.

MARY. Not surprising really.

JUNE. Here and there.

MARY. Sorry?

JUNE. Days. Away. A holiday.

A pause.

Getting bad, is he?

MARY. Not bad – you know. Bad. Just sick of that bloody house. He's got this motorbike. It's like it were a human being. He cleans it, every night. Almost loves it.

MARY *stands and walks to the pram*.

I wonder sometimes.

A pause.

JUNE. Wonder?

MARY. If he's a bit soft. (*She points to her head.*) Up here.

A slight pause.

Getting to know his mam a lot now. Didn't like her at first. I do now. We talk. Talk. Just chatter, you know, most of the time. About Barbara. About the house. About most things. Talk. Can't chatter to my own mam like I can to her. Different at first. Okay now. She told me, her and her husband, Barry's dad, had never really got on. Happy together most of the time, just never got on. Happy in their own way, I suppose. Told me they got married because she was expecting, having Shirley, that's Barry's sister. Never talk to each other, not like you and me. Says if any fella picked her up, even now, she'd leave him. Go with him. Leave Barry's dad.

MARY *walks away from the pram.*

Think in her own way she feels sorry for Barry and me. Every Friday afternoon she buys me a cream cake. She works part-time. Mornings. At first it was as if she didn't want me in the house. Now, we get on.

JUNE. Yeh.

MARY. I like that. She told me, Barry was once caught by the police. He'd thumped this lad up outside a club. Barry was only fifteen. They were both drunk. When the police brought him home, his dad belted him and broke his nose. They had to take him to a hospital, let a doctor see it. That's why his nose is crooked now. She told me that, she didn't have to, but she did.

MARY *sits.*

I can't ride on the motorbike. My leg. I think that's why he got it. Made some excuse about teaching himself to drive on it, to become a driver. His mam told him to build a sidecar. Says we haven't the money.

JUNE. We should go out together sometime. A day somewhere. You, me, Barry and Tom.

MARY. Don't think Barry would, he's not like that.

A slight pause.

He wouldn't.

JUNE. Ask him.

MARY. Could do.

JUNE. No harm in asking. (*Stands*.)

MARY. Do you want to go?

JUNE. No. Like it here.

    JUNE *looks in the pram*.

MARY. Barry's mother bought those baby clothes. Not second hand, not charity shops. She looks good in yellow.

    MARY *stands and goes to the pram*.

JUNE. Yes.

MARY. Don't Tom and you want children?

JUNE. I do. (*She walks away*.) It's Tom. When we've a better house, he keeps saying. I read in this magazine, the longer you leave it, the harder it gets. Psychological. Showed it to Tom, he didn't believe it. They made him foreman at work, we can afford it now, but –

    A slight pause.

    He's careful is Tom. About money. Careful.

MARY. Yes.

JUNE. Lucky in some ways. I don't know.

    MARY *walks away from the pram*.

MARY. I'll ask Barry.

JUNE. About going out?

MARY. To old castles.

JUNE. Ask him.

MARY. I will.

    A pause.

    You know, his mother told me –

    A pause.

    Told me I should leave him. Get a divorce.

    MARY *stands and walks to the pram*.

    We were drinking tea and she told me. About her own son.

    JUNE *stands*.

JUNE. Listen

MARY (*quietly*). That's about the only thing I hate her for.

A slight pause.

Saying that. To me. Saying it.

MARY *looks at* JUNE.

Looking me in the eye and saying it. Sitting there on the sofa. Cup of tea in her hand.

JUNE *walks to her.*

For me, I suppose, she told me. I hate her for that.

MARY *releases the brake and pushes the pram on a few yards.*

I didn't say anything. Not much. Didn't know what to.

A pause.

Just didn't.

A pause.

Barry threw a portable radio at her the other evening. It was giving off this high-pitched whine, he blamed her. Just picked it up – hit her leg. Batteries were flat. Or it was broken.

A slight pause.

He wanted to listen to something or other.

A slight pause.

Couldn't.

MARY *looks at* JUNE.

Divorce. I hate her for that!

JUNE *moves to her.*

(*Almost crying.*) She didn't have to say that to me.

MARY *looks up at* JUNE.

And I like her.

JUNE. Yes.

MARY. I do.

JUNE. Yes.

MARY. A lot.

JUNE. Let's walk.

They exit.

Lights fade to blackout.

Scene Five

One month later.

There is a baby's cot. Beside the cot, a toy dog. Somewhere else there is a motorbike.

Dim lights pull up on the cot.

BARRY *is standing looking at the baby.*

He doesn't move. He just stares.

A pause.

MARY *enters. She wears dressing gown and slippers.*

MARY. Don't breathe on her like that.

BARRY *ignores her.*

Don't put your face near hers.

BARRY. Want me to wear a gas mask? Want her to wear a gas mask? Stick it on her head? German style?

MARY. Can kill babies, bad air.

BARRY *ignores her.*

Don't, I said.

BARRY. Shut up!

MARY. My baby.

BARRY *tucks in the blankets.*

Leave her.

MARY *tries to stop him.*

I said leave her.

A pause.

Saw this programme about bad air and babies.

BARRY *stands*.

A pause.

I saw June again yesterday.

BARRY. Been seeing a lot of her.

MARY. Just yesterday.

BARRY. Suppose I'm not enough?

MARY. In the park. On the grass.

A pause.

She asked again, if we'd like to go out with her and Tom.

BARRY. No.

MARY. Barry.

BARRY. Told you, no!

MARY. You'll wake her, that noise.

A pause.

They won't ask us no more.

BARRY. No.

MARY. Give up asking.

A pause.

In their car.

BARRY. Go on my motorbike.

MARY. You know I can't. Couldn't we go?

BARRY. No.

A pause.

MARY. It's the fourth time they've asked us.

BARRY. So you can count! First time, second time – third time, fourth time – all the bloody time. Don't want to.

MARY. Yes, but I do.

BARRY. Go then.

A slight pause.

MARY. I am.

> BARRY *stares at her.*

> Boating, on a lake. Rowing.

BARRY (*laughing*). Feeding bloody ducks. (*Hard.*) Come here.

MARY (*she doesn't move*). Next Sunday.

BARRY. Leave me on my own?

MARY. What do you want? I don't know what you want.

BARRY. You're not going.

> BARRY *stares at her.*

> *A pause.*

MARY. I've decided. Decided, to go.

> *A pause.*

> Looks rude saying, saying no all the time.

BARRY. No.

> *A pause.*

MARY. Why don't you co–

BARRY. Bitch. Bitch!

MARY (*staring at him*). You'll bloody wake her.

BARRY. Fuck off! (*He looks away.*)

> *A pause.*

MARY. Barry, I decided to go with them, next Sunday.

> Boating.

> *A slight pause.*

> MARY *turns and exits.*

BARRY (*screams*). BITCH! BITCH! BITCH! BITCH! (*Spits.*)

> *Lights pull down leaving* BARRY *isolated in light.*

> BARRY *sinks to the ground, almost sobbing. He cuddles and strokes the toy dog. He talks to the dog.*

She's a bloody bitch. Yes she is. Cripple. Bet she was a very horrible little girl, with irons on her leg. You can pull her with a magnet, across a room. (*He laughs, looks up.*) Motorbike. (*He reflects.*) Motorbike.

He picks up the dog and crashes it to the ground.

MOTORBIKE!

He strokes the dog.

A pause.

This little doggy went to market and this little doggy stayed at home and this naughty little dog pissed against a lamp-post. (*He laughs.*) Call you Rover. (*He tries saying the name 'Rover' in different ways.*) Rover. Rover. Rover. Rover. Rover. Made a mess on the pavement. Naughty, naughty boy. (*He hits the dog.*) Bad Rover. Bad dog. Do it again and I'll smash your nose. (*He laughs.*)

Suddenly angry he raises the dog and crashes it to the ground.

BREAK IT!

He strokes the dog.

A pause.

Wouldn't hurt you, would I? No. Wouldn't I? No, course I wouldn't. No. Not hurt you. I wouldn't hurt you. Not Rover. Not my Rover.

He picks up the dog and crashes it to the ground.

Not my little dog. (*He cuddles it.*) Rover? Can you hear me?

He stands and picks up the dog.

That's my little girl. Asleep. Asleep in her cot. Little eyes tight shut for the night. Tight shut. She's called Barbara and you're called Rover. Two horrible names? Don't you think? (*He smiles.*) Eh? (*He holds the dog's face to his.*) Eh? Barbara and Rover? (*He puts the dog's face to Barbara's face.*) Look at her. Look. Eyes shut. Isn't she just so sweet? (*He pushes the dog nearer Barbara's face.*) Eh? So sweet? Pretty? Loveable? Eh? I could kill you and her. (*He cuddles the dog.*) But I won't. No. I won't. Could do, but I won't. Not that I'm a coward. Rover? You listening? Listening to me? Are you? Good dog. Nice doggy. Listening? (*Hard.*) You can't hear me, can you?

He throws the dog to the ground.

CAN'T HEAR!!

He puts his hands to his cheeks.

I've got a motorbike. Motorbike. Very very fast. (*He laughs.*) Fast. Fast! Faster than a train. Faster than a rocket to the moon. Faster. Than all of you. (*He laughs.*) Fast. Wind. Speed. Wind blowing. (*He laughs.*) Speed.

He staggers across to the motorbike.

Lights crossfade. They go down on the cot, up on the motorbike.

He sits on the motorbike. He kickstarts it three times. It finally fires.

The light begins to pull up and down as he changes up through the gears. The light begins to flicker.

He keeps his head low over the handlebars.

The wind blows his hair. His face is red. He is enjoying the speed.

The motorbike is extremely loud. When he speaks, he has to shout.

Speed. Hah! (*He laughs.*) Forty. Forty-five. Fifty. Fifty-five. Watch out. Fifty-five.

The sound of wind is now very loud.

Watch out, old ladies. (*Laughing.*) Sixty. Sixty-two. Sixty-three. Round a bend we go. (*He leans slightly.*) Sixty-five. Hah! Let me on the speedway. Speedway! (*He laughs.*) Seventy. (*He laughs.*)

In a daredevil movement he puts his hands on his head. He quickly grabs the handlebars again.

Show rider. I'm a police show rider. Daredevil. Could stand on my head. Turn a somersault. Steer with my feet. (*He laughs.*) Seventy.

His mood changes. A sudden urgency in his voice.

A bend! Big bend! A bend coming up. Slow up. Slow up. Fifty! Brake!

The sound of wind slowly fades.

Forty-five. Bend. Forty. (*He laughs.*) Thirty-five. Bend! Slow! Slow! Bend! Bend! Bend! Bend! Bend! BEND! BEND! Arr –

The motorbike crashes.

Instant blackout.

Scene Six

A lakeside.

JUNE, *her husband* TOM WILSON *and* MARY.

TOM, *his shoes and socks off, his trousers rolled up, is standing in the water.* JUNE *and* MARY *stand at the edge.*

TOM *is twenty-nine. He is smartly dressed, wears fawn trousers, a shirt open at the neck and a cardigan.*

Some distance from them, COLIN *and* DAVE.

They mime skimming flat stones along the water.

TOM (*shivering*). It's cold. Shouldn't be surprised if there aren't ice cubes floating around in here.

JUNE (*pointing*). What's that?

TOM (*looking*). Just an old bottle.

JUNE. Might have a message in it.

TOM. What? On a lake? Only get messages in bottles on the sea. (*He walks in a bit further.*) Ar, ar – it's bloody hard to walk, all stony.

MARY. If there's bottles, there's glass.

TOM. Yeh. Think I'll swim the channel one day. What animal do you think you are?

MARY. Eh?

TOM. What animal?

MARY. Animal?

TOM. What animal would you like to be?

MARY. Never thought about it.

TOM. I'd be a bloody dolphin. (*He walks a bit further.*) Think.

MARY. Can't imagine. Kangaroo, if I had to be anything.

TOM (*to* JUNE). What about you?

JUNE. Don't involve me.

COLIN *and* DAVE *refer to the number of bounces their stones have made on the water.*

COLIN. Five.

TOM. Come on.

JUNE. No.

   TOM *walks out of the water.*

TOM. Bring a towel?

DAVE. Four.

JUNE. Didn't think you'd be paddling.

MARY. Have to leave them to the sun.

TOM. Yeh.

COLIN. Six.

   TOM *sits.*

TOM. Barry heard about his job? Bus driver?

MARY. They turned him down.

TOM. Oh.

   MARY *sits.*

MARY. No, I knew they would.

JUNE. Went in yesterday, then?

MARY. Yeh.

COLIN. Look at that one, nine, ten, eleven. Beat that.

MARY. Just had the three days.

DAVE. Lucky.

COLIN. Do this in the Olympics and I'd have a gold medal.

MARY. He was alright, really. Just shock.

TOM. Was he bothered? About the job?

MARY. Didn't seem to be.

TOM. Never mind, eh.

MARY. Shock and a cut on his face.

   A slight pause.

   So, all in all.

   A slight pause.

   Barry's mother's looking after Barbara.

DAVE. Four again.

MARY. He's got a plaster on his arm where they took some of his blood.

DAVE (*sitting*). Bloody four.

MARY. Would have come today, but for the accident. He was coming. Wanted to come.

JUNE. Yes.

MARY. Said he was looking forward to it. It's a pity.

TOM. My feet are drying.

MARY. He keeps looking at this plaster as if he'd had a major operation, or something. A heart transplant. He changes it all the time when all there is is a little bruise. Bloody stupid.

TOM. Playing at hospitals? (*He smiles.*)

MARY. Playing at bloody something. He wanted a bandage on –

A slight pause.

I enjoyed that row, the splash of the oars.

TOM. Yeh.

MARY. Barry likes rowing, a proper little cox he is when he gets going. Watches the boat race. He's good with Barbara. Good with her now. Said he was sorry, sorry he couldn't come.

TOM. At night, in the sea, when you row, you get like little diamonds. It's the reflection of plankton. Like little jewels. It's nice. Solve all your problems, if you could pick them out and sell them. (*Smiles.*) Just have to buy a fishing net, go for a row, and you'd be rich.

TOM *starts to put on his shoes.*

Trouble is with that, everyone would do it and it wouldn't count. (*He thinks for a brief moment.*) Lots of diamonds would make them all nothing.

A slight pause.

(*Smiling. To* MARY.) Nothing for it, have to get an evening job as well. A barman.

JUNE *looks at him.*

Free drink. (*He smiles.*) Don't you fancy me as a barman?

JUNE. You know what I think.

TOM. Pulling pints?

   TOM *puts his arm around* JUNE*'s waist.*

   When I was a kid I thought they really were diamonds.

MARY. Never seen that.

TOM. Thought all I had to do was pick them like potatoes.

   He starts to put on his other sock.

JUNE (*to* MARY). He's not content with one job.

TOM. That's right.

JUNE. There ought to be a word for people like you.

TOM. There is. (*He thinks for a moment.*) Can't think of it.

JUNE. I can. Idiot.

TOM. Not idiot. There is a word, but not idiot.

   A slight pause.

   I'm serious.

JUNE. Bloody know you are.

   TOM *puts on his other shoe.*

TOM. Walking down the road the other day, I thought –

   A slight pause.

   (*Brighter.*) Have to be serious, that's what I say.

MARY. Serious?

TOM. Look at it in a way –

   A slight pause.

   Just look at it in a way that's –

   A slight pause.

   Well, serious. I mean you get some people who –

   A pause.

   They're the idiots.

   A pause.

MARY. Barry's going to lose his friends. Not that he has –

A slight pause.

A few friends.

A pause.

You know, his mam told me about his dad. She just told me. About the war, about Hitler and bombs – a lot of things, about them. His dad was born in that house, he hasn't moved. Stayed there. When they were married they moved in with his parents, just like Barry and me moved in with them. Told me, she did, how his dad hated it. Hated it. She hated it. Only difference in that house now, from seventy years ago, is the bathroom. That's all. His dad did all sorts of jobs.

A pause.

Even cleaned windows for a while.

TOM *stands.*

TOM. I enjoyed that.

JUNE. You keep saying.

TOM. I did.

TOM *bangs his feet once or twice on the ground. He takes a deep breath.*

Best be off. Getting dark, the moon'll be out shortly.

MARY *stands. She walks a few yards round the edge of the lake.*

MARY. I've enjoyed today, as well. It's nice to be quiet.

She walks on a few yards. She turns to face TOM.

Barry's too serious.

TOM. Didn't mean that about Barry.

MARY. No.

TOM. About me, I suppose.

MARY. No.

JUNE *stands.*

JUNE. Let's talk about something else.

MARY. I was wondering

A slight pause.

No, nothing.

A slight pause.

Nothing.

TOM (*brightly*). Come on then.

MARY. Yes.

TOM. Home sweet home.

MARY. Think I'll buy a choc-ice.

JUNE. Ice lolly.

They exit.

Lights dim slightly.

A pause.

DAVE. You asleep, Colin?

COLIN. Eh?

DAVE. Thought you must be asleep, lying like that.

COLIN. Yes, I'm asleep. Do you enjoy disturbing people?

DAVE. It's a habit.

COLIN. Caught it off a monk I suppose?

DAVE (*smiling*). Yeh.

A pause.

Isn't it quiet.

COLIN. It would be.

DAVE. The evening.

A pause.

Nice to leave the wife at home?

COLIN. Yeh.

DAVE. Cool. Looking at the water. (*He points.*) That a swan?

A pause.

Peaceful. Silence.

COLIN. Anybody ever call you bloody Wordsworth?

DAVE. Eh?

COLIN. All this bloody poetry.

DAVE. Did once sign myself Shakespeare.

COLIN. He wasn't a poet?

DAVE. Yes he was.

COLIN. Started going to libraries, have you?

DAVE. Piss off.

A pause.

(*He points.*) The sun reflecting off the water.

A pause.

Listen, mate.

COLIN. Mate now, is it?

A pause.

No.

DAVE. Haven't asked you yet.

COLIN. No, to whatever it is.

DAVE. About as generous as a heap of scrap iron –

COLIN. And twice as bloody handsome, I know.

A pause.

DAVE. It's this bloody fridge.

COLIN *turns to face him.*

COLIN. Look, you're not the only bugger who's a bit bloody short.

DAVE. It's almost funny.

COLIN. Wish it was.

A pause.

DAVE. Lent you a fiver once.

COLIN. Don't talk to me about history.

DAVE (*hard*). Well. Sod off!

A pause.

COLIN. Look, if I had it, I would.

DAVE. Forget it.

COLIN. Bit short myself.

DAVE. Forget it!

A pause.

COLIN. Honestly, I'm short.

DAVE. Wanted second hand, but she would have a bloody new one. We'll manage, she says. Bloody fridge.

COLIN. Yeh, I know.

A pause.

Do what I do and raid your kids' piggy banks and make out you're committing a daring bullion robbery at the same time. Exciting.

DAVE. Do you?

COLIN. Would do. Trouble is we never give them anything to put in the bloody money boxes to rob.

DAVE. Don't you?

COLIN. Do you?

DAVE. No.

COLIN. Talking about me.

A pause.

Owe it, do you?

DAVE. Yeh.

COLIN. Just don't pay it.

DAVE. Wish it was that easy.

COLIN. It is.

DAVE. Funny.

COLIN. Very funny.

A pause.

DAVE. This is the life.

COLIN. It would be, if only you'd bloody shut up.

Lights slowly fade to blackout.

Scene Seven

By the side of the M1.

A faint light from the moon. Clouds passing in front of the moon.

The sound of cars screaming past.

Car headlights flashing past.

BARRY *enters. He has a haversack over his shoulder. He stops and stands. He is bewildered by the light.*

A slight pause.

BARRY. Stop. (*Much louder.*) Stop! (*He raises his thumb.*) STOP.

Bloody stop.

He rushes on a few yards as if chasing a car.

Stop you bastards, stop.

He walks back.

A slight pause.

Stop. Stop! (*He raises his thumb.*) STOP. Why don't you bloody stop? Please, stop! Why don't you fucking bloody stop! (*He shouts.*) STOP!

He stands. He looks dejected.

A slight pause.

He runs his hands through his hair.

(*Quietly.*) Give me a lift. (*He shouts.*) Give me a BLOODY LIFT. You don't care. Don't CARE!

In rage he throws his haversack to the ground.

Well I don't bloody care! Yes, I don't. Want a lift. Want to stand here all night. Stand here – all night.

The sound of the cars begin to fade to silence.

All fucking night.

He thinks he hears a voice behind his left ear. He jolts his head.

What you fuckin' lookin' at? Watching me. Eyes. Eyes. (*Again he jolts his head.*) Where? (*Again, this time the jolt causes him pain.*) Where? Who? (*He turns.*) Who are you? (*He jolts his head.*) Where? (*In agony, holding his head.*) Where are you?

The cars have gone.

Over speakers a wind like sound. Electronic sounds. High pitched. Whines. Talking being re-played on a tape recorder at high speed. 33 records at 78. Sounds distorted from everyday reality.

BARRY *clutches his head. He doesn't know what they are. He can't make them out. They cause him great pain.*

(*He shouts.*) You. Know you. I know you. Go away. (*Getting calmer.*) Don't want you. Want to. Want to go back. (*He twists his fingers together.*)

The sounds are not loud. BARRY *does not have to shout.*

(*Looking up.*) Go back and do it, do it. (*He jolts his head to the left.*) Do you hear me? Yes. Yes I can. Yes I can hear you. (*Head jolts.*) Now. Go back and do it now. Go back and kill them. Do it – now. Do it now! (*Looks up, agony in his face.*) Kill them. Kill them.

A sudden break from the agony. He smiles.

Kill. Kill. Kill. Kill. (*Makes a violent stabbing motion through the air.*) Compass. Compass. A compass! Compass. (*His face begins to break.*)

Blood. Compass. (*His smile has gone.*) Blood. (*Quite quietly now, slowly getting louder.*) Blood. Saw it run like a tap 'til it was gone. Like a tap. Like a tap flowing to the sun. Sun. Sun of life. Empty. Empty sun. Sun. Blood goes. Goes to the sun. My blood to the sun. To the sun on fire. The sun of life – burning – on fire. Death. My blood of life. Red sun. My blood on fire. Hot, hot. Hot.

He rips off his jacket.

Hot. Hot. Hot. Hot. Hot. Hot. Hot.

He rips off his shirt.

Burning. Burning. Burning. (*He looks up.*) No. No. (*He screams.*)

NO. NO. NO. No, I didn't. (*He sinks to the ground*.) I didn't. I didn't. (*Quietly*.) Didn't kill them. Didn't kill them. Didn't.

The sounds fade to silence.

A pause.

I didn't. (*He looks at the sky*.) You're gone.

A slight pause.

Cold. I'm cold. (*Almost sobbing*.) I'm cold. (*He pulls his shirt over himself*.) Cold. Cold. Cold.

A pause.

He's gone. He's gone.

He pulls his jacket over himself.

Gone –

A pause.

I –

A pause.

Cold.

A pause.

I –

A pause.

I –

A pause.

(*Quietly*.) Want to be dead. Dead.

Silence.

Suddenly cars scream past. Their loudness increases.

BARRY *lies still.*

Moon light fades to blackout.

Silence.

Interval.

ACT TWO

Scene Eight

A bedroom.

A dim light pulls up as a church clock strikes four o'clock. MARY *is asleep in bed.*

A pause.

BARRY *enters. He drops his haversack on the floor.* MARY *stirs.*

A pause.

BARRY *picks up a mirror from beside the bed. He stares at his reflection.*

A long pause.

MARY *stirs. She wakes.*

MARY. Barry.

> BARRY *ignores her. He continues to stare into the mirror.*

> (*More emphatic.*) Barry.

> *He ignores her.*

> Nearly had the whole of Scotland Yard out. Looking. Nine, nine, nine, all that. Frogmen in canals. Searching. Barry!

> *He ignores her.*

> Police with your picture.

> *A pause.*

> Looking. For you.

> BARRY *puts down the mirror. He turns to face her.*

BARRY. Been to the shop. (*Taking out a packet.*) For a packet of Polos.

MARY. For three days?

BARRY. Ten minutes.

MARY. You're wet.

BARRY. Raining.

MARY. In the middle of the night?

BARRY. Rains in the night.

MARY. Shops are shut.

BARRY *turns away from her.*

BARRY *(quietly)*. Don't question me.

A pause.

MARY. I was going to get the police out.

BARRY *picks up the mirror. He stares at his reflection.*

Tell me, Barry.

BARRY. Tell what?

MARY. Been? Where you've been?

A pause.

BARRY *throws the mirror onto the bed.*

A pause.

One of your work mates came here. Colin Thompson. He told me
you hadn't been showing up some days, at work. Where've you
been going?

A pause.

Answer me.

BARRY. Been at work on the bus. Standing on the bottom deck only.

MARY. Where?

BARRY. Can I have a parrot? A green one with dirty feathers? *(He
smiles.)* Feed it. I like animals. *(He speaks quietly, not aggressively.)*
Remember, one day, when I was still at that school, uniform. *(He
takes off the other shoe.)* I stabbed all the white mice to death with a
compass. Left them in a heap on the table. In the biology class, it was.
(He pulls off a sock.) Then I electrocuted the goldfish.

MARY *lies face down on the pillow.*

In the afternoon, when I came home, pretended someone else had
done it, acted all weepy, like sometimes on the telly. Told me mam.
She believed me. *(He pulls off the other sock.)* Then I told my dad,

but he was listening to Joyce Grenfell being posh on the radio. I was going to pour nitric acid in the tropical fish tank, but I heard someone coming.

MARY. Shut up. (*She lifts her head off the pillow, tears in her eyes.*) Shut up for God's sake.

BARRY *has tears in his eyes. He looks sad and pathetic.*

BARRY. That's why I want a parrot.

MARY *has her head on the pillow. She is crying.*

MARY. You're a bastard.

BARRY *stands. He seems brighter.*

BARRY (*taking off his jacket*). I would really like a parrot. A real one, not a stuffed one. Don't like stuffed animals. It's cruel. I did that to those animals because they didn't deserve to go on living. I gave them better. Better.

MARY (*sobbing*). He told me, this man, that you're likely to lose your job. Doesn't that mean anything to you? (*She lifts her head to face him.*) Don't I mean anything to you?

BARRY. Our teacher, biology teacher, she cried when she saw it all.

A slight pause.

And no one knew it was me. Cleverer than you think, I am.

His face changes. His body starts to shake. He kneels.

A pause.

He looks up.

(*Quietly.*) Been? Where have I been?

A pause.

(*More quietly.*) Where?

BARRY *stands. He is brighter again.*

I enjoyed that walk, trees and that.

MARY. It's night, Barry.

BARRY *sits on the bed.*

BARRY. Want a Polo?

MARY. Do you know, where you've been?

Pause.

Do you? I –

A pause.

Got cotton wool in your ears?

A pause.

If you lose your job, it'll be the last of us getting somewhere on our own.

A pause.

Barry, I've been looking about for flats. We wouldn't get a house.

BARRY *stands. He walks away.*

BARRY. Haven't been anywhere.

A pause.

I'm not moving.

MARY. You don't like it here.

A pause.

BARRY. I want to stay in this house.

A pause.

MARY. What about work?

BARRY. Look, I've been out to buy Polos. Don't you understand?

MARY. Barry.

BARRY. Leave me alone. Please, leave me alone.

A pause.

MARY. First time you've been polite, said please.

BARRY *takes out a box of matches.*

First time.

She lies face down on the pillow.

BARRY *strikes the matches and throws them through the air.*

BARRY (*laughing*). Call the fire brigade.

MARY *looks up at him.*

Blackout.

Scene Nine

Six months later.

A wooden towpath along the edge of a canal.

COLIN *and* DAVE *enter.*

DAVE. Emperor Napoleon was sea sick.

COLIN. Cut the funnies.

DAVE. Learnt that at school.

> *A pause.*

> Always makes me think of sea sickness when I look at water. At the canal.

COLIN (*hard*). What happens when you have a bath?

> COLIN *moves along the towpath.*

DAVE. Look –

COLIN. Just don't try to be funny.

DAVE. Only trying to –

COLIN. I know.

> *A slight pause.*

> Don't need cheering up.

DAVE. Yeh, I'm sorry.

COLIN. Just feel, bastard, that's all.

> *A slight pause.*

> Doesn't feel funny any more. If they evict us.

DAVE. They won't.

COLIN. Get a court order. Bloody police in the street.

DAVE. Pay it.

COLIN. What with? Write a begging letter to an oil tycoon?

DAVE. Borrow it.

COLIN. Where from?

DAVE. Think of somewhere.

COLIN. I've thought.

DAVE. How long did they give you?

COLIN. Week on Monday.

A pause.

It isn't my fault.

DAVE. Isn't it?

COLIN. No. Well, my fault that I haven't been paying the rent. Didn't pay it one week, it was alright, next week I didn't alright. It went from there, I didn't care any more. Too bad to bloody care.

A pause.

I remember one day, in the park, we talked. (*He sighs.*) I said we were lucky.

DAVE. You're an idiot, you know that. Don't you know that?

COLIN. My life.

DAVE. Your life, yes.

COLIN. Thought it would never happen.

DAVE. A fuckin' idiot.

COLIN. A fuckin' idiot, so what?

DAVE. Just out of interest, what did you expect to happen?

A pause.

God to throw you down a bundle of five pound notes? Money tree to grow up in your garden?

COLIN. So I never thought they'd turn me on. The bastards.

A slight pause.

Let's change the subject.

A pause.

DAVE. I thought we'd try Bridlington this year.

COLIN. Oh, shut up.

A pause.

DAVE. A holiday. On the coast.

COLIN. Thought the sea would make you feel sick?

DAVE. Sitting on the sand.

A pause.

COLIN (*sighs*). We had thought of Wales.

DAVE. No sand on top of a mountain.

COLIN. Llandudno. Colwyn Bay.

DAVE. Knew a bloke in Colwyn Bay once.

COLIN. What's he do?

DAVE. Not seen him since I was ten.

COLIN. Thought he might have run a boarding house?

DAVE. Might do.

COLIN. Don't suppose you've any money?

DAVE. Oh, get lost.

A slight pause.

God hasn't thrown me any money either.

A pause.

Knew him at primary school.

COLIN (*sighs*). Or Scotland.

A pause.

Got too many commitments, that was all.

DAVE. Hire purchase? Loans? Stuff on the never-never?

COLIN. Yeh. All that.

BARRY *enters. He walks along the tow-path. He turns and walks back.*

DAVE (*shouting*). Oy! You!

A slight pause.

OY! (*To* COLIN.) Come on, I want a word with him.

COLIN. He can't hear.

DAVE. Want to know why he's hardly ever at work. (*Runs a few yards along the towpath.*)

COLIN. Obviously spends his days walking along the edge of this bloody canal.

DAVE. Seriously, he wants to get himself to work.

COLIN. Not surprising really.

DAVE. Eh?

COLIN. Him, Barry, like that. Living in that house. Have you seen it?

DAVE (*taking a deep breath*). It?

COLIN. The house! Bloody listen! It's hardly Buckingham Palace. (*Grabbing at his left ear.*) Open it.

A slight pause.

So small a family of mice would move out.

DAVE. Have you seen her?

COLIN. Yes.

DAVID. She's no Miss Holiday Camp. She's no bathing beauty.

COLIN. Looks isn't everything.

DAVE. Who said that?

COLIN (*sighing*). Some idiot. (*Changing the subject.*) Look, Dave –

DAVE. I don't know anyone with any money.

A pause.

An expert on their home, are you?

COLIN. Just like you are on Napoleon.

DAVE. Studied it, like in a class at school? Like science?

A pause.

COLIN. I like her.

DAVE. Oh?

COLIN. When he didn't show up at work once, about six months ago it was, I went round to his house, see if he was ill. Mates and that, at one time anyway. It was about the time he first started being off.

DAVE. Was he ill?

COLIN. She said he was away at funeral. One of his uncles died. Thought it strange then.

A pause.

She was okay, his wife.

DAVE. My brother was in the same class as him.

COLIN. Saw his dad. Nearly bald. Looks like a bastard.

DAVE. Yeh?

COLIN. Yes. Works shifts. (*He sits.*)

A pause.

Bet there'd be an old fridge for you in this canal.

DAVE. Got one.

A pause.

COLIN. I said *we* were lucky.

A pause.

Fancy a change.

DAVE. What to?

COLIN (*sighing*). Racing driver.

DAVE. In your bus?

COLIN. Serious though, I do.

A slight pause.

I mean shifts, working shifts all the bloody time – no bloody end to it – all the bloody time. You seen Barry's dad? He's a bloody cripple – because of shifts all the bloody time – cripple.

A slight pause.

Don't mean cripple with a walking stick. Not all due to shifts, some of it is.

A pause.

Like a change.

COLIN *stands and walks up the towpath.*

DAVE. Napoleon travelled by horse.

COLIN *(muttering).* Interesting.

DAVE. Eh?

COLIN. I said, how bloody interesting.

DAVE. Yeh, I thought it was.

A pause.

When I'm on back-shift I watch schools telly. History for eight-
year-olds.

A pause.

DAVE. Trouble is, when I'm on front-shift, I miss it. End up only
knowing half of it. Bloody annoying. Still don't know in what year
he became Emperor.

COLIN. Eighteen-o-four.

DAVE. Eh?

COLIN. I've watched it a few times.

DAVE *(laughing).* Be joining the Brains Trust next –

COLIN *(loud).* Jesus Christ, shut up!

DAVE. Listen, mate, don't shout at me! Not my bloody fault.

He exits.

COLIN. Did I say it was? Anyway I don't care, kick the copper's head
in when he comes to the door. *(He exits after DAVE.)*

A pause.

BARRY *enters along the towpath. He stops. He thinks. For a
moment he stands, his body rigid, his face tilted to the left. His
movements are becoming strange; his appearance is dirtier; the
words he uses make sense only to himself.*

BARRY. I could do with a swim. Hide and seek. Monopoly. And
Mayfair's mine. Two houses, one hotel. Two hundred pounds. The

Old Kent Road. Park Lane. I could jump. Jump. Big Splash. Water works. Take a chance. Community card. Jump. Jump! Little Jack Horner sat in a corner. Funny thing. Funny. Cluedo. Games. The Queen in the tower has blood on her finger. Could jump. Jump off here. Not funny, no. (*He forces himself back from the side.*) Not funny. Can't swim. (*He exits.*)

The lights dim down and then pull back up.

TOM (*off*). Yeh?

MARY (*off*). Yeh.

TOM (*laughing*). Good.

MARY *and* TOM *enter.*

MARY. His dad takes him to work, drives him to the depot in his van. An old mini-van – 1968. Was blue but it's going rusty now. That way Barry has to go.

A pause.

Got our own telly now in our bedroom. Three channels. Get lines across it on BBC One, but not bad.

TOM. Wants mending.

MARY. Portable, it is. All Barry knows is the television. All we all know is the television. Don't think I want to move out now. Sort of got used to it, green curtains, wallpaper. You know how you get used to places.

TOM. Yeh.

MARY. Got used to looking at those little fishes on the bathroom wall. Sharks.

TOM. Not little.

MARY. Big then. Suppose sharks must be big.

TOM *squats down. He looks into the water.*

TOM. This water's dirty.

MARY. Barry doesn't say very much. He's just quiet. Not dummy like, well – (*Reflects.*) bit like a dummy really. I'm pleased that he goes to work, pleased that his father takes him. Feel I can trust him now.

TOM. Yeh?

MARY. Trust. Don't get on with his mam like I used to.

MARY *walks up the towpath*. TOM *picks up a stone, he plays with it in his hands*.

Glad in a way, to get on with my own things. By myself. Barbara's started to walk now, been walking a bit. Just sits, does Barry.

TOM. Remember I felt like that once.

MARY (*pointing*). That an old fridge over there, in the canal?

TOM (*looking*) Cooker.

MARY. Oh.

TOM. Not as bad.

MARY. Yeh?

TOM. Bit wild. A wrecker.

MARY. Barry's not wild.

TOM. Was wild.

MARY. Might say that.

TOM. One day, hadn't a case, had to use a carrier bag, packed a couple of shirts and left. For Liverpool. Thought about going on a bloody boat, working on a boat. Cunard. Salty seas. Returned home the next day. Police wouldn't let me onto the bloody docks. Spent the night on Liverpool Station. (*He smiles*.)

A pause.

I don't see my family now – (*He stands*.) my mam and dad. Got two brothers. Haven't for five years. Don't blame them, blame *me*, I suppose. Change. It happens. Never want to see them again. Happens.

He walks to MARY.

Remember once, my father coming home from work, drunk. Couldn't bloody stand up. We just sort of left him, lying on the floor. Out cold, like a bleedin' light. I was only about eight. He'd been on the beer, got onto the whisky. He came in and he had this dead sparrow, picked it up from the road, he wouldn't let it go, kept holding it. Even kissed it. It was all wet, half its feathers hanging off.

TOM *walks along the towpath*.

Anyway, turned out he'd been given the push, sacked. Gone out and got drunk as celebration. Celebration, huh! He called it a celebration.

He throws the stone high in the air and catches it.

They have problems of their own.

MARY. Why Liverpool?

TOM. Liverpool, a place. A town.

He throws the stone and catches it.

Then I met June.

He throws the stone.

Got another job, my dad. He always did, eventually. Don't blame him for that even. (*He squats down.*) Hadn't been to Liverpool.

A pause.

That's why when June and I have kids –

He stands, throws the stone in the air and catches it.

Well –

He walks to MARY.

MARY. Yeh.

TOM. I saw my brother once. Trevor. He was just the same.

They start to exit along the towpath.

MARY. Do you think Barry might have gone to Liverpool?

TOM. Don't think so.

MARY (*off*). Might have done.

TOM (*off*). Might. Never been back.

MARY (*off*). No.

A pause.

BARRY *enters running along the towpath. He stops. He pushes his neck and head forward and stares at the water.*

A pause.

He points at something in the canal.

A pause.

He squats down and again points. He sees a fish. He follows it with his eyes as it swims.

BARRY (*quite quietly*). A fish, a fish, a fish. (*He moves along the towpath a couple of feet.*) There you are. I can see you. (*He listens. He smiles.*) I can hear you fish. (*He listens.*) Hear you. (*He smiles, half-laughs.*) Yes. Yes. (*His face changes.*) No! Throw a rock at you. Kill you.

He looks up, agony on his face.

Again the electronic sounds, distorted from reality.

Stop talking to me. (*Louder.*) Stop talking to me! (*He looks at the fish.*) Stop talking! Stop talking! Stop!

NO!

BARRY *backs away from the edge of the towpath.*

Lights go down. A rippling water effect on the canal. A light on BARRY.

(*At first quietly, getting louder.*) It was the horrible game because I am the fingers of a parlour that did it, of life, to life, in the arms of a funeral place about all of us of life, sitting together of life, about a game of life. A monopoly life. That is it. All about when you were a foot high and that's what I want to say now. A silly bit of life, is that what it all is? All about all of us of life.

Faintly in the distance the voice of a BOY.

It is that of BARRY, *aged eight.*

BOY. Mam, Mam, I want my own room. Why can't I have my own room? I want my own room, Mam, want my own room, Mam Mam Mam Mam –

BARRY. All about all of us life and wishing it would fall into the wishing well of life and wishing, isn't that true about life and outside it all is?

BOY (*getting louder*). Mam, Mam, where's my rabbit? Where's my rabbit, Mam? Where's my rabbit?

LYN (*over speakers*). You've eaten it, now shut up.

FATHER (*over speakers*). It's your own bloody fault.

BARRY (*shouting*). Today we eat in the sink and have it to do with life.

BOY. I hate you. I hate you both, you're horrible.

A scream from the BOY *as he is slapped.*

BARRY *feels the slap, he jolts his head.*

He waves his hands through the air.

The scream of the BOY *becomes that of the* BIOLOGY TEACHER.

BIOLOGY TEACHER. The mice, the mice, the mice they're all dead. The mice.

BARRY (*agony on his face*). Eat in the sink. Yes! (*He is sweating.*) Yes, I know in life. Life in a red sink beginning to watch the forces from life in the moon and sun is shining. In a red sink of life.

The voices in BARRY'*s head are getting louder.*

LYN. Shut up, Barry. Get out or I'll belt you. Do you hear?

A second scream from the BOY *echoes and fades.*

BARRY *again feels the slap.*

The BIOLOGY TEACHER *screams.*

BARRY *clutches his head with his hands.*

BARRY. This is all I do with life is twisting in a red sink of life. It's all very dirty. Dirty. Like a dance in the tree of life.

The voices echo more and more.

LYN. Don't you bloody go on at me!

FATHER. Sod off!

LYN. Fine bloody way to speak to your wife!

FATHER. Shut up!

LYN. Bloody fine. (*Echoing to silence.*) Bloody fine, bloody fine, bloody fine, bloody fine, bloody fine –

BARRY *looks up.*

BARRY (*screams*). NO!

A third and longer scream from the BOY.

(*Waving his hands violently through the air.*) GET OFF ME! GET OFF ME!

A slight pause.

LYN. He's leaving school tomorrow.

FATHER. Idle bastard.

LYN. What you doing, Barry? (*Echoing to silence*.) What you doing? What you doing? What you doing? What you doing? What you doing?

FATHER (*voice coming in on* LYN'*s echo*). Own bloody room now and he's still as dirty. Still as dirty, still as dirty, still as dirty, still as dirty, still as dirty, still as dirty –

The echoes fade.

A slight pause.

BARRY *again looks up. For the moment, the voices having gone he seems calmer, quieter.*

BARRY. I heard you fish. It's all to do with the warming of your feet in the wishing well. Calmer of life. Calmer.

Suddenly the sound of Barbara crying.

Loudly the voices come in again.

BARRY *doesn't know what to do. His face contorts. He stands. He twists his fingers together.*

MARY. Why do you have to make such a mess everywhere?

LYN. Pick all that up.

MARY. Why such a bloody mess?

LYN. He's always been a dirty little boy. Dirty little boy, dirty little boy, dirty little boy, dirty little boy, dirty little boy, dirty little boy, dirty little boy.

MARY (*joining* LYN'*s echo*). Why such a bloody mess, why such a bloody mess, why such a bloody mess, why such a bloody mess, why such a bloody mess, why such a bloody mess?

MAN (*joining their echoes*). Sorry Mr Jackson we don't want you as a bus driver. As a bus driver, as a bus driver, as a bus driver, as a bus driver, as a bus driver, as a bus driver –

Echoes of voices are gone.

BARRY (*throwing his hands through the air, screaming*). I HATE YOU! I HATE YOU! I HATE YOU!! I HATE YOU!!

A slight pause.

BARRY *falls forward into the canal.*

A splash and the sound of water.

Lights change. The canal ripples with light.

BARRY *moves in slow motion under the water. He mimes attempting to swim, half-drowning, half-succeeding.*

Occasionally he is able to bring his head up out of the water for air.

A pause.

He brings his head out of the water. He half-screams, half-groans.

Err – err – err! (*Goes under again, comes back up.*) Err – (*Under again, back up.*) Err – err! (*He coughs. Again under.*)

A pause.

(*Comes up.*) Arr – (*Again under.*)

TOM (*off. Shouting extremely loud*). WHERE ARE YOU?

BARRY (*up again*). Err – (*He coughs and goes under. Up again.*) Arr – arr –

TOM (*off*). WHERE?

BARRY (*screaming*). Arr – arrrrrrrr – (*He goes under.*)

TOM (*off*). WHERE?

BARRY (*up again*). Arr. (*He coughs and goes under again.*)

BARRY*'s movements in slow motion become more and more frantic – those of a drowning man.*

A pause.

TOM *enters. He jumps in and moves under the water.* BARRY, *not wishing rescue, pushes him away. They both go under.*

A pause in the scuffle as they both come up for air.

TOM (*shouting*). Bastard. (*He takes a deep breath.*)

They go under. TOM *again tries to grab* BARRY. *Again* BARRY *pushes him away, this time more violently.*

They scuffle.

A pause as they come up for air.

BARRY (*screaming*) Arr –

TOM. Bastard!

> *They go under.* TOM *in an attempt to pacify* BARRY *thumps him. We can see* BARRY *feels the punch by the expression of pain on his face.* BARRY *struggles.*

> *A slight pause in the fight as* TOM *comes up for air.*

> TOM *grabs* BARRY*'s head and pushes it down under the water.* TOM *keeps* BARRY *there, his cheeks bulging with air as he holds his breath.* BARRY *slowly becomes more and more passive until he is still.*

> *A pause.*

> TOM *lets* BARRY *go. They both float to the surface. They take in air. Immediately* BARRY *starts to struggle again.*

Bastard!

> *Again* TOM *pushes* BARRY *down. He holds him there for twenty seconds.* BARRY *becomes passive. Becomes limp.*

> *They slowly float to the surface.*

> *A slight pause as* TOM *takes a deep breath.*

> TOM *grabs* BARRY*'s limp body and slowly pulls him, half-swimming, half-treading water, to the edge of the canal.*

> *A pause.*

> *They flop down onto the towpath.*

> *Lights change. White light pulls up.*

> BARRY *and* TOM *both lie flat out. Both breathe very deeply.*

> *A pause.*

> MARY *enters. She stands for a moment and looks at them. She is almost calm as if she had been expecting this to happen. She goes to* BARRY.

MARY. It's alright.

BARRY (*groans*). Arr – (*Saliva drips down his chin.*)

MARY (*almost flippant*). Nothing.

> BARRY *stands, he walks away.* MARY *looks at* TOM.

TOM. Barry?

   MARY *walks to* BARRY.

MARY (*comforting voice*). Come on, my friend, my husband.

   BARRY *walks away*.

   What were you doing down by the canal?

   BARRY *walks further away*.

   Thought you were at work?

   BARRY *sits*.

TOM (*hard*). You want to learn to open your fucking mouth, you do, son.

   MARY *walks to* BARRY.

MARY (*comforting voice*). Eh Lone Ranger? (*She walks away*.) I can't talk to you! It's like you were a stuffed animal in a glass case, in a museum. Bloody museum. All still and rigid. You'll get the sack, Barry!

   TOM *starts to walk to* BARRY. MARY *pushes him away*. TOM *looks amazed*.

   No, he's my problem.

TOM. Mary –

MARY. Leave him!

   TOM *walks away*. MARY *goes to* BARRY, *she kneels down beside him*.

   (*Comforting voice*.) Listen to me, Barry.

   BARRY *looks at the ground*.

   (*Suddenly angry*.) Do something! Do bloody something! Hit me if you like – (*Shouting*.) Hit me if you like!

   A pause.

   (*Almost pleading*.) Tell me, what do I do? What have I to do? What are you going to do?

   MARY *stands*. *She walks away from him*.

   (*Angry*.) Buy me a house? Hah! A bloody famous oil painting on the wall to stare at?

TOM *looks at the ground.*

Hah! A house? Hah! Bloody house! Don't make me bloody laugh. House! Hah! (*She laughs.*)

BARRY *stands. He runs. He exits.*

(*Screaming after him.*) Barry! (*She runs after him.*) Barry!

TOM. Let him go.

MARY (*screaming*). Barry!

TOM. Mary.

MARY *turns and looks at* TOM.

MARY (*quietly*). What can I do?

TOM *goes to her. He comforts her, puts his arm around her waist.*

(*Quietly.*) I want the person I love, who used to love me.

TOM. Don't know.

MARY. Look at him.

MARY *looks up. Their eyes meet.*

TOM. I don't know.

TOM *breaks away. He walks a few yards.*

MARY. I remember seeing a house once. A white house, almost white, built of stone. (*She smiles.*)

TOM *looks at her.*

Not brick, but stone. It was very beautiful. Remember it now like it was standing over there.

TOM. When you were a child?

MARY. It had a garden, all planned, neat and tidy like a big garden that you pay to walk round. Nothing, not a flower out of place. Built of solid stone. (*She smiles.*)

TOM. Yes.

MARY. Have you seen a house like that?

TOM. No, I haven't.

MARY. When I saw the flowers in the garden, I wanted to run and pick them. A bowl to put them in. (*She almost sobs.*)

A slight pause.

Be about eight.

TOM. When you're eight you remember things like that.

MARY. Suppose so. (*She walks a few yards.*) Yes. I remember –

A slight pause.

Reading stories of frogs turning into princes. (*She laughs.*)

TOM *smiles.*

You're smiling.

TOM. Like to smile. Mary –

A slight pause.

MARY. Yes?

TOM. You'd be better leaving him –

MARY (*she interrupts him*). This white house was on top of a big hill.

TOM. Mary?

A pause.

Even if it was only for a while. Sort of bring him to his senses.

MARY (*angry*). What right have you to say that?

TOM. No right.

MARY. Look, I've been through all this before.

TOM. Yes.

A pause.

Let me tell you something, it sounds so bloody stupid, but I want that house on a hill. So bloody stupid.

MARY. You'll get it.

TOM. Will I?

MARY. Think so. A job.

TOM. A job?

MARY. What *you* do.

TOM. What do you mean?

MARY. Barry hasn't got a job like yours. A good job.

TOM. Because I'm in charge of a few people?

MARY. Yes.

A slight pause.

I don't know what I'm going to do.

A slight pause.

(*Looking at him.*) You'll get that house.

A slight pause.

I think Barry's mam is going to throw us out shortly, I can feel it. Feel it coming. Don't blame her.

(*Bitterly.*) She's a cow.

A pause.

When Barbara's older I can go out to work.

TOM. Yes?

MARY. Yeh.

A slight pause.

Yes. We'll find somewhere to live.

JUNE *enters. She carries a shopping bag.*

JUNE. Been waiting ages so I thought I'd look for you. (*To* TOM.) What's been happening?

TOM (*aside to* JUNE). Tell you later. Ssh.

MARY (*trying her best to seem brighter*). Coming.

TOM (*to* JUNE, *louder*). Talking. (*He smiles.*)

MARY. About houses.

JUNE. Oh?

MARY. Yeh.

JUNE (*to* TOM). I've got everything.

MARY. Shopping

JUNE. Yeh. Bloody shops. (*To* TOM.) You been talking about houses again? (*To* MARY.) He never bloody stops.

JUNE *takes a small parcel from her bag. She gives it to* MARY.

For you.

MARY. Me?

JUNE. Just something.

MARY *opens the parcel. She takes out a small baby's dress.*

For Barbara. Just saw it, thought it was nice.

MARY. Yes.

TOM (*turning to exit*). Come on.

JUNE. Wait a minute.

TOM. Come on.

MARY. Must have cost a lot.

JUNE. Not much.

MARY. It's nice.

TOM. I'll be walking on.

TOM *exits.*

JUNE. Come on. (*She moves to exit.*)

MARY. June –

JUNE *stops, turns.*

You keep it.

JUNE. No.

MARY. Go on.

JUNE. What for?

A slight pause.

MARY. Oh, I don't know.

They exit. Light fades to blackout.

Scene Ten

Four days later.

A park.

DAVE *and* COLIN *sitting on the grass.*

They wear their bus driver's uniforms.

DAVE *is reading a copy of* The Sun.

COLIN *is eating a meat pie.*

DAVE. What did the apple say to the orange?

COLIN. Core, you look juicy. (*He stares at* DAVE.)

DAVE. Oh.

COLIN. Funny!

DAVE. I thought it was.

COLIN. You would.

DAVE. How do they put the tea in teabags? Force it through the holes.

COLIN *stands. He walks away.*

COLIN. So you watched telly last night as well!

DAVE *laughs.*

What does a woman get when she uses a yellow sanitary towel?

DAVE. Give up.

COLIN. A sunny period. (*He walks back to* DAVE.) Listen, Dave, I've got this idea.

DAVE. Don't want to know.

COLIN. Something I said once about robbing piggy banks.

DAVE. Yeh?

COLIN. So we could.

DAVE. What's that?

COLIN. Rob a bank. (*He laughs. He sits.*) I've always had this ambition to see inside a fuckin' prison.

DAVE. Thought about answering one of those adverts, 'become a prisoner warder'? (*He laughs.*)

COLIN. Sod off. (*Reflecting*.) Rob a bank. Or a jeweller's shop in Bond Street.

A pause.

Given up, decided they wouldn't dare evict us.

DAVE *laughs*.

Glad you find it funny.

DAVE *laughs*.

(*Shouts*.) Glad you find it fuckin' funny!

DAVE *is silenced*.

(*Standing, walking away*.) Wife threatened to leave me last night, take the kids.

A slight pause.

Always thought that's just what I bloody wanted. Now –

DAVE. Wouldn't bloody work, would it?

COLIN. Wouldn't work for you. (*He turns to face* DAVE.) Just for a couple of weeks, that's all.

DAVE. Couple of weeks, a year –

COLIN. Few days.

DAVE. Few days, a year, goes on.

COLIN. If she leaves me –

DAVE. She won't.

COLIN. You shit in my face and I'll shit in yours. (*He walks away*.) Remember you asking me to borrow some money.

DAVE. Did I bloody get it?

A pause.

COLIN. If we could move in for just a couple of weeks.

DAVE. My house is my house. No room.

COLIN. Bastard!

DAVE. Don't call me a bastard.

A slight pause.

COLIN. Said she'd take her and the kids to one of her bloody cousins. Oh, Hollywood USA.

A slight pause.

Hollywood USA, I fancy that. I love her when I want to love her. I know I'm no good.

A slight pause.

No good me asking again?

DAVE. Arranged anything, have you?

COLIN (*laughing*). No.

DAVE. You're an idiot.

COLIN. Yeh. (*He smiles.*)

DAVE. Sally Army?

COLIN. Have to learn to play a fuckin' trumpet.

DAVE. Trumpet, so what?

COLIN (*laughing*). Never was any good at music.

DAVE. Somewhere to go.

COLIN (*hard*). For tramps.

DAVE. Seen a vicar?

COLIN (*hard*). When I was bloody christened.

DAVE *looks at* COLIN. COLIN *stares at him.*

I could kick you.

DAVE *looks at him.*

Could!

DAVE *looks away.*

Right in your bleedin' face.

COLIN *stares at him.* DAVE *is still avoiding his gaze.*

Could do!

DAVE. Sit down.

COLIN. Kick your fuckin' head in.

A pause

Said she's going today.

DAVE *looks at him*.

Leaving this moment, for all I bloody know.

DAVE. Wife?

COLIN. Who else? Her cousin is called Marjorie, Marjorie, a fuckin' idiot if ever there was one. Marjorie and Billy, her husband. Billy's hobby is fucking other people's wives. Not that I care about mine. Not that she cares about me.

A slight pause.

Thump his face in, break his nose, if he touches her.

A slight pause.

She'll be packing the suitcases, so –

A slight pause.

So –

DAVE. So?

COLIN. Shut up!

DAVE. You want to watch how you bloody speak to people.

COLIN (*hard*). Oh?

DAVE. Yeh.

COLIN (*hard*). Why's that then? (*He moves towards* DAVE.)

DAVE (*staring at him*). Just do.

COLIN. Been in the army, have you?

DAVE. No.

COLIN. Learnt how to be hard? (*He threatens* DAVE.)

DAVE. No.

COLIN. Screw fuckers about?

DAVE. No.

They stare at each other.

Never wanted to fight a war. (*He smiles*.)

COLIN *looks at his watch*.

COLIN. If she goes –

A pause.

COLIN *sits.*

Trouble is, how do you pay off debts with no bloody money?

DAVE. Overtime?

COLIN. Don't like overtime.

DAVE. No choice.

COLIN. Got a fuckin' choice. Fuckin' choice.

DAVE. What?

COLIN. Don't know. Become Royalty. (*He laughs.*) King Colin.

DAVE *looks at him.*

You're so bloody serious.

DAVE. Yeh.

COLIN *runs at him. He grabs* DAVE *by the back of the neck. They scuffle.*

DAVE *breaks away. He runs. For a brief moment they stare at each other.*

Sod off, Colin.

DAVE *exits quickly.*

COLIN. What did the apple say to the orange? (*Quietly.*) You give me the pip – (*Shouting.*) You give me the bloody pip!

A pause.

(*Calling.*) Sod off then!

A pause.

(*Calling.*) Fuckin' turd! Shit-faced twat!

A pause.

You give me the pip. You fuckin' git!

A pause.

(*Calling.*) Go on, bloody run!

A slight pause.

(*Shouting.*) SOD YOU! SOD YOU!

He stares off for a moment.

A pause.

He walks back.

A pause.

He looks at his watch.

Forget the poxy job.

A pause.

He sits down and starts to read The Sun.

He flicks through the pages, sees a joke and starts to laugh.

A pause.

He flicks over some more pages.

Light slowly fades to blackout.

Scene Eleven

The sitting room.

A baby's highchair. A baby's dish upon it.

Crumbs on the floor.

BARRY *standing a few paces from the highchair. He has a very faint smile on his face. Apart from occasionally moving his fingers he does not move a muscle.*

A pause.

MARY *enters. She takes the baby's dish and exits.*

A pause.

MARY *returns. With a damp cloth she wipes some crumbs off the highchair.*

She talks as much to herself as to BARRY.

MARY. I bought a paper. Went out and got it myself – five pence it was. Or was it four?

She works.

He's got it, your bloody dad. Looking at the telly page, why he can't buy one himself. Bloody paper.

She works.

TV Times. Happened to the paper I got yesterday. Worth my while buying them a *Radio Times.*

She works.

Not many adverts in there today. It's Saturday.

She exits.

A pause.

She returns and wipes the floor.

I didn't want any old job. (*Calls.*) Don't think you can keep that paper all night.

She works.

You can go on collecting your bloody money.

She works.

Barbara, well –

She pushes BARRY *away a few feet so she can wipe the area of floor where he was standing.*

Told you a million times about standing there all dirty, it's a bloody disgrace. (*She exits.*)

A pause.

She returns carrying a crumpled copy of the Evening Standard.

Your dad's decided he'll go out. Terrible a paper after he's read it, all crumpled.

She rests the paper on the highchair.

Oh damn, I've missed a bit. There's still some custard on here.

She wipes it with her finger.

Lights dim to blackout.

Scene Twelve

A street.

BARRY *lying dead on the pavement.*

BRIAN JONES *a passer-by is standing beside him.*

A slight pause.

A POLICE CONSTABLE *enters.*

BRIAN. Collapsed. I was just walking –

CONSTABLE. Take off his shoes – er, ambulance, have you called an –

BRIAN. Woman. A woman's gone, to the phone box.

> BRIAN *takes off* BARRY's *shoes. The* CONSTABLE *kneels. He takes a deep breath and blows into* BARRY's *mouth. He pushes on his chest to deflate his lungs. He does it six times.* BRIAN *watches.*

CONSTABLE. Er –

> *Again the* CONSTABLE *blows into* BARRY's *mouth. He puts his ear to* BARRY's *chest.*

> It's no use.

> *He starts to thump* BARRY's *chest.*

> *He thumps fast. His thumping gets faster, almost as if he were becoming angry at the lack of response from the dead* BARRY.

BRIAN. Fuckin' hell.

> *After thirty seconds the* CONSTABLE *stops.*

> *A slight pause.*

> *He takes a driving licence from* BARRY's *pocket.*

CONSTABLE. Licence to drive a motorbike.

> *A slight pause.*

> Name?

> *Lights change. Blackout. A light up on* MARY.

MARY. Barry Jackson.

CONSTABLE. Age –

MARY. Twenty-two years.

CONSTABLE. Cause of death?

A pause.

Any other relevant points?

MARY. No.

Scene Thirteen

The mortuary.

The stainless steel table and chair. The PATHOLOGIST*'s shoes by the hat stand.*

On the hat stand his jacket and tie.

BARRY*'s body on the trolley covered by the white sheet. The post-mortem is finished.*

A light on the body. Houselights to half.

The PATHOLOGIST *is standing by the trolley. He removes his rubber gloves.*

PATHOLOGIST. The body was taken away in an ambulance. No panic, no sirens screeching, no flashing lights. A doctor – (*He consults the clipboard.*) Dr Richard Clements, who came with the ambulance, certified him dead. At the hospital he lay on a trolley for three hours before a porter was instructed to wheel him down to the mortuary. (*He sits.*) At the mortuary, his socks and shoes, his jacket, trousers, and shirt were removed and placed in a numbered plastic bag. His underpants and vest were cut away. (*He changes into his shoes.*) After having been washed his body was placed, along with five others that had arrived that afternoon, in a large fridge for the night. It is not unusual for bodies to stay two or three days in these fridges. Because of his age and the circumstances of his death a post-mortem was asked for. For this, permission was sort and was finally reluctantly granted by the family. His mother and father in particular seemed bitterly opposed. Some next of kin will often only give their permission if an undertaking is made only to make one or two small incisions.

A slight pause.

He takes off the apron and puts on his jacket.

The examination of this body proved to be very interesting. It was not an easy job. I found no signs of any fatal disease, nothing that could be said to be, 'a principal cause of death.' I looked again. Certain tests were repeated and rechecked in the laboratory. Again nothing. The bacterial examination, though rarely profitable, was carried out and proved a blank.

A slight pause.

The body did seem to me, in one or two ways, to resemble that of an older man. Clinical evidence? Only slight. Instinct? Perhaps instinct, I don't know. A desire from the patient himself to age, to die? It has been known. To run away? If circumstances are bad enough I suppose that is possible. (*He puts on his tie.*) On his death certificate the doctor wrote, 'natural causes'. In my report which I must conclude twenty-four hours after completing the examination I shall write, 'cause of death unknown'.

Two PORTERS *enter and wheel off the body.*

The light on the body dims to blackout.

When the post-mortem is finished to the satisfaction of the doctor and the pathologist, and everything clinically has been learnt to aid society in the future, the body is returned to a shelf in the fridge to await collection and burial by an undertaker selected by the family. (*He takes some car keys from his pocket.*)

Thank you for your attention.

PATHOLOGIST *exits.*

Houselights up to full.

The end.

MUD

Mud was first presented under the title *Taking Stock* at the Royal Court Theatre, London, on 25 August 1974, with the following cast:

GEORGE HARDCASTLE   John Normington
HAROLD PIKE   Ian Marter
ALAN TODD   Brian Deacon
PAULINE SWAILES   Susie Blake
SQUIRE PIKE   Gerald James

Director   Chris Parr

Characters

GEORGE HARDCASTLE
HAROLD PIKE
ALAN TODD
PAULINE SWAILES
SQUIRE PIKE

The play takes place during one very hot August, eight hundred feet up on North Yorkshire moors near Whitby.

The play is in seven scenes with an Interval after Scene Three.

A moor. To the left, the ground rises to form a small hill. Upon this hill stands a dying tree. Right, at the bottom of the hill, is an area of marsh, a patch of waterlogged ground such as is found in numerous places on any moor.

The ground is rough and barren, covered sparsely in yellow scorched grass, moss and weeds. Only one or two small clumps of purple heather look at all fresh and alive. The ground is stony, especially up the sides of the hill.

Scene One

August the first. A very hot sunny day. In the distance the sound of birds. An aeroplane flies loudly over. The birds are scared and squawk more loudly as they take to the air. GEORGE HARDCASTLE *enters. He watches the aeroplane as it flies off into the distance.*

GEORGE *is sixty-five. He wears a dark brown suit and tie. A pause.* GEORGE *puts his hands on his hips and surveys the scene. He takes a deep breath, smiles. A pause. He puts down his carrier bag and fishing rod and stands for a moment in silence. Again he takes a deep breath. A pause. He starts to touch his toes.*

GEORGE (*touches*). Hup. (*Touches.*) Hup. (*Touches.*) Hup. (*In succession.*) One, two, three, four. (*Stops, out of breath.*)

A pause. He looks around to see if anybody is looking and then goes down into a sprinter's starting position.

On your marks. Get set. Go!

At the same time as he says 'Go!' there is a bang from a shotgun. GEORGE *runs a few yards and again stops out of breath. He takes a deep breath.*

No use me trying to stand on my head.

He takes a paperback fishing book from his pocket.

P for perch. (*He opens the book, reads*.) – drift float fishing!

A pause.

The method is self-explanatory!

GEORGE *is bafffled. He puts his book away and starts to make the necessary preparations for fishing. This is simple, all he has to do is take a slice of bread from his carrier bag and attach a small piece of it to the hook. The rod is already fitted with a fishing line.*

While he is doing this, HAROLD PIKE *is heard singing in the distance.*

HAROLD (*off*). I was born and bred on Yorkshire's soil
For thirty-one years I've learnt to toil
For my father who's squire,
He hunts on the moor
And he owns all the land in the valley.
When the August sun shines hot and high
I shoot at birds as they flutter in the sky –

HAROLD *enters. He is thirty-one, wears very smart working clothes, fawn trousers, tweed jacket. He carries a shotgun. In his hand he has a dead rabbit. He wears dark glasses.*

GEORGE *casts his line into the marsh.*

You a fisherman?

GEORGE. Yes, I'm a fisherman.

HAROLD. Nice. An expert fisherman?

GEORGE. Wouldn't say expert. Never been after the big ones, sharks and things like that.

HAROLD. No?

GEORGE. A hobby. Inland fishing. Perch. Prefer the inland waters, never much fancied braving the mid-Atlantic in a rowing boat. Too rough. Leave that to trawlers.

HAROLD. Couldn't land a three-hundred-pound killer shark?

GEORGE (*smiling*). Don't think I could. (*He settles back to fish.*)

A pause. HAROLD *walks on.*

HAROLD. You'll as likely catch a shark in there as a perch.

GEORGE. Oh?

HAROLD. In fact be lucky if you land a rusting old beer can. (*He looks into the marsh*.) Did once chuck an old McEwan's Export can in there. Filled it with tiny pebbles to make it sink. Stagnant. It's stagnant.

GEORGE. Don't think so.

HAROLD. Know so. Seen more life in a dead rabbit.

GEORGE. Oh.

HAROLD. Beer cans and dead sheep, that's all there is in there. That's all.

GEORGE. Well –

A pause. HAROLD *walks up the hill.*

HAROLD. You're not bothered?

GEORGE (*brightly*). It's the sport that's important, not the catch. The open air. Catching a fish would be a perk, I can do without perks. (*He pulls gently on the line with his fingers*.) Landed rainbow trout by the hundred once. From a beck.

HAROLD. Oh?

GEORGE. With a fly. Not here.

HAROLD. No?

GEORGE. Scotland. The north.

HAROLD. Yes?

GEORGE. By the hundred. Great big things, about that size. (*He holds his hands two feet apart*.)

HAROLD. You'll be telling me next about the one that got away.

A pause.

When motor vehicles have run them over, damaged them, killed them, hurl them in there. Dead sheep. Get rid of them. Usually stinks on a hot day like this, rotten blood.

GEORGE. Oh.

HAROLD (*he licks his finger, holds it in the air*). Wind's blowing from the east today.

GEORGE. Like to feel the open air when I'm fishing. (*He looks up.*) Watch the clouds chasing in the sky.

HAROLD (*he uses his gun as a shooting-stick and sits on it*). They say when the wind blows from the east on the first day of August we'll have storms by the first day of September.

GEORGE. Earth beneath my feet.

HAROLD. If they're not too bad we send them to the hunt to feed to the hounds. Dead sheep.

A pause.

GEORGE. You fish?

HAROLD *jumps up. He holds his gun as if about to shoot.*

HAROLD. I shoot! BANG. Rabbits. Anything! Find blowing little animals to bits very relaxing. When I was a boy I used to drown kittens. Would do it in the bath. Used to hold them under with the end of one of my toy battleships. (*Getting very excited he starts to move the gun from side to side.*) Taught this dog we had to catch rats. Called her Ratter. A pedigree spaniel. Used to wait, crouched by the haystack, Ratter on lead, saliva dripping from her chops, waiting. Father taught me. Slip the lead, Ratter'd get one in her mouth, crush it in her jaws. Bloody great brown rat dead in her mouth.

A pause.

Break a leg if you slip into a rabbit hole.

He offers GEORGE *the rabbit.*

Want it?

GEORGE. Haven't the facilities. For cooking in my caravan. Just a small oven. Portable gas.

HAROLD. Holidaying eh?

GEORGE. Yes.

HAROLD. Rented? Owned?

GEORGE. Rented. Answered an advert in *Exchange and Mart*. Make do with fish fingers, me.

HAROLD *throws the rabbit.*

HAROLD. Some fox will find it. From the south are you?

GEORGE. Yes.

HAROLD. Thought so. Nearer the Equator the south, the tropics, warmer. Retired?

GEORGE (*smiling*). Just.

HAROLD (*again sitting on his gun*). Used to call me Sherlock Holmes at school, being good at deductions, teachers and pupils alike, all called me Sherlock. Kept his books under my pillow. Studied them. Gold watch?

GEORGE (*smiling*). Fishing rod. Fishing rod from my mates, roses for the garden from my boss. Don't have a garden. (*He smiles*.) Bloody stupid.

HAROLD. On your own are you?

GEORGE. Yes.

HAROLD. Lonely?

GEORGE. Wouldn't say lonely.

HAROLD. I would.

GEORGE. Earned a break after all these years, turned enough earth. Time to settle down now. Not lonely. (*He gently pulls on the line with his fingers*.)

Silence. HAROLD *jumps off the the gun and walks to the marsh.*

HAROLD. Yes, when I was just a child, before I could walk, before the pit-patter of my tiny feet, father'd read to me from *The Hound of the Baskervilles*. Bloody story, people being poisoned, knifed. Find it fascinating. (*He looks at* GEORGE.)

GEORGE. Yes.

HAROLD. Pity Conan Doyle isn't still alive. I could tell him a story that would make his hair stand on end.

GEORGE *pulls on the line with his fingers. He takes a hanky and wipes his brow.*

GEORGE. I gave the roses away. A friend. Better that they be used. I always wanted a garden, cultivate prize chrysanthemums and cucumbers. Chrysanthemums on the floral side and cucumbers on the vegetable side. Had to make do with cactuses in plantpots.

HAROLD. Hah!

GEORGE *smiles.*

Children have you?

GEORGE. Two.

HAROLD. Girls?

GEORGE. Boys. One a garage mechanic. An expert on cylinder-heads. His life and hobby tampering with car engines. Other works for the Coal Board in Wales. Huh. (*He smiles*.)

HAROLD. Wife?

GEORGE pulls on the line with his fingers. A pause.

GEORGE. She's buried now.

HAROLD. I'm –

GEORGE. Don't have to be sorry.

HAROLD. Yes but –

GEORGE. Buried. Dead.

HAROLD. Sorry.

A pause. HAROLD sits.

Natural?

GEORGE. Natural?

HAROLD. Accident? Not a mishap with a lorry? Sorry, shouldn't have asked.

GEORGE. No lorry. You learn to forget.

HAROLD. Bus?

GEORGE (*hard*). I said you learn to forget!

A pause.

Nothing like that.

A pause.

HAROLD. The Royal Air Force fly over here.

A slight pause.

RAF jet fighters. Training practice. Scares the birds. If it wasn't for Moscow, the Communist threat, there'd be no need. My father blames the Kremlin.

A slight pause.

This is a National Park. Ruins the shooting. (*He points his gun.*)
Blast them from the sky like John Wayne in a war film. Big hole in
the wing.

A slight pause.

Get myself a blunderbuss.

GEORGE. She died natural, my wife. Natural!

A pause.

HAROLD. Why did you say you'd caught trout?

GEORGE. Did do once. When I was a kid. In the river with my bare
hands. Tickle them. Tickle them with my bare hand and slowly lift
them from the river – get the palm of your hand underneath their fat
bellies. Lifted as many as twenty a day some days. My hobby used
to be poaching fish when I were a kid. Poaching off the squire.
Caught us one time but we played innocent – only about eight. Lived
in the country then.

A pause.

My father worked on the land. When I were a kid I wanted to be a
farmer. Then I wanted to play an organ in a cinema. Huh! (*He smiles.*)

*A slight pause. GEORGE quotes from the 'Remembrances' by John
Clare.*

Summer's pleasures they are gone like to visions everyone,
And the cloudy days of autumn and of winter cometh on.

A slight pause.

John Clare. Poet. Farm worker. (*He smiles.*) Looks like my little
fishing book is wrong about there being perch in the ponds of
Northern England.

HAROLD. Ponds yes. Marshes no. No experience. (*He points his gun
at* GEORGE.) My father's the squire.

GEORGE. That thing loaded? Is it loaded?

HAROLD. Considers a bunch of five-pound notes small change. (*He
points the gun in a different direction.*) It's loaded.

GEORGE. Want to be careful, you do.

HAROLD. Owns over one thousand acres of rich pasture.

GEORGE. Just be careful.

HAROLD. Shoots both in and out of season. (*He points his gun at* GEORGE.) Will shoot at anything that moves. Anything that moves.

GEORGE. Just you watch it.

HAROLD *lowers his gun. He sits. A pause.*

I used to cook the fish I poached.

HAROLD. Even takes potshots at whisky bottles and silver coins. Just like in Westerns. Has holidays in exotic places. You been abroad?

GEORGE. Isle of Man. Once. For a weekend.

HAROLD. His estate will be mine when he's finally drunk himself to death. His bones swelling up – horrible gouty body.

GEORGE *pulls on the fishing line.*

GEORGE. You been overseas?

HAROLD. Up the Amazon in a canoe. Fighting off the pygmies all with big lips, chanting and throwing spears at me. (*He sighs.*) Not much. Never. Seen pictures.

A pause.

His estate will be mine. Then I can do what I want.

The sun goes in.

GEORGE. Sun's gone in.

HAROLD (*lifting his glasses slightly*). Behind a cloud.

GEORGE (*looking up*). Behind a white cloud. (*He holds out his hand.*) No breeze. Still. Hot.

HAROLD. Sweltering into the eighties I should imagine.

GEORGE. Humid.

HAROLD. Get pains across the top of my head. The sun. Fierce.

GEORGE. Wondered why –

HAROLD. Glasses? Sensitive eyes. Been prone since I was a child.

GEORGE. Winter? Wear them in winter, do you?

HAROLD. You know, you can be quite funny.

GEORGE *smiles. The sun comes back out.*

Winter's dark here, don't need glasses. Dark as a cave, a filthy dungeon. Known it fifty foot deep in snow. Nothing but snow.

A pause. HAROLD *lies back.* GEORGE *winds in a few feet of line. A pause.* HAROLD *sits up.*

You ever thought about being stupid?

GEORGE. Stupid?

HAROLD. Being stupid.

GEORGE. Not stupid.

HAROLD. Think so? You are Dr Watson to my Sherlock Holmes. Nothing. (*He lies back.*)

GEORGE. Known stupid people but I'm not stupid. You know you can be bloody rude.

HAROLD. What did the cat say to the dog with only one testicle?

A pause.

GEORGE. Aren't stupid.

A pause.

I like the quiet.

HAROLD *sits.*

The peace. Like thinking.

A pause.

HAROLD. About things?

GEORGE. About anything. Just idle thoughts. (*He smiles.*) Remember when I was a boy. Born in Oldham, near Manchester. My father was a shepherd. Anyway, up on the hills with a kite on a bright sunny day, beautiful. Kite, flying in the wind. Stone walls. Hedge backs. Solitary. White kite like a cloud, motionless. Went back there by Inter-City two years ago, saw the country from the train window, first time in twenty-odd years, place hadn't changed. Smells, still the same. Didn't like it though, I couldn't understand it. All the people I knew, still there. Mostly, anyway. Half the mills have closed. Derelict.

A pause.

Moved to London when I was twenty-two-and-a-half.

HAROLD. Smog down there. Thick. Yellow.

GEORGE. My father died in Oldham.

GEORGE pours himself tea from a flask. He takes a plastic bag containing sugar lumps from his pocket and stirs four lumps into his tea.

He almost died on the moor.

HAROLD takes a hip flask from his pocket.

Don't drink tea?

HAROLD. No.

They drink.

GEORGE. Walked over the old cobbles. (*He smiles*.) Oldham's all hills. Did you know that? That's why they're all so fit in Oldham, walking up and down the hills. Up and down, up and down, all the time. Old women, grandparents, everybody.

A pause. GEORGE puts down his rod and stands.

No smog in London. (*He takes a deep breath. He drinks*.)

Think I'll walk.

HAROLD. In those shoes?

GEORGE. Anything wrong?

HAROLD. No, no.

GEORGE. Aid the constitution.

HAROLD. Skin cracks on your toes in winter, here.

GEORGE. Not winter.

HAROLD. Legends on the moor. Mysteries unsolved. You study the stars? Planets? When Venus and Mars are in opposite poles you can never tell what is going to happen. I blame the moon missions. For the violence, for the unrest in the world. It's all around us.

GEORGE. Is it?

HAROLD. Yes. (*He jumps up*.) Given up?

GEORGE. Not a bite.

HAROLD. Might be able to find you something. A token.

Rolling up his sleeves, HAROLD goes to the marsh. He bends down and delves about within the mud at the side. Eventually he produces a sheep's skull.

GEORGE. Oh God!

He is distressed. HAROLD *laughs.*

(*Coughing.*) What is it? Get it away! GET IT AWAY.

HAROLD. Told you about the sheep. Bit rotten.

GEORGE (*calmer*). Sheep's?

HAROLD. Must be dozens in there. Summer months, cars on the road, trippers. (*He throws the skull back in.*) What d'you think it was?

GEORGE. Don't know.

HAROLD. Harmless.

GEORGE. Bloody pointless thing to do.

HAROLD. Don't swear at me!

GEORGE. Swear all I like, mate. (*He points at the rod.*) That was my rod.

HAROLD. Done nothing to that.

GEORGE. Never said you had. My leaving present.

HAROLD. Fibre glass?

GEORGE. Shut up! (*He coughs up some phlegm into his hand.*) You know I saw my wife's body laid out in a bright new coffin. Kissed her cheek, she smelt, not the sweet smell of angels. Horrible. I dropped a handful of earth onto the casket. Put soil on her. For a brief moment I saw her skull. Naked skull. You holding her rotting skull. Oh god.

GEORGE *coughs up some more phlegm into his hand. He bends down and wipes his hand on the ground. Lights fade to blackout.*

Scene Two

August the eighth. A similar sunny day. ALAN TODD *and* PAULINE
SWAILES, *a couple in their early twenties.* ALAN *is sitting, minus his
trousers, with his feet into the marsh.* PAULINE *is struggling to put
her short dress on.*

ALAN *watches her.*

ALAN. What d'yer think yer doin'?

PAULINE. What's it look like? Diggin' spuds? Puttin' me dress on
aren't a?

ALAN. Get it off easier than yer get it on. (*He watches.*) Yer a
beautiful shape. Ought to cast you in bronze, a statue in an art
gallery.

PAULINE. Have dirty old men fingering me. Get lost.

ALAN. Cast iron titties.

PAULINE. Be quiet.

ALAN. What yer puttin' it on for? I'nt cold.

PAULINE. Tramps around 'ere.

ALAN. Didn't bother yer a minute ago.

PAULINE. That were a minute ago, weren't it. Put yer trousers on. I'nt
a nudist are you? Feet'll get all mucky in there.

ALAN *kicks his feet.*

Stop that. You'll splash me dress, it'll stain. It's me best one. Stop
it!

ALAN. Take yer dress off.

PAULINE. No. I aren't a pin-up in a cheap magazine. Stop it, Alan.
(*She moves away.*) Yer no better than a five-year-old.

ALAN *acts like a five-year-old, sucks his thumb.*

Buy you a dummy next time I see one, a will.

ALAN *stops kicking.* PAULINE *has her dress on. A pause.*

ALAN. Pauline.

PAULINE. What you after now?

ALAN. Come here.

PAULINE. No.

ALAN. Love. (*It has no effect.*) Sexy.

PAULINE. Don't think yer can win me that way.

ALAN. Sexy. (*He pats the ground.*) Come here.

PAULINE. You're obsessed you are. Like our cat, yer never stop. Not good for you twice in 'alf an hour. It brings you out in spots.

ALAN *laughs*.

True as I'm standing 'ere. Promise you won't and I will.

ALAN. What?

PAULINE. Sit down. (*She sits.*)

ALAN. Wouldn't swap you. Not for the most beautiful woman in the world because you are the most beautiful woman in the world.

PAULINE. Want a wedding ring first. It in't proper. Not all the time. You will buy me a good ring, won't yer Alan? Gold.

ALAN. Thought you could make do with an old washer.

PAULINE. Be serious.

ALAN. Nick it off an old tap. (*Softly.*) Course a will. (*He puts his arm around her waist.*) Still got two left.

PAULINE. What?

ALAN (*whispers loudly in her ear*).You know.

PAULINE. Don't think you respect me. I'm just an instrument, a spanner. Love tractors more than you love me.

A pause.

How much gold, Alan? In the ring.

ALAN. Much as you like. A'll send abroad for it special. Even mine it for you if you like, with a pan in the bloody river.

PAULINE. Then a want three children.

ALAN. Got it all planned, 'aven't you.

PAULINE. Two girls, one boy.

ALAN. Boy first.

PAULINE. Three's a nice numher. Manageable.

ALAN (*he lifts a foot out*). Me feet are dirty.

PAULINE. 'Ho's fault's that? Not mine, that's for sure. You could get arrested being like that, locked up.

ALAN. Would yer come and see me?

PAULINE. Where?

ALAN. Prison.

PAULINE. Doubt if me dad'd let me. Wouldn't want to know yer if yer were in prison.

> ALAN *wipes his feet on a pink towel.*

> A brought that to sunbave on. Not much use now. Like pink. When we're married we're 'avin our bavroom pink. (*She puts her arm around his waist.*) Would you swim the China Sea to be with me?

ALAN. Can't swim. Comes of being frightened of the sea. Me brother was once stung by a jellyfish. Worse than nettles. (*He kisses her, once.*) If you were on the moon I'd go to America and become an astronaut. Be famous then as well. Have some moon rock above the fireplace.

PAULINE (*running her hands through his hair*). Your 'air i'nt 'alf dirty. Greasy. (*Looking around.*) See my tights?

> ALAN *points.*

> Fetch 'em for us.

ALAN. 'Aven't you legs? (*He gets the tights.*)

PAULINE. Would you risk death to save me from a fire?

ALAN. Depends 'ow bad the fire was.

PAULINE (*taking the tights*). Ta.

ALAN. You dun'alf go on sometimes. (*He sits.*)

> *A pause.*

PAULINE. Alan, why do we always come up here Sundays?

ALAN. It's good.

PAULINE. Couldn't we go somewhere?

ALAN. Where?

PAULINE. D'know.

ALAN. Buy me a car and I'll take you somewhere, where yer d'know.

PAULINE. Don't be stupid. Stupid only 'aving Sundays off.

ALAN. 'As to be sacrifices, working on the land. I don't mind.

PAULINE. Yeh, but I do.

ALAN. I like the farm.

PAULINE. I'nt normal. If you 'ad Saturdays off we could go away of a weekend.

ALAN. Where to like?

PAULINE. Away. Just away. Stay in a boardinghouse. Blackpool. I'nt seen the illuminations since I were a kid.

ALAN. Couldn't afford it, not on top of getting married.

PAULINE. Must be worth a fortune all that overtime, you must.

ALAN. I'nt a fortune. (*Changing the subject.*) Let's go down the old mines.

PAULINE. Tell me 'ow much you earn. Tell me. Alan.

ALAN. Fancy chucking a few bricks down the shafts.

PAULINE. Why won't yer tell me?

ALAN. Fancy the walk.

PAULINE. Too bloody far.

ALAN. Only a couple of miles. Come on.

PAULINE. No.

ALAN (*putting his arm around her waist*). Take yer dress off then.

PAULINE. Oh, get lost!

    ALAN *stands. A pause.*

    Thought the army was gonna blow them shafts up.

ALAN. With one bloody great bang, they are. (*He starts to put on his trousers.*)

PAULINE. Hope those bats have gone. Like a horror film down there, bats flying about.

ALAN. They're not bats. They're big hairy gorillas, about eight feet tall.

ALAN *puts the tights over his head and acts like a gorilla. His trousers fall to his ankles.*

PAULINE. If you ladder them you can buy me a new pair.

ALAN *attacks her. He grunts.*

Get off me. (*She laughs.*) I'll smack you one, in the mouth. Stop it. (*She laughs.*) They put people like you in mental places. St Luke's.

HAROLD *enters, they do not see him.*

People who attack innocent young girls.

ALAN *falls on top of her.*

I'll tell me dad. Tell him. (*She laughs.*) He'll bash you one, hit you, like he hits the dog with the bloody poker.

HAROLD. So this is what you do on your day off, Alan? (*He smiles.*)

PAULINE *and* ALAN *are startled. They stop.* ALAN *fastens his trousers and pulls off the tights. They don't know what to do.*

HAROLD *sits on his gun.*

(*He points.*) I noticed one of the sheep up on Sandale Ridge. It has a wonky foot. Lame, probably broken.

ALAN. It's strained.

HAROLD. Probably broken!

ALAN. I know about it. Fell.

HAROLD. Broken I'd say. Just looked at it. Definitely broken. (*Points.*) Up, over there.

ALAN. Yes.

HAROLD. Have her in tomorrow.

ALAN *nods.*

First thing. Send her to the butcher's. Foot's definitely a mess. No good.

ALAN. Yes.

HAROLD. Fine. (*He jumps up.*) Otherwise they look in good shape. Well done.

HAROLD *exits. Silence for a moment.*

PAULINE. Call him Hitler, do you?

ALAN. Not so loud! The boss's son.

PAULINE. A bloody cheek, I know that much. Like to bet 'e's been spyin' on us.

ALAN. Course 'e 'asn't.

PAULINE. Peepin' through a bloody bush.

ALAN. Sssh! I 'ave to work for 'im.

PAULINE. What's 'e do, anyway?

ALAN. Sort of manager. Really 'e does what 'is dad tells him.

PAULINE. Looks stupid.

A pause.

You told me you was the manager.

ALAN. Did a?

PAULINE. Yeh. You know you did.

ALAN. Well –

PAULINE. Said you 'ad people under you.

A pause.

Why did you tell me you 'ad people under you?

ALAN. Why is the sky blue? The grass green?

PAULINE. Cos it is. You lied to me, Alan. Told me a lie.

ALAN. White lie.

PAULINE. Fibbed. Tell me why?

ALAN. Just lied didn'a. A joke.

PAULINE. I'nt very funny.

A pause. ALAN sits.

ALAN. Anyway there is someone below me. This lad who comes to clean the stables on Saturday mornin's. Mr Pike said I'll be in charge of the potato-pickers next year. Said you 'ave to make them work or they stand about idle. Do nothing but talk. He told me. You 'ave to keep your eye on them. Ones that talk a lot they don't take on next day.

A pause.

I'm only at the beginning of my career. Ten years, you wait.

PAULINE. Ten years is a long time.

ALAN. Twenty years is longer. Can't rush.

A pause. PAULINE *sits.*

PAULINE. End up like me dad, you will.

ALAN. Yer dad?

PAULINE (*she looks at him*). Didn't mean that.

ALAN. Should bloody 'ope not!

A pause.

PAULINE. Me dad's going funny. Stupid.

ALAN. Soft.

PAULINE. I'nt soft. Think 'e was a bleedin' tape recorder 'alf the time, the way 'e goes on. About owt. First things that come into 'is 'ead most of the time. Did a tell you 'e bust the telly?

ALAN. No.

PAULINE. Threw a bloody ashtray at it. Right in the middle of this film with lots of singing. Tuneless, he said. The rent people didn't believe it was a accident, took it away. Bloody daft. Didn't give a bugger about the telly. Me mam told him.

ALAN. He's ignorant.

PAULINE. It made a bloody great hole in the screen. We're gettin' a new one, twenty-six-inch. Still watch it 'e will.

A pause. ALAN *looks at her.*

ALAN. I'm learnin', Pauline. Should see 'ow I can handle the sheep.

PAULINE. All yer need's a little mountain hut.

ALAN. When *I'm* a manager – (*He picks up a stone and throws it into the marsh.*) Won't be a boss though, that's all wrong.

PAULINE. 'Ave to be a little bit of one.

ALAN. No, Pauline.

PAULINE. If you 'ave people under you, you 'ave to be a bit of a boss. Else they aren't under you. Be in authority, giving out the orders.

ALAN (*lying back*). Be experienced then.

A pause.

PAULINE. Wonder if me dad ever 'ad ambition? Thinkin' of buyin' an old van, now 'e is. Drive me mam to work. On the lookout.

ALAN. Have my own farm.

PAULINE. Also wants to 'ave a couple of pigs on the allotment.

ALAN. Two hundred acres.

PAULINE. Breed them. Sell the babies. You listenin' to what I'm saying?

ALAN sits up. He looks at her.

ALAN. Perhaps we can emigrate to Australia?

PAULINE. Too hot down there.

ALAN. Yeh, rich though.

PAULINE. Sweat a lot. Bad for the skin.

ALAN. Go surfing.

PAULINE. 'Ave to learn to swim.

A pause.

You ought to 'ave a chat to me dad about 'is pigs, 'e'd like that. T'other day he went to the library, first time in twenty years. He got this book on pigs, put it under his jacket, nicked it. Want to keep it, he said, for study.

GEORGE *enters. He carries a small sketchpad and some charcoal. For a brief moment, silence.*

GEORGE *(out of breath)*. Fine day. *(He holds up the pad.)* Out sketching. Long walk up from the road, past that concrete thing.

ALAN. Trig point.

GEORGE. Oh. *(He takes a deep breath.)*

ALAN. Eight hundred feet.

GEORGE. Been wondering what it was. Walked past it several times this past week. Now I know. *(He takes a deep breath.)* Do you mind if I leave my things here?

PAULINE. Heavy?

GEORGE. Yes. Cumbersome.

PAULINE. No.

ALAN. Leave them.

GEORGE *puts down the carrier bag and the sketchpad.*

PAULINE. You an artist?

GEORGE. No. A hobby. Used to be football.

PAULINE. Ever sold any?

GEORGE. First day at it as a matter of fact. (*He takes a deep breath.*)

PAULINE. You all right?

GEORGE. Just out of breath.

PAULINE. You wonna sit down for a bit.

GEORGE. I'm okay. (*He sits.*) Fine now. (*He takes a breath.*) That hill
that does it.

A pause.

Lungs all soiled up. Took an X-ray once, they did. Few years before
I'll need the kiss of life. (*He takes a breath.*)

A pause.

PAULINE. Sketch do you?

GEORGE. Landscapes.

PAULINE. Good artists are usually French.

GEORGE. Use charcoal.

A pause.

You a farmer, around here?

ALAN. Yeh.

GEORGE. Everyone round here seems to be a farmer.

PAULINE. 'E's a manager.

GEORGE. My father was on the land. (*He coughs.*)

PAULINE. My father works in the docks. Unloads wood.

GEORGE. Seen a bloke around here? Glasses?

ALAN. Dark glasses?

GEORGE. Yes. Supposed to meet him.

HAROLD *enters. He carries some dead branches.*

HAROLD. Twigs, wood. Dry as a bone. Touch them with a flame and they'd be up before you could screech Guy Fawkes. George.

GEORGE *nods*. HAROLD *puts down the wood*.

(*To* ALAN.) We're having a barbecue here this evening. Roast a suckling pig. (*To* PAULINE.) Fun in the open air. Like to come?

ALAN. I don't –

HAROLD (*to* PAULINE). You?

ALAN. – know.

HAROLD. Food and beer in the open air – romantic night life. A glass of bubbly. The screech of the owls. (*He moves towards* PAULINE.) I could run you home in the car afterwards.

PAULINE. Alan could!

HAROLD. Has Alan a car?

PAULINE. We're thinkin' of buyin' an old car.

HAROLD. Only thinking?

ALAN. At the moment.

HAROLD. If Alan doesn't want to come I could run you home. I've a Volvo Estate – the Concorde of the roadway. Seventy-five in first.

A pause. HAROLD *moves to exit. He stops*.

An old car is four wheels and a rusty frame. Get a shiny new one. (*He exits*.)

PAULINE (*calling*). 'Ave to ask me dad.

HAROLD (*off*). See you tonight.

A pause.

PAULINE. Bleedin' cheek.

ALAN s*miles*.

Who does he think'e is? Bleedin' Prime Minister?

GEORGE. Gets headaches.

PAULINE. Fancy 'imself as Yorkshire's Casanova does 'e?

GEORGE. That's why the glasses.

PAULINE. Well *I* i'nt going, that's for sure.

ALAN (*to* GEORGE). He don't normally wear them.

PAULINE. Bloody cheek!

GEORGE. You sure? Told me –

ALAN. Past week, that's all. (*He puts his arm round her.*) Won't touch you.

GEORGE. Wonder why he told me?

PAULINE. Twisted that's why.

ALAN (*tickling her*). Away then, let's be off. Be dark before we get there, and then those bats, they'll get you by the throat, and suck out your blood. (*He laughs like Frankenstein.*)

PAULINE. I 'aven't put my tights on. Stop it. Stop it! Alan. If you don't give over tickling me, I'll –

ALAN *stops*.

(*Quietly.*) You won't ever be like him, will yer, Alan?

ALAN. A might be. (*Again he tickles her.*)

PAULINE (*laughing*). No, yer don't mean it.

ALAN (*laughing*). A do.

PAULINE. Get off me. Bloody great brute. Yer'll get me giggling. (*She giggles.*) A'll suffocate. Me dad'll hit yer. That's enough now! Alan! Say yer won't be like 'im, Alan. Say it. If I 'ave to bash you, yer'll be sorry. (*She starts to struggle.*)

GEORGE *is smiling*.

I'm warning yer, Alan. A'll punch yer one!

ALAN. Go on then.

PAULINE. Can yer know.

ALAN. Can't.

PAULINE. Bloody can. (*She laughs.*)

GEORGE *is laughing*.

ALAN (*to* GEORGE). D'yer think she dare punch me one?

PAULINE. Belted bigger people 'an you at school. (*She hits him, not hard.*)

ALAN. You been taking wrestling lessons?

PAULINE (*she hits him again*). That'll learn yer.

ALAN (*to* GEORGE). Come on, hold her hands.

PAULINE (*to* GEORGE). You dare.

ALAN. Come on. She's gonna tear me to bloody shreds. Her nails are like bloody fangs.

GEORGE *doesn't move.* PAULINE *is hitting all the time, getting harder and harder.*

She'll murder me. (*He laughs.*)

PAULINE. Jack the Ripper's got nowt on me! (*She thumps him.*)

GEORGE *stands.*

ALAN (*to* GEORGE). Hold her bloody hands.

PAULINE. I could hate you, Alan Todd, know that! That's enough now. I've 'ad enough. You 'ear me!

GEORGE *holds one of her hands. Slowly he starts to tickle her.*

I said that's bloody enough! Piss off!

ALAN (*to* GEORGE). Hold her other hand.

GEORGE *doesn't.* PAULINE *is now very angry, the fun for her having died completely.*

PAULINE. Get off me! Alan! A'll bite yer!

ALAN (*to* GEORGE). Grab her hands.

PAULINE (*struggling violently*). Stop it!

Slowly GEORGE *raises his spare hand to her breasts. His hand hovers above, as if about to caress her. In jerky movements he pulls his hand away. In the struggling and shouting neither* ALAN, *nor* PAULINE, *has noticed this.* GEORGE *moves away from them. He is distressed.*

ALAN (*to* GEORGE). Come on.

PAULINE. A'll kick yer! (*She kicks.*) Right where it 'urts the most.

GEORGE *is bent double. He coughs.*

STOP IT!

She spits in ALAN*'s face.* ALAN *breaks away and wipes his face with his hand.*

I tol' yer. Warned yer. (*To* GEORGE.) Said, didn' a?

ALAN *picks up the towel.*

ALAN. Filthy cow. (*He wipes his face with the towel.*) Slut.

PAULINE (*quiely*). Don't call me a filthy cow.

ALAN *throws the towel at her. He moves to spit at her but changes his mind.*

ALAN (*mutters*). Think you was the only mermaid in the ocean.

PAULINE. Yer what?

ALAN. I said you're not the only bloody mermaid in the ocean.

PAULINE. Wha's tha' suppose to mean?

A pause. PAULINE *stands.*

Yer like a little kid. Only difference between you an' a one-year-old is the nappy.

GEORGE *moves up the hill. He sits with his back against the tree.*

I'm off down the mines.

A pause. ALAN *and* PAULINE *stare at each other.* PAULINE *picks up her tights. She exits.*

ALAN. Sod!

A pause.

Suppose I'll 'ave ta go after 'er.

A slight pause.

She'll come back.

GEORGE. Do you have ambition?

ALAN. Bloody sod. (*He sits.*)

GEORGE (*muttering*). Did I have ambition? (*Louder.*) Do you 'ave ambition?

A long silence.

ALAN. Yeh. With 'er I sometimes wonder whether it's worth it. All for 'er.

GEORGE. Ambition?

ALAN. Yeh.

GEORGE. Look at me – sixty-five. I had three brothers, four sisters – all the same as me. Brothers like my father. Sisters like my mother. All the same. We weren't no different.

ALAN. She's like that, you know. Temperamental. I'nt me. (*He lies back*.) She'll come.

A pause.

I'll make a good farmer.

GEORGE. Think so?

ALAN. Yeh.

A pause.

See the way she spat at me?

A pause.

Yer don't need training, like school training. Know what I mean? Training to be a farmer. Not the sort of thing you can learn from a blackboard – sitting in hot smelly buildings, teachers breathing, bad breath, down the back of yer neck. Writing. Doing equations and that. A wasn't a bright kid, but I knew more than some. About 'ow to get on like. Teachers told yer – yer thick, Todd. Just like that – yer thick. Wear the black hat, Todd, dunce. Should see the way Harold clips sheep. Thinks he knows it all. Bloody mess he makes, literally blood. He's okay, though. A good laugh most of the time.

GEORGE. Been on the farm long?

ALAN. Year an' a 'alf, I've been here.

GEORGE. Why don't you go after her?

ALAN. She'll come back.

GEORGE. Dragging her tail behind her?

ALAN. More 'an likely.

ALAN *changes position and lies on his stomach. A pause.*

I 'ad this apprenticeship once, on the docks, wi' ships. Left after six month. Didn't get me articles or whatever they're called. In six months all we did was learn the names of bloody tools, that and paint the sides of ships. I mean, I know what a hammer looks like. As for painting, when I were a kid I painted our 'ouse from top to bottom. All in this light-blue colour. They showed us this lathe, never let us touch it though. For fear we'd smash it I suppose. Valuable instrument on the scrap heap. Did want to be a fitter, then. All it was, was bloody cheap labour. Still, I fancied working a lathe. Suppose I was stupid, naive, then. Skilled-job, though. Left and got this job as a driver's mate, delivering cookers, fridges, deep-freezes. I've bloody lugged more deep-freezes than you've 'ad 'ot dinners. Taken them through windows when they wouldn't go through doors. Got the push from that. Was a bit of a bad'n at the time. Used to get pissed past me eyeballs most nights. Rolling drunk. 'Ardly touch a drop, now. Went off it. Used to go with me old mates, on a crawl. Me mates from the docks. Used to learn 'ow many tankers they'd painted. Don't see 'em now, lost touch. You know 'ow you do? Just happens. You lose touch. After that I started my own sea-coal business – collecting coal on the beach. Went all along the coast. Tried to con people into buying it – said it would give a warmer fire. Daft really. Laid out thirty quid on a wheelbarrow and shovel. Didn't make a bloody cent. Not a bleedin' penny. Wheelbarrow went rusty with the salt. Early mornin', there I'd be, on the beach, tide washing round me ankles. Six o'clock, picking up lumps of coal. There before the housewives got there, picking it up for nowt. Coal Boards too big to compete against. Salt water's an alkali, that's why it rusted. School taught me something, I suppose.

GEORGE. Born round here.

ALAN. Weren't born nowhere else.

GEORGE. Seaside?

ALAN. Town. No little bloody cottage on the coast, not for us. Lived six miles from the coast, yet we only went twice a year. August Bank Holiday. The whole of our street'd be sittin' on the beach. Wonder why we bothered. Everyone on the same bus home.

GEORGE. Hah. (*He smiles.*)

A pause.

ALAN. After my sea-coal business I went to Hull an' worked the trawlers for a bit. Deck hand an' all the fish you could eat. Never eat fish, not now, prefer a steak pie. Steak pie and chips.

GEORGE. Older than you look?

ALAN. Eh?

GEORGE. You must be older than you look.

ALAN. Twenty-two.

GEORGE. Thought you'd have been older than that.

ALAN. No.

A pause.

Settled now. Definitely settled.

GEORGE. Remember my father.

A pause.

It was hard to change in my day.

ALAN. Learn a few things. Have my own farm one day.

GEORGE. I was brought up in a place like this. Frightening in a way.

ALAN. Frightening?

GEORGE. Makes you think. Like a flood up here. (*He points to his head.*) Come up here to forget the past and it all comes back. You know?

ALAN. No.

GEORGE. Old.

A pause.

This bloke, Harold. Your boss. He took a skull from there.

ALAN. Sheep.

GEORGE. Yes, so he told me.

ALAN *looks at his watch.*

She's being a long time.

ALAN. Yeh. (*He looks again.*)

GEORGE. Won't make her come any faster.

ALAN. No.

A pause.

GEORGE. You thought about death – no, I'm being silly.

ALAN. Yes, I've thought about death. We're all going to die. There is no little anti-death pill.

GEORGE. As you get older –

A pause.

Remember my father, sitting at the tea table, wondering if he'd still have a job the next day. Remember that vividly, up here. Like I say, like a flood. Up here. It was hard then. I once saw my father cry. I couldn't believe it, I was only very small. My father actually crying. I didn't know men cried, then. He didn't see me, he thought he was alone. Crying.

A pause.

When he died my mother had no money to pay for his funeral.

A pause.

There are times when I feel like cutting my wrists with a razor, watching the blood clot, slowly. (*He runs his hands through his hair.*) Think I ought to go and see my family.

A pause.

When my father had a job he was happy. Working with the sheep. That's what made happiness.

PAULINE *enters. She is carrying some dead branches. She looks at* ALAN *and places the wood with the other.* PAULINE *picks up her towel.*

PAULINE. Me mam's best towel.

HAROLD *enters. He too is carrying some dead branches.*

ALAN *jumps up and stares at him. Lights fade to blackout.*

Scene Three

That evening. A red cloudless sky. The moon casting eerie shadows.
Over the marsh, a thin ground mist. Centre, the remains of a fire, still
spitting and glowing. On a spit over the fire a half-eaten suckling pig.
HAROLD *is standing by the tree drinking from a can of McEwan's*
Export. PAULINE *is sitting beside him.* GEORGE, *a coat over his*
shoulders, is sitting halfway up the hill. ALAN *sits by the fire.*

HAROLD *and* PAULINE *are drunk.* HAROLD *sings.*

HAROLD. It was in the month of August
  At the ending of the day,
  A young maiden I espied
  As she wandered on her way,
  I won her and I took her
  From a labourer down the lane,
  I caressed her cos he left her
  And now her love he can't regain.

  HAROLD *laughs. He stops. His mood changes.*

  I feel ill.

  He slides down the back of the tree and ends in a sitting position by
  PAULINE.

  Like an elephant with diarrhoea. Can you imagine the mess?

  He smirks.

GEORGE (*to* ALAN). Cold?

ALAN. Eh?

GEORGE (*rubbing his hands*). Cold?

ALAN. I'nt tropical, a'll give you that.

HAROLD (*to* PAULINE). Do you believe in Martians? Little Mars men?

  ALAN *looks at them.*

  Little men with telly aerials sticking out the top of their heads?
  Tuned into BBC Two. (*He smirks.*)

PAULINE. Yer mad.

HAROLD. Who only say, buzz buzz. Only say, buzz buzz. Buzz buzz
  all the time. Nothing but, buzz buzz. Buzz buzz buzz. Buzz buzz.

PAULINE. Oh, shut up.

HAROLD. Buzz buzz buzz buzz. Seen them through my telescope.

PAULINE. 'Ho 'as?

HAROLD. Me.

PAULINE. Get out.

HAROLD. Buzz buzz buzz buzz. All the time. You see, that's how they communicate. By buzzing. Buzz buzz, like that. They all walk around buzz buzzing. Constantly, buzz buzz. It's like our talking, only they buzz. I've seen them.

PAULINE. If you've only seen them, how d'yer know they buzz.

HAROLD. I've heard them as well. On the BBC Home Service. (*He smirks.*) Buzz buzz buzz buzz –

PAULINE. Yer bonkers.

HAROLD. Come here.

PAULINE. No.

HAROLD. Buzz buzz. (*He kisses her.*)

GEORGE. I wish he'd be quiet.

ALAN. I'm going to kick his head in, before long.

    HAROLD *and* PAULINE *start to snog.*

GEORGE. You the time?

ALAN. Eleven-thirty.

GEORGE. Late.

ALAN. Too late.

PAULINE. 'Ere, you can stop that!

HAROLD. That's what Martians do.

PAULINE. No wonder they bloody buzz.

GEORGE. You catch cold easy?

ALAN. Eh?

GEORGE. Cold. No coat.

ALAN. No coat, no.

GEORGE. Hardy then?

ALAN. You might say.

GEORGE. Evening's cold here.

PAULINE *slaps* HAROLD*'s hand.* HAROLD *laughs.*

ALAN (*quietly*). Kick his face in. Push it to the back of his head.

GEORGE *looks at them.*

Spoilt bitch, her.

PAULINE *laughs.*

Do owt for spite. Can't take a harmless joke.

GEORGE. Why don't you?

ALAN. What?

GEORGE. Hit him. Deserves it, I should say.

ALAN. Why don't I? Why bloody don't I? Know why?

A pause.

Never done this to me before.

GEORGE. Her idea of a joke.

ALAN. Kick his face from here to bloody Mars, and back.

PAULINE. Move yer 'and.

HAROLD. Pardon?

PAULINE. Yer 'and!

HAROLD. Them people on Mars, they don't have sex. All virgins. It's all done by remote control. By electric charges. I know, see.

PAULINE. 'Ow old are you?

HAROLD. That's got nothing whatsoever to do with you.

ALAN *picks up a stone and throws it into the marsh.*

PAULINE. What's that?

HAROLD. Nothing.

ALAN *throws another stone, this time a lot harder.*

ALAN. Caused by the heat radiating from the earth, that mist. Physics. Law of mass an' all that.

ALAN *throws another stone, again harder. A pause.*

GEORGE. Monday morning.

ALAN. Work.

GEORGE. Hated Mondays as a rule.

ALAN. Don't mind. Same as any other day.

GEORGE. First day.

A pause.

ALAN. What you do?

GEORGE. Eh?

ALAN. A job?

GEORGE. Was a porter. Railway porter. King's Cross Station. Carried cases, full of odds and ends. Bric-a-brac. Put mail parcels onto trains. Did all that. Much of the mail going north I handled, Edinburgh, far-away places.

ALAN. Interesting?

GEORGE. Like to share my coat?

ALAN. Stay by the fire.

GEORGE. Up to you.

A pause.

ALAN. We i'nt fixed a date, but it was definite. Me an' 'er. Been into this pub a know, t'get costs. Know the barman who works there, might get it a bit cheaper, like.

A slight pause.

Gonna cost us nigh on a hundred quid. Got this cottage on the farm to live in. Goes with the job, a house. Good that. Been decorating in my spare time, evenin's, want it nice. Put in a new sink-unit, all by mesel'. Cheaper t'do it yersel'.

A pause.

Couldn't afford to buy a 'ouse. Couldn' afford that. 'Is father 'as four cottages they give to workers. Not give, 'ave the use of.

A pause.

GEORGE. Was at King's Cross practically all my working life. Stepped off the train when I got there and stayed. (*He smiles*.) Not very funny really.

PAULINE (*about* HAROLD*'s glasses*). What d'you wear these for?

HAROLD. Leave them.

PAULINE (*she touches them*). What for?

HAROLD. Keep the sun out.

PAULINE. I'nt no sun. (*She touches them*.)

HAROLD. Leave them, I said.

PAULINE. Keep yer 'air on. Only askin'.

A pause.

You got funny eyes or something? Bet you've got funny eyes. Le's 'ave a look. Never know a bloke with funny eyes before. Go on.

HAROLD. No.

PAULINE. Go on.

HAROLD (*moving away*). Get off. (*He kneels a few feet from her*.)

PAULINE. You allergic to light, or something? Is that what it is? Eh? Eyes like a little dog's?

HAROLD. Don't be sick.

PAULINE (*laughing*). All clouded up and horrible.

HAROLD. Sensitive, that's all. I was a sensitive child.

PAULINE. Cry baby?

HAROLD. Leave me alone. I feel sick. Elephants being sick. (*He smirks*.) Imagine it. Buzz buzz. Oh god. Feel awful.

PAULINE. Do you have to put drops in your eyes? 'Ave to buy you a white stick to walk around with. (*She laughs*.)

HAROLD. Shut up!

PAULINE. Like a spastic. Let's 'ave a look.

PAULINE *tries to grab his glasses. She does not succeed.*

HAROLD *slaps her, hard.* ALAN *stands, he runs at* HAROLD. ALAN *kicks him hard in the stomach. An aeroplane flies loudly over.* HAROLD *is winded, he lies flat-out, groaning loudly.*

ALAN *stares at him, his nerves making him shake.*

Everyone is still.

ALAN (*quietly to* HAROLD). Serves you right. You hear me? Serves you right.

HAROLD (*coughs*). Oh –

ALAN (*quietly*). Shouldn't 'ave done that t'me. Serves you right.

PAULINE (*quietly*). Alan.

ALAN. You 'ear me?

HAROLD (*coughing*). Oh –

PAULINE. Alan.

HAROLD. Blood.

ALAN. Shouldn' 'ave done that to me. Made me feel like that. You asked for it. You all right?

HAROLD. Oh –

ALAN. You all right?

HAROLD (*quietly*). Go away.

GEORGE (*bending down, looking*). There's no blood.

ALAN. Asked for it, that's all.

HAROLD (*turning to look at* ALAN. *Shouting*). YOU BASTARD!

Silence. HAROLD *starts to cry.*

Bastard.

A pause.

GEORGE. He's just winded. A bit drunk.

ALAN (*quietly*). It's your fault.

PAULINE. Mine?

ALAN. Your fault.

PAULINE *moves away.* GEORGE *bends down to help* HAROLD. HAROLD *pushes him away with his hand.*

ALAN (*to* HAROLD). Shouldn' 'ave done that to me.

HAROLD *stands.*

HAROLD. Get my dog and she'll rip you to shreds. She isn't no
Lassie, isn't my Killer.

An aeroplane flies loudly over.

Trained to lacerate limbs! Pull them off! Trained on the postman,
my Killer. Call her Killer, because she kills. Kills! You haven't seen
her when she's aggressive, my dog. Oh yes, my dog. Pounces with
the claws of a mountain lion, big teeth in her mouth to tear. Tear and
rip open the red flesh. Blood spilling. My Killer. My dog. Alsatian to
the core, she is.

A pause. He slowly sinks to the ground.

(*To* GEORGE.) As you'll have gathered, not the friendliest of dogs.
Keep it constantly muzzled. (*He puts his head in his knees.*)

A long pause.

ALAN (*quietly to* GEORGE). Those planes flying over. Practice night
flying. Fifty feet above the ground. Practice flying under radar.

HAROLD (*looking up*). You know, I fell and damaged myself on a
gate. That's it! A gate! The white one at the entrance to the drive.
Tripped! Gate in the way! Smash! Fell over and damaged my eye.

He pulls off his glasses. His left eye is badly bruised. He sobs.

See it? My eye. Bruised. My father said, tell them you fell on a
gate. Well I didn't. Shall I tell you? My father, he hit me! Swiped
at me in anger. Now I've a bad eye. Not the first time he's hit me.
Bad eye.

A pause. He puts the glasses back on.

You know why he hit me? Because I wanted two weeks' holiday
and it turns out he wanted one, at the same time. He hit me for that.
He was rolling drunk, pissed as a fart. Someone has to look after the
estate while he's away. He's having his holiday. Next day he was
sorry. He's always sorry after he's hit me. Seen more sympathy in a
sick cow.

An aeroplane flies loudly over. HAROLD's *father,* SQUIRE PIKE,
enters. He is fifty-four and fat. They don't see him.

PAULINE. Think we'd better be off.

A pause.

Getting late.

PIKE. Late enough.

> HAROLD *stands*. PIKE *walks forward*.

> Harold.

HAROLD. Just finishing, Father.

PIKE (*to* PAULINE). Hello.

> PAULINE *nods shyly*. PIKE *nods at* GEORGE.

> (*To* PAULINE.) Had a good evening's sport?

PAULINE. Eh?

HAROLD. Very good.

PIKE. Eaten the fatted calf? This piggy seems to have been well molested.

PAULINE. Pardon?

PIKE. Eaten.

PAULINE (*not in cheek*). Looks like it, doesn't it.

PIKE. That's what I just said. Suckling pig leaves little to the imagination. Does it? Stomach juices rumbling. (*To* GEORGE.) When he was a boy Harold's stomach used to rumble, in time to a well known Elvis Presley record. (*To* HAROLD.) My Land-Rover is parked over on the track.

HAROLD. Yes.

PIKE. Home, I think, Watson.

> *A slight pause.*

> I think it's time you were in bed, Alan, if you hope to give a full day's work tomorrow. (*To* HAROLD.) Yes, Harold's mummy used to be particularly fond of this old Bing Crosby number. Give him a bottle and while his mummy was crooning away, Harold's tummy would start to rumble. A sort of human percussion accompaniment. We had this old gramophone. (*To* GEORGE.) There was a child star with ringlets who made him feel sick. (*To* HAROLD.) Sick. Come, Watson.

> PIKE *exits*. HAROLD *follows him*.

GEORGE (*sighing*). God.

PAULINE. That's it then, i'nt it? (*She sits*.) Stuck. How do I get home?

GEORGE. How do I get home?

PAULINE. All bloody mouth. His father bashes him up.

GEORGE (*sitting down*). Nearly twelve. (*He winds his watch.*)

PAULINE. Bloody twelve. How'm I gonna get to work tomorrow?

ALAN. That's your problem.

PAULINE. A like that.

ALAN. See 'ow 'is father is?

PAULINE. Nowt excuses 'em. Leavin' me like this.

A pause.

I 'ave to look afta me self, why shouldn' 'e.

ALAN. What you rabbitin' about?

PAULINE. Him. Goin' off like that. It's a four-mile walk. (*She sighs.*)

A pause.

GEORGE. Look at the stars.

PAULINE. Stars?

GEORGE. In the sky. Miles away. Light years from here. Millions of light years. Gives you an idea of distance.

A pause.

Feel strange this evening.

ALAN. Oh?

GEORGE. Yes.

ALAN. All 'ave to feel strange sometimes.

A pause. ALAN *walks to the tree.*

When I've me own farm.

GEORGE. That'll be the day. (*He smiles.*)

ALAN *smiles. A pause.*

ALAN. When a were a kid, me mates and me, we used to go to this sweet shop and steal Smarties. Nothing to do with that really, but I knew then, what I wanted. To feel I'd built it, run it, myself. That it were my own. At first it were to build a sweet factory, then a fag factory, then my own dock, then –

GEORGE. A farm?

ALAN. A farm. Will one day.

> GEORGE *coughs up some phlegm into his hand. He wipes his hand on the ground.*

PAULINE. You never told me you were a thief.

ALAN. You ever felt, you wanted to build something of your own?

> *A pause.*

You ever felt that?

GEORGE. Maybe I did. Maybe. Once. A lot of water has entered the sea from the river since then.

ALAN. Yeh.

GEORGE. Don't think I had the capabilities to redesign King's Cross Station. (*He laughs.*)

> ALAN *smiles.*

PAULINE (*standing*). We off then?

ALAN. You off?

PAULINE. I'nt we going together?

> *A slight pause.*

ALAN. Suppose we are.

> ALAN *and* PAULINE *look at each other.*

PAULINE. Will yer carry me?

ALAN. No, yer can carry yer sel'.

GEORGE (*standing*). I feel like a walk.

PAULINE. Piggy-back.

ALAN. Wish you'd jump off a high building.

PAULINE. And the same to you. (*She exits.*)

GEORGE. Beautiful, the stars.

ALAN. Come on.

GEORGE (*pointing*). The plough.

ALAN. We'd better catch her up.

PAULINE (*off*). Yer an idiot you are, Alan Todd.

ALAN (*calling*). Shut up.

GEORGE. Which is your best foot?

ALAN. Don't think I've got a best foot.

GEORGE. Right or left?

ALAN. D'know.

GEORGE. That's the plough. (*He points.*)

ALAN. All look the same to me. Just a load of stars.

> *They exit. An aeroplane flies low overhead. Lights fade to blackout.*
>
> *Interval*

Scene Four

August the ninth. Morning. Again a sunny day. Heard, the occasional bleat of sheep. PIKE stands by the tree. He watches as HAROLD treads into the ground the last piece of turf where the fire was.

HAROLD. Not a sign of last night's fire now, Father.

> PIKE *nods and exits. A pause.* HAROLD *lifts his glasses and rubs his eyes, being very careful of his bad eye. The sound of sheep increases.*
>
> ALAN *is heard offstage, whistling at his sheep dog.*

ALAN (*off*). Hold it, lass. Stay, stay, lass. That's it, good girl. Stay. Quiet now, lass.

> HAROLD *watches him. Sound of sheep increases for a brief moment as the dog goes too near them.*

(*Off.*) Stay! Stay, lass! (*He whistles.*) Hold it. (*He whistles.*)

Gently forward, now.

> *The dog barks.*

(*Off.*) Sssh! Sssh. Leave it, lass! Leave it. Gently forward.

HAROLD (*calling*). Don't you know how to pen a flock of bloody sheep? It's like the docking of two space craft, needs precision.

ALAN (*off*). Yer what?

HAROLD. Don't know how to pen a flock of sheep!

Again sound of sheep increases for a moment.

Watch that dog! Do you want it to take a leg off that animal?

ALAN (*off*). It's all right.

HAROLD. Don't know what you're doing! Haven't a bloody clue.

ALAN (*off. Whistles*). Stay now, lass. Good girl. Good girl. Gently now.

A pause.

There yer are, penned at the first attempt.

HAROLD. Could have been done in half that bloody time.

ALAN (*off*). Come, lass. Come. (*Louder.*) A'll bring in the second flock.

A slight pause. GEORGE *enters.* HAROLD *exits in haste after* ALAN, *nearly knocking him over.*

GEORGE (*muttering*). In a hurry.

GEORGE *is out of breath. He stands gasping for air. Sheep fade to silence. A pause.* GEORGE *sits and starts to draw in his sketchpad. He sketches like a professional, holding the charcoal at arm's length to gain perspective. A pause.*

HAROLD *enters. He comes up behind* GEORGE *and looks over his shoulder.*

HAROLD. Not very good.

GEORGE (*startled*). Eh?

HAROLD (*pointing*). What's that supposed to be?

GEORGE *closes the sketchpad.*

They're teaching monkeys to paint, in zoos. Join the class. Join the chimps' tea party.

GEORGE. Be quiet.

HAROLD. That an attempt at impressionism?

GEORGE *looks at him.*

That mess.

GEORGE. Be quiet.

HAROLD. Were you painting that ridge? (*He points.*)

GEORGE. What if I was?

HAROLD. Not like what you've drawn.

GEORGE. So?

HAROLD. So.

GEORGE. So, I wasn't painting that ridge.

HAROLD. Sorry.

A pause. HAROLD *walks.*

I paint.

GEORGE. Oh?

HAROLD. Yes, I paint.

GEORGE. Paint as well as the way you behaved last night?

HAROLD. SHUT UP!

A long pause. HAROLD*'s mood changes.*

Last night –

GEORGE. Didn't –

HAROLD. Last night –

GEORGE. Didn't bother me.

HAROLD. Was drunk.

HAROLD *lifts off his glasses and rubs very gently his bad eye.*

Just drunk.

GEORGE. I –

HAROLD. Drunk. You know, drunk.

A pause.

GEORGE. I forget. (*He sighs.*)

A pause.

Remember silly things. Only silly things. Did you know, Crystal Palace has a ground capacity of fifty-one thousand? Bolton Wanderers, sixty thousand one hundred and thirty- six?

GEORGE *looks at* HAROLD.

Once attempted to learn the ground capacities of all the football clubs in the four divisions. Something to do. Like reading the Bible from cover to cover. An exercise. Followed Crystal Palace – October the tenth, 1959, in the fourth division – beat Barrow nine bloody nil. No toilet rolls or knives then. You follow football? Most folks are only interested in their Littlewoods Lit-Plan. Not the game any more. Even in the summer it's Australian soccer, not cricket.

HAROLD. Freddy Trueman.

GEORGE. It's the West Indies. Gary Sobers. Play cricket on the pavement there, in the streets. That's how you start. In the streets. Cricket all year round, play cricket while they're eating their dinner. Play cricket in their sleep, some of them. All year round, that's love. Enthusiasm. The crowds went wild at Crystal Palace, what there was of a crowd, went wild. Nine nil. All attack. That was in the day of wingers. Get a sprinter out there, all you needed was a good header of the ball. A winger who could cross, mind. Not all of 'em could. Good wingers, you can't beat 'em.

HAROLD. Thought you'd have played bowls?

GEORGE. Bowls?

HAROLD. Rubber pads on perfect lawns, pushing balls at a marble thirty feet away.

GEORGE. And a half bitter at the end? No. For old men.

HAROLD. Oh?

GEORGE. Yes.

A pause.

Oldham Athletic's ground holds forty-one thousand two hundred. My old place. (*He forces a smile.*) Remembering now –

A pause.

Aston Villa, sixty-two thousand two hundred and fifty. Peterborough United, thirty thousand. Middlesbrough, forty-two thousand. Mansfield Town, twenty thousand five hundred. Queen's Park Rangers, thirty-five thousand, Preston North End, forty thousand one hundred – Exeter City, forty-five thousand – Newcastle United, sixty-one thousand five hundred – Southampton, thirty-one thousand –

GEORGE *is now very excited.*

Doncaster Rovers, forty-four thousand three hundred and eighty-two – Arsenal, seventy-three thousand, two hundred and ninety-five – Millwall, forty thousand – Lincoln City, twenty-three thousand one hundred and ninety-six – Cardiff City, fifty-eight thousand. (*He laughs.*) Hah. Ask me one!

HAROLD *just looks at him.*

Cambridge United, sixteen thousand.

GEORGE *coughs up some phlegm into his hand. Silence.*

I knew them. Knew them all. Every single one. Without a doubt, I knew them. Knew them! Ask me. Go on, ask me. I challenge you. Put a pound on you asking me. Put my life on it. And I knew the team records and the players and the team records. Knew every player's Christian name. (*Angry.*) ASK ME!

HAROLD (*taken aback. Quietly*). I don't know.

GEORGE *laughs.*

GEORGE. Manchester United, sixty-one thousand five hundred. You see, I know. It was my sport football, my sport. And now it's like that – (*He spits.*) Filth on the ground. Filth. (*Calmer.*) Can't you ask me one? (*Almost pleading.*) Ask me.

HAROLD (*quietly*). Don't know.

GEORGE. Filth on the ground. Remember seeing Charlie Chaplin, on the screen. On the flickering screen, up above the stalls. Charlie Chaplin. The laughter catcher on the flickering screen. And the organ music. And the captions, up there – Dolly Perkins has fallen in love – and, Dolly Perkins admiring her prince, in silence. Felix the Cat. Charlie Chaplin. The whole of the audience'd be on the floor, as the poor man carried on. Trouble after trouble. Never smiling, but carrying on. And we'd be on the floor, laughing. Laughing, in the stalls. Always a poor man. Laughing at ourselves, at our own comedy – (*Shouts.*) IT ISN'T FUNNY.

A pause. HAROLD *doesn't know what to do, or where to look. He stands looking bemused.*

I wasn't very old then. When the screen went blank we'd go home, down the old streets. Then came the stars of the silver screen, and the glamour. White robes. Jewels. Pearls. And the film stars came to England, looking very expensive. Delicately dressed. We'd be

humming the numbers of their musicals, hum them between
mouthfuls of watery soup. Admiring of the whole expense, of the
riches. We looked up to the glamour. (*Twisting his face*.) We looked
up to the glamour. Horrible!

A pause.

Yes, I recall, one night. Night after night. After my wife died,
dreaming of this great desolate plain. Just like the Sahara, miles of
nothing. Nothingness. Empty – not like the beach. Sand that just
carried on for miles. No trees. You know how you imagine
cactuses? Well, it was empty.

HAROLD *slowly exits.* GEORGE *does not see him go.*

Quite suddenly out of the silence, came the sound of this hunting
horn. (*He imitates the sound of a hunting horn.*) Slowly in the
distance, I saw these hounds, millions of them. They were running
after this fox and fox was running like hell, like a wild dog trying to
escape them. Behind the hounds were huntsmen on horseback, in
red coats and drinking white wine from slender glasses, as they
galloped along. I saw them. Coming towards me. Getting nearer and
nearer. I felt my body, I was becoming hairy. Covered in brown hair.
(*He feels his legs.*) My nose began to change shape. (*He feels his
nose.*) Became pointed. My vision seemed strange, as if I was nearer
the ground and I realised I was on all fours. When I felt behind I had
a bushy tail.

*His face is contorted. He laughs, a sad, pathetic laugh. His
laughing dissolves into silence.*

(*Quietly.*) And the hounds came nearer, nearer and nearer.

ALAN *enters.*

ALAN. Seen Harold?

GEORGE *looks up at him.*

Seen Harold? I've found a sheep with a broken leg, need him to
help me carry it.

GEORGE (*looking around*). Er – er. He was here a minute ago.

ALAN. D'yu know which way?

GEORGE. Way?

ALAN. He went.

GEORGE *doesn't answer.*

Which way he went? You okay?

GEORGE (*pointing*). That way I think.

ALAN. Thanks.

ALAN *exits.* GEORGE *coughs up some phlegm into his hand.*
A long pause. He groans. A pause. He stumbles up onto his feet and
stands looking up.

GEORGE. Look at the sun. Bright. Alive. See if you can touch your
toes, old son.

A pause.

He tries to touch his toes, only managing to get halfway down.

Think I'm stuck. (*He straightens up.*) Oh God.

A pause.

(*More brightly.*) Oh God.

He coughs up some phlegm into his hand. Lights fade to blackout.

Scene Five

Early that evening. The sky just beginning to darken. GEORGE *is*
asleep.

PAULINE (*off*). 'Ang on a minute, will yer.

ALAN (*off*). Come on. You wouldn't need a snail to win the snail
championships, wi' you around.

PAULINE (*off*). I'm a girl. What's the rush?

ALAN (*off*). There's gold in them there hills.

PAULINE (*off*). Oh, shut up.

ALAN *enters.*

ALAN. Come on.

PAULINE (*off*). I i'nt in training for the Olympics.

ALAN. Going to get yer a pair of them parallel bars.

　　PAULINE *enters*.

PAULINE. 'Ad enough walkin' t'other night. Wish we'd stayed in and
　　watched the telly, or done my hair.

ALAN. Good for you, walking.

　　They notice GEORGE.

PAULINE. It's 'im again. Must live on the moor, does he?

ALAN. Ssh!

PAULINE. Wonder 'ow long 'e's been 'ere?

ALAN. Sssh.

PAULINE (*more quietly*). All right.

ALAN. He's asleep.

PAULINE. Think I'm thick or something?

ALAN. No. Just don't make a noise.

PAULINE (*barely audible*). All right.

ALAN. Yer what?

PAULINE. I said, all right.

ALAN. Oh.

PAULINE. 'E's a funny old bloke.

ALAN. Eh?

PAULINE (*normal voice*). This i'nt 'alf stupid.

ALAN. Sssh!

PAULINE. Yer worse than a bloody steam engine. Sssh, all the time.
　　(*She looks at* GEORGE.) Let's go. I think 'e's a bit, you know –
　　(*She twists her finger on the side of her head*.)

ALAN. Nice bloke. (*He sits*.)

PAULINE. Come on.

ALAN. Sittin' now.

PAULINE. Come on.

ALAN (*quite hard*). Don't order me about!

They stare at each other. A pause.

PAULINE. Alan –

ALAN. That's all I'm sayin'. Like I say, it's forgotten. Like it i'nt
never happened.

PAULINE. Alan – (*She stops.*)

A slight pause.

ALAN. Do it again and it's the finish.

PAULINE. Yeah, well –

ALAN. Mean it.

PAULINE. Said sorry, 'aven' a?

ALAN. Yeh.

PAULINE. You and me.

ALAN. Yeh.

PAULINE. Nothink else.

A pause. ALAN *smiles.*

ALAN. Let's forget it.

PAULINE. Yeh.

A pause. PAULINE *looks at* GEORGE.

'E's dirty yer know? Look at 'is neck, it's all dirty. (*She pulls his
collar away from his neck.*) Could grow plants on the side of his neck.

ALAN (*standing*). Where?

PAULINE. Err! (*She lets go of the collar.*) Disgusting.You could grow
carrots and spuds.

ALAN (*looking*). No soap.

PAULINE. Probably got worms. Like cats. (*She smells his hair.*)
Never'd thought 'e was like that.

GEORGE *grunts. A pause.*

ALAN. Thought he was wakin'.

PAULINE. Feel sorry for 'im really.

ALAN. Yeh.

PAULINE. 'Is shoes are a right mess, an' all.

ALAN *sits*.

You ever get like that an' it'll be the end, I tell yer that.

ALAN *laughs*.

Not hygienic. We used to 'ave hygiene classes at school, cookery and hygiene. All about the right amount of soap liquid to use. (*She sits by ALAN*.) Think we ought to wake him?

Can't stay like that all night, can 'e.

ALAN. Later.

A pause.

PAULINE. You see – (*She stops*.)

ALAN. Eh?

PAULINE. Nothin'.

A pause.

I was gonna say, you seen 'im today.

ALAN. 'Im?

PAULINE. Harold. You know.

ALAN. Yeh, I've seen him.

PAULINE. Say owt?

ALAN. Not a bloody word.

A slight pause.

PAULINE. Didn' 'alf kick 'im one.

ALAN. Asked for it.

PAULINE. Never seen you like that before.

ALAN. When I'm riled.

PAULINE. Yeh.

A slight pause.

Long as 'e didn' take it out on yer.

ALAN. Harold? Wouldn't dare. 'Is father might, but then 'e don't know a kicked him.

A slight pause.

Bloody twit 'e is. Don't know nowt. Harold doesn' 'ave a say in what goes on. It's 'is father says that. 'Is father's boss.

PAULINE. Good.

ALAN. Thinks 'e knows more than me, but he don't. Not big headed, that. Should a seen 'im with the sheep this mornin', trying to tell me I done it wrong. Knows he can't handle 'em as well as I can.

PAULINE. Good.

GEORGE *waves, moves, grunts and groans.*

GEORGE. Err – (*He rubs his eyes.*)

PAULINE. Was going to wake you.

GEORGE. Must have dropped off. What time is it?

ALAN. About eight.

GEORGE *stands.*

GEORGE. Oh God. (*He forces a smile.*) Spent a week in Brighton once, on the sands and dozed off every day. Watched the tide go in and out – ate ice lollies and candy floss. All sticky. Working on the railway I got free travel. One of the benefits.

ALAN. Yeh?

GEORGE. Yes. Suppose you didn't know that?

ALAN. No.

GEORGE. Great, if you wanted to travel. Trouble was I didn't, all that much.

A slight pause.

As I say, went to Brighton. (*He rubs his eyes.*) Oh – (*He sits.*) Went to Oldham once or twice. (*He takes off his shoes.*) Feet get cramped up.

ALAN *takes out a packet of Players No6.*

ALAN. You smoke?

GEORGE. Used to.

PAULINE *takes from her bag a Benson & Hedges. They light up.*

Not any more. (*He takes off his socks, his feet are dirty.*) All hot my feet. Feel like they've been in a furnace.

A pause. GEORGE *wiggles his toes.*

These could have been tap-dancing feet, you know. Could have been. Could have tapped at the Royal Ballet.

GEORGE *stands. He attempts to tap-dance.*

That's what they call the soft-shoe shuffle, something like that.

A pause. GEORGE *sits, rubs his eyes.*

(*Resigned.*) My feet could have been meant for stardom. Could huh.

ALAN *smiles.*

(*Friendly.*) You may smile.

A slight pause.

See this toe? If things hadn't taken a different course, might have ended up insuring that toe for one million pounds. An insurable asset, that's what they call it.

ALAN *smiles.*

Don't smile.

ALAN *laughs.*

All I'm saying is that this toe could have been world-famous. Photographs of it in magazines.

ALAN *looks at* PAULINE. *They smile. A pause.*

That's all I'm saying.

A pause.

GEORGE *looks at his hands. He stares at them.*

Your hands scratched?

ALAN (*looking*). No.

GEORGE. Hard.

ALAN. Be able to make rabbit hutches for my kids with these hands.

GEORGE. Hard skin.

ALAN. Knock up a thing or two. Made for building things, my hands. That's what our woodwork teacher used to say – your hands were made for building things, go into building. Still remember 'ow to mortice and tenon.

PAULINE. Sounds like a dance.

ALAN. Isn't a dance. I'd really like to be a designer. Design farm machinery, new battery-hen system.

GEORGE. Don't know what you want.

ALAN. Want to be a farmer.

GEORGE. Idle dreams?

ALAN. A farmer, that's all. Not idle.

GEORGE. No? No, no, suppose not.

ALAN. Just a farmer.

A pause.

GEORGE. I worked with my father when I was a child. When I left school, like everyone else, I went into the mill – hot, sweaty and sticky. You smelt the stale stink of sweat? At first I quite enjoyed it. Huh, enjoyed. Trouble was some of us had to go, so I went. South. Not the work, no jobs. Had to go. That's my life story, hardly enough for an autobiography, a book.

ALAN *smiles.*

My big toes had it as regards being a famous object. (*He coughs up some phlegm into his hand.*)

PAULINE. You spit all the time?

GEORGE (*coughing*). My throat.

PAULINE. Saw this film on the telly once, about cancer. You know, up here in the – (*She points at her breasts.*) Thought perhaps you'd – (*She tails off realising that it is not appropriate.*) got-it-in-the-throat. (*Quietly.*) A lump.

GEORGE. Smoked too much.

PAULINE. Said forty-three was a dangerous age.

GEORGE. I'm okay.

PAULINE. This film. Told us about things like that at school, in school. Sent me mam and dad a letter. Me dad said he didn't believe in sex lessons, said we should learn it in the home. Left to learn it from the dogs, more or less.

A pause.

Then we learnt how to sew and make meat-and-potato pie. We had this very fat mistress for cookery called Mrs Nicholson. We called 'er Dumpling, on account of her size anyway, she was always getting us to make apple crumble so she could sample it. Honest.

GEORGE *forces a smile*.

She 'ad this kid 'ho was at the same school. 'E was dead thin. We reckoned she probably starved 'im. Called him Marcus. 'E passed the thirteen-plus and left. Dumpling was dead 'appy and pleased, we didn't see 'im no more. She didn't like 'im 'aving to associate wi' the likes of us.

GEORGE *forces a smile*.

First weeks at school, senior school that is, we made this apron in sewing to use in cookery. Dumpling and Miss Sampson, she was the sewing mistress like, must 'ave 'ad this agreement. Anyone 'ho came to the school after that, 'ad t'buy an apron. First week in cookery all we did was talk about pots and pans and 'erbs – never used a 'erb in me life. Bloody stupid learnin' it really. Then we did sums and English and things like that. Used to 'ave to read in front of the class, those that were best, good at it like, then 'ad to read in assembly. Me, a read bad on purpose. Didn' wan' ta end up 'aving to read in front of the 'ole school.

GEORGE *forces himself to laugh*.

We 'ad this games mistress. Called her Sprinter. True. Honest as I'm sittin' 'ere. Real hard case she was. Stronger than most of the lads. She 'ad to be tough, mind, wi' us around. Don't blame 'er. She could chuck a bloody javelin further than the PE master.

GEORGE *smiles*.

Don't believe me?

GEORGE. Don't know.

PAULINE. No lie. Honest as I'm sittin' here now. Boy was nearly killed at our school with a javelin. One nearly 'it 'im. 'Eadmaster didn' 'alf go off about it.

GEORGE *smiles. He has a fit of coughing*.

Go and see a doctor if I were you. Mean it.

GEORGE *stops*.

I would.

GEORGE. Know about cancer.

PAULINE. Saw that film?

GEORGE. My wife died of cancer. So they said.

PAULINE. They can tell.

GEORGE. Yes.

A pause.

Cancerous body. I didn't realise. I just watched her grow thin. In the end, when she died, she was just over six stone. By the time I realised, it was too late. Pale – her skin was white, a virgin-white pale face. (*He speaks very slowly.*) Wrinkles on her face, like wrinkles on the sand after the tide has gone out.

A pause.

Hurts now you know. Hurts to think about it. Hurts to think about her body bleeding inside, the digestive system letting blood slip away. Her birthday was on the fifth of April. She was buried in a coffin – in a coffin in the ground. Every year on the fifth of April I take a spring daffodil and place it on her grave.

A pause.

In her youth.

A pause. GEORGE *stands, slowly, with obvious difficulty.*

Sometimes I feel very angry. (*He raises his hand.*) Want to raise my hand and hit, like that. (*Demonstrates.*) Trouble is, I'm too old, it wouldn't hurt any more. Haven't the strength. When you're young you can put up with it. (*Quietly.*) I just want to hit hard. (*He again raises his hand and forces it through the air.*) Don't know why.

A pause. He takes off his jacket.

You know what I would have like to have been?

ALAN *and* PAULINE *look at him.*

A heavyweight boxer. A tightrope walker in a circus or a foreign diplomat. The life on the high wire. A military governor somewhere. Any of those. Could have been our ambassador in Peking, a foreign envoy, regular visits to the Home Office. (*He takes off his tie.*) They're what I could have been. Instead –

A slight pause.

Could have owned a car factory. Look down with awe at my workers on the assembly line, sweating it out, bolting bolts. Could have been a station manager. Could-have-been.

He takes off his shirt. His vest has holes in it.

Who wants a fight? (*He starts to shadow-box.*) Who wants a fight? Come on. Come on.

He punches near ALAN. ALAN *raises the palms of his hands and* GEORGE *hits them with his fists.*

Is that the best you can do? Fight me. Come on. What are you, yellow? Come on. (*He stops, out of breath.*) Fight me.

A pause.

PAULINE. Yer'll catch yer death.

GEORGE *tries to flex his muscles.*

You will.

GEORGE. Won't you fight me?

ALAN. Why?

GEORGE. Want a fight. Come on. Prizefighter, me. Body jabs my speciality. No holding. (*He shadow-boxes.*)

A pause.

PAULINE. Yer will yer know. Catch yer death.

Slowly GEORGE *raises his shaking hand and runs it through his hair. He sinks to the ground. A pause. He takes an old photograph from his jacket pocket and smiles looking at it.*

That of you?

GEORGE. When I was twenty. (*He passes it to* ALAN.)

ALAN. Old.

GEORGE. One of the very first ever taken. Was very proud of the suit. The first suit I ever owned, the suit I left home in. Won that cup at the local boxing championships – the silver shining, reflect the sun round the world and back, that silver would. I polished it. Didn't have the makings of a big-time boxer, but I was proud. Proud. Good eh?

ALAN. Yeh. (*He moves to pass the photograph back to* GEORGE.)

PAULINE (*stopping him*). Le's us 'ave a look. (*Looks.*) Good.

GEORGE *takes the photograph and puts it back into his pocket.*

ALAN. Weren't the chances in your day.

A pause.

GEORGE. Of course, when Henry Cooper was heavyweight
champion, I taught him a thing or two. Oh yes, yes.

ALAN *smiles.*

He didn't develop that left hook from Scotch mist. Oh no. I said to
him one day, I said – Henry, you need a big punch, with a big punch
you'll do fine. Make it to the top, I said. So we spun this coin to
decide which punch we'd develop, the left or the right. Left won. Was
a time when his left hand was the most famous left hand in the world.

A pause.

PAULINE. You going 'ome shortly?

GEORGE (*looking up*). Erm?

PAULINE. 'Ome? London?

GEORGE *puts on his shirt.*

We'll write to yer. Won't we, Alan?

GEORGE. No.

PAULINE. Will.

GEORGE. No.

PAULINE. Cross my heart and 'ope to die.

GEORGE. No, you won't.

PAULINE. Will.

GEORGE. Better things to do, you have.

PAULINE. Like writin' letters.

A pause.

You going home?

GEORGE. First of Septemher. Three weeks yet.

Slowly GEORGE *puts on his jacket. He puts the tie in his jacket
pocket and starts to put on his socks.*

Going to Australia?

ALAN. Mebbe.

GEORGE. Wish you luck.

Silence. GEORGE *puts on his shoes. Slowly he stands up.*

I wish you luck. You'll need it. (*He looks at the sky.*) Getting late.

A pause. GEORGE *puts his hand to his brow, looks.*

Got to walk all the way down there. Long way. Still – (*He starts to exit, he turns to them.*) Wish you luck.

He exits. Long silence. ALAN *puts his arm around* PAULINE.

PAULINE. We will 'ave luck, won't we?

ALAN. We got luck now. Good job.

A pause.

PAULINE. Me dad's gettin' a bit like 'im.

ALAN. So?

PAULINE. Just tellin' yer.

ALAN. I'nt worth thinkin' about.

PAULINE. You 'aven't 'alf got a warm stomach.

ALAN. You don't like the old sod anyway, d'yer?

PAULINE. Not the point. Our Bess didn' 'alf yelp when he 'it 'er with the poker.

ALAN. No prospects in 'is day too.

PAULINE. Worst of it was 'e didn't give a bugger.

ALAN. Who?

PAULINE. Me dad. Beltin' our dog. Don't you listen?

ALAN. Thinkin', that's all. Come here.

They snog.

PAULINE. We won't end up like 'im, will we, Alan?

ALAN. He's just bitter, because 'e didn't get on. Get on in life.

PAULINE. Don't want you to be like 'im.

ALAN. They're the exception.

They snog. ALAN *sits.*

I mean, you only 'ave to look at George to see that. Old man, i'nt
'e. When yer old, that's it. Fact of life. Anyway, it's different now.
Technology and that, times change – in twenty years there'll be men
miles out in space, livin' up there. Bein' born up there. Fifty year
ago everyone was like him, today, well –

A pause.

'Ow could there be men on the moon and things not change?
Obvious, i'nt it? I'nt it?

PAULINE. I d'know, you're the clever dick.

ALAN. Bound to be. Men like 'im left school when they was ten.
I mean, 'ow could they learn a proper trade? The skill of a proper
trade? Being a porter on a station is just riffraff, rubbish. Anybody
can do that. It's the job that you 'ave, that makes all the difference.
'E didn' 'ave a good job, that's all.

PAULINE. Honest?

ALAN. Yeh. Know I'm right.

A pause.

PAULINE. What we gonna do then?

ALAN. Now?

PAULINE. Can't sit all night like this.

ALAN (*sexily*). Come here.

PAULINE. Don't start any a yer antics.

ALAN. 'Ho said owt about antics.

PAULINE. I know you when you start.

ALAN. Start what?

They snog.

PAULINE. I was sorry, Alan.

ALAN. Sorry?

PAULINE. 'Bout last night.

ALAN. Forgotten.

They snog.

PAULINE. Alan, I could go and see the vicar tomorra! A church
wedding.

ALAN. Oh yes?

PAULINE. Yeh, I could.

They snog.

Could take an hour off in t'afternoon.

They snog.

ALAN. Better do that then, 'adn't yer.

PAULINE. I will. You fix the reception?

ALAN. Yeh.

They snog. Lights fade to blackout.

Scene Six

August the 31st. The weather has broken, it is dull and grey. PIKE *and* HAROLD *both have double-barrelled shotguns, they are out shooting.* HAROLD *is standing by the marsh, the dark glasses gone, his eye healed.* PIKE *is crouched by the tree.*

An intense silence.

Suddenly PIKE *moves his gun, following the flight of a bird. He shoots twice in quick succession. A pause. A pheasant falls onto the stage as if from the sky. (Pheasants fall onto the stage several times in this scene, it is meant to seem slightly ludicrous and above all funny.) A pause.* PIKE *reloads his shotgun.*

An intense silence.

PIKE. It has always been a thing of no little remorse to me, the fact that I was never knighted. Never honoured by Her Majesty.

A pause.

One nil to me.

A pause.

When you think of some of the utter ninnies who have received titles.

A pause.

Doddery old men in wheelchairs with Sir before their name. Makes me want to think of turning seriously towards the Church. (*He sighs.*) Fifty-four years of waiting for a letter.

A pause.

Think if I risked my neck on some foolish endeavour they'd give me a title?

A pause.

A feat similar to that of Tenzing on Everest?

A pause.

I'm an old man. An old fuddy-duddy.

HAROLD. Not old.

PIKE. Old. I feel like becoming a Roman Catholic.

A pause.

I suppose after reading *Country Life* the Bible is the only other natural thing to turn to.

With the agility of a man of twenty, PIKE *moves. He shoots twice in quick succession.*

Damn! Skimmed it. Sent its little heart thumping, thump, thump, thump.

HAROLD. Missed it.

PIKE. Gave it a bad attack of the collywobbles. (*He sighs.*)

A pause. PIKE *reloads his gun.*

Pheasant, they are so bloody tame. What I long for is an African lioness in my sights.

A pause. HAROLD *moves his gun, he shoots twice in quick succession.*

(*In despair.*) Oh God.

A pheasant falls onto the stage as if from the sky.

One each.

HAROLD. Level pegging.

PIKE. How humiliating, drawing a bloody competition. It's like being caught with one's flies undone at the church fête. Your mother's so keen on the bloody fête. (*He points his gun at* HAROLD.)

HAROLD *looks at him, worried.*

Playing Hoopla. Putting her hand in the sawdust of the lucky dip. Winning some small token item that we have no use for. I could shoot you.

HAROLD *smiles, a worried smile.*

I could. Then there's that bloody brass band, marching up and down the lawn like regimented fleas.

A pause. PIKE *lowers his gun.*

No, I need my son and heir. There's nothing for it but to accept the humiliation. The degredation of drawing a competition with my son.

A pause. PIKE *points his gun off.* HAROLD *reloads his gun.*

I could be shooting monkeys in some jungle swamp in deepest Asia. (*He sighs.*) Or travelling up the Amazon on some small rubber inflatable craft, shooting crocodile and dodging rapids. Watching some naked Amazonian peasant dancing to the sole accompaniment of a single bongo. Tossing tiny trinkets at their feet, worthless knick-knacks or other. Adventure –

A pause.

(*Smiling.*) Retirement –

A pause.

Even that's been spoilt. I was reading in *The Express* of some firm organising package holidays to the Amazon river. Is there nothing sacred? In ten years they'll have holiday camps up there.

A pause.

Harold, I've decided to retire.

HAROLD. Fifty-four.

PIKE. I don't want to start wetting my bed, fouling my sheets. The white linen stained. I am told old men in hospital foul their sheets, make a mess in the night. They call it, having a messy night. I'll fly away. Fly away to the sun.

A pause. HAROLD *stretches out his hand.*

HAROLD. Thought I felt rain.

A slight pause.

Coming in cold now.

PIKE. Wouldn't want to end up soiling my bed in some geriatric ward, next to some leaky-bowelled general or other from the First World War. Some human relic.

A pause.

Why is it that people always have to spoil the fun? Some bloody idiot sets up a game reserve to stop me hunting lion. Too many people wanting to do good deeds. Too many do-gooders. Smart men and women with social consciences, they'll be the downfall of this world. Feeding neglected mongrel puppies like they're pedigree dogs. Oh God. Why can't they leave things alone?

A pause.

None of life's simple pleasures are left.

A pause.

Having this general talking to me of the medals he won in the Mesopotamia War, during the first advance on Baghdad. Cuddling his bayonet in bed and dreaming of battles lost and won. Shouting, forward, and, stick 'em up the arse there.

A pause.

It's all gone.

A pause. PIKE*'s mood changes, he is much brighter.*

The farm's looking good, Harold. I walked across the moor this morning, sheep are in great shape. Four sturdy feet, one at each corner. That's the way I like it.

HAROLD. Do my best.

PIKE. Your best is good.

A pause. HAROLD *looks up.*

HAROLD. Clouds are grey. Cumulus.

PIKE. All the same?

HAROLD. The same?

PIKE. Clouds.

HAROLD (*holding out his hands*). Thought I felt rain a minute ago.

A pause.

PIKE. Did you give Alan a reference?

HAROLD. He never asked.

PIKE. No?

HAROLD. He didn't blink so much as an eye. Then he turned round and told me to sod off.

PIKE. Would you have done?

HAROLD. Sodded off?

PIKE. Given Alan a reference?

HAROLD. No.

PIKE. Best to stay out of things. Best to stay out.

HAROLD. Best too.

PIKE. Live life without interference.

A pause.

Did you ask where he was going?

HAROLD. Didn't ask. Didn't care. (*Looking up.*) Sure they're cumulus.

A long intense silence as they wait for pheasants to fly up.

PIKE. Going abroad for a year.

HAROLD. You really going to shoot a lion?

A pause.

PIKE. Soiling my bed because I can't kill a lion.

A pause.

There was a time when England, dear old England, was respectable. When we could tramp through the jungle in tropical kit and the natives would bow. Tramping in one's colonial baggy shorts.

A pause.

Now all people care about is happiness. Fun. I'm not happy. Am I happy? Harold?

HAROLD *looks at him, a vacant expression on his face. A pause.* PIKE *looks down his gun.*

Who's that?

HAROLD (*looking*). That old man.

PIKE. Thought it was a ghost.

HAROLD. Not a ghost.

PIKE. Looks bloody silly. Trying to catch butterflies. (*He points his gun.*) How many points is a human worth? (*He lowers his gun.*)

Thought I'd seen a ghost.

HAROLD. Just that old man.

PIKE. He looks ridiculous, trying to catch butterflies in a net made for tadpoles.

A pause.

God was English once upon a time. Once upon a time.

A pause.

I once wrote this article for the parish magazine entitled: 'God was English' – was English. The Vicar found it slanderous, contemptuous.

A pause. PIKE *points his gun at* HAROLD.

Think you can handle the estate?

HAROLD *points his gun at* PIKE. *A pause.* PIKE *lowers his gun.*

You handled the Alan situation very well. (*Pointing.*) Sure that isn't a ghost?

HAROLD *lowers his gun.*

HAROLD. He had to go.

PIKE. Alan. Go.

HAROLD. Hadn't respect.

PIKE. Respect.

HAROLD. Took us for granted. His job for granted.

A pause.

PIKE. Harold –

A pause.

I am told that some deprived children cannot use a lavatory properly. That they miss. Oh dear, it's a disgusting subject. What I'm trying to say, Harold, is that if I've been cruel to you, it was for a reason. If I hit you –

A slight pause.

I read this article about the lavatory habits of the adolescent working class. Quite outrageous. It was to teach you respect. Respect for what we have. Respect for what we are.

A pause.

My father used to beat me, Harold. I thanked him for that.

HAROLD. Yes.

PIKE. The estate is yours.

HAROLD. Mine.

A pause.

Another ferret was dead this morning. Probably died in the night.

PIKE. That gamekeeper of mine starves them.

HAROLD. Of mine.

PIKE *looks at* HAROLD.

He starves them.

PIKE. Gamekeeper of yours. (*He lies back.*) Think he feeds his family on what he should be feeding to the ferrets. That's why they are all so bloody fat. That's what is wrong with this country, it's fat. Fat. No longer are people prepared to go without. Without –

A pause.

HAROLD (*looking up*). Getting stormy. Rain clouds.

PIKE. Rain clouds?

HAROLD. Yes.

PIKE (*pointing*). That old man is still there.

A pause.

Where are all the bloody pheasant?

A pause.

Of no little remorse, the fact that I was never honoured by the Queen.

A pause.

I'll buy a house in Spain, situated by some sun-drenched private beach. I want to forget the world, put up a 'trespassers will be prosecuted' notice and enjoy the seclusion. In the distance, some Spaniard playing a guitar.

A pause.

Your mother will be able to forget the bran-tub at the church fête.

A pause.

And enjoy a peaceful retirement.

HAROLD (*holding out his hand*). Starting to rain.

They are now in exactly the same positions as in the beginning of the scene. A long, tense silence. Suddenly PIKE *raises his gun. He shoots twice in quick succession.*

PIKE. Missed the blighter!

HAROLD. There it goes! (*He shoots twice.*)

PIKE *stands.*

PIKE. You shot it.

HAROLD. I shot it. (*He jumps up.*) You missed.

PIKE. Missed the blighter.

HAROLD. Two one to me.

A flash of lightning. A loud clap of thunder. It starts to rain.

Come on, we'd better find shelter.

PIKE. The first of the winter rain.

The rain is very loud. They have to shout.

What about these?

HAROLD. What about what?

PIKE. The pheasant.

HAROLD. Leave them.

PIKE. What?

HAROLD. Leave them.

PIKE. It's a waste.

HAROLD. So, what's important about a bit of waste? Come on.

PIKE. The Land-Rover up on the track.

HAROLD. Yes. Come on.

PIKE. Right.

HAROLD. Run.

> *They exit. A flash of lightning. A clap of thunder. Lights fade to blackout.*

Scene Seven

A few moments later. A flash of lightning. A clap of thunder. GEORGE *is standing in the rain, he is soaking wet. In his hand he holds a child's fishing net. He moves about with the net, very slowly, as if catching butterflies. He brings the net down.*

GEORGE. Got one. (*He brings the net down somewhere else.*) Another one. (*Again in a different place.*) And another one. (*Again.*) Got two that time.

> *An aeroplane flys low overhead. For a brief moment* GEORGE *stops to watch it. He brings the net down.*

Got one. (*Again.*) That makes two thousand I've caught. (*Again.*) Cabbage White. Red Admiral. (*Again.*) And another one. (*Again.*) I'd like to keep them in matchboxes.

> *He thinks he sees a butterfly flying over the marsh. He rushes at it, rushing through the mud. He swings his net at it and in doing so falls in the mud.*

Got it.

> *He crawls out. Again he brings the net down in a different place.*

The day I graduate to moths will be a great day.

> *He stops still. A pause. The rain eases off slightly, gets quieter.* GEORGE *looks at his feet. A slight pause. He raises the net and smashes the stick on his leg. The two pieces he throws violently to the ground. A flash of lightning. A clap of thunder.* GEORGE *sinks to the ground, he sits. A pause.*

> PAULINE *enters. She wears a plastic mac and a headscarf. Her best white shoes are covered in mud. She looks at* GEORGE. *A pause.* GEORGE *looks up at her.*

PAULINE. Yer soaked.

GEORGE *nods*.

You okay?

GEORGE *doesn't answer.*

You can't be okay.

She takes off her plastic mac and puts it round his shoulders.

Bloody stupid thing to do, walk off an evenin' like this. I wanted to walk. Wanted to walk up 'ere.

A pause.

You okay?

A pause.

Not much on t'telly now. Load of old rubbish, if you ask me. A don't mind gettin' wet. Feel like gettin' all wet.

A pause.

Me mam always used to say it was dangerous, gettin' soaked to the skin. S'pose it is. Don't care. In't bothered about illness. Not no more.

A pause.

I was reading in a magazine about this bloke 'ho owned this industry somewhere. Boring if you ask me, load of old tripe. It was just a lot of words.

GEORGE. Yes.

PAULINE. Yeh. Think you 'ad better go 'ome.

GEORGE. Think I had. (*He does not move.*)

A pause.

PAULINE. Don't know 'ow people gets the money to buy magazines like that.

GEORGE *looks up at her.*

It was in the dentist's.

GEORGE. Yes.

PAULINE. Yeh.

GEORGE. Get it from somewhere.

PAULINE. Load of bloody rubbish on the telly. That's why I come up here. To walk. I want to leave here one day and see the world, every corner of it.

A flash of lightning. A clap of thunder.

GEORGE. I like walking. Did like walking.

PAULINE. Yeh?

GEORGE. Walked miles. Used to do cross-country running, boxing training. You're getting wet.

PAULINE. Don't care.

GEORGE. Want this. (*He offers the mac.*)

PAULINE. You keep it. You and me, we must go walking one day. When it's fine, like. We can walk wherever we want.

GEORGE. I'm going home tomorrow. I don't care about the rain.

PAULINE. Right old storm.

GEORGE. Like it. Refreshing.

PAULINE. You fallen in the mud?

GEORGE. Yes.

PAULINE. Filthy. (*She bends down to wipe the mud off his trousers.*)

GEORGE. Leave it. Don't care any more.

PAULINE *stops. A pause.*

Are there no butterflies up here?

PAULINE. Not often, on the moor.

GEORGE. That's why I haven't caught any. I was trying.

PAULINE. Tryin'?

GEORGE. Nothing to catch. That's my life story.

PAULINE. You want a good bath.

GEORGE. Yes.

PAULINE. Warm you up a bit.

GEORGE. Yes.

PAULINE. Sit by the fire, get warm.

GEORGE. What you could do with.

PAULINE. Suppose yer right really. We still 'ave a coal fire in our 'ouse.

GEORGE. Yes.

PAULINE. We in't all electric.

GEORGE. No.

A flash of lightning. A clap of thunder.

PAULINE. No. Easier 'avin all electric, like. No grate to clean in't mornin's.

A pause.

My Alan's gone down south.

GEORGE. I know.

PAULINE. Gettin' a job down there.

GEORGE. Yes.

PAULINE. Not any old job, like. A good job. He don't take riffraff, don't Alan. 'E'll get a good job. Left day before yesterday, got the nine-forty out of Darlington for King's Cross. Like, you know about King's Cross.

GEORGE. Yes.

PAULINE. Home ground for you.

GEORGE. Not any more.

PAULINE. No.

GEORGE. Not any more.

PAULINE. He's gonna write me. I 'aven't 'eard from 'im yet, but a will. You're shivering.

GEORGE. The cold.

PAULINE. Is cold.

A pause.

Trouble was I couldn't go with 'im, cos of accommodation an' that. 'E'll 'ave to find 'imself a boardinghouse.

A pause.

Fancy livin' in London, going to see all the shows an' that. Neon lights. Find some nice place t'stay, 'ave my own 'ouse. Be able to choose me own things. Never 'ad my own 'ome.

A pause.

Tomorra a think a should get a letter. One every day 'e's gonna write. Love letters, just like at school.

A pause.

See, I 'aven' an address to write to 'im. I'm not bad at love letters. Only thing a was good at at school, was love letters. Plenty a practice.

A pause. A clap of thunder.

Was best for 'im to move from 'ere. Gettin' t'push. Probably find a much better job. Got a good 'ead on 'is shoulders, 'as my Alan. My Alan. Did right thing, going south. Better down there, better prospects. A still like 'ere though, wouldn' change where I was born. Like it up 'ere a lot. I told 'im to go. My choice.

GEORGE *flops over onto his side. He is dead.* PAULINE *does not see him.*

I brought a file this mornin', to keep all 'is letters in. I know 'e'll write every day. 'E's kind is Alan. His mam's a bit funny, though. She 'as bad veins in 'er leg. Ought to 'ave an operation really, 'ave them cleared. Sittin' too near the fire, that's wha' does it. Alan told 'er, but she don't take a blind bit a notice.

A pause. See bends down to GEORGE.

You okay? Eh? You all right? Eh? You aven't fallen asleep, 'ave you? (*She shakes him.*) You i'nt fallen asleep? George? George, you all right? (*Quietly.*) You 'ave fallen asleep, 'aven't you? George?

A flash of lightning. A clap of thunder. It is now raining very hard.

George!

She puts her hand to her mouth to stifle a scream. A pause. She pushes GEORGE *over onto his back. A clap of very loud thunder.* PAULINE *starts to scream, she screams and screams. Lights slowly fade to blackout. Silence.*

The End.

OTHER WORLDS

Other Worlds was first performed at the Royal Court Theatre, London, on 6 May 1983, with the following cast:

The Fishermen

JOE WATERMAN	Paul Copley
ROBERT STORM	Paul Luty
MOLLY STORM	Anita Carey
PETER STORM	John Holmes

The Farmers

ANNE WHEATLEY	Rosemary Leach
BETSY	Juliet Stevenson
JOHN WHEATLEY	Jim Broadbent
JOHN, *as a child*	John Holmes
RICHARD WHEATLEY	Jim Broadbent
EMMA BRAYE	Juliet Stevenson
MARY	Lesley Dunlop
STOCKTON	Peter O'Farrell
WILLIAM ELDERBERRY	Peter O'Farrell
Director	Richard Wilson

ACT ONE

Scene One: The beach at Bay Ness. Early Tuesday morning, 11 July 1797.

Scene Two: Anne Wheatley's kitchen at Middlewood Farm. An hour later.

Scene Three: Later that morning.

Scene Four: The beach and town at Robin Hood's Bay. The same morning.

ACT TWO

Scene One: Middlewood. Twenty years earlier. Mid-afternoon of Christmas Eve, 1777.

Scene Two: Mid-afternoon of Boxing Day.

Scene Three: The night of New Year's Eve.

ACT THREE

Scene One: Anne Wheatley's kitchen. Twenty years later. The evening of 11 July 1797.

Scene Two: The beach and town at Robin Hood's Bay. A few moments later.

Scene Three: The beach at Bay Ness. Midday, two days later.

The play takes place near the village of Fylingthorpe and the small town of Robin Hood's Bay on the North Yorkshire coast, during the time of a threatened invasion by France.

Characters

The Fishermen

ROBERT STORM, *fifty*
JOE WATERMAN, *forty-three*
MOLLY STORM, *forty-one*
PETER STORM, *twelve*

The Farmers

ANNE WHEATLEY, *fifty-nine*
BETSY, *nineteen*
JOHN WHEATLEY, *thirty-two*
JOHN, *as a child*
RICHARD WHEATLEY, *forty-four* (*in 1777*)
EMMA BRAYE, *twenty-six*

MARY, *fourteen*
STOCKTON, *a gorilla*
WILLIAM ELDERBERRY, *early thirties, a dwarf*

ACT ONE

Scene One

The beach at Bay Ness. Very early Tuesday morning, 11 July 1797.

The beach is empty apart from a small, rough, tent-like shelter which has been constructed from driftwood, old pieces of cloth, and canvas. Around the base of the tent seaweed has been placed to hold it down.

The tent has an opening at the front, inside can be seen the figure of a child, MARY.

Darkness, almost no moon. A raging storm is blowing. A high wind. Driving rain. A wild sea is pounding violently against the shore.

ROBERT STORM *enters from Bay Ness. He has a lantern.*

ROBERT *is a big, stocky, square, broad-shouldered man of fifty. He has a round, ruddy face which is sunburnt from his work outside, big hands, and big feet. His clothes are of poor quality; breeches, shirt, waistcoat, neck-tie, hat; no stockings and no shoes.*

ROBERT *staggers forward through the wind and rain, he is looking along the beach. He stops.*

ROBERT (*shouting over the storm*). Is that you, Joe?

ROBERT *holds the lantern up to illuminate his face.*

JOE WATERMAN *enters from Robin Hood's Bay. He also has a lantern.*

JOE *is a small, thin, pinched-looking man of forty-three. His bones seem to stick through his flesh, especially on his face which is brown and sunburnt. He has a thick crop of dark hair. His clothes are of better quality; breeches, shirt, waistcoat, neck-tie, stockings, but no shoes.*

JOE *is blown forward with the wind. He holds the lantern to his face.*

JOE (*shouting, his voice not as strong as* ROBERT*'s*). Robert?

ROBERT. A've bin watchin' fo'yer.

ROBERT *walks forward. They meet.*

Yer've lost yer hat?

JOE. It got blown away.

ROBERT. D'know if a've sin a storm like this. It's a hundred devils were out.

JOE (*nodding*). Aye. What's 'appenin'?

ROBERT. Thess a boat of Bay Ness rocks.

JOE *listens.*

Shiz a wreck unless we do summat. Shiz flounderin'. Lookin' f'shelter.

JOE. What sort of boat?

ROBERT. Can't see properly. Two or three masts. A schooner. Shiz sailin' on just 'er jib.

JOE. D'yer recognise 'er?

ROBERT (*shaking his head*). No.

A flash of lightning.

They both look at the sky for a second.

Shiz a wreck, Joe, unless we do summat.

JOE *nods.*

JOE. Which way is she comin' from?

ROBERT. Down the coast from Whitby.

JOE (*thinking*). I keep wonderin' –

ROBERT. What?

JOE. She might be a French boat.

A loud clap of thunder.

They look at the sky and wait for it to finish.

ROBERT. You know best, Joe.

JOE. It's jus' the sort a'night the French would come. A night like this. Tryin' to catch us out. When we're not expectin' 'em.

ROBERT *looks perplexed.*

MARY *comes out of her shelter.*

MARY *is a small, thin girl of about fourteen, though she looks and is dressed like a boy. Her hair is roughly cut and her skin is ingrained with months of dirt. Her clothes are ill-fitting and ragged: trousers, shirt, waistcoat, jacket, a cap on her head; no stockings and no shoes.*

MARY *staggers forward towards* ROBERT *and* JOE.

A don' know what t'do. Are the beacons ready?

ROBERT (*nodding*). Yeh.

ROBERT*'s hat nearly blows off, he pulls it back on.* MARY *is beside them.*

MARY. What yer doin' 'ere?

ROBERT (*gruffly*). Thess a boat in trouble, boy.

JOE. If we light the beacons does she stan' a chance?

ROBERT. More'n she do now.

JOE (*shouting more loudly*). A wish a could be sure it weren't the French. (*After thinking for a moment.*) Alright, light 'em. We'll tekk the risk.

ROBERT *walks a pace or two towards Bay Ness. He waves his lantern from side to side.*

JOE *and* MARY *watch.*

MARY (*pointing, excited*). Look, there the' go. I ain't seen tha before, Master.

A flash of lightning. MARY *covers her head with her hands.* ROBERT *stops waving the lantern.* JOE *walks to him.*

JOE. I hope it's not the French army?

ROBERT. Aye. Are yer comin' or a'yer goyn back?

JOE. I'll come with yer.

ROBERT. We'll go then.

ROBERT *and* JOE *walk towards Bay Ness.*

MARY. Where yer goyn? Can I come?

ROBERT *and* JOE *have exited.*

A loud clap of thunder. MARY *covers her head with her hands.*

Why can't a come? Yer all the same you fishermen.

The moonlight fades to blackout.

The sound of the storm remains.

Scene Two

ANNE WHEATLEY*'s kitchen at Middlewood Farm. An hour later.*

The kitchen is quite small and has a stone floor. The walls have been roughly plastered and whitewashed. In the back wall there is a sash window which is set in a small recess. When it is light an oak tree can be seen growing outside. At the base of the window, set in the recess, is a rough oak ledge which serves as a kitchen work surface. In front of the window is an oak table and a wooden bench. Beside the window, to the left, is the outside door. The door is secured from the inside by a bar of wood; at the moment the bar is resting against the wooden door frame. In the left-hand wall is a brick oven, the chimney-breast leads upwards from it. The oven is newer than the rest of the kitchen, it was built ten years ago. On the chimney-breast are two wooden shelves. Standing against the right-hand wall is a fine oak dresser. Downstage of the dresser is a door leading to the rest of the house, and upstairs. Near the dresser is a rocking chair.

ANNE *keeps her kitchen clean and tidy. On the ledge below the window are various cooking items; a sugar loaf; various dried herbs, some hanging free, some in small wooden boxes; a copper jelly mould; an iron toast rack; a wooden butter pat; wooden and iron spoons, copper ladles, etc. Leaning against the oven is a pair of firetongs. Above the oven on the two ledges are cooking-pots, skillets, saucepans of various sizes, the bigger ones are made of iron and the smaller ones of copper. Standing on the oven is a kettle and a toasting fork. The dresser is decorated with china and pewter plates, wine glasses and goblets. Dotted throughout the kitchen are candles and rushlights in holders. On the table, covered by a muslin cloth, are various cooked meats, bread and pies.*

A faint moonlight through the window.

The storm is still raging, though now the scene being inside, it is muffled.

MARY *appears outside at the window.*

A flash of lightning.

MARY *covers her head with her hands for a moment. She tries the window, it opens. She lifts it up and clambers in. In doing so she knocks various items off the window ledge, they clatter to the floor.*

Thunder outside.

MARY *closes the window. She looks about the kitchen, peering into things. Eventually she lifts the muslin cloth on the table and sees the food. She picks up a meat pie and starts to eat it. She is starving; bits of pie drop onto the floor.* MARY *has a canvas bag with her, while she is eating she packs the bag with the rest of the food. Suddenly she stops. She has heard someone upstairs, she goes to the window and tries to open it. The window is stuck.* MARY *hides under the window ledge.*

The door to the rest of the house opens. ANNE WHEATLEY *peers round, she has a candle.*

ANNE *is a plump woman of fifty-nine. She has a gentle, intelligent, homely face and her hair has gone grey. Her hands and fingers are slightly red with rheumatism. She is wearing a white nightdress and a woollen shawl.*

ANNE *steps gingerly into the kitchen. In her other hand she has an iron poker.*

She is followed in by BETSY. BETSY *has a candle in one hand and a broom handle in the other, she looks frightened.*

BETSY *is a slim, attractive girl of nineteen. She is taller than* ANNE, *and has a clean, bright, alert face, and short blonde hair. She is wearing a white nightdress. The kitchen has brightened with the candlelight.*

BETSY. See anyone?

ANNE. You've gone white, girl.

BETSY. I don't think I heard anything after all, Aunt.

ANNE. Close the door.

    BETSY *nervously closes the door.*

    Stay by it.

BETSY (*staying by the door*) Please, Aunt, it must've been the storm.

ANNE (*walking to the table*). Look at this. There is someone in here.

BETSY. I hope he's escaped.

ANNE (*walking to the outside door*). The door's unbolted.

BETSY. I heard Master John go out.

ANNE puts the wooden bar across the door.

ANNE. You've done very little sleeping, have you, girl?

A flash of lightning.

BETSY jumps. They both look towards the window.

I've never seen such a night, Now, where is this thief? You didn't hear him go out?

BETSY. No.

Thunder outside.

BETSY jumps. ANNE starts to search the kitchen, looking under and over things.

(*Nervously.*) I know who it is.

ANNE. Who?

BETSY. Appleyard's lad.

ANNE. Tim Appleyard?

BETSY. I've seen him hiding in the trees, he's bin watching us.

ANNE. Come out, Tim Appleyard, if you're in here, we know it's you.

MARY tries to push herself further under the window.

BETSY. I've seen you, Tim Appleyard.

ANNE puts the candle on the table. She holds the poker in both hands and searches the kitchen again.

Be careful, he's a big lad.

ANNE. I've some puff in me still.

BETSY (*calling*). Did you hear that, Appleyard's boy?

ANNE looks by the dresser.

ANNE. A good-for-nothing since the day of his birth, that's Tim Appleyard.

BETSY. I'm glad your poker's brave.

ANNE. Don't prattle, Betsy.

> MARY *comes out*.

BETSY (*screaming*). Aunt! There 'e is!

> MARY *climbs onto the window ledge*.

ANNE. I've got 'im.

> MARY *tries to open the window. Before she can succeed* ANNE *has got to her.* ANNE *hits out at* MARY *with the poker. The blows are quite hard across* MARY*'s back*.

BETSY (*shrieking*). You've done it, you've done it! You've got 'im, you've got 'im!

> MARY *falls off the window ledge onto the floor, she rolls up into a ball*.

> ANNE *continues to hit out*.

> BETSY *goes to the table and puts her candle down*.

> ANNE*'s blows slowly cease. She stops*.

ANNE. He's had enough now.

> ANNE *looks dishevelled, her hair has fallen out of place, and her shawl has fallen on the floor. She picks it up and puts it back across her shoulders. She is breathing deeply*.

BETSY. Are you all right?

ANNE (*walking to the rocking chair*). I haven't as much puff as
    I thought.

> ANNE *sits in the rocking chair*.

I'll be all right in a minute.

> *A slight pause*.

BETSY. You hit him quite hard.

ANNE. Yes.

> *A slight pause*. BETSY *looks at* MARY.

BETSY. It's not Tim Appleyard.

ANNE. No.

BETSY. I've never seen 'im before. I don't know who 'e is, d'you?

ANNE. No, child.

BETSY. He's just a child 'imself. You were brave.

ANNE is breathing more easily, she stands up and walks back towards MARY.

ANNE. We'd best find out who he is.

BETSY. He hasn't moved. You don' think he's dead?

ANNE. He's breathing, thank goodness.

BETSY. Yes.

ANNE. I let my arm take over. Let it be a lesson f'you.

A flash of lightning.

BETSY *jumps.*

BETSY. I wish the lightning'd stop.

ANNE. What is your name, child?

A slight pause.

Tell me where you've come from?

A slight pause.

BETSY. Nowhere, Aunt.

ANNE. You're not from Flyingthorpe or the farms round about, are you? (*Looking up at* BETSY.) He's not a fisherman, I hope?

BETSY (*worry in her voice*). How could he be?

ANNE. It's a silly thought.

BETSY (*to* MARY). We don't talk to the fishermen.

ANNE. You're not a fisherman from Robin Hood's Bay, are you?

A slight pause.

BETSY. He's not, Aunt.

ANNE. I don't know what to think. (*To* MARY.) Tell me your name, child, and I won't hurt you more.

MARY *is still silent.*

BETSY (*picking up* MARY*'s canvas bag*). He must've been hungry.

BETSY *puts the bag on the table and starts to unpack the food* MARY *has taken.*

All he's taken is the food.

ANNE (*after a moment's pause*). What am I going to do with him, Betsy?

ANNE *bends down and takes hold of* MARY*'s shoulders.*

Stand up, child, let's see you more clearly.

MARY (*wriggling, shouting*). Ge' off me.

ANNE. But you can't stay there all night.

ANNE *lets* MARY *go.* BETSY *has put the food on the table.*

BETSY. He's eaten one pie.

ANNE (*taking* MARY*'s shoulders again*). Stand up, come on.

MARY (*wriggling, shouting*). No.

ANNE *tries to lift* MARY *up.* MARY *kicks out with her feet.*

Ge' off! Stop it!

ANNE. You're going to stand up.

BETSY. Be careful, Aunt, he's kicking.

ANNE. I know where he's kicking, he's going to do as he's told.

MARY. Ge' off me!

ANNE (*smacking* MARY*'s bottom*). Stop it.

MARY *stops struggling, she stands up.* ANNE*'s hair has fallen out of place.*

Now then, that's better.

MARY *spits at* ANNE.

I'm doing you a kindness, child. (*Pushing her hair back.*) For such a little mite you're very strong.

MARY *spits at* ANNE.

Thunder outside.

Thunder outside an' thunder in here. Would you pick those things up off the floor, Betsy.

BETSY *goes to the window. She starts to pick up the things* MARY *knocked off and returned them to the ledge.*

MARY. This is my kitchen.

ANNE. It is, is it?

MARY. Well it ain't yours. Yer hurt me.

BETSY. I think he must be living wild, Aunt.

MARY (*aggressively to* BETSY). 'Ow would you know?

ANNE (*to* MARY). Let's have no more.

MARY. Who's she?

ANNE. Betsy is my niece.

MARY. Bit funny, ain't she?

BETSY. Not as funny as you.

ANNE. Would both of you cease. I want the boy to talk, Betsy,

MARY. I ain' a thief, Mistress.

ANNE. Then why are you in my kitchen?

MARY. Cos – cos I'm 'ungry.

ANNE. When did you last eat something?

MARY (*pointing at it*). That pie. All I've 'ad f'days'n days.

ANNE. And are you living wild as my neice said?

MARY. On the beach, Mistress,

ANNE. With the fishermen?

    MARY *is silent.*

    With the fishermen, child?

MARY (*not sure what to say*). Aye. A like them lot.

    BETSY *stands up and listens.*

ANNE. Have they talked to you?

MARY (*looking between* ANNE *and* BETSY). All the time, Mistress. The' give me food.

ANNE. Then why are you starving now?

MARY. D'know.

ANNE. Did the fishermen send you here?

MARY. Yeh, the' did.

ANNE. Why did they send you?

MARY. D'know, Mistress. The' didn't.

BETSY *starts to pick up the last of the things off the floor.*

ANNE. How long've vou been like this, child?

MARY. Weeks'n'weeks. Months.

BETSY (*standing up*). I've picked those up.

ANNE. Thank you, Betsy.

BETSY. D'you think he is with the fishermen?

ANNE. I'm sure not.

MARY (*looking at* ANNE). What yer goyn t'do wi' me?

ANNE. I don't know.

BETSY. He doesn't seem very old t'me.

ANNE. How old are you?

MARY *shrugs*.

MARY. Can' count, Mistress. 'Bout thirty-two, summat like.

ANNE. My son's thirty-two. He's a man.

MARY. 'Bout eighteen then.

ANNE (*gently*). Sit down.

MARY *sits down on the bench.* ANNE *walks to the rocking chair and sits.*

If you're not from Bay Town where are you from?

MARY *shrugs*.

Don't you know that either?

MARY. Stockton.

ANNE. Whereabouts is Stockton, child?

MARY (*pointing*). That way.

BETSY. Shuvv up, boy.

MARY *moves along*. BETSY *sits down on the bench*.

MARY. A've bin walkin' a lot.

ANNE. 'N' what's your name?

MARY. The' call me Jack. Skip-Jack. Cos I used t'skip all the time.

The storm is slowly beginning to blow itself out and quieten.

Where abouts am a?

ANNE. You're near the village of Fylingthorpe on the North Yorkshire coast.

MARY. Is this a farm?

ANNE (*brightly*). My son John runs the farm.

MARY. 'Ave you any cows?

ANNE. Three.

MARY. A can milk cows. 'Ave you a job, Mistress?

ANNE. I don't think so, child.

MARY. A can milk cows till me fingers drop off. A c'd live in the barn.

BETSY (*shivering*) I'm cold.

MARY. A've slept wi' pigs, a c'd live wi' them?

ANNE. My son decides such things.

MARY. Only want a home.

ANNE. I expect you do, child, but how can I have you?

MARY. Oh please, please.

BETSY. He's some politeness about 'im now.

MARY. A'd eat the pigs' food.

BETSY. I'm cold, Aunt, why don't we let 'im go?

ANNE *thinks*.

It's not as if he's Appleyard's lad, we won't see 'im again.

ANNE. I don't want him at Bay Town, Betsy.

BETSY. It don't matter, do it?

ANNE. How I wish it didn't very of'en.

MARY. This is my home now, ain' it?

ANNE. We don't know anything about you, you can't stay here.

ANNE *is thinking*.

BETSY. I'll be bold. Aunt, I think you're being silly.

ANNE. Choose your words with care.

BETSY. I'm sorry.

ANNE *thinks for a moment longer and then looks at the window*.

ANNE. Thank the Lord the storm is ceasing.

BETSY. It seems t'be.

ANNE (*leaning forward*). If I let you go, boy, will you run away and not go back to the fishermen?

MARY *shrugs*.

We had a feud with Bay Town many years ago.

BETSY (*to MARY*). They stink you know, with the smell of fish. One fisherman has two heads.

ANNE (*standing up*). Who on this earth told you that?

BETSY. Stephen Cheese at 'Thorpe village.

ANNE. Such tales belong in books.

BETSY. He had a pipe in one mouth an' was eating with the other.

ANNE (*turning, walking to the dresser*). Gossip, Betsy. The villagers only make things worse.

BETSY. The villagers believe him, Aunt.

ANNE. I expect they do in their foolishness. Is that reason f'us to?

BETSY. No.

ANNE *picks up a small wooden box from the dresser, it contains yarrow leaves*.

ANNE (*putting some leaves into a small bowl*). Stephen Cheese was not alive those twenty years ago. He's never been to Bay.

ANNE *adds a few drops of water to the bowl from the kettle by the fire*.

BETSY. The villagers believe him because it was he who saw the soldiers comin'. (*To* MARY.) The press gang came here.

MARY looks blank.

Don't you know about the war?

ANNE has found a wooden spoon, she is mixing a paste with the yarrow leaves and water. She sits down.

We're at war with France. A platoon of soldiers arrived here in their gleaming blue uniforms an' took away those that didn't hide quick enough.

ANNE. Don't exaggerate f'the boy. Some men wanted t'go, child.

BETSY. Only the faggers, Aunt, the poor. Only those fit for nothing else.

ANNE (*leaning back in the chair*). I tire of your prattle.

ANNE closes her eyes.

The poor deserve our respect. What else could they do?

BETSY. I know we're lucky, Aunt, I didn't mean it that way.

A slight pause.

I do respect the poor. I thank the Lord every night in my prayers.

ANNE opens her eyes. MARY scratches her aching back.

Why doesn't the lad go in the army?

ANNE. D'you really not know about the war?

MARY shakes her head

The army is a good life for a boy your age. The faggers, their lads went, all boys like you. They're fighting France.

MARY (*scratching her back*). Soldiers chased me once. At the market town of Guisborough. A ran off.

ANNE. Does your back sting?

MARY nods.

Come here, child, and I'll rub some yarrow leaves on it.

MARY. No.

ANNE. The yarrow leaves will help soothe it. (*Standing up.*) Stand up'n take your shirt off.

MARY (*hesitantly standing up*). No, a don' wan' it.

ANNE (*walking to* MARY). What's the matter with you now?

MARY (*walking away a step*). Ge'off me. Leave me alone.

ANNE (*gently*). All right, child.

BETSY. The boy doesn't want to be naked in front of two women.

There is a loud knock at the outside door.

ANNE. Who's that?

BETSY. It'll be Master John come back.

ANNE *puts the wooden bowl on the table and goes to the door.*

ANNE. Is that you, John?

JOHN (*from outside*). What's going on?

ANNE. Wait a minute, I bolted the door.

ANNE *removes the wooden bar and rests it against the door frame.*

The door opens. JOHN WHEATLEY *enters, he is soaking wet.*

JOHN *is a tall, broad-shouldered man of thirty-two. He has rough hands, thick dark hair, and a sunburnt face. His clothes are of good quality; shoes, stockings, breeches, silk shirt, waistcoat, jacket, neck-tie, and a hat.*

JOHN (*closing the door, taking his hat off*). I saw the candlelight, now the door, what's going on?

JOHN *turns and sees* MARY.

Who's that?

ANNE. He broke into our kitchen.

JOHN *puts his hat on the table and walks towards* MARY. MARY *backs away.*

BETSY. Don't, Master John, he's had a sound thrashing from the Mistress here.

JOHN *stops.*

JOHN (*looking at his mother*). Ma?

ANNE. Betsy spoke the truth.

JOHN (*looking at* MARY). What does the boy say?

MARY *is silent*

(*Going to* MARY.) I'll lock him with the hens.

ANNE. Then what?

JOHN (*taking* MARY *roughly by the arm*). Take him to the Justice in Whitby when it's light.

MARY *kicks* JOHN.

He kicked me.

JOHN *increases his hold on* MARY.

ANNE. Would you go to bed please, Betsy.

JOHN. I'm not having a row, Ma.

ANNE. Yes, you are.

BETSY *walks to the upstairs door.*

MARY (*trying to kick* JOHN *again*). Ge' off me.

JOHN. Don't you go.

BETSY. This time I agree with the Mistress. Goodnight.

ANNE. Goodnight, Betsy.

BETSY *exits upstairs and closes the door.*

MARY *is struggling.*

Will you let the boy go.

MARY *stops struggling.*

I shouldn't have to ask you again.

A slight pause.

Will you let the boy go please.

JOHN *lets* MARY *go.* MARY *struggles free of his hands.*

(*To* MARY.) Come here.

MARY, *a little bewildered, walks to* ANNE.

He's spending the rest of the night in here. If in the morning you still want to take him to the Justice, that's up to you.

JOHN. I haven't done anything. What've I done? Tell me. Ma?

ANNE. I'm tired. John.

JOHN *looks down for a moment.*

JOHN. I come back, there's a boy in the kitchen who's a thief, what am I expected t'do?

ANNE. I'm not only talking about now.

JOHN. What are yer talkin' about?

ANNE. Wilf Meadows, yesterday morning. I saw you shouting at him in that terrible manner. I felt ashamed.

JOHN. Wilf Meadows is our shepherd. He'd lost five sheep.

ANNE. But you found them again.

JOHN. I found 'em. In Middlewood. Is that what this is all about?

ANNE. Only partly, John.

JOHN. Yer find funny ways of goyn about it. What else?

ANNE. I've tried to say – your manner and your bullying.

JOHN *takes his pocket watch from his waistcoat pocket.*

JOHN. It's four o'clock in the morning.

JOHN *puts the watch away.*

The storm is now much quieter, it has almost blown itself out.

ANNE. Where've you been?

JOHN. I couldn't sleep. I wen' out to look at the farm.

ANNE (*to* MARY). Sit in the chair.

MARY *walks to the rocking-chair and sits down.*

Is the farm in a mess?

JOHN (*walking to the bench, sitting down*). Most of the wheat is down.

ANNE (*walking to the bench, sitting down beside him*). Will the faggers be able to cut it?

JOHN. It'd begun to ripen, Ma. It's now as flat as the mill pond. Five Acre was yellow with ripening.

ANNE *looks tenderly at* JOHN.

(*Slightly more brightly.*) Aye it'll cut if it don't rot first. A harder job f'the faggers, that's all.

ANNE *smiles.*

At least yer smilin' now. Yer won't be when a tell yer this. Lightning struck one o' your cows.

ANNE. Which one?

JOHN. Celandine. The silly beast got 'ersel' beneath the oak tree in Bottom Meadow.

ANNE. Is she dead?

JOHN. Aye, she is. I'm sorry, Ma. The trees down an' all. A were fond of that oak tree.

ANNE. So was I.

JOHN. Celandine was your favourite, wasn't she?

ANNE. She'd the best disposition,

JOHN. Will you buy another cow?

ANNE. I'd like to, John. Her milk was always best for the butter, too.

JOHN. Aye, well, we'll do that. (*Smiling*.) I'll grumble till I'm sick about the money.

ANNE. I'm sorry if I sometimes seem harsh.

JOHN. Yer do'n all. 'N' why send Betsy t'bed?

ANNE *smiles*.

I know why an' that smile proves it. T'get yer own way.

ANNE. I haven't yet, have I?

JOHN. No, an' we'll see if yer do.

Silence for a moment.

ANNE (*turning, looking at the window*). The storm has stopped, thank goodness.

JOHN (*standing, walking to the oven*). I went up t'Bay Ness.

ANNE. What on earth for?

JOHN (*holding his hands above the oven*). The fishermen were on the beach, tryin' t'save a boat.

ANNE. Did they?

JOHN. No, it was wrecked.

ANNE. I hope God has mercy upon them.

JOHN. By the time the' lit the beacons the boat didn' stand a chance. (*Gingerly touching the top of the oven.*) The oven's not in.

JOHN *touches the oven with the palm of his hand.*

ANNE. I was going to relight it at dawn. Why did you go to Bay Ness?

JOHN (*turning to face* ANNE). I don't trust 'em, Ma. If the French do come, it'll be a night like this. 'N' if they're not watching –

ANNE. I think they will watch, John.

JOHN. Yer've faith f'a dozen. Farmer Wood had the same idea. I met him there.

ANNE *pulls a face.*

The strong wind'd blown the thatch from 'is barn. All his hay inside.

ANNE. Farmer Wood is an idle drunkard.

JOHN. It's no wonder 'e don't like you.

ANNE. I wouldn't expect to be liked by any of the Wood family. They're all as idle as a stopped clock.

JOHN. I think yer do it on purpose.

ANNE (*huffily*). What?

JOHN. Everyone talks about yer, Ma.

ANNE. Do they. Let them. It's gossip with no meaning.

JOHN. They've started to say yer a witch.

ANNE. Who're they?

JOHN. The villagers at 'Thorpe.

ANNE. Bring those villagers to me. I speak my mind. Always have done. I won't change now. I'm not on God's earth to be loved by the villagers of 'Thorpe. And I hope you defend me.

A slight pause.

Do you defend me?

A slight pause.

Obviously you don't.

JOHN. I try to, Ma.

ANNE. Witch is a very strong word.

JOHN. I know that.

ANNE. I'll have to go the village.

The first faint light of dawn can be seen through the window.

(*Standing.*) It's beginning to get light.

JOHN. I've to muck out the pigs. Sally is lookin' restless, 'er litters near due.

ANNE *walks to* MARY.

'N' I'll bring up Celandine from the meadow. We'll have some beef, all be it a bit tough, she was an old lass.

ANNE. Have you decided about the boy? The Justice will have him whipped from one end of the village to the other.

JOHN. If he's with a band of sheep stealers, Ma.

ANNE. He's not.

JOHN *thinks for a moment.*

JOHN. A whipping is no less than he deserves.

MARY. I've bin whipped before. At the market town of Guisborough. A put some paper down me breeches.

JOHN. D'you promise me t'run away? Somewhere else 'n' never come back.

ANNE. The boy will run. He's been running. He's used to running.

A slight pause.

JOHN. Alright, Ma, but this is the last time. (*Walking to the upstairs door.*) I'll go upstairs 'n' change these wet clothes.

ANNE. I'll make breakfast, John.

JOHN. It's against my better judgement.

JOHN *exits through the upstairs door and closes it behind him.*

ANNE *goes to the table und starts to pack the canvas bag with the food.*

ANNE. Think yourself lucky, child.

MARY (*standing up*). Wha'?

MARY *walks to* ANNE.

ANNE. Run away. And never come back as the Master said.

MARY. A don' want t'.

ANNE. Don't be silly. (*Putting the bag over* MARY*'s shoulder.*) I can't help you.

ANNE *pushes* MARY *towards the outside door.*

MARY. Why can't a stay?

ANNE *opens the door.*

ANNE. Go on run, child, run.

MARY (*staying put*). Where am a runnin' to?

ANNE. Away from here. Run, go on, run.

MARY *runs through the door.*

As fast as your legs will carry you.

A slight pause.

That's it.

ANNE *stands watching through the open door.*

In the dawn light the two candles are still burning.

Scene Three

ANNE WHEATLEY*'s kitchen. Later that morning.*

The sash window and the outside door are open.

Sunlight is streaming in. It is a bright, warm, sunny day.

On the table is a plate of sweet pig meat, some butter in a dish, and a milk jug.

A song thrush sings outside.

BETSY *enters through the open door, in one hand she is carrying a wooden pail which is half full of water, and in the other she is clutching four big apples, an onion, and a carrot. She is wearing shoes, a gown, an apron, and a cap on her head.*

BETSY *puts the pail down near the table. The apples, onion, and carrot she puts near the pig meat. Next she starts to find, and bring to the table, all the things she will need to make a pie: bowls, spoons, etc.*

She lays them out ready. When she has finished she looks at the table for a moment.

BETSY *goes to the upstairs door and opens it.*

BETSY (*calling through*). Mistress, are you back yet?

No answer. BETSY *walks to the outside door and looks out for a moment.*

The song thrush sings again.

BETSY *goes to the dresser and takes a broken china cup from the top ledge. She takes a key from the cup, bends down, and opens one of the cupboards at the bottom of the dresser. From the back of the cupboard she takes a notebook (it is* ANNE's *diary), she goes to the table, clears a space, and sits down to read. She turns the page, reading with great interest.*

JOHN *appears at the outside door. He is wearing shoes, stockings, breeches, shirt, neck-tie, and a hat. His hands and clothes are covered in pig muck.* JOHN *watches* BETSY *for a moment.*

JOHN. Betsy.

BETSY. Oh, Master John, you gave me a shock. Don't do that. (*Trying to hide the notebook.*) What's happened t'yer!

JOHN. I've fell in the pig muck.

BETSY *smiles and stands up.*

Don't you dare laugh.

BETSY *smirks and tries not to laugh.*

(*Severely.*) Betsy.

BETSY. Don't you come in here for goodness' sake. the Mistress will have a blue fit. (*Almost laughing.*) If you could see yourself.

JOHN. That stupid sow, Sally, knocked me right over.

BETSY *sniffs.*

BETSY. I can stink you from here, Master John. Go'n rub yourself with parsley, that'll help rid of it. (*Laughing.*) Otherwise yer'll stink f'weeks.

JOHN (*walking into the kitchen*). If I'm going to suffer, you will.

BETSY (*trying to be firm, but laughing*). No, Master John, don't be annoyin'. If the Mistress –

JOHN. I'm the head of the house, Betsy. (*Sitting down on the bench.*) Make me a cup of tea. (*Seeing the notebook.*) What're you doin'?

BETSY. Nothin'.

JOHN (*pulling the notebook towards him*). This is the Mistress's diary.

BETSY. I know.

JOHN. Reading it again? One day, she'll catch you.

BETSY. She won't, I only read it when she's not here.

JOHN. Don't look t'me if she does.

BETSY. She's gone t'Thorpe, t'see Appleyard's wife about our washin' next week.

JOHN. Has it never occurred t'yer that she might know?

BETSY. What?

JOHN. She might know yer read her diary.

BETSY (*taking the notebook from* JOHN). Of course she don't.

JOHN. The Mistress is cleverer than that.

   BETSY *closes the notebook.*

   She don't do much that's not on purpose.

   BETSY *walks with the notebook to the dresser.*

   Where's this tea yer mekkin' me?

BETSY. I can stink yer, Master John,

   BETSY *puts the notebook back in the cupboard.*

JOHN. Why didn't you support me las' night?

BETSY (*locking the cupboard*). I was tired.

JOHN. Tell me why the Mistress crosses me?

BETSY (*putting the key in the cup*). Your bad temper, I should think.

   BETSY *replaces the cup on the dresser.*

   (*Walking back to the table.*) I've to busy myself. Where's the knife.

   A knife is not on the table, she finds one on the window ledge.

JOHN. Why doesn't she like me, Betsy?

BETSY. Such nonsense I've never heard. (*Starting to cut the pig meat into cubes.*) You are right in my way, Master John.

JOHN *moves out of her way towards* ANNE*'s chair.*

Do you like the Mistress?

JOHN. She's my mother.

BETSY. If you don't like her, how can she like you?

JOHN (*angrily*). I'm head of the house.

JOHN *sits.*

Why don't folk like me, Betsy? Thess only David Wood an' 'e's a drunkard according to my mother.

BETSY. He is a drunkard, the Mistress is right.

JOHN. Even you think so.

A slight pause.

All the village girls spurn me.

BETSY. Would you like to take a wife, Master John? The Mistress would like you to wed. She worries about you.

JOHN. I worry too.

A slight pause.

BETSY. A girl likes to be courted gently. Be given some flowers from the field 'n' treated fair. (*Her face breaking into a smile.*) Not wooed by a silly pig man with shite all over 'im. (*Putting down the knife, laughing.*) I'm sorry. I can't help it, you're so funny sometimes.

JOHN. I can keep my temper.

BETSY. I'll have to look the other way.

BETSY *looks away from* JOHN, *she picks up the knife and continues to cut the meat. She stops laughing.*

JOHN. Finished with your fun:

BETSY *nods, holding back the laugh.*

I've a temper, have I?

BETSY. You know you have, Master John.

JOHN. I've my father's temper. It will go, it will vanish like a morning mist.

A slight pause.

And when it's gone completely, which may take a few weeks, my mother will do exactly as I say. As will you.

BETSY *nods*.

There'll be no more thieving boys set free from this kitchen.

A slight pause.

No longer will the folk of 'Thorpe say I sleep in my mother's bed. Nor say my mother's a witch.

BETSY *holds back another laugh. She has finished cutting the meat, she starts to peel the four apples with the knife.*

I'll go the village, t'the New Plough Inn. Give ol' Chris Smith twopence t'play his fiddle. 'N' I'll dance, mighty jollily, with all the girls. I'll be the gossip of 'Thorpe for my changed manner. I'll sow hemp seed beside Harriet Woodforde's door, because she's the girl of my fancy. We'll be married within eighteen months.

BETSY. I should tell 'er first.

JOHN *holds his temper.*

JOHN. I won't have to force her to kiss me any more. Or get her drunk which costs money. Or get drunk myself.

A slight pause.

What're you makin'?

BETSY. A pig meat pie.

JOHN. F'dinner?

BETSY (*still holding back the laugh*). Yes.

JOHN. Yer a fine cook.

BETSY. Thank you, I do my best.

JOHN (*standing up*). Don't turn against me, Betsy. My father was never disobeyed.

BETSY. I didn't know 'im, did I. I was four when he had his riding accident, and died.

JOHN (*wiping the chair clean*). He was a fine 'n' strong man. With the intelligence of an eagle. He would have had the boy whipped.

BETSY *nods slightly.*

I loved my father. Never believe what my mother sez.

JOHN *walks to the window and looks out.*

BETSY. She never talks about 'im, Master John. But if your father had had that boy whipped he would've been cruel.

JOHN. Wilf Meadow's arrived back from the moor. He's two sheep with him. I won't have time for tea.

JOHN *walks towards the door.* BETSY *stops peeling the apples.*

BETSY. Master John.

JOHN *stops and turns.*

The Mistress loves you more than you know. Just as she loves me. 'N' if she does know I read her diaries, it's because she wants me to. Your father was a cruel man. She's lived the years since his death brooding on it.

JOHN. You've a foul tongue, Betsy. One day someone will cut it out.

JOHN *turns and exits through the open door.*

After a moment BETSY *picks up the knife and continues to peel the apples. The song thrush sings. A slight pause.*

ANNE *enters through the outside door. She is wearing shoes, a gown, a red cloak, and a bonnet. Her shoes and the bottom of her gown are muddy.*

ANNE. John's jus' sped past me in a ferocious mood.

BETSY. He fell in some pig shite, Aunt.

ANNE. Is that what it was. (*Taking off her cloak.*) I can cope with his temper, it's a bright sunny day. The path to the village is muddy after all the rain. (*Putting the cloak over her arm.*) You have got on well.

BETSY. Daisy and Hawthorn didn't give much milk.

ANNE (*taking off her bonnet*). I wouldn't expect them to. (*Walking to the upstairs door.*) The lightning scares them and dries them up.

BETSY. They must be missing Celandine. Did you see Appleyard's wife?

ANNE. She's coming on Tuesday f'the washing, a week today. (*Opening the door.*) She'll sleep the night here. That way we'll make an early start.

ANNE *goes out.*

BETSY *finishes peeling the apples, she walks to the dresser, finds a wooden bowl and brings it back to the table. She starts to core the apples and cut them up into the bowl.*

The song thrush sings.

BETSY *whistles, imitating it.*

ANNE *returns minus the cloak and bonnet. She sniffs.*

The stink is still here.

ANNE *goes to the dresser and opens another cupboard at the bottom. The key is already in the lock.*

Tim Appleyard is a bad sort.

BETSY. Did you challenge 'im about hidin' in the woods?

ANNE (*taking an apron and a cap from the cupboard*). I did. He told me some terrible lies.

BETSY. What lies?

ANNE (*closing the cupboard door*). All in front of his mother as well. (*Standing up.*) His mother scolded him roundly.

ANNE *starts to put the apron on.*

BETSY. What lies, Aunt?

ANNE. I'm not sure I should say, they were so terrible. Appleyard's wife is a grand sort, it's not fair.

ANNE *starts to put the cap on.*

He's an eye for you, that's what it amounts to.

BETSY. Tim Appleyard has?

ANNE. A big and roving eye.

BETSY. What did he say?

ANNE. He said he's been watching you.

BETSY. Me? (*Suspiciously.*) What for?

ANNE. As I say the lies are terrible.

BETSY (*looking at* ANNE). Tell me truthfully, Aunt?

ANNE (*looking at* BETSY). Well, Tim Appleyard said he's been following you through Middlewood, towards Bay Town.

BETSY. 'E said that?

ANNE. Indeed he did, child. An' that in Middlewood you meet a fisherman, and there you make passionate love to one another,

BETSY. I don't believe it.

ANNE. He's been roundly scolded. It's not so, is it?

BETSY. Of course not, Aunt.

ANNE. Then I want to hear no more.

> BETSY *nervously continues to cut the apples up into the bowl.*

He's an eye for you, of that there's no doubt. He admitted to sowing hemp seeds by our door. You've gone red, girl.

BETSY (*quietly*). I haven't, have I?

ANNE. Scarlet. (*Turning, walking to the dresser*). Is there not a boy at 'Thorpe who takes your fancy?

BETSY. I like it here.

> ANNE *takes a bowl off the dresser, she walks to an earthenware casket below the window ledge.*

ANNE. Sometime soon we must sit down and talk about your future.

BETSY. Why?

ANNE. One day you'll want a home of your own. (*Lifting the top off the casket.*) We must find someone suitable who'll give you that.

> *The casket is full of flour.* ANNE *proceeds to spoon some into the bowl.*

BETSY. I'd like to talk to you, Aunt.

ANNE. Would you?

BETSY. Yes. (*Hesitantly.*) I want to know the truth about me. I know I'm not your niece.

> *A slight pause.*

Aunt, I've been reading your diaries.

ANNE. Good.

> ANNE *replaces the top on the casket. She takes the bowl of flour to the table.*

(*Brightly.*) This war with France is making us all uppity. We'll talk soon, girl.

ANNE *puts butter into the bowl and starts to mix it into the flour with her hands.* BETSY *finishes cutting the apples, starts to peel the carrot.*

BETSY. I wish they'd come. At least we'd know.

ANNE. What a terrible thing to say.

The song thrush sings.

BETSY. D'you think Squire Boulby knows what's happening?

ANNE. He is our Landlord. He sits in The House of Commons, with Mister Pitt.

BETSY. I wonder why France wants to come here?

ANNE. To take our land from us.

BETSY. I hate them.

BETSY *finishes peeling the carrot, she starts to chop it into the wooden bowl.*

ANNE. Have you ever thought why we bear hatred, Betsy?

BETSY. What?

ANNE. And time exaggerates so, doesn't it?

BETSY *has finished cutting the carrot, she starts to peel and chop the onion.*

BETSY. What d'you mean?

ANNE. I've been thinking about what you said las' night, about the fisherman with two heads. Our hatred for Bay Town is still growing. What happened, happened twenty years ago, not this day. You weren't even born.

BETSY. I know.

ANNE. It's up to the young folk to put an end to it. And yet it's the young folk who are the worst.

A few tears come into BETSY's *eyes.*

What's the matter?

BETSY. The onion. (*Screaming.*) A mouse!

BETSY *jumps onto the bench.*

ANNE. Where?

BETSY (*pointing*). Goyn beneath the dresser.

ANNE (*looking at* BETSY). Don't be silly, girl, and come down.

   BETSY *slowly gets off the bench.*

   (*Still mixing the pastry.*) Where's that silly cat?

   BETSY *puts the chopped onion into the wooden bowl.*

BETSY. Was there any other gossip at Fylingthorpe?

ANNE. I tried to stop some men gambling.

   A slight pause.

   Farmer Wood was there. Hirin' faggers t'mend his barn roof.
   I pity the faggers, he's a worse temper than John.

   BETSY *puts the chopped pig meat into the bowl.*

   Oh, and Wilf Meadow's wife has had her baby. During the storm of
   all nights.

BETSY. What was it?

ANNE. A girl. They're going to risk the wrath of the village and call
   her Anne after me.

   BETSY *smiles. She picks up a wooden spoon and starts to stir the
   mixture together in the bowl.*

   I promised them a silver guinea. His son is coming to collect it this
   afternoon.

   ANNE *is making pastry.* BETSY *is stirring the mixture in the
   wooden bowl.*

   The lights slowly fade to blackout.

Scene Four

The beach and town at Robin Hood's Bay. The same morning.

A beach. Sand, stones, pebbles, driftwood, and seaweed. Towards the back the sand becomes soily and the ground grassy. Standing on the grass is the house belonging to ROBERT *and* MOLLY STORM. *The house is made of stone with a brick slated roof. On the roof is a chimney pot and small wisps of smoke can be seen drifting from it. The house has a door, painted faint green, with sash windows either side. On the sand, a short distance from the house, is a bench and two wicker baskets.*

The sun is high in the sky. A strong bright light.

MOLLY *is sitting on the bench. She is shelling various sea creatures (crabs, limpets, whelks, mussels, oysters, etc.) with a sharp knife.*

MOLLY *is a plump, tallish woman of forty-one. She has a rough, earthy face, and straggling hair. Her hands and face are brown and dried from the sun. Despite the heat she is overdressed and her clothes are of a poor quality; several petticoats, a gown, an apron which is dirty, and a bonnet: she is not wearing any shoes.*

MOLLY *takes a limpet from one basket, removes the shell, the shell drops onto the sand, and places the flesh in the second basket.*

MARY *enters walking across the grass towards the house. Her canvas bag is on her shoulder. She knocks at the door.* MOLLY *looks up from her work.*

MOLLY. Yeh, wha' is it?

MARY. This your 'ouse, Mistress?

MOLLY. Aye.

MARY. Want yer windas cleanin'?

MOLLY. I 'ave 'ands f'that mesell.

MARY. F'a penny?

MOLLY. Like yer thoughts, eh?

MARY. D'know.

MOLLY. A did 'em mesell not two days since.

MARY. Oh.

MOLLY. You the boy livin' on the beach?

MARY. Yeh.

MOLLY. Yer bin goyn roun' all the houses?

MARY. Yeh.

MOLLY. Thess n'pennies fo'yer here. Thess 'ardly a coin f'us.

MARY hesitates for a moment, she decides to stay.

MARY. Where's all the men?

MOLLY. The're at the wreck. What's left of 'er.

MARY. Any work wi' them, Mistress.

MOLLY. Yer ears mus' need a clean, I've told yer.

MARY. Will the' be back soon?

MOLLY. The'll be back as fancy tekks 'em. Or the tide comes in. The'll be drunk, I imagine. Very drunk. The first thing the' found this mornin' was the port wine.

MARY (*walking down towards* MOLLY). I could do wi a drink.

MOLLY. Drink ain' f'lads o'your years, it's a ruinous thing.

MARY is standing near MOLLY.

D'yer stay where yer not wanted?

MARY (*shrugging*). D' know.

MOLLY. Go t'the farmers'n pester them.

MARY. Gi'us a drink, Mistress.

MOLLY (*smiling*). Yer a bright'n a half, aren't yer? Bright as a silver button on a rich farmer's coat.

MARY smiles.

Jus' like one o'my lads, you are. I imagine 'is cheek'll do fer 'im an' all. The army took 'im. 'Eard a sound, nor seen a sight, f'six months. Poor little beggar.

MARY sits down on the sand.

It's one less mouth t'feed.

A slight pause.

Don' yer wish you were a farmer?

MARY *shrugs*.

Thess one farmer up there got so much money 'e built a barn o'gold keep it in. They reckon it's watched over by hobgoblins from India. Thess me left, 'ere.

MOLLY *smiles to herself*.

We're equal when we die, except f'the coffin.

MARY. What yer doin'?

MOLLY. A'll mekk a big pie wi' these.

MARY. Never eaten owt like 'em.

MOLLY (*smiling*). Bright, but not used t'the world, eh?

MARY. Ain't bin by the sea before.

MOLLY. 'Aven't yer?

MARY *shakes her head*.

Well I never.

MARY. It were like seein' a big monster when a first came.

MOLLY. Were it?

MARY. A didn' know what it was.

MOLLY. Rum'n, rum'n.

MARY. Yer wha'?

MOLLY. Yer a rum'n, boy.

MARY. No one'd telled me before.

The bugle-like call of a herring gull, as the bird flies over their heads.

MOLLY. Yer do what the sea sez. Yer don't argue wi' it. Too many lives're lost. The sea's calm t'day. So calm yer can 'ardly 'ear it.

They listen. Silence.

But there it is look, it's still there. It's foolin' yer.

MARY looks at the sea. The bugle-like call of the herring gull, as the bird flies back over their heads.

The herring gull knows when it's going t'be stormy, 'e goes inland. That's 'ow we knew about the storm las' night. We were waitin' for it. (*Looking at the sky.*) The're all back this mornin', shrewd as the writers of books.

MOLLY *puts down the knife, she reaches down to the bottom of her petticoats and lifts them up. Underneath, lying on the sand, is a small baby.* MOLLY *picks him up.*

Keep 'im from the sun.

MOLLY *opens her gown. The baby suckles at her breast.*

I should be passed 'avin' bairnes b'now.

MARY *watches.*

This one's good as gold. What d'you reckon to us 'ere?

MARY. D'know.

MOLLY. D'know much, d'yer?

MARY. Suppose not.

MOLLY. We don't see many strangers. Yer've got t'row t'Whitby f'that. D'yer know Whitby?

MARY *shakes her head.*

Whitby's a fine large town with a big harbour. (*Pointing.*) Up the coast, about four mile beyon' Bay Ness. We row there t'the markets. There yer might get yersell some work, on the big fishing boats. Can yer read'n write?

MARY *shakes her head.*

A wish a c'd say I could. Are yer God-fearing?

MARY *nods.*

It's wise t', God is master o' the sea. Heard o'John Wesley?

MARY *shakes her head.*

Mister Wesley came 'ere. If yer see 'im, you scatter. Like strong drink 'e brought religious ruin t'the town. Except the men don't reckon so. Mekken 'em feel bad wi' 'is preachin'. Tellin' 'em t'mekk peace wi' the farmers. It's the farmers who wronged us. Fillin' their 'eads wi' guilt. A'd curse the name o' John Wesley but the Lord might strike me. Fearin' God is one thing, John Wesley summat else. Not that boys like you know owt.

MARY. Is there a fisherman wi' two heads, Mistress?

MOLLY. Thess a farmer wi' five hands – mekkin' light work of everything. 'N' another wi' a tongue that spits fire. Mind, the' all d'that.

MARY. Jus' wondered.

> MARY *takes a cloth rag from her pocket. The rag is filthy.*
> MARY *mops her brow.*

MOLLY. Yer hot?

MARY. Aye.

MOLLY. It is hot t'day. The earth's an oven. A d'know which is muckier, you or the rag.

> MARY *puts the rag away.*

I'm a winter woman if the truth be told. 'N' when it gets t'winter, a long f'the summer.

> MOLLY *looks along the coast towards Bay Ness.*

What're your eyes like, boy?

MARY (*following* MOLLY*'s gaze*). The sea's shiny.

MOLLY. I'm as blind as a bat. Is that our cobbles comin' back?

MARY. What's a cobble?

MOLLY. Fishin' cobble, our rowin' boats.

MARY (*looking at* MOLLY). The've bin at the wrecked boat, 'ave the'?

MOLLY. They should 'ave some plunder wi' 'em.

MARY. What's plunder?

MOLLY. Stuff the'll've tekkn off. Plates, cups, bowls. Mekk our life easier.

MARY (*looking along the coast*). Thess a load of 'em.

MOLLY. A'the rowin' straight?

MARY. The're in a line.

MOLLY. I wondered 'ow drunk the' were. I 'ope not very drunk. (*Mopping her brow with her hand.*) Yer mekkin' me sweat now, rum'n. (*Looking down the beach towards Bay Ness, squinting.*) Who's this hurryin' down the sand?

MARY *looks*.

The're back. I'd get off if I were you.

MARY *stays put*.

(*Taking the baby off her nipple*.) Sorry, sweet'n.

MOLLY *stands up, the baby in her arms*.

(*Calling*.) What yer got?

A slight pause.

What yer got? Owt good?

ROBERT *and* JOE *enter from Bay Ness. They are dressed for the sun in breeches, shirts and neck-ties. There is nothing on their feet.*

ROBERT *and* JOE *are carrying between them a long wooden crate*.

What's in there?

ROBERT. Yer'll get a shock, Molly. We hurried back.

ROBERT *and* JOE *put the crate down*.

MOLLY. What's in it?

ROBERT. The rest're in the cobbles.

MOLLY. What?

ROBERT (*taking the top off the crate*). We found crates'n crates of these, Molly.

The crate is full of infantry muskets.

ROBERT *picks one up*.

The French're here.

MOLLY (*taking a step back*). Oh, The Lord God, whatever next.

ROBERT. An' do yerself up, woman.

MOLLY *pulls her gown over her naked breast*. MARY *stands up*.

JOE (*calmly*). We don't know it's the French, Robert.

ROBERT (*his voice booming*). I do. They're hidin' in the caves'n woods. I saw somethin' earlier. (*Trying to cock the musket*.) I'm ready for 'em.

MOLLY (*to* JOE). What else is there?

JOE. There's no sign of a living or dead soul. They either jumped'n were drowned –

ROBERT. The didn' jump.

JOE. Or somehow they've got ashore.

ROBERT. The' here, waitin' for us. (*Not succeeding with the musket.*) The' don't frighten me.

MOLLY. What're we goyn t'do?

ROBERT. Fight 'em off.

JOE (*calmly*). We do what we came ahead for.

ROBERT (*walking towards the town*). I'll go and tell 'em to ring the church bell.

JOE (*calling after him*). And come straight back. Tell everyone yer see, this is where we'll meet.

ROBERT. Aye. (*Holding up the musket.*) I'm tekkin' this with me. Keep the French from my wife, Joe.

    ROBERT *exits*.

MOLLY. Is the boat badly wrecked?

JOE. The rocks're right through her hull. (*Putting the top on the crate.*) Can yer help me wi' this. I want it hidden and safe.

MOLLY. D'you think they're watching us, Joe?

JOE. If they are they'll show themselves soon.

MARY. Who's watchin' us?

JOE. You come too, boy.

    MOLLY *and* JOE *pick up the crate.* MOLLY *has the baby in her other arm.*

    They exit with the crate towards the town.

    MARY *stays and watches them go.*

    The bugle-like call of a herring gull as the bird flies overhead.

    MARY *stoops down and picks up her canvas bag.*

MARY (*calling*). All right.

    MARY *stoops down and picks up her canvas bag.*

    (*Calling.*) All right.

MARY *walks towards the town, as she does so a gorilla enters, walking on all-fours from the direction of Bay Ness.*

In a few moments MARY *will christen the gorilla* STOCKTON. *He is black and furry: a real gorilla. He is wearing a blue woollen sailor's jumper.*

STOCKTON *sneezes a kind of snort.* MARY *hears this, Stops, and turns. She steps back a pace in fear.* STOCKTON *looks briefly at* MARY *and sits down on the sand.*

Who're you?

A slight pause.

Where did you come from?

A slight pause.

(*Pointing.*) I was supposed t'be goyn wi' them.

STOCKTON *is watching* MARY *from the corner of his eye.*

I'm not frightened, 'r you? (*Taking a few steps towards* STOCKTON.) A don' want t'harm yer. I'm friendly.

STOCKTON *sneezes.* MARY *stops.*

A slight pause.

STOCKTON *looks at* MARY *from the corner of his eye.*

Yer shy, aren't yer?

STOCKTON *stands and walks on all-fours towards* MARY. MARY *backs off.*

(*Frightened.*) No, don't come near me.

STOCKTON *stops and sits down again.*

A thought yer were goyn t'get me.

STOCKTON *watches* MARY *from the corner of his eye.*

Yer weren't, were yer? (*Warily taking a few steps towards him.*) You're my friend. We'll both be friends.

STOCKTON *sneezes.*

'Ave you got a cold?

MARY *reaches out and touches* STOCKTON's *head. She moves warily forward, stroking him.* STOCKTON *enjoys it.*

I'm goyn to call you Stockton. After where a come from. I'm goyn t'look after you.

MARY *kneels down and continues to stroke him.* STOCKTON *watches her from the corner of his eye.*

You'n me, we're together.

STOCKTON *sneezes.*

Er, yer sprayed me wi' water, yer have got a cold. Where yer goyn? Don' yer like me?

STOCKTON *lets out a loud call.* MARY *steps back.*

Don' do that. I don like it when yer do that.

A slight pause.

(*Walking towards* STOCKTON, *warily.*) Is that all yer can say? Can yer say owt else?

STOCKTON *is watching* MARY *from the corner of his eye.* MARY *reaches* STOCKTON *and strokes him again.*

MOLLY *enters from the town, she has the baby in one hand, a piece of wood in the other. She stops.*

MARY *puts her arms round* STOCKTON'*s neck and tries to pull him.*

Come on, come wi' me, we'll go t'my tent.

STOCKTON *doesn't move.*

(*Pulling him again.*) Why won't yer come? Yer heavy.

MARY *looks up and sees* MOLLY.

MOLLY. Stay with 'im, boy.

MARY (*standing up*). 'E won't arm yer. 'E's my friend, 'e's friendly.

STOCKTON *walks on all-fours towards* MOLLY. MOLLY *raises the piece of wood and backs off.*

MOLLY (*screaming*). Ge' back, ge' back, ge' back.

Before STOCKTON *reaches* MOLLY *he sits down again.*

(*Screaming.*) Don't do that again.

MARY (*going to* STOCKTON). Why don't yer like 'im?

ROBERT *and* JOE *enter from Bay Ness. They have a large fishing net.*

ROBERT. Joe?

JOE. I don't know, Robert.

MARY (*looking at* ROBERT *and* JOE). What's goyn on? (*Stroking* STOCKTON, *confused*.) I've seen one before. In a fair.

ROBERT *spits*.

ROBERT. Frenchman!

MARY (*looking between the three of them*). No, it did tricks. Like standin' on its 'ead. Then it collected pennies from people.

JOE (*calmly*). It looks like an animal.

MARY. It is. Honest.

MOLLY. The boy's lying.

MARY. 'N' I'm not a boy, I'm a girl really.

ROBERT. Now the boy sez 'e's a girl.

MARY. I am a girl. I've jus' been pretending. These were all the clothes I 'ad.

JOE. What's your name?

MARY. Mary. Honest.

ROBERT. Boys aren't called Mary.

MARY. I am.

ROBERT. The boy's a spy f'the Frenchman. He's bin waitin' fo'im. Why yer livin' on the beach?

STOCKTON *gets up, he walks on all-fours in a small circle.*

MOLLY, ROBERT *and* JOE *step back*. STOCKTON *sits down again. He watches them all from the corner of his eye.*

MARY (*looking between the three of them*). A ran away see. With me brother. Only me brother died o'the fever, so a took 'is clothes.

MOLLY. The boy's a liar.

MARY. No. A left me brother in a hedge back somewhere.

ROBERT *spits*.

ROBERT. Frenchman!

STOCKTON *stands up and walks a pace towards* ROBERT. *He sits down again.*

(*Aggressively, frightened.*) Stop 'im doin' that.

MARY. A can't. (*Going to* STOCKTON.) Yer musn't do that, the' don't like it.

The church bell starts to toll from the distance.

ROBERT. What're we goyn t'do, Joe?

MOLLY. The boy's a spy.

JOE. If he was armed he'd have tried to shoot us by now. (*To* MARY.) Where did 'e come from?

MARY (*pointing*). Down there. His name's Stockton.

JOE. Where're the rest of them?

MARY. A don't know.

MOLLY. The boy's lying,

STOCKTON *lets out a loud call.*

ROBERT (*stepping back*). He's goyn to attack us, Joe, 'e's callin' 'is friends.

JOE. Tell us the truth, child, where are they?

MARY *is beginning to feel upset, she shakes her head.*

ROBERT (*to* JOE). Shall I shoot 'im?

STOCKTON *lets out a loud call.*

They're all around us, Joe.

JOE. Is he a Frenchman?

MARY *looks at* JOE, *she has tears in her eyes.*

Is he?

MARY *nods.*

Why did you bring 'im 'ere?

STOCKTON *lets out a loud call. He stands up and walks quickly on all-fours in the direction of the town.*

MOLLY (*screaming*). He's escapin'.

ROBERT *and* JOE *chase after* STOCKTON. *They throw the fishing net over him.* STOCKTON *yelps, falls, and starts to rush blindly in all directions.*

In doing so he tangles himself further in the net.

MOLLY, ROBERT *and* JOE *back off watching.* STOCKTON *comes to a final halt, he can move no more.*

ROBERT *points the gun at* STOCKTON.

ROBERT. We've got 'im, we've captured a Frenchman.

The church clock is still tolling.

MARY *has tears in her eyes.* STOCKTON *is panting. They are all still.*

The lights fade to blackout.

ACT TWO

Scene One

Middlewood. Twenty years earlier. Mid-afternoon of Christmas Eve, 1777.

A sheep enclosure (clearing) in the middle of the wood. A rough stone wall runs in a U-shaped arc round the perimeter of the stage. In the wall, to the left, is a gateway with a wooden gate. Behind the wall, oak, ash, and sycamore trees are growing. The enclosure is free of any woody vegetation. To the right is a small low stone building (a small barn) with an open front and a sloping thatch roof. The barn is stacked with hay.

There is thick snow on the ground, and on the trees. The snow has drifted heavily against the stone wall and a path has had to be cleared to the gate.

The sky is thick with snow. It is quite dark.

JOE *is standing at the opening to the barn. He has a book, wrapped in an old cloth, in his hand.*

JOE *doesn't quite look the twenty years younger; his face is pinched and old-mannish, but it is somehow cleaner, brighter. His skin is white. His clothes are of very poor quality and he is inadequately dressed for the cold; breeches, shirt, waistcoat, neck-tie, jacket. He has no shoes on his feet and instead has bound old pieces of cloth round them with string.*

JOE *blows into his hands, and stamps his feet, to keep warm. He hears someone coming and steps back into the barn.*

RICHARD WHEATLEY *enters followed by the young* JOHN. RICHARD *is carrying a dead sheep across his shoulders.* JOHN *is carrying a spade.*

RICHARD *is a tall, strong, burly man of forty-four. He has broad shoulders, a fat gut, and a powerful, intelligent face. He is dressed richly for the cold in boots, stockings, breeches, shirt, waistcoat, jacket, top coat and a hat.*

The young JOHN *is twelve. As yet he shows little sign of the donkey-like adult he will become. He has a clean face with alert eyes. His clothes are of good quality; boots, trousers, shirt, waistcoat, jacket, and a top coat.*

RICHARD *and* JOHN *stop.*

RICHARD. Who's there hiding?

JOE (*comes out from the barn*). Me, Mister Wheatley.

RICHARD. It's you, Joe. Good afternoon.

JOE (*nodding, shyly*). Afternoon t'yer both.

RICHARD. Might I ask what your purpose is?

JOE. I'm waitin' f'Emma.

RICHARD. Is that all?

JOE. We meet 'ere, Mister Wheatley.

RICHARD (*smiling*). Up to the devil's mischief, John.

    JOHN *smiles.*

    I hope it's not mischief yer up to.

JOE. We've bin courtin' f'over a year.

RICHARD. Remember whose land you're on.

JOE. A will.

RICHARD. Don't trespass more than yer need.

JOE. No, Mister Wheatley.

RICHARD. There are sheep stealers in this part of Yorkshire. Moving north from Scarborough. The snow will be stopping them – but, I like to know who's on my land.

    JOE *nods.*

    RICHARD *drops the sheep to the ground.*

    (*Brightly.*) So yer meet the lass here in the cold?

JOE. Aye.

    JOE *blows into his hands.*

RICHARD. Is there nowhere else where it's warmer?

JOE. It were warm in summer, Mister Wheatley.

RICHARD. I did my courtin' in all weathers.

> JOE *quietly stamps his feet.*

> 'N' 'ave yer nothin' f'yer feet?

> JOE *is silent*

> Why don't yer meet 'er at the farm? It would be better than here.

> JOE *stops. He is still.*

> The Mistress wouldn't mind yer usin' her kitchen. I'm sure of that.

JOE. It's kind of yer, Mister Wheatley.

RICHARD. What's the matter? Our kitchen's not good enough, John?

JOE. I don' mind the cold.

RICHARD. The look of you tells another story. Emma's a fine lass.
What about her and the weather?

JOE (*quietly stamping his feet again*). She don' mind, Mister Wheatley.

RICHARD. Have you asked her, Joe?

JOE. Of course.

> JOE *looks down at the snow.*

RICHARD. Emma's a good maid, the best maid we've had. I don't
want to see 'er wronged.

JOE. I love 'er, Mister Wheatley.

RICHARD. As long as yer do.

> EMMA BRAYE *enters between the trees.*

> EMMA *is a slim, attractive woman of twenty-six, and although her
> face has a mature, hard-worked look to it, there has remained
> something vibrant and girlish.*

> *She is dressed for the cold in* ANNE*'s cast-off clothing; shoes,
> a gown, a grey cape, and a bonnet.*

> EMMA *hides behind a tree. They do not see her.*

> Come to the kitchen next time.

JOE. I'll tell 'er. I will.

RICHARD. I hear you're a good worker, Joe? (*Walking towards him.*) 'N' you say you love Emma.

RICHARD *stands beside* JOE.

Is being wed to the girl in your mind?

JOE. One day, Mister Wheatley.

RICHARD. Is it indeed.

JOE. I'd come t'yer first, f'yer permission. Emma's parents bein' dead, 'n' you lookin' after er. 'Avin' no folks of 'er own.

RICHARD. There'd be trouble from Mistress if Emma was to leave us.

JOE *looks down at the snow.*

If Emma was t'stay, 'n' help in the kitchen now'n again, 'n' help in the dairy with the butter makin'. But set up home with you in one of my cottages – would you com'n work for me?

JOE *looks up. He is silent.*

There's an offer, John, isn't it?

JOHN *smiles.*

A farmer's life is different from yours. What d'yer say, Joe?

JOE. I d'know, Mister Wheatley.

RICHARD. I'm offering yer the chance t'better yerself.

JOE (*quietly stamping his feet*). A can't think in the cold.

RICHARD (*turning, walking back to* JOHN). Think about it. Let me know. But don't think too long.

JOE. A will.

RICHARD *puts his arm round* JOHN. EMMA *is listening intently behind the tree.*

RICHARD. We're looking for a shepherd.

JOE. What 'appened t'Tom Meadows?

RICHARD. 'E died las' week.

JOE. Poor ol' Tom Meadows.

RICHARD. If I don't tekk you I'll tekk his son Wilf.

JOHN. Yer haven't told him the pay.

RICHARD. You tell him.

JOHN. Nine pounds a year.

JOE. Did 'e die from cold?

RICHARD. This winter is taking many.

JOE. The old an' the sick, Mister Wheatley.

RICHARD. Aye.

JOE. If I'll be your shepherd, what 'appens t'young Wilf?

RICHARD. He'll join the faggers at 'Thorpe.

JOE. An 'is family will lose their cottage?

RICHARD. The parish cares f'the poor, Joe. I'm not a ruthless man. (*Moving from* JOHN, *standing back*.) I've lost six of my sheep in this snow. This one found shelter against a wall, the snow blew in an' covered 'er.

JOE. She'll feed you, Mister Wheatley,

RICHARD. Aye, but she'll bear no lamb.

JOE (*gaining courage*). We're starving at Bay Town. The sea's froze over, our boats're stuck in the ice.

EMMA *puts her hands in front of her eyes to hide them.*

RICHARD. I've seen them.

EMMA *takes her hands away.*

JOE. We can't fish. Only by mekkin' holes. An' dangling a hand line.

RICHARD. Ave yer nothin' put by?

A slight pause.

Come t'me, Joe, I'll feed yer.

JOE. The whole town needs feedin'.

A slight pause.

RICHARD. I didn't know you were so bad.

JOE. Since the snow came.

RICHARD. A month?

JOE. Summat like, Mister Wheatley.

JOHN. I saw the girls skating.

RICHARD. 'N' yer starving?

JOE. Near starving.

RICHARD. Thess nothing I can do, Joe. Yer must plan.

JOE looks at the snow for a moment.

JOE (*looking back up*). A feel like begging, Mister Wheatley.

RICHARD. Take my job.

JOE. A'll think on.

RICHARD. You do that.

A slight pause.

(*Picking up the dead sheep.*) Come on, John, let's be home t'your mother. She'll be thinkin' we've died in a drift ourselves.

RICHARD *carries the sheep towards the gate.* JOHN *follows with the spade.*

Open the gate, Joe.

JOE *goes to the gate and opens it.*

RICHARD *and* JOHN *exit towards the farm.*

EMMA *comes out from behind the tree.*

EMMA. Joe.

JOE looks up, sees her.

I 'eard. I was 'idin'.

JOE (*turning, walking away from the gate and* EMMA). Is hatred too strong a word f'what I feel about 'im?

EMMA *comes through the gate, she stops.*

EMMA. Yer cold, Joe.

JOE (*turning to her*). Warmer with you.

They walk towards each other. They kiss. They embrace. EMMA *rubs her hands vigorously up and down his back.*

EMMA. I'll 'ave yer warm as an oven in a minute.

JOE. Oh, that's nice.

They continue the embrace for a moment and then break it.

'E dun'alf mekk me mad.

EMMA *holds out her hand,* JOE *takes it.*

A seem t' wither away when a see 'im.

EMMA. Yer don't. I expected 'is temper any time.

JOE. What d'yer mean?

EMMA. Yer stand up to 'im. 'E's a foul temper. 'E likes yer.

JOE. Oh.

EMMA. Don't be surprised.

JOE. Can' 'elp it.

EMMA. Why yer surprised?

JOE. A thought a weren't me in front of 'im.

EMMA. 'E ain' a bad sort, Joe.

JOE. Don' start.

EMMA. Wait on.

EMMA *smiles.*

JOE. What yer want t'say? Emma –

EMMA. I 'eard 'im about the job.

JOE (*turning, walking away a pace or two*). Thought that was it.

EMMA (*walking to* JOE). F' year or two.

JOE. No.

EMMA (*looking at him*). Please, Joe.

JOE *turns and walks away a few paces.*

JOE (*turning to her*). I ain't changin' the plans. We're leavin' 'ere.
I'm tekkin' yer.

EMMA. I'm not sayin' change 'em.

JOE. What are yer then?

EMMA. Put 'em off f'a bit.

JOE. That's change 'em t'me.

EMMA *looks at* JOE.

We're goyn in the spring.

EMMA. Ye know in the autumn, Joe – what we've bin doin'?

JOE *looks* blank.

Yer do. Not now cos it's t'cold.

JOE. What?

EMMA (*touching her stomach*). I've a child in 'ere.

JOE. A don't believe yer.

EMMA. Yer'll 'ave to, cos it's so.

JOE. Who said?

EMMA. Mistress Wheatley tol' me.

JOE. She's tellin' yer lies, Emma.

EMMA. She ain't. Joe.

JOE. Wait 'till a see Robert Storm, a were swallowin' the ten worms.

EMMA. A tol' Mistress Wheatley, she said that don't do nowt. It's in me belly, Joe. It mekks a difference to us now.

JOE. Why?

EMMA. F'me. 'Avin' the child in my own village.

JOE. Course it don't, Emma.

EMMA. It do t'me.

JOE. Yer enjoyed it right enough.

EMMA. That's not like you, Joe.

Silence between them for a few moments. EMMA *walks to* JOE.

JOE (*stepping back a pace*). No, a don't want yer.

They stop a short distance apart. Silence for a moment.

Course a want yer, a don't want the bairne.

EMMA. Mebbe it'll die.

JOE. Did yer tell Mistress Wheatley who the father were?

EMMA I 'ad to.

JOE. Is that why 'e offered me the job?

EMMA. 'E don't know. She said it could be worse. You bein' the fine man you are. If not s'fine f'doin that.

JOE. We'll 'ave t'wait then. I wanted t'go t'the city, Emma. I hate this place.

EMMA. Don't, Joe.

JOE. It's easy f'you. You've food in your belly. A child as well I suppose.

EMMA. It ain't easy.

JOE. Waitin' fo'yer, a were all merry. Now it don't seem like Christmas Eve.

EMMA. Will yer tekk 'is job?

JOE. A can't, Emma.

EMMA. F'me, at Christmas?

JOE. I'm a fisherman.

EMMA. 'E'd treat yer well.

JOE (*turning, walking away a pace*). Course'e wouldn't.

EMMA. 'E would, Joe.

JOE (*turning to* EMMA). The way he's treated Bay. The way we've been treated.

EMMA. A were talkin' about you.

JOE. All this land were common land! Look at it now! Fences on it! It belongs to the farmers! That's why we're starving! (*Silence. Still shaking with anger.*) I ain't gonna say sorry either. Not while 'is stomach is full. If yer want me, yer come t'Bay. Cos I ain't comin' t'Thorpe.

Silence.

EMMA *looks down and walks a pace or two away from* JOE.

Silence.

JOE *blows into his hands*.

EMMA. I'll go then, Joe. Are we still meetin' on Boxin' Day?

JOE. If yer want.

EMMA. I can get angry too yer know.

JOE. Why don' yer?

EMMA. Per'aps a can't get angry then.

JOE. This land belonged to all of us, Emma. Fishermen 'n' farmers alike. The farmers took it.

EMMA. It were by Act of Parliament in London.

JOE. What d'we know about London? Them folk in London don't give us food.

JOE blows into his hands.

EMMA. Squire Boulby took the land not Mister Wheatley.

JOE. 'E tills the soil, don' 'e? Puts 'is livestock on it.

EMMA. 'N' 'e pays the rent.

JOE. You 'ave t'be starvin' to understand.

A slight pause.

I ain' eaten t'day, Emma. A didn' eat yesterday.

EMMA looks down at the snow.

If I 'ad, a don't suppose a'd care.

EMMA (*looking up, gently*). A reckon yer would, Joe.

JOE. A want food.

EMMA. Why won't yer tekk 'is job then?

JOE. Inside me, a can't.

EMMA. Why?

JOE is silent.

Yer too proud.

JOE. I want to.

EMMA. Do it, Joe.

JOE No.

Silence.

EMMA. Talking never helps us, does it?

EMMA *walks to* JOE. JOE *takes her hand. They kiss. They embrace.*

JOE. A brought the book wi' me.

EMMA. A noticed.

JOE. Thess some words a don' understand.

EMMA. Let's look at 'em then.

They break the embrace. JOE *walks to a log which is lying on the ground, he clears the snow off the top of it with his hand. He sits down.* EMMA *sits down beside him.* JOE *starts to unwrap the book from the cloth.*

It is Jethro Tull's The Horse-Hoeing Husbandry. *The book is marked with little slips of paper, he opens it at page 73.*

JOE. Thess a word 'ere. (*He puts his finger on the line and reads out the sentence.*) All weeds, as such, are perni-ice-ous; but some much more than others. Perni-ice-ous?

EMMA *looks at the word.*

EMMA. A don't know. It mebbe means like bad.

JOE. Bad?

EMMA. Well yer don' want weeds in a field, d'yer?

JOE. That don't make sense.

EMMA. A'm only trying, Joe.

JOE (*reading the sentence again*). All weeds, as such, are bad; but some much more than others. Mebbe it does.

EMMA. I'll ave to ask Mrs Wheatley.

JOE. A thought yer knew every word.

EMMA. Don't be silly.

JOE. A thought yer did.

EMMA. Thess more words than anyone can remember.

JOE. Don' tell me lies then.

EMMA. What's the next one?

JOE *turns to page 79. He puts his finger on the line and reads.*

JOE. 'Tis but of late years that turnips have been introduc'd as an improvement in the field. All sorts of land, when made fine by tillage, or by manure and tillage, will serve to produce turnips, but not equally; (*Enjoying himself.*) for chalky land is generally too dry (a turnip bein' a thirsty plant); and if they are too long in such dry poor soil before they get into rough leaf, the fly is very apt to destroy them, yet I have known them succeed on rough land, tho' rarely.

JOE *takes his finger off the page and smiles.*

A've bin practisin' that bit.

EMMA *kisses* JOE *on the cheek.*

A'll soon know more words than you.

EMMA (*smiling, happy*). We're different, Joe.

JOE. Won' a?

EMMA. Aye.

JOE. Then I'll teach 'em t'you. It'll be other way round.

EMMA. Of course yer will.

JOE. What were yer sayin'?

EMMA. A were sayin' we were different.

JOE. A will know more words, Emma, yer'll 'ave to accept that.

EMMA. Can we 'ave one conversation, not two.

JOE (*excited*). A did it, a did it. Me readin'.

EMMA *smiles.*

(*Looking at the front cover.*) Jethro Tull's *Horse-Hoeing Husbandry.* Can't yer get me books about summat else? I'm sick o'farming.

EMMA. They're the only books Mister Wheatley has.

JOE. Soon I'll know more about farmin' than 'e does.

EMMA *smiles.*

(*Picking up a handful of powdery snow and throwing it into the air.*) A did it, Emma. A didn' reckon a would.

EMMA. I knew yer would.

JOE. Did yer? I didn't.

EMMA . I know, calm down.

JOE. A did it, a did it, a did it.

EMMA *laughs*.

A did it, Emma.

JOE *laughs. They are both laughing*.

(*Standing up*.) It's jus' 'avin' the confidence, isn' it? T'know the words. I ain't no fear now. I 'ave 'ad before.

EMMA (*standing up*). We belong in another world, Joe.

JOE. Yer what?

EMMA. We ain't part o' this one.

JOE (*putting his hand on* EMMA*'s stomach*). Come wi' me t'the city.

EMMA. I 'ave fears, Joe.

JOE. Yer wha'?

EMMA. I 'ave fears.

JOE. Yer've learnt me, Emma.

EMMA. Mistress Wheatley taught me.

JOE. I alwez reckoned it were me that were scared.

EMMA. No.

JOE. Mistress Wheatley is a good sort, ain't she?

EMMA. The've given me a home.

A slight pause.

We're special, Joe. You'n me. We're special here. We can make another world, but at the farm.

JOE *looks down at the snow*.

We don't know what's at the city, do we?

JOE. No. Yer right. (*Turning, walking away a pace*.) I'm sick o'yer bein' right.

JOE *stops, turns, and walks back*.

All right, I'll tekk the job.

EMMA. Joe.

JOE. Of course a will.

EMMA (*hugging him*). Oh, Joe.

JOE. Careful, yer'll knock me over.

EMMA. It is Christmas now.

JOE. It were Christmas before.

EMMA (*pulling back slightly from the embrace. Looking at him*).
Think better of yerself. Alwez think better.

JOE. Yer goyn again, tellin' me what t'think. (*They hug*.) I suppose I'll
learn t'like Mister Wheatley.

They are still, holding one another.

The lights fade to blackout.

Scene Two

Middlewood. Mid-afternoon of Boxing Day.

The sky is still thick with snow. It is quite dark.

EMMA *is near the barn waiting for* JOE. *She is stooping, making
a snowball. Beside her is a box tied with a ribbon. She is wearing a
red cloak, apart from this her clothes are the same.* EMMA *puts the
box under her arm and stands up with the snowball. She blows into
her empty hand. She sees* JOE *coming and puts the snowball behind
her back.*

JOE *enters hurrying nervously. He is out of breath. He looks once
behind his back.*

JOE. Did anyone follow yer?

EMMA. Eh?

JOE. Did anyone follow yer?

EMMA *smiles and throws the snowball. It hits him.*

(*Brushing the snow away.*) Don', Emma.

EMMA. I'm sorry. A made it f'you.

JOE *grabs* EMMA*'s hand.*

What's goyn on?

JOE *pulls* EMMA *into the entrance way of the barn.*

What's 'appened?

JOE. Don' mekk a noise. Please, Emma.

EMMA. Wha' is it?

JOE (*still catching his breath*). I tell yer in a minute. Where's Mister Wheatley?

EMMA. A d'know, 'e's round wi' the sheep somewhere. They all are. Why?

JOE. Thess trouble. Thess gonna be trouble.

EMMA. Get yer breath back'n tell us prop'ly.

JOE *takes a few deep breaths.*

JOE. We've 'ad a meetin' in The Anchor. All of us.

EMMA. Yeh?

JOE. D'know 'ow y'tell yer.

EMMA. Jus' tell us.

JOE. We're goyn t'come'n raid the farms.

EMMA. Yer what?

JOE. We're goyn t'com'n raid the farms.

EMMA. What fo'?

JOE. Tekk back the land that were ours. Knock the fences over.

EMMA. Then what?

JOE. It'll be our land like before.

EMMA. Who said?

JOE *shrugs.*

JOE. We did. All of us.

EMMA. You?

JOE *shrugs.*

JOE. Suppose me.

EMMA. You said that?

JOE. We were all sat round, what could a'say?

EMMA (*shaking her head*). A don't believe yer.

JOE. Yer'd better.

EMMA. 'N' you said nowt?

JOE *looks at the snow for a moment.*

JOE. A wanted t'say we should come'n beg. A near got on me knees. A would a'done, a were a coward.

A short silence.

Yer don't understand, d'yer?

EMMA. No. (*Walking out of the barn.*) I thought yer were stronger than that.

JOE. Please come 'ere, Emma. If the' see yer. A were told not t'come.

EMMA *walks back into the barn.*

Someone might've followed me.

A slight pause.

EMMA. When d'they plan it?

JOE. T'night.

A slight pause.

EMMA. One of us 'as got t'do summat.

A slight pause.

Are yer goyn t'tell Mister Wheatley?

JOE *looks down at the snow.*

Then yer not tekkin' is job.

A slight pause.

JOE. You could come wi' me.

EMMA *looks at* JOE.

A short silence.

EMMA *takes the box from beneath her arm.*

EMMA. It's Boxing Day. I brought these from Mister Wheatley.

JOE *takes the box from her. He unties the ribbon and takes the lid off the box. He takes out a pair of* RICHARD*'s cast-off shoes.*

JOE. A don' wan' 'em, Emma.

He puts the shoes back in the box, and gives the box to EMMA.
EMMA *takes a small, neatly wrapped packet from her cloak pocket.*

EMMA. An' this is from me. It's not much.

JOE. No thank you.

EMMA (*tears swelling from her eyes*). Don' be so pig headed an' tekk it.

JOE (*taking the packet*). Thanks. I can smell it from here. (*He smells the packet*.) It's tobacco. (*After a moment's pause*.) I made you a brooch. From a piece of jet a found. I forgot it. (*He sniffs the tobacco*.) I'll enjoy smokin' this.

He puts the packet in his waistcoat pocket.

Yer wearin' a new cloak, aren't yer?

EMMA (*showing it off, she is proud of the cloak*). The Mistress gave it to me. It's her old one.

JOE. It looks nice on yer.

A short silence.

EMMA (*her tears gone, she has held them back*). We've a Frenchman comin' t'stay. It's good news, unlike yours.

JOE. Oh aye?

EMMA. He's here to study our farms. A letter's come from Squire Boulby in London.

JOE. Yer'll hear talk of another country.

EMMA. I'll be sent out, I expect. I'll go then, Joe.

EMMA *walks from the barn towards the gate. After a moment*
JOE *steps from the barn. He stops.*

JOE. Don't go, Emma.

EMMA *turns to face him.*

Won't yer tell me you understand?

EMMA. I can't, Joe, 'cos I don't.

JOE *gets down onto his knees.*

JOE. If I do this t'yer.

EMMA. What for?

JOE. It's other people messed it up, not us.

EMMA. It's us.

JOE. I'm on me knees, Emma. What more can a do?

> JOHN *enters running. He has a snowball in his hand which he throws at* EMMA.
>
> JOE *stands up.*
>
> *The snowball hits* EMMA.

JOHN. I got her.

> RICHARD *enters followed by* ANNE.

Did you see it? I hit her.

> ANNE *looks twenty years younger; her whole appearance is of a more agile, sprightly woman. She is thinner, her hair has yet to grey. She is dressed for the cold in shoes, a gown, a new red cloak, gloves and a bonnet.*
>
> *The sun starts to come out from behind the clouds.*

ANNE. I hope Emma didn't mind.

JOHN. You didn't mind, did you, Emma?

EMMA. No.

JOHN (*bending down, ready to make a snowball*). Let's have a snowball fight.

ANNE. Not now, John.

JOHN. Oh, why?

ANNE. Because I'm your mother, 'n' I said so.

> JOHN *looks at his father.*

RICHARD. Do as your mother sez.

> JOHN *pulls a disappointed face and stands up.*
>
> *The sun is shining through the trees.*

(*Walking to* JOE.) We hoped t'see you, Joe. (*Turning briefly to* ANNE.) Didn't we?

ANNE. Yes. (*To* JOHN.) Come here to me this is men's talk.

JOHN *goes to* ANNE *and stands beside her.*

RICHARD (*standing beside* JOE). Did the shoes fit you all right?

EMMA. I've them 'ere, Mister Wheatley. I was carryin'um fo' 'im.

JOE. Thanks, Mister Wheatley.

ANNE (*walking with* JOHN *towards* EMMA). The snow is beautiful when the sun shines.

RICHARD. Have yer thought about the job?

EMMA. 'E needs more time t'think, Mister Wheatley.

ANNE *and* JOHN *stand near* EMMA.

RICHARD. Joe can answer for 'imself. Joe?

JOE. I'd like t'tekk it, Mister Wheatley –

RICHARD. That's settled then.

JOE. But –

RICHARD. But what?

JOE. I'm a fisherman.

RICHARD. We're all the same people, Joe.

ANNE. If 'e doesn't want to, don't make 'im.

RICHARD. No, a want this sorted out. (*Looking* JOE *in the eye*.) What've I done?

JOE *is silent*.

What 'aven't I given yer? Tell me'n I'll mekk it right.

JOE (*plucking up the courage*). Will yer give us our land back, Mister Wheatley?

RICHARD. Aye, a thought that might be it. And what mekks yer think it's your land?

JOE. Cos we've a right to it.

RICHARD. What right is that?

JOE. My father's right, Mister Wheatley, that was his father's and should be mine. 'N' the fair justice that goes with it.

RICHARD *raises his hand to hit* JOE *across the face*.

ANNE. Leave 'im be, Richard.

RICHARD*'s hand stops momentarily and then it comes down powerfully, hitting* JOE *across the cheek and jaw.* JOE *doesn't resist, he falls to the ground.*

EMMA *hides her eyes.* JOHN *lets out a quiet shriek before closing his.* ANNE *watches sadly.*

JOE (*picking himself up*). And if you don't give us it we're goyn t'tekk it.

EMMA. Don't, Joe.

JOHN (*frightened*). Don't, Dad.

ANNE. Is that the way to treat someone?

RICHARD. Stay out of this, woman! (*Back to* JOE.) Yer think yer goyn t'tekk my land?

JOE. Aye.

RICHARD *raises his hand, he brings it down powerfully across* JOE*'s face.* JOE *falls to the ground again.*

(*Picking himself up. A small trickle of blood is running from the corner of his mouth.*) I'm weak, Mister Wheatley, not strong like you.

EMMA *makes a dart towards* JOE. ANNE *quickly grabs her hand and stops her.*

ANNE. Don't, girl.

RICHARD *raises his hand, he brings it down powerfully across* JOE*'s face.* JOE *falls to the ground.*

JOHN. What's 'e doin' it for? What's 'e done?

RICHARD *walks away from* JOE *and away from the other three.*

ANNE *is still holding* EMMA*'s hand.* ANNE *lets her go.* EMMA *rushes to* JOE.

EMMA (*bending down beside him*). Joe.

JOE *is unconscious. Blood is coming from his mouth.*

JOHN. Is 'e dead?

EMMA (*nursing him on her lap*). Joe.

JOHN (*tugging at* ANNE*'s sleeve*). Did yer hear me? Is 'e dead?

ANNE. I don't know, John.

JOHN (*proudly*). He could fight anyone.

ANNE. Don't you ever fight, d'you hear?

RICHARD. I don't know what came over me. Any learnin' yer do don't make yer less angry. I treat people fair. I'm a good man.

EMMA. You've killed 'im.

RICHARD *is looking at* ANNE. ANNE *is silent.*

RICHARD. I know it's not the way your God behaves. I'll walk on my own back to the farm.

RICHARD *exits, quite slowly, through the gate and through the trees.*

JOHN (*tugging at* ANNE*'s sleeve*). Are we goyn too?

ANNE. In a minute. I want to help Emma first.

ANNE *walks to* EMMA.

EMMA. It's all right. I'll do it.

ANNE (*taking* EMMA*'s arm*). Come here, girl.

EMMA *stands up and falls into* ANNE*'s arms. She sobs.* JOHN *watches.*

Sssh.

A slight pause.

JOHN. I'm goyn after him.

ANNE. Don't get lost now.

JOHN *walks through the gate, as he exits through the trees he starts to run.*

A slight pause.

Sssh.

EMMA *sobs more loudly.*

Eh, shush now, shush.

The sunlight fades to blackout.

Scene Three

Middlewood. The night of New Year's Eve.

A full moon is shining through the trees casting quite a bright light. There are one or two eerie shadows.

EMMA, *wearing the same clothes, is sitting alone on the tree trunk.*

WILLIAM ELDERBERRY *enters.*

WILLIAM *is a dwarf in his early thirties. He has a kind, lively face and he speaks without a trace of an accent. He is dressed for the cold in shoes, stockings, breeches, shirt, waistcoat, neck-tie, and a top coat.*

EMMA *sees him and stands up, she looks frightened.* WILLIAM *stops.*

WILLIAM. Don't be frightened. I don't mean you harm.

EMMA (*taking a step backwards*). A've bin waitin' fo'yer.

WILLIAM. My name's William Elderberry. I'm with the fair.

EMMA. Where're your friends?

WILLIAM. They're back along the road there. Our caravans are stuck in the deep snow. I was looking for someone to help us pull them out.

EMMA. I thought you lived in the ground.

WILLIAM. No. I realise it's late. We shouldn't have been on the road at this time, especially on New Year's Eve.

EMMA. Where yer goyn t'tekk me?

WILLIAM. I don't understand.

EMMA (*taking a step backwards*). Now I've seen you, a'm scared. A thought a wouldn' be. You are a boggart, aren't you? Where're your horns?

WILLIAM *feels the top of his head.*

WILLIAM (*smiling*). I don't have any. What are boggarts?

EMMA. The little men who live in these woods. (*Taking a step backwards.*) Yer horns must've dropped off, like cows, when you were fightin'.

WILLIAM. I'm not a boggart.

EMMA. Yer live in the roots o'trees, don' yer? 'N' tekk people away t'yer den?

WILLIAM. Who told you this?

EMMA. Folk've seen yer from the village.

WILLIAM. D'you wish a boggart to take you?

>EMMA *nods*.

>(*Taking a step towards her.*) I really am not a boggart.

EMMA (*taking a step back*). Boggarts are liars.

>*They stop.*

WILLIAM. Are you so unhappy? What's your name?

EMMA. Emma. Emma Braye.

WILLIAM. I am with the fair.

>WILLIAM *takes three balls from his pocket. He juggles with them.*

>This is how I make my living.

>EMMA *watches blankly.* WILLIAM *catches the balls and stops juggling.*

>Come to me, Emma.

EMMA. Do I 'ave t'do as you say?

>EMMA *walks to* WILLIAM.

WILLIAM. Feel the top of my head.

>EMMA *tentatively feels the top of* WILLIAM'*s head.*

>Are there any horns there?

EMMA. No.

>EMMA *takes her hand away.* WILLIAM *produces one of the balls from his mouth.*

>'Ow did yer do that? D'you eat those?

>WILLIAM *puts out a hand to* EMMA'*s ear.* EMMA *jumps back.*

WILLIAM. Don't move.

>WILLIAM *produces a ball from behind* EMMA'*s ear. He coughs. Another ball drops from his mouth. He catches it.*

>Mrs Elderberry taught me.

EMMA. Who's Mrs Elderberry?

WILLIAM. My wife.

EMMA. Is she as small as you?

WILLIAM. She's smaller than me. (*Putting the balls in his pocket.*) Won't you tell me what the matter is?

EMMA *looks down, turns, and walks away a pace.*

(*Blowing into his hands.*) It's jolly, jolly cold here. Are there any men to help us move our caravans? (*Rubbing his hands.*) Mine's at a steep angle, I'd be rolling out of bed if I went to sleep.

A slight pause.

Please tell me.

A slight pause.

Let me consult Mrs Elderberry.

WILLIAM *puts his hands to his temples and thinks for a moment.*

I think you've been in love, haven't you?

EMMA. 'Ow did you know?

WILLIAM. Mrs Elderberry told me.

EMMA. Yer can't do nowt. No one can. 'E's dead. The boggarts've taken 'is body.

WILLIAM. Where have they taken it to?

EMMA. A don't know. We left it 'ere. When a came back it'd gone. A came back wi' the pony. It's all my fault. Joe was right. 'E would be alive if it weren't f'me.

WILLIAM. Don't distress yourself.

EMMA. I've 'ad enough.

A slight pause.

WILLIAM. You loved him very much, didn't you?

EMMA *nods.*

EMMA. We were goyn t'the city. I were wrong, I stopped us. We were goyn t'go to York.

WILLIAM. York has a castle. We pitch our fair on the green nearby.

EMMA. What's it like?

WILLIAM. York is crowded with people. All seeking work like you and your – Joe?

EMMA *nods*.

Like you and Joe would have been. The streets of York are littered with destitute men. The poverty and disease I've seen should be a crime. I much prefer the country. Thousands of people have gone to the cities. This is the place for you.

EMMA *smiles slightly*.

EMMA. D'you travel a lot?

WILLIAM. All over Yorkshire. We're on our way from Scarborough. We should be in Whitby now for the New Year.

EMMA. I've never bin t'the fair.

WILLIAM. Haven't you?

EMMA *smiles*.

You're beautiful when you smile.

EMMA. Yer jus' sayin' that.

WILLIAM. I understand why Joe loved you.

EMMA (*surprised*). D'you think 'e did?

WILLIAM. Yes.

EMMA. I weren't sure. Especially after what I did. (*Feeling upset again*.) I wondered if yer stopped lovin' when you were dead. I want 'im still t'love me.

WILLIAM. I've upset you again.

EMMA. Yer haven't. Yer not a boggart, are you?

WILLIAM. I'm beginning to feel like one, the way you keep saying it.

EMMA. I wonder where they are?

WILLIAM (*blowing into his hands*). Wrapped up warm I imagine.

EMMA. What happens at a fair?

WILLIAM (*going into his act*). Jolly up, jolly up, step right this way, ladies and gentlemen. See the moving waxworks, the dancing horse, the impersonators. Tumblers, musicians, fire-eaters. Our troop of tightrope-dancing children. (*Bowing to her*.) Step right this way, my girl.

EMMA *laughs*.

Come on, step this way.

EMMA *walks past him*. WILLIAM *does part of his act; he produces a long red handkerchief from the inside of his mouth.* EMMA *watches*.

(*Bowing*.) Thank you. People usually clap.

EMMA *claps*.

Who's this?

WILLIAM *impersonates George III*. EMMA *looks blank*.

That's George the third, our King.

WILLIAM *impersonates The Archbishop of York; he sticks his bum out and makes a loud farting noise*.

EMMA. I don't know.

WILLIAM. The Archbishop of York, farting.

EMMA. I haven't seen them.

WILLIAM (*standing upright again*) Haven't you seen pictures of them?

EMMA. No.

WILLIAM. They have in the towns. People like it when the Archbishop farts.

EMMA. I know what he does.

WILLIAM. You are a funny girl.

WILLIAM *smiles. They look at one another for a moment.* EMMA *looks down and walks away a pace*.

I had better be going back really.

EMMA (*turning to him*). Don't go yet.

WILLIAM. Mrs Elderberry will be wondering where I am.

EMMA. I'd like to meet your wife.

WILLIAM. Would you?

EMMA. Yes.

WILLIAM. Have you no hope?

EMMA *shakes her head slightly.*

Another man will cross your path, won't he?

EMMA (*sitting down on the log*). It's not jus' Joe.

WILLIAM. What is it then?

EMMA. I can't live 'ere any more.

WILLIAM. Why?

EMMA. Cos of what's 'appened. It's terrible. (*Looking at* WILLIAM.) There was a big fight between us and the fishermen.

WILLIAM (*sitting down beside her*). I don't understand.

EMMA. The fishermen came up t'take their land back. They fought in this field. (*Her voice rising.*) They must think I tol' Mister Wheatley, but I didn', 'e guessed. About thirty or forty fishermen came up from the Bay. All they were armed with were sticks. The farmers 'ad guns. When the fishermen tried t'pull down the fences, our farmers charged 'em. They were lyin' in wait. The fishermen 'ad no chance.

WILLIAM. Go on?

EMMA. In the end the fishermen jus' fled. Anywhere they could run where the snow weren't too deep. Our farmers were stronger'n chased 'em. Pockets o'men jus' fightin' wi' their bare fists. 'N' gunshots ringin' out.

WILLIAM. What happened?

EMMA. One farmer was killed, one fisherman and another six fishermen caught. The rest of 'em got away.

WILLIAM *looks down at the snow.*

The six that were caught were taken to the Justice.

WILLIAM. Oh dear.

EMMA. The villagers raised a flag of victory in the village square. A couldn't stand the celebration of it. The fishermen're t'be taken t'York assizes. Mister Wheatley is travelling there tomorrow. He wants them all hanged to set an example.

WILLIAM. Joe was a fisherman, was he?

EMMA *nods.*

EMMA. He weren't in the fight though. 'E were killed before.

A slight pause.

Joe would 'ave liked you an' all. What do I do? I 'ave t'live with Mister Wheatley.

WILLIAM. Let me consult Mrs Elderberry.

EMMA. D'you alwez do that?

WILLIAM. Yes.

WILLIAM *puts his hands to his temples and thinks for a moment.*

Firstly, she says you musn't let the boggarts get you. Because Joe's not with them. Secondly, she says you must think about the future.

EMMA. Is that all?

WILLIAM. And have some hope.

EMMA. Why?

WILLIAM. Because when you've lost hope, you've lost everything, haven't you?

EMMA *looks down and thinks for a moment.*

EMMA. Is Mrs Elderberry dead?

WILLIAM. I was in love too.

EMMA. She is, isn't she?

WILLIAM (*standing up*). I ought to be back to my caravan.

EMMA. Tell me. It'll give me hope if she is.

WILLIAM. She died of the fever five years ago. (*He has heard something.*) Listen. What's that?

They listen.

A church clock can be heard chiming faintly from the distance.

It's New Year's Eve. It must be midnight. A drink.

WILLIAM *produces two small glasses from his pocket.*

EMMA. Where did yer get those from?

WILLIAM (*giving them to her*). You hold them please.

EMMA *holds the glasses.* WILLIAM *produces a small bottle of wine. He pours wine into the glasses and puts the bottle away.*

The clock is striking midnight.

WILLIAM *takes one glass from* EMMA.

To the New Year.

EMMA (*standing up*). To the New Year.

They drink and empty their glasses.

WILLIAM. If you could send some men in the morning I'd be grateful.

EMMA. I will.

WILLIAM. Look after yourself.

EMMA. I'll try to.

WILLIAM *turns and exits towards his caravan.*

(*Calling after him. Holding the glass at arm's length.*) You've forgotten your glass.

A slight pause.

Good luck, William Elderberry.

EMMA *stands holding the empty glass.*

The moonlight fades to blackout.

ACT THREE

Scene One

ANNE WHEATLEY's *kitchen at Middlewood farm. Twenty years later. The evening of 11 July 1797.*

The light from a full moon is shining through the window.

ANNE *is sitting on the bench at the table. Beside her is an inkpot, and with a quill she is writing her diary in her notebook. A candle nearby is giving quite a lot of light.*

The cupboard in the dresser where she keeps her notebooks is open. A rushlight is burning on the dresser itself. The outside door is not bolted, the bar of wood is resting against the frame.

ANNE *is wearing the gown, she has the woollen shawl across her shoulders. She writes slowly and purposefully, thinking about every sentence.*

An owl hoots outside.

ANNE *blows on the ink to dry it. She turns the page and writes another line.*

There is a muffled knock on the outside door.

ANNE *looks up.*

A short silence.

ANNE *writes.*

The knock again, this time louder.

ANNE (*going to the door*). Who's there?

　　A short silence.

　　It's late. Who is it? Is it you again, boy?

　　A short silence.

　　I'm not opening the door until you say who you are.

　　The knock again.

　　I should warn you I've a dog beside me.

ANNE *slowly opens the door.*

JOE *is standing there. He is dressed in his best clothes; shoes, stockings, breeches, waistcoat, shirt, neck-tie, and a jacket.*

JOE. Mrs Wheatley?

ANNE (*she doesn't recognise him. Suspiciously*). Yes?

JOE. Do you remember me?

ANNE. No. Who are you? What d'you want at this time of night?

JOE. You don't recognise me?

ANNE. No.

JOE. I'm Joe Waterman, Mrs Wheatley.

ANNE *looks at* JOE, *she takes a step back from the door.*

ANNE. I don't know who you are, but go please.

JOE *takes a step into the kitchen.*

JOE. I haven't come here to frighten you, Mistress.

ANNE. Joe Waterman, but you're dead.

JOE. I was left for dead twenty years ago.

ANNE (*sharply*). Go away from here. What d'you want?

JOE. I've come for your help.

ANNE. Help! How can we help you?

A short silence.

JOE. Emma mentioned t'me once about a Frenchman who came here.

ANNE. What of it?

JOE. I wondered what he looked like, Mistress?

ANNE. Who?

JOE. The Frenchman who came.

ANNE. Why?

JOE. We think we've a Frenchman at Bay Town.

ANNE *goes white. She walks to the rocking chair.*

JOE. I beg of you, Mrs Wheatley.

ANNE. Go. Please go.

> ANNE *sits in the chair.* JOE *shuffles nervously, he stays.*

> Why did you come here? If it is you, Joe.

JOE. I had t'come now. It will be too late tomorrow.

ANNE (*softly*). How could I ever forget you.

> ANNE *closes her eyes, she rocks in the chair.*

> *A slight pause.*

JOE. If you'd jus' tell me what the Frenchman looked like.

ANNE. Emma said you were alive. We didn't believe her.

JOE. Do you remember?

ANNE (*opening her eyes*). The Frenchman? Yes, I do. He was an older man. Squire Boulby brought him to Richard. He was here to learn the new farming, he kept slipping in the snow.

JOE. Was he covered in hair?

ANNE. He was bald. Wigged.

JOE. A'yer sure?

ANNE. Why?

JOE. The Frenchman we have is covered in hair. A boat was wrecked las' night –

ANNE. We know.

JOE. Oh?

ANNE. We watch you, Joe.

JOE. Well, we reckon 'e's from that. But I think he's an animal. Did your Frenchman walk upright?

ANNE. Yes.

JOE. Ours walks on his hands and knees.

ANNE. He was like you or me. He spoke slightly different, with an accent.

JOE. Ours grunts'n groans, 'n' shrieks now'n again. Yet he looks human. Sometimes, anyway. He has this way of lookin' at yer. 'N' 'e's strong like a man. The town's in panic.

ANNE. Where is he?

JOE. We have him in a cage. He's not a Frenchman, Mistress. We're being made t'look so stupid.

ANNE. Is that why you came?

JOE. T'be certain.

ANNE. It must've taken courage?

JOE. I waited 'till dark, so no one would see me.

A slight pause.

Thank you.

JOE *turns and walks towards the open door.*

ANNE (*standing up*). Don't go, stay.

JOE. The whole town is watchin'. I should be there myself.

ANNE *walks to* JOE*, she feels his arms.*

ANNE. You are real, aren't you.

JOE. I don't know what we've got t'say to each other, Mrs Wheatley.

ANNE. It is you, Joe.

JOE *looks embarrassed, he shuffles.*

Will you stay?

JOE. A few moments.

ANNE *walks to the door, she closes it.* JOE *walks into the kitchen. They turn and look at one another.*

What happened to Emma?

ANNE. She died, Joe, giving birth to her child.

JOE. A waited for her, but she never came. A waited, for a year a waited. Then a stole up one night an' found her stone in the graveyard.

ANNE. The girl'd whittled away t'nothing out of grief f'you.

JOE. What happened to the child?

ANNE. She's upstairs. Asleep I hope.

A slight pause.

JOE. That's quite a shock. That I didn't know.

ANNE. I brought her up.

JOE. Is she like her mother at all?

ANNE. I'm not very good at comparing people. Yes, I think they are. They've the same spirit.

JOE. Does she know about me?

ANNE. I've tried to tell her. In my own way. Recently I've tried.

JOE turns, he walks one pace. He stops and looks at ANNE.

I'm getting older, Joe. I won't be here for very much longer. I didn't want to go without her knowing.

A slight pause.

And it's time she was married an' knew the truth. She'll marry well, she'll make a good wife.

A slight pause.

All these years I've written a diary. Just my thoughts, the day t'day things. I discovered they were being moved. I let her go on with it.

JOE. Why didn't you tell'er when she was little.

ANNE. How could I, Joe? Would you have done? The spite in the village, they wouldn't have let the child live.

JOE. No.

ANNE. I wanted to tell her.

A slight pause.

But it takes courage after so long.

JOE turns, he walks the one pace back. He stops and looks at ANNE.

JOE. I should be goyn.

ANNE. We're not strangers, Joe.

JOE. I don't know why a came. A shouldn't o'come.

The upstairs door slowly opens. BETSY peers round, she has a candle.

BETSY. I've been listening at the door.

BETSY steps into the kitchen. She is wearing the white nightdress.

Is that my father?

ANNE. Back to bed this instant.

BETSY. No, Aunt, I'm not a child.

JOE *is staring at* BETSY.

(*To* JOE.) Are you my father?

ANNE. Don't be silly, girl.

BETSY. Please, Aunt.

ANNE. Of course he's not your father.

BETSY. Why're you denyin' him?

BETSY *looks at* JOE.

Are you my father?

JOE *looks at* ANNE.

A slight pause. ANNE *and* JOE *look away from one another.*

Why're you both quiet? I know. I could tell from the conversation. What do it matter?

A short silence.

I've of'en tried to picture you. Yer not at all like I imagined.

BETSY *walks to the table. She puts the candle down.*

(*To* JOE.) The Mistress alwez told me I was her sister's child.

ANNE. You've seen now, back to bed.

BETSY. Why can't you talk about it, Aunt?

ANNE. Mister Waterman was going, we're keeping him here.

BETSY. Were you?

JOE. I was goyn, yes.

BETSY *walks to the outside door and stands in front of it.*

BETSY (*to* ANNE). Why don't we have that talk now?

A short silence. BETSY *looks between* ANNE *and* JOE.

JOE. Yer should praise yer Aunt f'what shiz done.

BETSY. Will yer tell me about you?

JOE *looks at* ANNE *and then back to* BETSY.

JOE. It was your mother really who taught me everything I know. (*To* ANNE.) D'you mind if I sit down?

ANNE. No. Do.

> JOE *sits down on the bench.* ANNE *walks to the rocking chair and sits down.*

JOE. We were goyn to marry, an' then that bad winter came. (*To* ANNE.) Didn' it?

ANNE. Yes.

BETSY. All that is in the diary.

ANNE. Come away from the door, child, the draught will give you a chill.

> BETSY *walks to the bench and sits down.*

JOE. At that time I worked with my father and three brothers. We had the one cobble. We starved.

BETSY. I know about the fences.

JOE. After the battle, all we decided we could do, was to become fishermen proper. With more boats. 'N' store food f'the winter. We'd been farmers y'see, as well. (*To* ANNE.) Hadn't we?

> ANNE *nods.*

> We cut down trees, stolen off the farm land. An' built cobbles. (*Looking at* ANNE.) We're still poor, but we're better than we were.

BETSY. What about you?

JOE. I've jus' sold my cobble.

BETSY. What for?

JOE (*slightly tentatively*). I'm hoping to open a school.

BETSY. Someone told me that.

> JOE *looks sympathetically at* BETSY. *He smiles.*

JOE. For the children of the town. Teach them t'read'n write.

ANNE. How will you make a living?

JOE. The towners who send children will have to pay me. It'll be a struggle because we've a new preacher at the town. A methodist. I dislike their preachin', they think children should work. He's made them suspicious. A few have promised to help. Enough to begin with. (*Proudly.*) It'll be the first school at Bay Town.

BETSY (*smiling*). They'll come.

JOE (*smiling at* BETSY). I hope so.

ANNE. I wish we had a school at Fylingthorpe.

JOE. School is a new idea t'the likes of us. It'll take gettin' used to.

ANNE. All the new ideas are like that.

JOE. I think so.

 A short silence.

BETSY. Am I like you imagined?

ANNE. Don't pester Mister Waterman, Betsy.

JOE. It's alright. I don't reckon you are because I didn't know you see. I didn't know what had happened. I didn't know there was a you. I've wondered.

BETSY. I wondered all the time.

 JOE *smiles.*

ANNE. Have you married?

JOE. No, unfortunately.

ANNE. Why not?

JOE. It didn't seem right to.

BETSY. D'you know a fisherman called Andrew Cove?

JOE. Yes, I do. Thomas Cove's son.

 BETSY *plucks up her courage and stands up.*

BETSY. I want t'tell yer both something.

ANNE (*closing her eyes*). Don't, Betsy.

 ANNE *rocks in the chair.*

BETSY (*looking at* ANNE). Tim Appleyard were right.

ANNE. I don't want to hear, child.

 BETSY *looks at* JOE.

BETSY. I've bin meetin' Andrew Cove. We're goyn t'get married one day.

 ANNE *stops rocking and opens her eyes.*

ANNE. Get out of this house!

BETSY. Yer knew, didn't yer?

ANNE. Of course I didn't know.

BETSY (*tapping the side of her head*). Yer can keep things up here.
    But as soon as the' said, yer can't talk any more. Why?

ANNE *closes her eyes and rocks in the chair. A slight pause.*

(*To* JOE.) I met 'im in the woods. I was pickin' mushrooms one day.
He were poachin' rabbits.

JOE *looks down.*

(*To* ANNE.) It's you who believe the fishermen 'ave two 'eads. Not
me. Yer can't stand up f'the truth.

ANNE. Tim Appleyard was too convincing.

BETSY. A bet 'e were. Idle layabout.

ANNE. I don't want to hear it.

ANNE *closes her eyes.*

I'll have to apologise to him. He was roundly scolded.

A slight pause.

BETSY. D'yer want me t'go, Aunt? If yer want me to, a will.

ANNE. You're a disappointment to me.

BETSY. A can't do much about that, a'm sorry.

A slight pause.

D'yer want me t'go?

ANNE. Why did you do it, Betsy? Why have you ruined everything?

BETSY. I haven't.

ANNE. But you have. You could've been such a good girl.

BETSY. No, Aunt.

A slight pause.

I understand what my mother felt. I'm goyn t'do what she should
have done.

BETSY *walks to the upstairs door and goes out leaving the door
open.*

ANNE. What a terrible mess.

   ANNE *closes her eyes, she rocks in the chair.*

   Silence for a moment.

JOE. Did you know, Mistress?

ANNE. I guessed.

JOE. Then what do it matter?

ANNE. Does it not bother you?

JOE. I've wanted t'come here f'a long time.

ANNE. Have you told anyone?

JOE. No. I admit that. We could start, Mrs Wheatley?

   The owl hoots outside.

ANNE. I'm not an intelligent woman, Joe. I've alwez lost the things
   I treasured most. My husband. Emma. My son. And now it seems
   I'm to lose Betsy.

JOE. We've lost them because of conflict, Mistress.

   ANNE *is thinking.*

ANNE. Things seem to repeat themselves. As spring and sowing,
   follows autumn and ploughing.

JOE. We can change that. Stop that. Emma was right all those years
   ago. It's no good running away. The city wouldn't've been f'us.

   A slight pause.

   She's beautiful.

ANNE. Who?

JOE. Betsy.

ANNE (*proudly*). Is she?

JOE. She does remind me of Emma. In my mind Emma is still as
   young. I meant what I said about praisin' yer, Mistress.

ANNE. You're a better man than me, Joe.

   JOE *sits back.*

   What is this boy like?

JOE. Andrew Cove? Don't you remember his father?

ANNE. No.

JOE. His father was one of my pals. He was one of those hanged.

ANNE*'s gaze drops to the floor.*

Andrew 'imself is a bright lad.

ANNE. D'you think they'll have talked together?

JOE (*shrugging*). Wouldn't you 'ave done?

ANNE. I wonder what they've said about me.

JOE. He's not the cheeky sort.

ANNE. What does he do?

JOE. 'E fishes a cobble with Edward Tideswell.

ANNE. How old is he?

JOE. He's about twenty.

ANNE. And he's bright, you say?

JOE. He's a sense of good fun, Mistress.

ANNE. I'm glad. I was trying to picture him.

A slight pause.

What d'you think I should do?

BETSY *enters through the open upstairs door. She has dressed hastily in shoes, a gown, and a red cloak. The bonnet on her head is crooked. She is carrying a canvas bag.*

ANNE *stands up.*

(*Brightly.*) Here she is.

BETSY *stands in the middle of the kitchen and puts her bag down.*

BETSY. I'll go then, Aunt.

ANNE *looks at* JOE. JOE *stands up.*

I don't know why you came but thank you, Mister Waterman.

ANNE. Won't you wait until morning?

BETSY. No.

A slight pause.

ANNE. Your bonnet's crooked. Untie it, let me set it straight.

BETSY unties the bonnet. ANNE puts it straight on BETSY's head. She starts to tie the ribbon.

I see you've taken my bag.

BETSY. I don't have one of my own.

The ribbon is fastened. BETSY picks up the bag and walks to the outside door.

ANNE. Please don't, Betsy. At least wait until it's light.

BETSY opens the door.

BETSY. If I wait, I'll never go. Thank you for all you've done.

BETSY goes out. She closes the door slowly behind her.

A short silence.

ANNE. Will she ever come back, d'you think?

JOE. I don't know.

ANNE. Half an hour ago everything was all right.

ANNE walks to the window and looks out.

JOE. I should really go with her, Mrs Wheatley. If they see 'er 'n' realise where shiz from –

ANNE. Why didn't you stop her then?

JOE. I couldn't have stopped 'er.

ANNE. What if they stone her, Mister Waterman?

JOE. It would be no worse than what you did to us.

ANNE. But she's your daughter.

JOE. She might've been my daughter twenty years ago.

ANNE. How can you stand there and say that?

JOE. Because it's what I think.

ANNE. So you'd let them stone your daughter?

JOE. If Andrew Cove came here, would you stone him?

Silence for a moment.

ANNE. No, I'd try'n stop them.

JOE. Then I will try'n do the same.

A slight pause.

I'm listened to at Bay Town. It's for the best.

The outside door opens. JOHN *enters. He is drunk.*

JOHN. Where's Betsy? (*Closing the door.*) I got Harriet Woodforde drunk'n she danced with me. (*Looking at* JOE.) Chris Smith played 'is fiddle. Who's he?

JOE *looks at* ANNE. *Silence for a moment.*

(*To* ANNE, *angrily.*) Who's he? Who's that in my house?

A moment's pause.

(*Lurching forward towards* ANNE.) Tell me, woman!

ANNE. It's Mister Waterman.

JOHN. Mister Waterman who?

ANNE. Mister Waterman from Bay Town.

JOHN. If he's a fisherman, hang 'im!

JOHN *lurches forward towards* JOE *with his fists clenched.* JOE *moves out of the way.* JOHN *falls to the ground.*

(*Picking himself up.*) I don't know a Mister Waterman.

ANNE. You're drunk.

JOHN. Of course a'm drunk. The whole of New Plough Inn were drunk. I paid for 'em. They like me now. (*Pointing a finger at* ANNE.) You don't mean anythin' to 'em any more.

JOHN *hangs his head.*

JOE. I'll go, Mrs Wheatley.

JOHN. I remember you. You're dead. (*Turning to his mother.*) He's dead, Ma.

JOHN *collapses in a heap on the stone floor.* JOE *walks to the outside door.*

ANNE. Will you bring me news of Betsy.

JOE. I'll try.

ANNE *opens the door.* JOE *is looking at* JOHN.

ANNE. Don't worry about him, I can manage sufficiently well.

ANNE *and* JOE *look at one another.*

JOE. Goodnight then, Mistress.

ANNE. Goodnight, Joe.

JOE *exits.* ANNE *slowly closes the door.* JOHN *picks himself up.*

JOHN. I remember Joe Waterman. Where's he gone? Where's the ghost?

ANNE *is looking at him.*

A mus' be dreaming. Yer can't hang a ghost. What're yer lookin' at me for? (*Angrily.*) Stop lookin' at me!

JOHN *straightens up, he tries to be sober.*

Joe Waterman's come back to haunt us. I'm drunk. You should get drunk.

ANNE (*tenderly*). Is this your answer to everything, John?

JOHN *stumbles backwards towards the table. He props himself up on it.*

JOHN. Don't treat me like a little boy. I'm not a little boy.

JOHN *sees the notebook. He looks at* ANNE. *He pulls the notebook towards him.*

Betsy's been reading these you know.

ANNE. Don't touch them please.

JOHN. All the lies in here, she believes.

JOHN *looks at the notebook.*

ANNE. Leave them, John.

JOHN. All the lies about my father. What've you put for t'day.

ANNE (*walking to him*). I asked you to leave them.

JOHN (*pushing her away, quite roughly*). Ge' off.

ANNE. Is this the way to treat your mother?

JOHN. I'm a new an' different man.

JOHN *picks up the diary.*

ANNE (*going to him*). Don't John, please.

JOHN (*pushing her away, roughly*). Ge'off!

ANNE *falls to the floor.* JOHN *rips the notebook in half.*

That's what I think about you an' your lies.

JOHN *throws the two halves of the notebook towards* ANNE. ANNE
picks them up, her hair has fallen out of place, she stands up.

JOHN *collapses down, he sits on the bench.*

Why d'you hate me, Ma?

ANNE *is close to tears. She says nothing. She pushes her hair back
into place.*

That was naughty, weren't it?

ANNE *walks to the table.*

Why don't you love me?

ANNE *puts the two halves of the notebook down.*

ANNE. I do love you.

JOHN. Why didn't you love my father?

ANNE. I loved him too.

ANNE *sits down on the bench.*

I loved him with all my heart. When he died, I died.

A slight pause.

JOHN. It's you who's made me like this.

A slight pause.

A didn' mean t'rip yer diary.

A slight pause.

Where're the others?

ANNE. In the cupboard.

JOHN. A didn't rip them. I'll glue it back together. Where is it?

ANNE. Leave it now.

JOHN *stops. A slight pause.*

JOHN. Did my father love you?

ANNE. No, I don't think he did.

JOHN. I'm like 'im, aren't I? That's what you didn't want. 'N' yet you loved him.

A slight pause.

I loved 'im as well. He was the apple of my eye.

ANNE. I loved him, but I hated what he did.

JOHN. Jus' like yer hate me? F'being like 'im.

ANNE. Yes.

A slight pause.

We should've talked a long time ago.

The owl hoots outside.

JOHN (*imitating it*). Twit-twoo.

A slight pause.

I think I'm very drunk.

The two candles and the rushlight are burning.

Scene Two

The beach and town at Robin Hood's Bay. A few moments later.

Sand. The house of ROBERT *and* MOLLY STORM. *Grass. Standing on the grass is* ROBERT'*s clinker-built fishing cobble. The cobble is called 'Molly', it is painted on in rough white lettering. Near the house, on the sand, is an old cart. On top of the cart is a wooden cage.*

The light from a full moon is shining.

A gentle sea can be heard lapping against the shore.

STOCKTON *and* MARY *are inside the cage. They are still.*

ROBERT *is sitting on a bench a short distance from the cage. He has the musket beside him. He is smoking a clay pipe.*

MARY *talks to* STOCKTON.

MARY. Me brother were the Skip-Jack, turning the jack on our Master's skip-roastin' fire. A were the scullery maid. 'E didn't treat us proper. One day 'e were beatin' me brother, so me brother pushed him in the fire. All 'is clothes set alight. We ran off f'fear what 'e'd do to us.

MOLLY *appears from the house carrying two tankards of ale. She walks down towards* ROBERT.

ROBERT. You go to bed, love.

MOLLY. I'll 'ave one with yer.

MARY. I still 'aven' 'ad that drink, Mistress.

MOLLY. You be quiet, boy.

MARY (*standing up*). A'm a girl, a've told yer.

ROBERT (*standing up. His voice booming towards* MARY). Eh, you be quiet, an' don't be cheeky.

MOLLY *gives one tankard to* ROBERT.

Ta, thank you. (*Sitting down.*) If my boys were as cheeky as 'im, a'd thrash them.

MARY. Yer daren't come near me, dare yer? Yer frightened.

ROBERT *stands up.*

MOLLY. Leave 'im be.

ROBERT *sits down.*

MARY. Told yer.

MOLLY *sits down beside him.*

ROBERT (*his voice booming to* MARY). Yer'll be 'angin' by mornin' you boy.

MARY. A won't.

MOLLY *drinks.* STOCKTON s*tands up, he walks round in a circle.*

You'll be 'angin' by evenin'.

ROBERT *drinks.* STOCKTON *sits down again.*

Wait till our friends get 'ere.

MOLLY (*calling to* MARY). Thess a few people tryin' sleep in this town.

PETER STORM *appears at the door of the house. He looks tired.*

PETER *is twelve years old. He is wearing a nightshirt.*

ROBERT. What d'you want, Peter?

PETER. A'm frightened.

ROBERT. Yer should be in bed, tucked up.

MOLLY. Let 'im come down 'ere, 'e won't hurt.

    PETER *walks towards them.*

    'Re yer brothers asleep?

PETER. Yes, Mam. Tom's snorin'.

ROBERT. A boy of mine frightened, Peter?

MOLLY. Sit down. D'yer want a drop o' this?

    PETER *sits down on the sand near the bench. He takes the tankard from* MOLLY. *He drinks half of it.*

PETER. I kept 'avin' bad dreams.

    PETER *drinks the other half.*

MOLLY. A said a drop, not all of it.

PETER (*giving the tankard to his mother*). Ta, Mam.

    MOLLY *holds the tankard upside down. It is empty.*

ROBERT. Do 'e alwez drink like that?

MARY. Is 'e your boy?

PETER. A were thirsty.

MOLLY. I'll 'ave 'alf o'yours.

ROBERT. See what trouble yer cause by yer drinkin'.

    ROBERT *pours half of his ale into* MOLLY*'s tankard.*

MOLLY. Peter's my favourite. 'E'll soon be a man. It's time 'e learnt t'hold 'is ale.

ROBERT. Yer alwez sayin' drink is ruinous?

MOLLY. So it is, too much of it.

    ROBERT *drinks.*

ROBERT. I understand 'im bein' frightened, a small'n like 'im. 'E's far from a man. I'd 'ave bad dreams mesell.

MARY. Why do 'e get a drink?

ROBERT (*to* MARY). I've warned you, boy.

    PETER *looks at the cage, and then at his father.*

PETER. Where're the other Frenchmen, Dad?

ROBERT. If a knew that, Peter, a'd be fightin' em. Yer can feel safe.

PETER. A were dreamin' they chopped our heads off.

MARY (*still standing watching them*). The' will do.

ROBERT (*his voice booming to* MARY). We're Yorkshire folk. No
    Frenchman's gonna do that.

PETER. A'yer sure?

    PETER *stretches out on the sand.*

ROBERT. 'E ought t'be in 'is bed.

MOLLY. Let 'im be. Thess summat special about t'night.

ROBERT (*suspiciously*). What d'yer mean, Molly?

MOLLY. Thess summat Christmas.

ROBERT. A don't reckon the' is.

MOLLY. Thess a ringle in the air. 'Aven't yer felt it?

ROBERT. I 'aven't.

MOLLY. A celebration.

ROBERT. I believe they're about us, Molly.

    PETER *curls up into a ball.*

    A d'feel proud though, bein' the one set to guard 'im.

    MOLLY *smiles.*

MOLLY. I feel good t'night. It's a victory, ain' it?

ROBERT. Yer might learn true those words.

    PETER *closes his eyes.* MOLLY *moves closer to* ROBERT.

    A bit o'love makin' an' all, is it? Yer've not got another one on the
    way?

MOLLY. No.

ROBERT. I've bin thinkin', Molly. A don't think swallowin' them ten worms does any good.

MOLLY *cuddles* ROBERT.

Not in front of the boy. Remember what Mister Wesley said.

MOLLY *stops*.

MOLLY. D'yer mean it?

ROBERT. Aye, a do. I'm not 'avin' that. Supposin' that new Preacher Man were seein' us?

MOLLY. 'E's not 'ere, 'e's in Scarborough.

ROBERT. Aye, well it mekks n'difference.

MOLLY. D'yer like 'im?

ROBERT. He's a man of my heart.

MOLLY *looks at* ROBERT.

It's no use sayin' owt, a've decided.

MARY *sits down in the cage.* STOCKTON s*tands up, he walks round on all-fours in a circle.*

MOLLY. Look at the boy, 'e's gone t'sleep.

ROBERT. Peter?

A slight pause.

'E'as an' all. Fallin' t'sleep on the sand. Shall a pick 'im up'n tuck 'im in?

MOLLY. Leave 'im. It's warm t'night.

ROBERT. The sky is 'is blanket.

STOCKTON *sits down. He settles, he is still.*

MOLLY. A want Peter t'go t'Joe's school.

ROBERT. We've 'ad this before, Molly.

MOLLY. He's a delicate lad.

ROBERT. Yer spoil 'im wi' too much affection.

MOLLY. Mebbe a do, Robert.

ROBERT (*suspiciously*). What's that mean?

MOLLY. Agreein' wi' yer.

ROBERT. Why?

> MOLLY *puts her fingers on* ROBERT*'s knee, she 'walks' them up his leg.*

MOLLY. A won't rest till Peter's at that school.

ROBERT. Where yer tekkin' them fingers?

> ROBERT *watches.* MOLLY *continues.*

> I'll 'ave t'go'n dig up worms in a minute.

> MOLLY *stops.* STOCKTON *lets out a loud shriek.* MOLLY *and* ROBERT *jump. They look at the cage.*

> I don't like it when 'e does that.

> PETER *stirs. He changes position in his sleep.*

> MOLLY *and* ROBERT *look at him.*

MOLLY. 'E's 'avin' bad dreams again.

> PETER *stops, he is still.*

ROBERT. I'd like t'read'n write.

MOLLY. Would yer?

ROBERT. Aye, a would. Be like some o'them farmers. Be like Joe.

> BETSY *enters from the direction of Bay Ness. She is carrying the bag.*

> *She starts to cross quietly in front of the house.*

> It ain't to be.

MOLLY. Wouldn't you like yer son to?

ROBERT. Aye, a would. It'd mekk me proud.

> ROBERT *turns slightly towards the house.* BETSY *stops, hides in a shadow.*

> (*Looking back to* MOLLY.) 'E'd be a proper gentleman, wouldn' 'e?

> MOLLY *smiles.* BETSY *continues on her way.*

> Yer need breedin' t'read'n write, it's not f'us, Molly.

> BETSY *exits towards the town.*

ROBERT *turns to the house*.

Did you 'ear summat jus' then?

MOLLY. No.

ROBERT. Must 'ave imagined it. Me ears're workin' too well.

STOCKTON *lets out a loud shriek*.

Quiet, Frenchman.

PETER *stirs. He is still again*.

MOLLY. Yer get breedin' by learnin' t'read'n write.

ROBERT. Yer born with breedin', woman.

MOLLY. Joe Waterman weren't.

ROBERT. A like Joe, 'e's my friend, but 'e don't know it all.

MOLLY. Who d'folk turn to?

ROBERT. The' turn t'Joe. 'E's a fanciful man, woman.

MOLLY. Yer a strange'n, Robert Storm.

ROBERT. A'm a fisherman. A were born t'fish. A can see mesell now, Molly. A can see me place. Wi' me own cobble. A'm in charge o'mesell at last.

A slight pause.

Young Peter by me side. Young Thomas, young James, young Ned. Young Robin when 'e's back from the war.

MOLLY *smiles*.

All of us out there on the shiny sea.

MOLLY *looks at the sea*.

MOLLY. It's calm night.

ROBERT. Aye. As it should be.

MOLLY. Better than las' night?

ROBERT *nods*. MARY *stands up in the cage*.

MARY. Can I 'ave some food?

ROBERT. Ignore 'im, Molly.

MARY. I'm hungry. What yer goyn t'do with us?

ROBERT. Not up t'me, boy.

MARY. I saw a hangin' once, at the market town of Guisborough.

A slight pause.

MARY *sits down again.*

I don't like 'em, Stockton, d'you?

STOCKTON *is still.*

ROBERT. Tekk the boy t'bed.

MOLLY *stands up. She stoops down.*

MOLLY (*tapping him on the shoulder*). Peter. Peter.

PETER *stirs and groans.*

Peter. Wake up.

PETER *opens his eyes.*

Stand up, love, yer can't sleep there.

PETER *slowly stands up. He groans.*

ROBERT. You go yersell an' all, if yer like.

MOLLY. A'll come back.

MOLLY *puts an arm round* PETER*'s shoulder, they walk towards the house.*

JOE *enters from Bay Ness.*

(*Calling to* ROBERT.) Joe's here.

MOLLY *stops with* PETER. ROBERT *sees* JOE *and stands up.*

ROBERT. Yer dressed in yer finery?

JOE. I've bin goyn round the watches, checkin' the men.

ROBERT. Seen anythin'?

JOE. Nothin'. Anything here?

ROBERT. No. The boy natters on like a woman.

MOLLY. Yer reckon we're safe, Joe?

JOE. Yes. I want to have words.

ROBERT. Speak yer mind.

JOE. Where are they?

ROBERT. Who?

JOE. The French soldiers.

ROBERT. In the caves'n woods.

JOE. We've searched the woods an' caves.

> ROBERT *looks at* MOLLY.

> (*Looking between them.*) We haven't seen them because there aren't any. He's not a Frenchman.

ROBERT. Not a Frenchman?

> ROBERT *looks at the cage*.

JOE. He's an animal. I said so when we first saw him.

ROBERT. I ain't seen an animal like that?

JOE. Neither've I.

> ROBERT *thinks for a moment*.

ROBERT. No, Joe, yer wrong this time. I ain' a cruel man but they deserve t'hang.

> MARY *stands up, she watches them*.

JOE (*looking at her*). Molly?

ROBERT. She's my wife, she don't say nowt.

MOLLY. In any case I agree with 'im.

PETER. I know he's a Frenchman.

JOE. Eh?

PETER. I know he's a Frenchman.

JOE. D'yer? How?

PETER. Me dad said so.

ROBERT. See, even the lad knows.

> *A slight pause*.

JOE. I'm jus' sayin' what a think.

ROBERT (*sitting down*). A like yer, Joe, but sometimes yer stupid. Despite yer learnin' from all them books.

JOE. Aye.

A slight pause.

MOLLY. I'll say goodnight.

JOE. Goodnight, Molly.

MOLLY *exits with* PETER *into the house.* ROBERT *and* JOE *look at one another.* JOE *walks to the bench. He picks up* ROBERT*'s tankard and drinks.*

I've been good to Molly and you, haven't I?

ROBERT. Aye.

JOE. Setting you up with my old cobble. Helpin' yer.

ROBERT. What yer gettin' at, Joe?

JOE (*pointing to the cage. Firmly*). That's an animal. He's no spy. Tomorrow, at the meeting, that's what I'm going to say. Are you goyn to support us, Robert?

ROBERT. 'Ow can a? Jus' lately yer've been mekkin' a big fool o'yerself.

MARY. They're goyn to hang us, Stockton.

STOCKTON *lets out a loud shriek.*

A slight pause.

JOE (*putting the tankard on the bench*). I'd best go t'bed myself. I'll see you in the morning.

ROBERT. Aye.

JOE. Think about what I've jus' said. I'll expect you to support me. Goodnight.

ROBERT. Goodnight, Joe.

JOE *exits towards the town.*

A moment's pause.

MOLLY *appears from the house. She walks down towards* ROBERT.

Is Peter tucked up?

MOLLY. He fell straight back t'sleep.

MOLLY *sits down beside* ROBERT. *She cuddles him for a moment, they stop, they gently hold one another. They are still.*

MARY *sits down in the cage.*

MOLLY *closes her eyes.* ROBERT*'s eyes are open.*

An owl hoots.

MARY. They're goyn to hang us, Stockton.

STOCKTON *walks on all-fours towards* MARY. *He sits down beside her.* MARY *strokes him.*

They're goyn to hang us.

STOCKTON *looks at* MARY. *He speaks without a trace of an accent.*

STOCKTON. I know.

MARY *stops stroking him.*

Do not blame them.

MARY. Can' 'elp it, can a. I hoped you would talk.

ROBERT (*without turning round*). Quiet, boy.

ROBERT *taps out his pipe on the side of the bench.*

MARY. Tekk no notice. Are you really called Stockton?

STOCKTON. No, my real name is Mister Africa. My master, Captain Anderson, bought me from a Zulu warrior. I was his mascot. We travelled the seas together.

MARY *strokes* STOCKTON *for a moment.*

We've carried tea from India, spices from China, coffee from South America and carpets from Persia. It's been a good life.

MARY *strokes* STOCKTON.

My master's schooner was pressed into naval service. We were carrying soldiers to London.

ROBERT *closes his eyes.*

MARY (*hugging* STOCKTON). I love you.

STOCKTON. Do not blame these people, Mary.

MARY. I'll try not to.

STOCKTON. It isn't their fault. Look at them – what do they know of the world?

MARY. They've gone t'sleep. (*Stroking him.*) They're stupid, Stockton.

MARY *stops.*

(*Calling to* ROBERT *and* MOLLY.) Let me out.

ROBERT *and* MOLLY *are silent.* MARY *strokes* STOCKTON *for a moment.*

It's no good shouting, is it?

STOCKTON. No.

MARY *stops.*

These people are good people, Mary.

MARY. Are they?

STOCKTON. Would you be doing any differently?

MARY. A wouldn't be 'angin' meself.

STOCKTON. We'd do exactly the same. We are no better.

MARY *strokes* STOCKTON.

MARY. A don't want t'die.

MARY *stops.*

STOCKTON. In another world, you wouldn't. In this one, you will. We'll leave them our wisdom.

MARY (*hugging him*). I love you.

MARY *breaks the hug.*

Don't you mind dyin'?

STOCKTON. Of course.

The moonlight fades to blackout.

Scene Three

The beach at Bay Ness. Two days later. Midday of Thursday 13 July.

An almost empty beach. Sand.

The sun is high in the sky. A strong bright light.

A gentle sea can still be heard lapping against the shore.

At the back of the beach the bodies of MARY *and* STOCKTON *are hanging from two separate hanging posts. At the front, washed up, lies the body of a British soldier dressed in his uniform.*

JOE *enters slowly from the direction of Bay Ness. He is wearing his working clothes.*

The loud bugle-like call of a herring gull as it flies overhead.

JOE *walks to the British soldier, he turns the body over, he looks at the face.*

ANNE *enters from the direction of the town. She is wearing her best clothes; shoes, a gown, the red cloak, a bonnet.*

JOE *sees* ANNE.

JOE (*surprised*). Mistress?

    ANNE *stops. They are some distance apart.*

ANNE. A young girl at the town told me where you were.

    A slight pause.

JOE. The bodies are being washed up. Some are ours, from Bay.

    A slight pause.

    I don't recognise this one.

    ANNE *walks to* JOE, *she looks at the body.*

ANNE. It's Stephen Cushion, one of our faggers.

JOE. There are bodies the length of the beach. They are English soldiers. How could we not have known?

    JOE *walks away from* ANNE *towards the town. He stops.*

    The French won't come here.

ANNE. France is near the southern coast of England.

JOE. Is it?

ANNE *walks a pace or two from the body.*

Did no one at the town stop you?

ANNE. I walked straight through.

JOE. Why've you come?

ANNE. I came for news of Betsy.

JOE. They've gone, disappeared.

ANNE. Where to, d'you know?

JOE *shakes his head.*

JOE. They disappeared yesterday before the hanging.

ANNE *looks at* MARY *and* STOCKTON.

ANNE. One of them is that boy.

JOE. Yes.

ANNE. I also came for another reason.

Takes a bundle from beneath her arm. They are her notebooks, they are tied with string.

I've brought you these. They are my diaries. I don't want them. They're written about Emma.

A slight pause.

If you would like them? If not, I'll throw them away. They're too much about the past.

JOE. No thank you, Mistress. For the same reason.

ANNE *puts the diaries back underneath her arm.*

The bugle-like call of a herring gull as it flies overhead.

Has Bay Town changed?

ANNE. I tried not to look. I kept my eyes straight ahead.
I was frightened.

A slight pause.

This school, Joe?

A slight pause.

I can promise nothing, but I'd like to help. There's a large old barn in Middlewood. We don't use it. It's half way between Fylingthorpe and Bay Town.

A slight pause.

I can read. I can write. I could teach. With you? For all our children? If you would do me that honour.

A slight pause.

Don't dither, Joe.

JOE. It's such a new idea. I can't believe it would happen.

ANNE. If we want it to.

A slight pause.

JOE. Come with me to the town?

ANNE *hesitates.*

ANNE. I'm not sure I can face them openly.

ANNE *walks to* JOE. *She looks at the sea.*

I hadn't noticed until now, the men are fishing. (*Looking at* JOE.) What will happen?

JOE. We'll see, won't we?

ANNE *and* JOE *exit towards the town.*

The bright sunlight fades to blackout.

The End.

TODAY

To Paul and Natasha Copley

Today was first performed by the Royal Shakespeare Company at
The Other Place, Stratford-upon-Avon, on 23 October 1984, with the
following cast:

PEGGY SMITH	Penny Downie
VICTOR ELLISON	Roger Allam
RICHARD HURLL	David Whitaker
THOMAS ELLISON	George Raistrick
LUCY ELLISON	Amanda Root
WILFRED FOX	Jimmy Yuill
DOROTHY ELLISON	Rowena Roberts
CONSTABLE PRICE	Donald McKillop
REBECCA ELLISON	Kelly Gregory / Charlotte Williams
EDWARD LONGRESSE	James Simmons
ELIZABETH BRADLEY	Polly James
ERNEST HURLL	David Whitaker
HEINZ BAYER	Simon Templeman
PETER DEAN	Jim Hooper
SISTER MARY-JOSEPH	Katharine Rogers
Director	Bill Alexander

Characters

PEGGY SMITH
VICTOR ELLISON
RICHARD HURL
THOMAS ELLISON
LUCY ELLISON
WILFRED FOX
DOROTHY ELLISON
POLICE CONSTABLE PRICE
REBECCA ELLISON
ELIZABETH BRADLEY
EDWARD LONGRESSE
ERNEST HULL, *Richard's twin brother*
PETER DEAN
HEINZ BAYER
SISTER MARY-JOSEPH

ACT ONE
1936
1920
1923

ACT TWO
1937
1946

ACT ONE

In the half-light, the COMPANY *sing the traditional song on which* VICTOR *will base his piece of music.*

This play is partly about a composer, and the music might be simple to begin with, slowly becoming more symphonic as the drama progresses. The notes VICTOR *dictates in Act Two, Scene Four, are an English folk tune. It might be sung simply at the beginning and in an arrangement at the end, and is given as an example to indicate intention.*

Scene One

The lights are snapped up.

A secluded place on the vast lawns of Guisborough Priory.

Monday, 5 October 1936.

The sky is overcast and full of cloud.

On the grass there is a small wicker basket. The handle of an umbrella protrudes from it.

PEGGY SMITH *is standing near the basket. It also contains her purse and a few personal things.*

PEGGY *was born in 1908. She is a well-heeled woman with a fine bone structure. Her face is bright and alert. She is wearing an autumn coat with a matching hat.*

VICTOR ELLISON *is standing near her.*

VICTOR *was born in 1902. He is a big, squarely-built man with thick black hair. He is wearing a good, nut-brown suit which is chalk-marked from a school classroom. He has chalk on the ends of his fingers and a yellow nicotine stain.*

VICTOR *is bent almost double, breathing deeply. He has just entered. He has his hat in his hand.*

VICTOR. I'm sorry. Rebecca's had an accident. I've been at the hospital most of the morning.

PEGGY (*gently, concerned*). Don't worry, what's she done?

VICTOR. Only cut her finger, the little fool.

PEGGY. Victor –

VICTOR. I was more sympathetic with her. (*Showing* PEGGY *the side of his left index finger*.) Here.

PEGGY. How?

VICTOR. On some plateglass.

PEGGY. At school?

VICTOR. Yes. One of the little boys was larking about. On a door. He pushed her into it. She put her hand out to steady herself.

PEGGY. Poor Beccy.

VICTOR. Her headmistress telephoned me. I've so much on, what with the Christmas concert and everything.

PEGGY. Have they stitched it?

VICTOR. No. It's worse than that, unfortunately. That's why I'm in a state.

PEGGY. Which doctor saw her?

VICTOR. A junior doctor. Then your father.

    PEGGY *is looking at* VICTOR. *There is a moment's silence.*

    Yes, that's what I thought.

PEGGY. You didn't say anything?

VICTOR. Yes, Peggy, I told him all about us.

    A slight pause.

PEGGY. Poor you.

VICTOR. I expect it's one of those things.

    VICTOR *holds out his hand.* PEGGY *takes it; their hands fumble together.* VICTOR *straightens up.*

PEGGY. She needs surgery?

VICTOR. Mmm. (*Brightly.*) Well, Dr Smith?

PEGGY. It's not my field, Victor. He's good. I should trust him.

They are holding hands. PEGGY *points to the side of her own left index finger.*

Here? What's Daddy said?

VICTOR. As little as possible.

PEGGY. She's severed the tendon?

VICTOR. Yes. Is it serious, or very serious?

PEGGY. Quite serious.

A slight pause.

Would you like me to be at the hospital?

VICTOR. I don't see how we can. When I took her in I was praying you'd be there.

PEGGY. Didn't you know I wouldn't be?

VICTOR (*brightly*). Yes.

PEGGY (*after a moment's pause*). I'd have to wander in unbeknown. What time's he operating?

VICTOR. This afternoon. I don't even know what he's going t'do.

PEGGY. Try and find the two ends of the tendon and stitch them back. They're difficult things. (*Pointing to the top of his palm.*) It's most likely that the free end will have sprung up here. The first thing he'll have to do is to find it – it'll be lying somewhere in the soft tissue of the palm.

PEGGY *looks at him.*

VICTOR. Go on.

PEGGY. That means opening up the length of her finger until he comes across it.

VICTOR. Is it as vague as that?

PEGGY. Yes.

PEGGY *hesitates.*

VICTOR. You were going to say something else?

PEGGY. The pattern of the suture he'll use to reattach the tendon is very complicated.

VICTOR. I thought you said it wasn't your field.

PEGGY. It isn't.

VICTOR. Go on.

PEGGY. I live with Daddy – we obviously talk with one another.

VICTOR (*leaning forward*). Stop hiding, Peggy.

PEGGY (*looking at him*). Am I?

> *Their hands fumble together. They kiss each other. They embrace in a longer kiss.*

VICTOR. Is it a new operation?

PEGGY. Yes, quite new. He'll be keen to do it.

VICTOR. That makes sense.

PEGGY. It's an operation pioneered in America. He's been waiting. The best results have been obtained with children.

VICTOR. How good a surgeon is he?

PEGGY. Brilliant.

> *They kiss.*
>
> *A slight pause.*
>
> *Their lips move apart.*
>
> *A slight pause.*
>
> *Their hands fumble together.*

Especially with hands. He's a genius.

VICTOR (*smiling*). He skipped around like a spring lamb. I think he thought it was Christmas.

PEGGY. I could wander in.

VICTOR. Not you as well.

> PEGGY *frees her hand. She walks away a pace.*
>
> (*Stepping behind her, putting his arms round her waist.*) I'm sorry.

PEGGY. Yes, that was very unfair.

> PEGGY *turns round. They rub noses.*

VICTOR. I want to make love to you.

PEGGY. I want to make love to you.

RICHARD HURLL *enters.*

RICHARD *was born in 1910. He is a small, squat, broad-shouldered man with sunken eyes. He seems to be wearing all the old clothes he possesses. There is an old rucksack on his back and thick walking boots on his feet.*

VICTOR *and* PEGGY *move apart slightly.*

RICHARD. Could yer tell us the way to Whitby, please?

VICTOR. Er – which road d'you want?

RICHARD. That's what I thought I was askin' you like?

VICTOR. If you go out of the priory. Turn left. Follow the road down t'the market cross. Turn left again. Yer'll be on it.

RICHARD. Left. The market cross. Turn left.

VICTOR. There is another road, depending which you want?

RICHARD. I'm after gettin' t'Whitby. The quickest, yer know.

PEGGY. Are you on foot?

RICHARD. Aye.

PEGGY. I can give you a lift part of the way. (*To* VICTOR.) Am I going to the hospital?

VICTOR (*surprised; it takes him a second to think*). No.

PEGGY. I can take you to the Castleton turn-off.

RICHARD. That'd be great like if yer could.

PEGGY. There's a Riley parked by the church. It is open.

RICHARD. Aye.

A slight pause.

Where's the church like?

PEGGY. Turn right instead of left. It's facing you. Sit inside.

RICHARD. A will. Ta very much.

PEGGY. I might be a few minutes.

RICHARD. You take yer time like.

RICHARD *goes.*

VICTOR. Where the hell did he come from?

PEGGY (*walking away a pace*). I don't know.

VICTOR. I think I ate my heart. Where are you going?

PEGGY. I thought I might go to an auction this afternoon, at Danby. There was some particularly nice silver in the catalogue. Daddy wants me to bid for some cutlery.

VICTOR *is looking at her.*

VICTOR. This can't go on, can it?

PEGGY. Why not? I'm happy.

VICTOR. Are you?

PEGGY *is looking at him.*

PEGGY. I'd hate to lose you, Victor.

VICTOR. Me, too.

There is a moment's silence between them.

VICTOR *holds out his hand, their hands fumble together.*

The operation will be safe, won't it?

PEGGY. He wouldn't do it if it wasn't.

VICTOR. I was meaning the anaesthetic.

PEGGY (*smiling*). I know.

VICTOR. It seems a dangerous event for one little finger.

PEGGY. Stop worrying.

It starts to rain. It happens suddenly. It is raining hard.

(*Going to her basket.*) I've got an umbrella.

PEGGY *puts it up. They stand beneath it.*

VICTOR (*smiling*). Thank goodness for you.

PEGGY (*smiling*). Thank goodness for me.

VICTOR (*taking her hand*). I love you, Peggy.

There is a moment's silence between them.

It hasn't sunk in yet about Beccy.

PEGGY. That's quite usual.

VICTOR. Is it? I hope I've done the right thing. The decision to go ahead didn't seem to involve me.

PEGGY. Trust him. Have faith.

VICTOR. I find having faith very difficult. I never used to. It's age.

PEGGY *smiles*.

What're you smiling at?

PEGGY. Worrier.

VICTOR (*smiling*). Give over, woman.

PEGGY. I'd feel out of place pushed in front of a class of rowdy schoolboys.

VICTOR. They're not rowdy in my class.

PEGGY (*a twinkle in her eye*). Are you harsh with them?

VICTOR. Firm.

PEGGY *moves to kiss him*.

Today we're specialists, aren't we?

PEGGY. What?

VICTOR. Specialist knowledge. Today there's so much it would take a lifetime to begin to understand.

PEGGY *puts her free hand inside his jacket, round his waist*.

We have to begin to accept and not question.

PEGGY. What are you talking about?

VICTOR. Helplessness. (*Smiling*.) Ignore me.

PEGGY. I don't want to ignore you.

VICTOR. I feel happier ignored.

PEGGY. Victor.

VICTOR. No, I do.

PEGGY. Why?

VICTOR. That's not the complete truth.

PEGGY. Nothing ever is.

VICTOR. No.

The church clock nearby begins its chime, ready to strike the hour.

Is it two o'clock already?

PEGGY. Yes.

A slight pause.

If ever you want anything, you know I'm here.

VICTOR. Thanks, love.

PEGGY. D'you mean it?

VICTOR (*looking at her*). Of course I do.

They kiss.

The clock strikes.

I'd better go and teach those boys some music.

VICTOR *exits towards the school.*

The sky has become very dark.

Sudden blackout.

Scene Two

The lights are snapped up.

The moors a few miles from Guisborough. Beside the grassy verge of the Whitby road is a dry-stone wall which has fallen down in the middle.

Two hours later. Four o'clock.

It has stopped raining. The sky is brighter. There is a rainbow.

THOMAS ELLISON *is repairing the wall with a stonemason's hammer. He works methodically, slowly, reshaping the stones, and then fitting them back.*

THOMAS*'s jacket is resting on tap of the wall. His bicycle is leaning against it. The bicycle is a travelling toolkit. Fastened to it in all sorts of ingenious places are saws, chisels, wooden planes, a set square, spirit levels, hammers, mallets, screwdrivers, wood drills, rulers, etc.*

THOMAS *was born in 1880. He is a smallish, broad-shouldered man with bright, alert, mischievous eyes. He Iooks considerably younger than his fifty-six years. His shirt sleeves are rolled up and he is wearing his oldest clothes.*

RICHARD *is standing some distance away. He has just entered.*

THOMAS *hasn't seen him. He works. Slowly he becomes aware of* RICHARD*'s presence. He has turned. He stops work.*

THOMAS. Yer wantin' somethin'?

RICHARD. No, no, you carry on like.

> THOMAS *works. He feels self-conscious.*

> (*Walking towards him.*) A could watch people work all day. Us, yer know. That yer job?

> RICHARD *stops near* THOMAS.

THOMAS. Sometimes. Where yer from, laddie?

RICHARD. Newcastle.

THOMAS (*stopping work*). I thought so.

RICHARD. I was wonderin' if yer could tell us where a was like?

THOMAS (*smiling*). The moors, near Guisborough. Yer lost?

RICHARD. Not lost.

THOMAS. What're you askin' for then?

RICHARD. Confirmation, yer know. I'm tryin' to get to Whitby. It's bloody killin' us this.

THOMAS. Have you walked from Newcastle?

RICHARD. Aye, worst luck. I've had a few lifts. Includin' five miles in a Riley.

THOMAS. You've about another fifteen.

RICHARD. Will a mekk it by tonight, d'yer reckon?

THOMAS. If it's killin' yer, a doubt it.

RICHARD. I shouldn't have opened me gob.

THOMAS. How long've you been out of work?

RICHARD. Two and a half years.

THOMAS. A long time.

RICHARD. Aye, it is, a don't need tellin'. It's bad up in Newcastle. Still bad.

THOMAS. What're you going to Whitby for?

RICHARD. Lookin' for me brother.

THOMAS. Is he there?

RICHARD. Aye, he is, I hope. Me twin like. He left at the back end of
August.

THOMAS. Hoping for what?

RICHARD. The trawlers. Fishin', yer know. Or so we'd heard. I believe
they go all the way up to Iceland?

THOMAS. He's not come back?

RICHARD. No like. All he's had to do is to write a letter. Which is
why he might be in Iceland.

THOMAS *smiles*.

Is there work d'yer know?

THOMAS. I don't.

RICHARD. I asked a bloke in Guisborough – he didn't know either.
It's full of ignorance this part of the world. (*Realising*.) Sorry like,
a didn't mean you.

THOMAS. I always think of the Geordies as being ignorant. I think
you might be wasting your time.

RICHARD. How's that?

THOMAS. If there was work, we'd have heard about it.

RICHARD. You're nearer like?

THOMAS. Yes.

RICHARD. As I've got nearer, that's what I've thought.

THOMAS. It's worth you going to find out.

RICHARD. Aye, thanks mate, thanks.

RICHARD *walks on*.

Thanks, mate. See yer.

THOMAS. What work did you do in Newcastle?

RICHARD *stops and turns*.

RICHARD. The docks, yer know. That's why we thought boats,
trawlers. Bit of a dream mebbe?

THOMAS *smiles*.

Yer have to have yer dreams, don't yer? I worked a chain horse.

THOMAS *looks blank*.

I was right, you are bloody ignorant.

THOMAS. No, I don't know what a chain horse is.

RICHARD. You've no docks, have yer? With a steep hill up from 'em.

THOMAS. No.

RICHARD. Yer put an extra horse on the front to help pull the load. It takes two horses. At the top yer tekk the chain horse off. Yer go up and down, yo-yo like. Used to. The petrol wagon saw the end of me. (*Angry*.) Me brother wrecked a petrol wagon. I couldn't be bothered.

A slight pause.

(*Calm*.) I saw the point of it all like.

THOMAS. I know.

RICHARD (*challengingly*). D'yer?

A slight pause.

(*Calm*.) Blame me feet, mate, this isn't me talking.

THOMAS (*going to his jacket*). Would you like some chocolate?

RICHARD. No thanks like. Aye, all right, go on.

THOMAS (*taking his jacke*t). Are you married?

RICHARD. Aye. Two little lasses. Thankfully only the two, yer know.

THOMAS (*taking a bar of chocolate from his jacket pocket*). Is this the furthest you've looked?

RICHARD. Where d'yer want us to go? Southampton?

THOMAS. It's hard fo'yer.

RICHARD. I sometimes reckon it doesn't do yer any good to talk about what yer already know.

LUCY ELLISON *enters on her bicycle. She is ringing the bell.*

LUCY *was born in 1919. She is a fresh-faced young girl with a wide-eyed expression. There is something of the tomboy about her. She is wearing her school uniform of a blue check, cotton gingham dress over which is an open black coat. She has wellingtons on her feet.*

THOMAS. What do you want, pet?

LUCY (*coming to a halt*). Come to find you. (*To* RICHARD.) Hello.

RICHARD (*shyly*). Hello.

THOMAS. Has school finished?

LUCY. Hours ago. (*Getting off her bicycle.*) Is that chocolate?

THOMAS. I was just going to share it with –

RICHARD. Richard.

THOMAS. Richard.

LUCY (*taking her bicycle to the wall*). I didn't want any anyway. I hate it. I'll watch you.

   LUCY *leans her bicycle against the wall*

   (*Turning.*) By the way, Dad. I've felt another premonition. Something's happened to our Rebecca.

THOMAS. Stop it, Lucy.

LUCY (*going to him*). This time I'm absolutely serious. (*To* RICHARD.) Rebecca's my niece. I hate her. (*To* THOMAS.) Don't I?

THOMAS. No.

LUCY (*linking her arm through his*). I'm sure she's come top in a spelling test or something. Or sums. (*To* RICHARD.) Does that ever happen to you?

RICHARD. What d'you mean like?

LUCY. It happens to me.

   THOMAS *raises his eyebrows.*

RICHARD. It sounds like yer've a vivid imagination.

THOMAS. Let me give Richard his chocolate.

   LUCY *frees her father's arm.* THOMAS *breaks the chocolate into three. He gives a third to* RICHARD.

RICHARD (*taking it*). Am I disturbin' yer?

THOMAS. No.

LUCY. Am I?

THOMAS. Yes.

LUCY. Good.

> THOMAS *gives* LUCY *her third of the chocolate. The three of them eat in silence for a moment.*

> RICHARD *raises his hand.*

RICHARD. Thanks. See yer.

THOMAS. See yer.

> RICHARD *exits along the road towards Whitby.*

> That was rude.

LUCY. What?

THOMAS (*annoyed*). That.

LUCY (*linking her arm through his*). I'm sorry. Forgive me?

THOMAS. No, I don't. I was talking to him.

> LUCY *removes her arm.*

LUCY. I didn't stop you talking.

THOMAS (*angry*). That was rude.

> *A slight pause.*

LUCY. Why was it rude, it wasn't –

THOMAS (*interrupting her*). Because I was talking to him.

LUCY. You keep saying that. I didn't stop you.

THOMAS. You'll get a belt in a minute.

LUCY. Don't be silly, Dad. (*Walking away a pace.*) I wish I understood what the fuss was about.

THOMAS. The fuss is because you've been getting very rude lately.

LUCY (*looking him in the eye*). When have I been rude?

THOMAS (*looking her in the eye*). Just now. I mean it, Lucy.

LUCY. I sometimes wish I was a boy. I mean that.

> *A slight pause.*

> I'd love to be rude, but you're always telling me off when I haven't been. It's not very fair.

THOMAS. I wish I had treated you like a boy. This would never have happened. (*After a moment's pause*.) I loved you a year ago.

LUCY. Now you're being even sillier.

LUCY *links her arm through his*.

Was Victor this much trouble? I bet Victor was good as gold.

LUCY *kisses* THOMAS *on the cheek*. THOMAS*'s eyes flash in both directions*.

(*Insistent*.) Stop looking to see if there's anybody there.

THOMAS (*protesting*). I wasn't.

LUCY. Were.

LUCY *kisses her father on the cheek*.

You're so old-fashioned, Daddy.

LUCY *clings onto his arm*.

It's not as if we were snoggin'.

THOMAS. Lucy.

LUCY. What?

A slight pause.

I remember Victor and Dorothy snoggin'. When I was very little. I didn't know what it was.

A slight pause.

I used to snog my dolly.

THOMAS (*having to hide a smile*). Lucy.

LUCY. I did. Honestly. Don't you believe me?

THOMAS (*putting his hand on hers*). I do. That's the awful thing.

LUCY. I got a splinter in my lips. No, I didn't. That was a joke.

THOMAS *pats* LUCY*'s arm*.

THOMAS. I'm worried about Dorothy and Victor.

LUCY. Why?

THOMAS. Victor's not happy, pet.

LUCY. What's he said?

THOMAS. He hasn't. Not in words.

LUCY. Tell me.

THOMAS (*smiling*). This is where we need a premonition.

LUCY. I agree with you. I think you're right.

THOMAS *looks at her.*

I know you think I'm still a girl. I'm not.

THOMAS. Let me ask your advice then.

LUCY. Oh please, Dad.

THOMAS (*after a moment's pause*). Maybe we're both imagining it?

LUCY. Rebecca said something interesting.

THOMAS. What?

LUCY. She said her daddy had another country in his eyes. I don't
think she knew what she was saying.

THOMAS. When?

LUCY. Oh, a few weeks ago. When he was reading all his Left Book
Club stuff. One evening at home. Rebecca was on his knee. Dorothy
was upstairs. I was at the table doing my homework. Victor looked
far, far away.

THOMAS. He spends too much time with his books. Let's plot
together.

LUCY (*excited*). Please.

A slight pause.

What's the plot? This is like being Guy Fawkes.

THOMAS *smiles.*

I always knew you were sneaky really. (*Whispering in his ear.*)
Sneaky, sneaky, sneaky. (*Hand suddenly shoots into the sky.*) Look.
Look at that.

THOMAS. Where?

LUCY. An aeroplane. See it?

THOMAS *looks.*

THOMAS. Yes.

The aeroplane passes over their heads. It makes a roar as it goes.

LUCY *and* THOMAS *instinctively duck down slightly.*

The aeroplane goes.

LUCY *and* THOMAS *straighten up.*

LUCY. Bloody hell.

Sudden blackout.

Scene Three

The lights are snapped up.

Whitby, by the harbour. A flagstoned quayside.

Six hours later. Ten o'clock.

A bright moon is shining.

The very, very faint sound of the sea. It is like listening to it through a cowrie shell.

An old wooden fish crate is lying discarded on its own.

RICHARD *is standing back from the edge of the quay.*

A slight pause.

He walks forward, past the fish crate, to the edge and looks down at the water. He takes the rucksack from his back and puts it down.

A slight pause.

A seagull cries. It flies across the quay above his head.

RICHARD *walks to the fish crate. He picks it up and brings it back. He turns it long side up so that he can use it as a seat. He sits on it, balancing precariously.*

A seagull cries. It flies back across his head the other way.

RICHARD *is looking at the harbour.*

A pause.

Sudden blackout.

Scene Four

The lights are snapped up.

Guisborough, High Cliff. A few twinkling lights from the town can be seen down below.

A few seconds later. Ten o'clock.

A moon is shining.

VICTOR *is lying sprawled on the grass. He is wearing an overcoat over his suit. There is a handwritten music score in front of him and he has a pencil in his hand. He has a torch.*

WILFRED FOX *is standing quite a distance away. He has just entered from the surrounding woods.*

WILFRED *was born in 1910. He is a little, slightly tubby man, with a strong physique. His hair is always dishevelled. He is thickly dressed in all his old clothes, on the top of which is a loosely hanging poacher's coat.*

VICTOR. It's you, Wilf. I couldn't see who it was.

WILFRED. Only me.

WILFRED *walks forward.*

VICTOR. I thought you were a ghost for a minute.

WILFRED. I wondered who it bloody was sittin' up here. (*Squatting down.*) What yer doin'?

VICTOR. Studying this.

WILFRED *pulls the music score towards him.*

As nosy as ever.

WILFRED (*looking at it*). Yer don't know owt if yer not nosy.

WILFRED *scratches his head.*

VICTOR. Satisfied?

WILFRED. What is it?

VICTOR. A music score.

WILFRED. A can see that much.

VICTOR. It's a carol. Christmas carol.

WILFRED. It's a bit of a waste of time is this, Victor.

VICTOR. I'm doing some work with the boys at school.

WILFRED. Yer read this like? Yer hear the music in yer head?

VICTOR. Yes, I do.

WILFRED. No, no. It tekks all sorts t'mekk the world spin. (*Touching a note*.) What's that one?

VICTOR *sings the note*.

Bloody hell, I thought that was opera.

WILFRED *touches another note*.

VICTOR *sings it*. WILFRED *touches the note next to it*. VICTOR *sings. This snowballs*. VICTOR *is soon singing the tune of the carol*.

After a short while WILFRED *joins in. He sings a harmony to it in perfect pitch. They sing together for a moment*.

VICTOR. How do you know that?

WILFRED. Everyone knows it. It's 'While Shepherds Watch Their Flocks by Night'.

WILFRED *taps the side of his head*.

VICTOR. No, how did yer know? I thought I'd found it.

WILFRED. Come t'me when yer want t'know owt.

VICTOR. Tell me.

WILFRED. My old dad used to 'ave a load of these things, when he played the piano. Stuck in the stool like.

VICTOR. What happened to them?

WILFRED. I've got 'em.

VICTOR. You wazzack.

WILFRED. I didn't know yer were interested.

VICTOR. Can I have them?

WILFRED. Yeh, if yer want 'em.

VICTOR. I'll pay you.

WILFRED. Don't be daft. They're useless

VICTOR. T'you.

WILFRED. Yer can 'ave 'em, on a promise.

VICTOR. What?

WILFRED. That yer remember my old dad when yer mess about with 'em. My old dad was dear to me.

VICTOR. I want them for school.

WILFRED. Yer too bloody fancy, Victor.

VICTOR. Stop playin' the bloody idiot.

WILFRED (*putting his hand up*). Please, sir, yer shouldn't swear in the classroom.

   VICTOR *laughs*.

How's that headmaster of yours?

VICTOR. Don't.

WILFRED. I tripped him up the other day.

VICTOR. Yer what?

WILFRED. Accidentally on purpose.

   VICTOR *smiles*.

Flat on his nose. Outside Dixon's pawnshop. Me bloody gun's went again. I'm sick of pawning the bloody thing.

VICTOR (*smiling*). Idiot.

WILFRED. Aye, a like bein' an idiot, Victor. It's easier. (*Touching the score*.) No, it's a bit of all right is that.

VICTOR. Have yer bin at the top?

WILFRED. Aye. I'm left wi' me hands now like.

   WILFRED *takes a dead rabbit from one of the deep inside pockets of his poacher's coat.*

Four t'night.

VICTOR. Where d'yer take them?

WILFRED. The Seven Stars. The Anchor. I vary it.

VICTOR. What's happened t'yer ferrets?

WILFRED. Had t'sell 'em. Weeks ago.

DOROTHY ELLISON *enters from the town. She is carrying a blanket under her arm.*

DOROTHY *was born in 1902. She is a thin, rather beautiful woman and, although there is something soft about her, she is not frail. She is well-dressed and is wearing a topcoat.*

VICTOR *turns.*

VICTOR. Hello, love.

DOROTHY. Hello. Hello, Wilf.

WILFRED (*nodding*). Now then.

DOROTHY. I've brought us all a rug to sit on.

VICTOR *and* WILFRED *stand up.*

DOROTHY *spreads the blanket.*

WILFRED. Yer reckon we're gettin' dirty then, Mrs Ellison?

VICTOR *and* DOROTHY *sit on the blanket.* WILFRED *sits on the grass.*

DOROTHY. Sit on, Wilf.

WILFRED. No, yer all right.

DOROTHY. What were you talking about?

WILFRED. Ferrets.

DOROTHY. Ferrets?

WILFRED. I was sayin' what buggers the' could be.

DOROTHY. Your language, Wilf.

WILFRED. When the' nip yer fingers.

DOROTHY. My Uncle Victor had ferrets. Not this Victor, another one. In Cambridgeshire. He was the family rogue.

WILFRED. Oh aye?

DOROTHY. Yes, I rather liked him. (*To* VICTOR.) Don't you remember?

VICTOR. Mmm.

DOROTHY (*to* WILFRED). He was a gamekeeper. The rest of my family were books.

WILFRED *nods*.

A slight pause.

Isn't it rather cold sitting here?

VICTOR. I was coming back.

A slight pause.

DOROTHY. Has Victor told you Rebecca had an operation this afternoon?

WILFRED. No, the bugger didn't.

DOROTHY. It seems to have gone very well, we gather. We have been very worried.

WILFRED. What's the lass done?

VICTOR. Cut her finger.

WILFRED (*pulling a face*). Badly like?

VICTOR. Unfortunately.

DOROTHY. The surgeon's very highly regarded, so we're optimistic. (*To* VICTOR.) Isn't he?

VICTOR. Yes.

DOROTHY. Mr Smith, you know. Medicine has been in the family for generations, apparently. I've talked to his daughter in the butcher's.

WILFRED. She'll be all right?

VICTOR. Yes.

DOROTHY. Mr Smith wouldn't let us see her this evening. That's understandable. (*Turning to him*.) I'm surprised you didn't say anything, Victor.

VICTOR. It's early days yet. We don't want to build our hopes up.

DOROTHY. We thought it was remarkable how far surgery has advanced.

VICTOR. She has to have her arm in a splint for a month.

DOROTHY. It's a new operation.

WILFRED. It's goin' t'cost yer a penny or two.

VICTOR. Mr Smith's doing it for nothing.

DOROTHY (*jumping in*). We've money put by for a rainy day. It's what everybody should save for.

WILFRED. Them that can like.

DOROTHY. Everybody can save at least something.

WILFRED. Yer might find us arguin' wi' that like.

DOROTHY. I can argue, too.

WILFRED. A won't, cos o' your lass.

DOROTHY. Victor and I have always been very careful with money.

WILFRED *closes his mouth. He holds his lips together with his fingers.*

VICTOR. Give over, Wilf.

DOROTHY. Wilf knows I'm not accusing him.

WILFRED (*still holding his lips*). Yer've money t'be careful with, Mrs Ellison.

VICTOR. Stop it, Wilf.

WILFRED (*taking his fingers away*). You're as bad an' all.

VICTOR. He's doing it for nothing because it's an operation he's not done before.

DOROTHY (*trying not to be upset*). He hasn't done it for nothing, Victor.

VICTOR. He can't guarantee success.

DOROTHY *looks down.*

A slight pause.

WILFRED. If yer pull the other one yer'll find it rings.

VICTOR (*firmly*). What?

WILFRED. Yer really believe that, don't yer.

VICTOR. I believe what I'm told by people who know better.

WILFRED (*challengingly*). Tut.

VICTOR. You're off your head, Wilf.

WILFRED. I am, am I.

DOROTHY (*looking up*). Let's not argue.

WILFRED. What if it hadn't been your lass, but somebody else's? Not a school teacher's?

DOROTHY. I think you've got the wrong idea.

WILFRED. I have, have I?

DOROTHY. Victor's done more than anyone in this town for people like you.

WILFRED. People like me?

DOROTHY (*apologetically*). I can't help the words I choose sometimes.

WILFRED. Aye, a know.

A slight pause.

VICTOR. Why d'you think I became a teacher, Wilf?

WILFRED (*shrugging*). Search me.

VICTOR. I've pushed for scholarships.

WILFRED. Tut.

DOROTHY. And what's more we've bought shoes for children.

VICTOR (*really angry*). Stop it.

DOROTHY. I won't. It's time he knew these things. We've bought shoes and books and pencils for children. For one family in particular. A very bright boy. His family have ever so little, but they've tried. It is quite terrible the way you speak to us, Wilf.

WILFRED *holds his lips together with his fingers.*

It doesn't do to make a joke of it all the time. It doesn't befit you. (*To* VICTOR.) Does it?

VICTOR. Wilf's only not saying what he thinks.

DOROTHY. He seems to be saying it very precisely.

VICTOR (*he has seen someone in the surrounding trees*). Away.

WILFRED *looks. He pushes the rabbit back into his coat. He stands up and walks away.*

POLICE CONSTABLE PRICE *enters. He is wearing his uniform.*

PRICE *was born in 1886. He is a large, squarely-built man with a moustache.* PRICE *has a flashlight. He turns it off.*

PRICE. Good evening.

VICTOR. Good evening, constable.

WILFRED (*trying not to be nervous*). Now then, Willy.

PRICE *nods.*

PRICE. I'm glad to see you as a matter of fact, Wilfred. Given that Mr and Mrs Ellison don't go poaching.

WILFRED. Yer never know, d'yer?

PRICE. I think I've a shrewd idea in this case. (*To* VICTOR *and* DOROTHY.) I'm sorry about this. (*To* WILFRED.) Is it just rabbits?

WILFRED. We tried takin' the plough-horse, but he didn't want t'go.

PRICE. The Squire up there's been 'avin' a lot of trouble, Mr and Mrs Ellison. (*To* WILFRED.) Where's t'night's thievery? I don't want t'see 'em if they're rabbits. They're wild. It's the geese I'm after. Someone's been gettin' a bit above themselves.

WILFRED. It's just rabbits, yer know that.

PRICE. There's more rabbits in The Seven Stars some nights than customers. There can't be many left.

A slight pause.

These Christmas geese then. What we gonna do about it?

DOROTHY. How many have gone?

PRICE. Half a dozen so far.

DOROTHY. Is it you, Wilf?

WILFRED. Look, it ain't me.

PRICE. I think a might believe yer, Wilf, if yer weren't such a bloody liar. Who, then?

WILFRED. Yer must think a'm stupid, even if a knew.

PRICE. I don't think you're stupid, Wilfred, I know you are.

WILFRED *goes red.*

I'd like one left f'the wife t'buy on December the twenty-third. So, yer can tell Colin Gibson and his scrawny mate, that I know. Got it?

WILFRED (*quietly*). Yes.

PRICE. Has it sunk in? I know it has to fight its way through layers of ignorance.

WILFRED (*can't restrain himself*). Fuck off.

VICTOR (*quickly standing up*). I'll see it's done, constable.

PRICE (*his finger pointing*). I'll do you one day, my lad.

A pause.

VICTOR. I'll see it's done.

PRICE. Thank you, Mr Ellison. If I see them, I'll have to charge them.

A slight pause.

(*To* WILFRED.) Do you ever wonder to yourself why I haven't been promoted?

PRICE *turns the flashlight on.*

Yer reckon I'll go t'heaven, d'yer, Wilf?

WILFRED. Aye, Willy.

PRICE. Goodnight.

VICTOR. Goodnight, constable.

DOROTHY. Goodnight.

PRICE *exits the way he came, back towards the town.*

After a moment VICTOR *sits again.*

Was it you?

WILFRED. I went up with 'em one night. We couldn't catch the bloody things, there were feathers everywhere. They've been goin' back with a net.

DOROTHY. Why, Wilf?

WILFRED (*walking towards* VICTOR). Why is glass opaque?

DOROTHY (*mystified*). So that you can see through it.

WILFRED (*looking at her*). Glass isn't opaque, Mrs Ellison.

DOROTHY. I'm sorry, you're confusing me.

A slight pause.

I wish you'd call me Dorothy.

A slight pause.

It's stealing.

WILFRED (*squatting down*). Aye, mekks it excitin'.

A slight pause.

DOROTHY. It's against the law, taking what doesn't belong to you.

A slight pause.

What do you think, Victor?

VICTOR. He knows anything I would think.

VICTOR *winks at* WILFRED.

WILFRED *smiles.*

DOROTHY. What was that?

VICTOR. Nothing, love.

DOROTHY. You did something. You did something behind my back.

VICTOR. I didn't. Don't be silly. Don't get so upset.

DOROTHY. You did. (*To* WILFRED.) What did he do?

WILFRED. Nothing, Dorothy.

DOROTHY. He did. I wish to know.

VICTOR. I winked at him.

DOROTHY. Why? (*After a moment's pause.*) Why, Victor?

VICTOR. Because I wanted to, love.

DOROTHY. I don't know why, I must say. It just isn't good enough to say you wanted to. I want to do all sorts of things.

VICTOR. Let it rest.

DOROTHY. I won't let it rest. I'm always the one who does that. It just isn't fair. Not fair at all.

VICTOR. Oh, stop it for God's sake.

DOROTHY. No, I won't stop it.

VICTOR. We're in front of Wilf.

DOROTHY. Wilf might as well hear.

A slight pause.

VICTOR. I winked at him, that was all.

DOROTHY. I know I'm naive, it just isn't fair. But there has to be right and wrong sometimes. Someone has to stand up for that.

VICTOR. Nobody's saying the opposite?

DOROTHY. Then why wink, Victor?

VICTOR. We're embarrassing Wilf.

WILFRED. I am a bit like.

Silence.

DOROTHY. And it's no good thinking it doesn't matter.

Silence.

WILFRED *stands up.*

VICTOR. See yer, Wilf.

WILFRED. Aye, see yer.

WILFRED *exits towards the town.*

Silence.

VICTOR. Aren't you cold?

DOROTHY (*still furious*). I'm hot. I'm bloody hot. And why are you always up here?

Silence.

Meeting your friends without me.

Silence.

Why don't we make love any more? I miss you next to me. Your father's noticed.

A slight pause.

Lucy with her bloody impossible questions all evening.

VICTOR. I like it up here.

DOROTHY (*trying not to be upset*). I don't know about us any more, Victor.

VICTOR *takes off his overcoat. He puts it round* DOROTHY*'s shoulders.*

You'll be cold now.

VICTOR. It doesn't matter.

A slight pause.

DOROTHY. That seems to express it very well.

A slight pause.

Why don't we play the piano together? Like we used to in Cambridge? I used to enjoy those evenings so. I felt like Queen Victoria.

A slight pause.

Have those evenings gone forever?

A slight pause.

Why won't you let me look at your music?

VICTOR. It's no good.

A slight pause.

DOROTHY. That seems so negative.

VICTOR. When it's good, I'll tell you.

A pause.

DOROTHY. I feel like an outsider. Is that how musicians write – by being peculiar?

A slight pause.

By having feelings and disappointments they can't explain.

VICTOR. I think any artist wants to get his own back on the world.

DOROTHY. On me?

A slight pause.

VICTOR. Not you, love.

A slight pause.

DOROTHY. I've always thought of music as a joyous thing.

VICTOR. It's irrelevant.

A slight pause.

DOROTHY. It's not irrelevant. Not to us.

VICTOR. There's too many people having too hard a life. (*Instantly changing his mind.*) That was silly.

DOROTHY *puts her hand inside his coat. She runs her fingers beneath the top of his trousers.*

DOROTHY. If we could start making love again. Maybe we'd feel better?

A slight pause.

I miss your penis. If we got one of those rude books out again?

DOROTHY *takes her hand away.*

What you don't seem to realise, is that I want an escape too. (*Trying not to be upset.*) It's easy for you, you don't care about appearances. I know that's very modern. (*Tears coming into her eyes.*) I have to walk down the street knowing that people are looking at me.

VICTOR *looks at her.*

And they are, Victor. Please let's go to London.

VICTOR. Nobody's looking at you.

DOROTHY. Yes, they are. There are eyes in every corner. In London I would be modern. Everyone's modern there.

DOROTHY *wipes some tears from her eyes.*

I'd let you have affairs in London, as long as I could keep you.

VICTOR *looks down.*

I expect you do. Though I've no sort of proof. I could easily have found some. I am right, aren't I?

VICTOR *looks up.*

I feel the eyes on me in this town, knowing that. Don't worry, I haven't told anybody else.

A slight pause.

I should also say that I don't want to know who she is.

A pause.

Sudden blackout.

Scene Five

The lights are snapped up.

The moors. The Whitby road. The dry-stone wall is now complete.

Five days later. Saturday, 10 October. Midday.

The sky is full. It is raining.

WILFRED*'s old bicycle is resting against the wall. Beside it, on the grass verge, there is a large hessian sack with something in it.*

WILFRED *is sitting on the wall. He is wet.*

RICHARD *is standing a short distance away. He has his knapsack on his back. He is wet. He has just entered.*

WILFRED. It's bloody weather for October, isn't it?

RICHARD. Aye like.

WILFRED (*taking an egg from the pocket of his poacher's coat*). Want an egg?

He throws it to RICHARD. RICHARD *catches it.*

RICHARD. Where d'yer get these?

WILFRED. Pilfered 'em.

WILFRED *takes another egg from his pocket. He cracks it on the wall, tilts his head back, opens his mouth, and swallows the contents.*

RICHARD *has walked to the wall. He has done the same.*

(*Taking a third egg from his pocket.*) Want another?

RICHARD (*pulling a face*). One's enough like.

WILFRED *cracks the egg. He eats the contents.* RICHARD *watches him.*

That'd make us feel sick like.

RICHARD *clambers on to, and sits on the wall.*

WILFRED t*akes a bottle of stout from one of the inside pockets of his coat. He takes the stopper out with his teeth. He drinks.*

WILFRED (*passing the bottle*). Where've yer come from?

RICHARD. Whitby.

RICHARD *drinks.*

WILFRED. I went t'bloody Whitby.

RICHARD (*holding the bottle*). I was lookin' for me brother. He's never there, of course.

WILFRED *holds his hand out*.

RICHARD *gives him the bottle*.

Me twin brother, yer know.

WILFRED. No, I didn't know yer'd got a brother. What's yer name?

RICHARD. Richard.

WILFRED. Wilf. Now then.

RICHARD (*smiling shyly*). Now then.

WILFRED (*jumping down from the wall*). What happened to 'im?

RICHARD. From Newcastle t'Whitby, from Whitby to Spain.

WILFRED *lies full length on the grass verge*.

Are you all right, mate?

WILFRED. T' Spain?

RICHARD. Aye. I reckoned he might be in Iceland.

WILFRED. Looks like 'e's gone the wrong way.

RICHARD. Aye, that's what I thought. There's a war on, yer know.

WILFRED *sits up, he drinks from the bottle. He changes position, leaning back against the wall.*

WILFRED (*passing him the bottle*). Yer married?

RICHARD (*taking it*). Aye. You?

WILFRED. Yeh.

RICHARD. Any bairns?

WILFRED. Yeh.

RICHARD. How many?

WILFRED. Two. Two boys.

RICHARD. I've got two lasses.

WILFRED. My biggest lad's just started school.

RICHARD. Mine are littler than that.

WILFRED. Yer gonna finish it?

RICHARD. Aye. Ta.

WILFRED. If yer not, I'll 'ave it.

RICHARD *drinks, finishes the bottle of stout.*

WILFRED *stands up. He takes the hessian sack and walks away a few feet. He turns the sack upside down. A swan tumbles out. It is dead, but unmarked, and perfectly white.*

RICHARD *looks in disbelief*

(*Holding up the long neck.*) Isn't she beautiful?

RICHARD. Where did you get that?

WILFRED. Along there, there's a reservoir.

RICHARD. What yer goin' to do with it?

WILFRED. Eat it. A couldn't stop meself. Know what a mean?

RICHARD. Yeh, but a swan, yer know.

WILFRED. I've got t'pluck the bloody thing yet. Tekk hours.

WILFRED *lays the neck on the ground.*

I hated doin' it.

RICHARD. Yer shouldn't have done it.

WILFRED (*looking at him*). Yer think yer better than me, d'yer?

RICHARD. I didn't say that, mate.

WILFRED. What did yer say?

RICHARD. Nothin'.

WILFRED *stands up.*

WILFRED. I'll break that fuckin' bottle over your fuckin' head.

RICHARD *goes red.*

RICHARD (*nervously*). I don't fight.

WILFRED (*pointing at himself*). I do, I do. I get sick of bein' taken f'a fuckin' idiot.

A slight pause.

RICHARD. I never said you were an idiot.

A slight pause.

WILFRED *kneels down. He starts to stroke the swan.*

You're strange.

WILFRED (*bellowing*). Yer what?

RICHARD (*raising his hands*). I didn't say anythin'.

WILFRED (*jumping up, going to him*). Get off that wall.

RICHARD (*not sure what to say*). No.

WILFRED. Get off, or I'll push you off.

A moment's pause.

RICHARD *gets off the wall. He stands.*

What did yer say?

RICHARD. Listen, mate, I've said, I don't want a fight with yer.

A slight pause.

It's best if I go like before we have trouble.

A slight pause.

All right?

WILFRED *starts to cry. He turns his head away. He sobs.*

A long, long pause.

WILFRED *turns, he lifts his head up.*

Yer should walk somewhere, mate.

A slight pause.

Yer never know what yer puttin' up with, do yer? (*After a moment's pause.*) Till yer've put up with it. Or yer've walked somewhere.

A slight pause.

Yer scared us, I can tell yer. I'll remember today.

A slight pause.

All right?

WILFRED. Yeh.

A slight pause.

It's me, I'm goin' mad.

A slight pause.

I'm fuckin' violent. A weren't like, when a were a bairn, just after the war.

RICHARD. Yer lose yer dad?

WILFRED. No.

RICHARD. I lost mine like.

WILFRED. It didn't 'elp 'im; 'e died a few years after.

RICHARD. Maybe I'll walk to France to find his grave. (*After a moment's pause.*) I hardly remember him, yer know.

A slight pause.

It's important. History. Our lives.

WILFRED (*heartfelt*). Yeh, but the' think a'm stupid.

RICHARD. I weren't meaning school, mate. Yer have to look at history for yourself.

WILFRED. Yeh, but if I'm stupid.

RICHARD. They want yer to think you're stupid.

A slight pause.

WILFRED. It don't make no bloody sense.

A slight pause.

Yer from Newcastle?

RICHARD. Aye.

WILFRED. Yer goin' back?

RICHARD. Aye, a suppose so.

WILFRED. What fo'?

RICHARD. For me bairns, mate, and me wife. (*After a moment's pause.*) I went to Whitby for me dreams. To tell you the truth like, it's been a nightmare.

A slight pause.

See yer.

WILFRED. See yer, mate.

RICHARD *walks away.*

Take me bicycle, if yer want.

RICHARD. No thanks like. Aye, all right, go on.

RICHARD *gets on the bicycle, he has his foot on the pedal.*

Yer sure yer sure?

WILFRED. Yeh, why not. Watch the front brake, it doesn't work.

RICHARD *bicycles off towards Guisborough.*

WILFRED *watches him go.*

A slight pause.

Sudden blackout.

Scene Six

The lights are snapped up.

The garden of the Chaloner Hospital.

Sunday, 1 November.

The sun is shining.

REBECCA ELLISON *is sitting in a wheelchair under the boughs of a tree. She is wearing a white nightdress and a dressing gown, and there is a blanket over her knees and legs. Her left arm is in a sling, it keeps her hand on her right shoulder. She is reading a book.*

REBECCA *was born in 1928. She is a pretty little girl with fair hair.*

PEGGY, *in a white coat, is kneeling on the grass in front of her.*
PEGGY *is holding a pair of spectacles.*

PEGGY. What are you reading?

REBECCA. *Oliver Twist* by Charles Dickens.

PEGGY. What's it about?

REBECCA. Oliver, who has terrible things happen to him. You must have read it?

PEGGY. Yes, I have.

REBECCA. Mummy says I have to be clever.

PEGGY (*putting the spectacles on*). May I look at your hand, Rebecca?

REBECCA. Yes.

> PEGGY *helps* REBECCA *take her arm from the sling.*

> REBECCA's *forearm is in a long splint which pushes her wrist into thirty degrees of flexion. The whole forearm, and especially the hand, are heavily bandaged.*

Why don't we put *Oliver* on the grass?

> PEGGY *takes the book from* REBECCA's *lap.*

It still smells a bit. (*Smelling it.*) Pooh.

> PEGGY *examines the hand, delving very carefully with a pair of tweezers into the bandages across her palm to reveal the bottoms of her fingers.*

PEGGY. This hand needs a very good wash.

> REBECCA *looks as if she is about to move them.*

Keep your fingers still, love.

REBECCA. Yes.

PEGGY (*after a moment's pause*). It's healed very nicely where the stitches were.

REBECCA. Am I still a guinea pig?

> *A slight pause.*

PEGGY. Is your wrist aching?

REBECCA. A little bit. I've got used to it.

PEGGY. The splint can come off tomorrow.

REBECCA (*excited*). Can it? Oh, good. Just in time for bonfire night.

PEGGY (*still concentrating on her work*). You'll need to be here for another six weeks yet, Beccy.

REBECCA. Don't they have fireworks in a hospital?

PEGGY. I think I might be able to find some. One or two because you're special.

DOROTHY *enters. She is wearing an autumn coat.*

REBECCA. Mummy.

DOROTHY. Hello.

PEGGY (*leaving* REBECCA*'s hand, sitting back on her haunches. Brightly*). Hello, Mrs Ellison.

In the same movement PEGGY *stands up.*

She takes her spectacles off and puts them in her coat pocket.

REBECCA. I'm going to have a bonfire.

PEGGY. Fireworks, Beccy. If we had a bonfire we might set the hospital alight.

DOROTHY (*smiling*). That's nice, isn't it?

REBECCA. Yes.

DOROTHY. Thank you.

PEGGY. There are three or four children in the public wards who could come too. It's strictly against the rules.

DOROTHY. Mr Ellison's not called here, by any chance?

PEGGY. I was expecting him with you.

REBECCA. Where's Daddy?

DOROTHY. In a minute. (*After a moment's pause.*) I'd like a word with you, if I may.

PEGGY *and* DOROTHY *walk away.*

REBECCA. Where are you going?

DOROTHY. Mummy won't be a moment, darling.

The two women have stopped.

PEGGY. You're upset?

DOROTHY (*calmly*). No. Yes.

PEGGY (*gently*). Why don't you tell me what it is?

DOROTHY. I know what I'm going to say must seem a frightful imposition. A cheek, almost.

PEGGY. Yes?

DOROTHY. I have very few women friends. It's so silly, I'm so worried. Victor – Mr Ellison's – gone.

PEGGY *is not sure how to react.*

PEGGY. He's gone. Where's he gone?

DOROTHY. I don't know.

PEGGY. Perhaps he wanted to be by himself for a few days.

DOROTHY. Why should he?

A slight pause.

He's not been to see Rebecca?

PEGGY. No.

DOROTHY. How could he do this to a child?

PEGGY. I don't know, Mrs Ellison.

REBECCA. Shall I put my arm back in the sling?

PEGGY. Yes. Be careful.

DOROTHY (*after a moment's pause*). I thought if I had a word with you it might make me feel better. It has already. I feel so, so alone without him.

PEGGY. When did he go?

DOROTHY. Yesterday morning. There was nothing. No note. Not anything.

REBECCA *is putting her arm back into the sling.*

PEGGY (*calling to her*). Are you managing?

REBECCA. Yes.

PEGGY. Don't move those fingers, will you.

REBECCA. No.

DOROTHY. Why did you say he might want to be by himself?

PEGGY (*after a moment's pause*). Men like Mr Ellison do from time to time.

DOROTHY. Have I been cruel to him?

PEGGY (*after a moment's pause*). No.

A slight pause.

DOROTHY. You see, doctor, I think he might have gone to Spain. Now I know that sounds ridiculous. Victor's a socialist. I'm not, I'm afraid. These socialist people are sometimes very selfish, and Victor is easily led. He goes to meetings.

A slight pause.

If he has gone to Spain, there is a war being fought. It will do them no good, I think. (*After a moment's pause.*) But cost people money. And possibly their lives.

REBECCA *picks up her book. She starts to read.*

If we became friends I'd tell you the whole truth. It really is just terrible. (*After a moment's pause.*) I've felt, forgive me, that I've been getting to know you.

A slight pause.

PEGGY. I don't know what to say, Mrs Ellison.

DOROTHY. I think I'm beginning to hate men. (*After a moment's pause.*) Yes, I do, I hate men, Dr Smith.

PEGGY. Have you tried telephoning his school?

DOROTHY. It's Sunday.

PEGGY. Yes, of course. (*After a moment's pause.*) I obviously didn't know Victor.

DOROTHY. No. I'm sorry. (*After a moment's pause.*) What shall I tell Beccy?

PEGGY. I wouldn't say anything for the time being.

DOROTHY (*smiling*). I haven't asked about her.

PEGGY (*smiling*). She's doing just fine.

DOROTHY. We'll know tomorrow whether the suture's held?

PEGGY. Yes. My father's big day.

DOROTHY. What next?

PEGGY. The hard work begins, to get a very tired finger active again. It's an extensive programme. Beccy's going to have to work really really hard.

REBECCA (*looking up from her book*). What's that about me?

DOROTHY. Mummy shan't be long.

REBECCA reads her book.

PEGGY holds up a pair of crossed fingers.

PEGGY. Let us hope, Mrs Ellison.

DOROTHY. If there are problems, what might they be?

A slight pause.

Shouldn't I ask?

PEGGY. We think the main thing to watch for is if the tendon itself has adhered to the tunnel in the finger down which it glides. And the profundus muscle will need re-educating. The idea of the splint is to halt muscle and flexor tendon function.

DOROTHY. Yes.

PEGGY. But in halting the function you immediately set up the chances of adherence. Because the tendon is still. Like any wound it will repair and fasten to its surrounding surface. Which is why we must get it moving. Get it gliding, to stop that. We couldn't do it before the fourth week because the tendon repair would snap under even the tiniest amount of pressure from flexion.

DOROTHY. Yes.

PEGGY. If active, and later passive, movement of Beccy's finger fails to produce improvement

A telephone starts to ring in one of the adjacent offices.

I'm sorry, there's my telephone ringing, I must go. But it is possible to try tenolysis as a secondary procedure.

PEGGY dashes off.

REBECCA looks up from her book.

REBECCA. My tendon's been a lot of trouble, Mummy.

DOROTHY. Yes.

DOROTHY walks to REBECCA.

REBECCA. Would you read to me?

DOROTHY sits on the grass.

(*Passing her the book, her finger on the place.*) From there.

DOROTHY (*reads*). 'The Dodger sighed again, and resumed his pipe:
as did Charley Bates. They both smoked, for some seconds, in
silence.

"I suppose you don't even know what a prig is," said the Dodger
mournfully.

"I think I know that," replied Oliver, looking up. "It's a th– ; you're
one, are you not?" inquired Oliver, checking himself.

"I am," replied the Dodger. "I'd scorn to be anything else." Mr
Dawkins gave his hat a ferocious cock, after delivering this
sentiment, and looked at Master Bates, as if to denote that he would
feel obliged by his saying anything to the contrary.

"I am," repeated the Dodger. "So's Charley. So's Fagin. So's Sykes.
So's Nancy. So's Bet. So we all are, down to the dog. And he's the
downiest one of the lot!"'

Sudden blackout.

Scene Seven

A spotlight is snapped up.

*The attic at the Ellisons' house. A light bulb hangs from the cobwebbed
rafters of the low ceiling.*

Christmas Eve.

THOMAS *is sitting on the only chair.*

*In front of him is a small wooden box in which there are letters. He has
one letter in his hand.*

LUCY *is behind him. She is wearing a pair of trousers and a shirt which
are far too big for her. Her hair is pushed up inside a cap. She is leaning
on* THOMAS *with her arms around her neck.*

LUCY. I've brought you a hat.

LUCY *stands up. She puts a paper hat on his head.*

THOMAS. Don't I look silly?

LUCY. That's the idea.

He takes it off.

Oh, don't.

THOMAS (*putting it back on*). I must look almost as foolish as you.

LUCY. They're Victor's. Like them?

THOMAS. No.

LUCY. Why not. What do I look like?

THOMAS. A boy. I wish you wouldn't, Lucy.

LUCY. It does you good. Beccy's helping with the Christmas tree.

THOMAS (*smiling*). I will come down.

LUCY *is looking at him.*

A pause.

I will.

A pause.

LUCY. No, you won't.

A pause.

THOMAS. I will.

A pause.

(*Picking up a few letters.*) I was reading Victor's letters.

He puts them down.

Pause.

LUCY. No, you won't, Daddy.

THOMAS. The Cambridge ones. Looking for a clue.

LUCY. What is the point of that?

THOMAS. I loved him.

A slight pause.

Victor has had most of my life, Lucy.

A slight pause.

LUCY. No, you won't, Daddy.

THOMAS. You're behaving as if you don't care.

LUCY. He's gone.

THOMAS *starts to take the paper hat off.*

Leave it on your head, and do as you're told.

THOMAS *puts the hat back.*

A pause.

(*With* THOMAS*'s line.*) I don't see the point of sitting up here.

THOMAS (*with* LUCY*'s line*). I don't want to talk about it, Lucy.

A pause.

LUCY. I'm not going.

A slight pause.

Stillness.

The lights fade to half-light.

ELIZABETH *and* EDWARD *enter.*

They hum the opening folk tune.

THOMAS *and* LUCY *leave.*

Scene Eight

The lights travel up.

A small wooded coppice adjoining ELIZABETH BRADLEY*'s house by the River Thames in Twickenham.*

Saturday, 9 October 1920.

A warm autumn sunlight is filtering through the trees.

EDWARD LONGRESSE *is lying asleep on the ground, he has his head on a large yellow cushion.*

EDWARD *was born in 1902. He is a tall, good-looking boy with fair hair. He is wearing white trousers and jacket, and a white shirt.*

ELIZABETH BRADLEY, *with a long peacock feather in her hand, is standing some distance away. She has just entered.*

ELIZABETH *was born in 1874. She is a petite woman, but she has none of the feyness that might go with that. Her face has quite a hard edge to it. She cares little for her appearance, but nevertheless her clothes are fine.*

ELIZABETH *walks forward, she tickles his chin with the feather.* EDWARD *opens his eyes.*

ELIZABETH. Here you are, Edward, this is a surprise.

EDWARD (*still*). I trust a nice surprise, Aunt.

ELIZABETH. Yes, I shall sit with you.

>   ELIZABETH *starts to sit.* EDWARD *jumps up.*

EDWARD. Would you like the cushion? I stole it from the drawing room.

ELIZABETH (*sitting*). You're young, you keep it, dear.

>   EDWARD *sits.*

>   Yes, Pickles would tell you I've been lunching with that awful Mrs Wilson.

EDWARD. She said.

ELIZABETH. Of course if you'd told me you were coming I would have cancelled the thing.

EDWARD. I didn't know until this morning.

ELIZABETH (*strongly*). I would have telephoned her. (*Smiling.*) Goodness me, I haven't told you off since you were fourteen. What had you done then, I wonder?

EDWARD. Put itching powder in Pickles's vests.

>   ELIZABETH *laughs.*

ELIZABETH. Yes, Mrs Wilson has one of those toy thingummies, Edward. What are they called? You know.

EDWARD (*shaking his head*). I don't. What?

ELIZABETH. It sits on her lap like a spare hand.

EDWARD. A dog.

>   ELIZABETH *makes a playful swipe at him with her hand.*

ELIZABETH. It's a special dog. A special thingummy.

EDWARD. You're dotty, Aunt.

ELIZABETH. She gloats over it like a meal. It quite put me off my shepherd's pie.

EDWARD *laughs*.

So, Edward, here you are. Haven't you a telephone?

EDWARD. I thought you'd be delighted to see me.

ELIZABETH. I am, dear, I am. That's why I'm annoyed.

ELIZABETH holds out her hand.

EDWARD *takes it*.

I've missed you.

EDWARD. Me, too.

ELIZABETH (*smiling*). Isn't that a little like a lie?

EDWARD. Don't be silly.

ELIZABETH *laughs. Their hands part.*

ELIZABETH. What do we do if we live alone like Mrs Wilson?

EDWARD. Be doggyless.

ELIZABETH. I think so. The truth is I've given up caring about what the world thinks about me. (*Smiling.*) You've changed, Edward. Haven't you?

EDWARD (*smiling*). What are you talking about?

ELIZABETH. Good. I'm very pleased.

EDWARD. I've only been away for a month.

ELIZABETH. We sometimes change more in one day than we do in ten years.

EDWARD. What nonsense.

ELIZABETH. Is it?

EDWARD. What nonsense.

ELIZABETH (*after a moment's pause*). Yes, dear, I'm sure you're right.

A slight pause.

What about some lemonade?

EDWARD. I'm fine, Elizabeth.

EDWARD *smiles*.

ELIZABETH. That smile is hiding something. I'm not sure what. Forget my little jealousies. Did you have luncheon?

EDWARD. Yes, Aunt, in a public-house. A very rowdy place, fully of jolly men singing.

ELIZABETH. Oh dear.

EDWARD. No, it was wonderful. I did feel foolish, being on my own. And having a car which everyone looked at. And then spending over an hour taking rides. And then not feeling foolish, but very upper-class. And trying to explain that I wasn't. And after the rides yet another drink of beer, and then another. Which is why I was sleeping. This is 1920, well and truly.

ELIZABETH (*smiling*). Take care of your youth. Don't have age hurry you.

EDWARD. I will.

EDWARD *smiles*.

ELIZABETH. Such a reticent smile.

EDWARD (*laughing*). What are you talking about.

ELIZABETH. A smile full of doubts. When I was eighteen I wanted to rush.

EDWARD. I can't think of you at eighteen.

ELIZABETH. I was beautiful.

EDWARD. Like Mother?

ELIZABETH. No, much, much more than your Mother.

EDWARD. Mother was lumpy?

ELIZABETH *makes a playful swipe at him with her hand*.

ELIZABETH (*smiling*). As lumpy as a fish.

EDWARD. I shall tell her.

ELIZABETH *laughs. She takes* EDWARD*'s head and places it in her lap*.

ELIZABETH. So, Edward, tell me about Cambridge?

EDWARD. What is there to say?

ELIZABETH. Tell me everything.

EDWARD (*brightly*). Apart from the truth that I hate it.

ELIZABETH (*surprised*). Oh?

EDWARD. I don't hate it. It hates me.

ELIZABETH. Isn't Cambridge a collection of buildings like any other.

A slight pause.

Places are what we make of them. Not they us.

A slight pause.

How long have we known each other, Edward? As adults, not as adult and child?

EDWARD. Since I put the itching-powder in Pickles's vests.

ELIZABETH *makes a playful swipe at him with her hand. She moves his head and stands up.*

ELIZABETH. Have you run short of money already?

A slight pause.

(*Walking away a pace.*) I shan't know unless you tell me?

ELIZABETH *turns and looks at him.*

Don't hate yourself, whatever it is. Hatred is such an ugly thing.

EDWARD (*quite enjoying it*). I'm in love. With a boy. It's beastly.

ELIZABETH. Boys are there to be loved.

EDWARD. Are they?

ELIZABETH. Sometimes by girls, sometimes not.

EDWARD. I thought you might be shocked.

ELIZABETH. I cannot pretend it's what I expected to hear.

EDWARD. What would you do?

ELIZABETH. I'd do whatever I wanted, dear.

EDWARD. I haven't spoken to him.

ELIZABETH. Is he at Kings?

EDWARD. Yes, Aunt. He's a working-class boy.

ELIZABETH. Is that his appeal?

EDWARD (*brightly*). I think I might jolly well like being one of those.

ELIZABETH *smiles. She walks to him.*

ELIZABETH. I fell in love with our post-boy.

EDWARD (*shocked*). Aunt Elizabeth.

ELIZABETH (*leaning forward*). As did your mother. But I was the one who saw his bottom.

ELIZABETH *puts a finger to her lips.*

Don't you dare tell anyone that. It was said in confidence.

EDWARD (*calling, not very loudly*). Pick-les.

ELIZABETH. Edward, you promised.

EDWARD. I didn't. Pick-les.

ELIZABETH. Edward.

EDWARD. What?

They are looking at one another. ELIZABETH *makes a dive for him.* EDWARD *stands up.*

(*Still quietly.*) Pick-les, Pickles, Pickles, Pick-les.

ELIZABETH (*looking up at him*). Oh, you are naughty. I shall tell you nothing else.

EDWARD. How old were you?

ELIZABETH *is silent.*

Pick-les.

ELIZABETH. Nineteen, Edward.

ELIZABETH *suddenly laughs.*

It was a spotty bottom.

EDWARD. How on earth did you see it?

ELIZABETH (*putting a finger in front of her lips*). Sssh.

ELIZABETH *motions.* EDWARD *bends his head.* ELIZABETH *whispers something in his ear.* EDWARD *straightens up.*

EDWARD (*a sing-song voice*). Pick-les. Elizabeth saw twenty spotty bottoms, swimming in the river.

ELIZABETH (*jumping up*). Stop it, Edward.

EDWARD (*getting louder*). Pickles. Pickles.

ELIZABETH (*jumping up, trying to put her hand in front of his mouth*). Stop it, don't, stop it.

EDWARD. Pickles. Pickles.

ELIZABETH. Stop it.

They stop.

ELIZABETH *laughs.*

Oh dear.

EDWARD (*looking about*). Has someone pruned the apple trees?

ELIZABETH. Yes, I got Jack to do them. They do look better, don't they?

EDWARD (*nodding slightly*). Mmm.

ELIZABETH. He did them all in two days. It's time I did these things. (*Looking about.*) I was thinking of getting a goat.

EDWARD. A goat. What for?

ELIZABETH. I thought she'd keep the grass down in summer. I'd milk her, too. I've seen such similar things in Italy.

EDWARD. Well, yes.

ELIZABETH. In Italy they make cheese with the milk.

EDWARD. You're not going to try that as well?

ELIZABETH. I thought I might, Edward.

EDWARD. But what on earth for? Aren't they a rather beastly, smelly animal? I mean, a goat.

ELIZABETH. Or a pig. I can't eat all the apples.

EDWARD. Please, Aunt, a goat.

ELIZABETH. Two goats.

EDWARD. It's two now.

ELIZABETH. They will be company for one another. Good.

A slight pause.

Bring that young man here soon, Edward.

The lights fade.

Scene Nine

The lights fade up.

A lawn beside King's College in Cambridge.

Two days later. Monday, 11 October.

A warm, autumn sunlight.

VICTOR, *in a new suit, is lying on his stomach on the grass. He is surrounded by open textbooks, and he is writing an essay.*

EDWARD *is some distance away, upside-down, standing on his hands. He has just entered.*

EDWARD *'walks' forward.* VICTOR *hears him and looks up from his essay. When he is a short distance away,* EDWARD *rights himself.*

EDWARD. Isn't it such beautiful weather for October?

VICTOR (*shyly*). Yes.

EDWARD. We haven't been formally introduced. (*Leaning forward, stretching out his hand.*) I'm Edward Longresse.

VICTOR (*stretching forward*). Victor. Victor Ellison.

Their hands can barely stretch the distance, but they manage to shake.

EDWARD. We share the same staircase, you and I.

VICTOR (*shyly*). Yes, I know.

EDWARD *feels suddenly shy.*

EDWARD. I've asked the porter if he can't mend the stair rail where it's broken. How are you finding King's?

VICTOR. Well, hard work, at the moment.

EDWARD. I don't seem to have got into the swim of things. I'm not absolutely sure which way to dive.

EDWARD *goes red.*

VICTOR. There's so much t'do, isn't there?

There is a moment's shyness between them. EDWARD *sits.*

EDWARD. Why do you work out here on the lawn?

VICTOR. My rooms get stuffy.

EDWARD. Oh yes?

VICTOR. I used to work outside at home.

EDWARD. Where do your people live?

VICTOR. In Yorkshire.

EDWARD. I haven't been to Yorkshire, unfortunately.

EDWARD *goes red.*

VICTOR. North Yorkshire. Near the Cleveland Hills. Guisborough. It's a little market town, yer know.

EDWARD. My family are in India. In the Punjab.

VICTOR *nods.*

It's a beastly place. Where the cockroaches scuttle over your food. My father is a lawyer in the Civil Service.

EDWARD *goes red.*

I hope I'm not sounding like a perfect fool.

VICTOR. No.

EDWARD. I saw a hanging in the Punjab. A coolie was led, handcuffed, through the streets to the gallows. One saw the whites of his eyes through the wet, early morning air. He was a Hindu, held by a man with a fixed bayonet. At eight the bugle called, and the Hindu fell. The doctor present had to pull his legs because he didn't want to die.

VICTOR. That's awful.

EDWARD. I've written an account of it. What is your father?

VICTOR. He's a joiner.

EDWARD. Oh yes?

VICTOR. In Guisborough, yer know.

EDWARD (*smiling*). In Yorkshire?

VICTOR (*smiling*). That's right. Yer get the impression with 'im that he should be doin' more than that.

EDWARD. What do you mean?

VICTOR. If he'd been born like us, he might be here. He left school early.

There is a moment's shyness between them.

EDWARD. You're a music scholar?

VICTOR. Yes.

EDWARD. Is your father musical?

VICTOR. No. I don't know why it suits me. I was encouraged.

EDWARD. So very modest. The provost told me you were a brilliant pianist.

VICTOR (*shrugging*). I don't know.

EDWARD. You're going to play the organ in chapel?

VICTOR. Yes.

There is a moment's shyness between them.

EDWARD. The provost is an old friend of my father's. I had tea with him.

There is a moment's shyness between them.

VICTOR (*smiling*). I find it difficult making friends.

EDWARD (*smiling*). I have been asked to the parties. I've decided not to go.

VICTOR. Why?

EDWARD. It will be like school.

VICTOR. It seems to be a place f' parties – for enjoying yourself. It surprised me. I enjoy working. Are you on a scholarship?

EDWARD. Yes. My family are comfortable, but not rich. My aunt in Middlesex is the one with all the money.

VICTOR. I reckon it's the sort of place you only come to once.

EDWARD *smiles*.

A lot of it's like another language to me. All these toffs. I knew
there'd be a few. I'm sorry, I didn't mean you.

EDWARD. Don't apologise, I am a toff.

There is a moment's shyness between them.

Isn't it so superficial? Like you I would like to work hard. It seems
important.

VICTOR. I've noticed the light under your door on quite a few nights.

EDWARD. I have a wish to find my own coterie.

There is a moment's shyness between them.

EDWARD *stands up.*

I should leave you if you're working.

They shake hands.

The lights fade.

A slight pause.

The lights fade up.

The wooded coppice at ELIZABETH BRADLEY's *house in
Twickenham.*

The following weekend. Sunday, October 17th.

The sky is overcast.

VICTOR *and* EDWARD *are standing on the grass a yard or two
apart. They are wearing scarfs.* EDWARD *has an old croquet
mallet which he leans on, and swings from side to side,
occasionally.*

VICTOR. How did your auntie acquire the house?

EDWARD. My uncle bought it for her. Elizabeth saw it, and fell in
love at once.

VICTOR. Is she very rich?

EDWARD. Extremely. She's a millionairess.

VICTOR (*pulling a face*). Really? Phew.

EDWARD. From my Uncle John. She married money. Before the
house here in Twickenham, she lived in London. My Uncle John,
was the Bradley Bicycle.

VICTOR *pulls a face*.

Have you heard of them?

VICTOR (*interrupting him*). My father has a Bradley. He goes to work on it.

EDWARD. It was the very first safety bicycle. He mass-produced them, and made a fortune. He was an engineer. A thousand accountants run the company now.

VICTOR *nods*.

Uncle John was killed in an aeroplane crash.

VICTOR *pulls a face*.

VICTOR. When?

EDWARD. Six, seven years ago, in the January before the war.

VICTOR (*under his breath*). Phew.

EDWARD. He flew them as his hobby.

VICTOR (*shaking his head*). All this is beyond me.

EDWARD. I hope I'm not seeming pompous?

VICTOR. No, go on, like.

EDWARD. He was trying to beat the altitude record set by Georges Legagneaux of France. I was in preparatory at the time. Uncle and Aunt were in Tunis in Africa.

VICTOR. What happened?

EDWARD. No one is quite sure. He had to reach over twenty thousand feet.   '

VICTOR. Phew.

EDWARD. The wreckage of the aeroplane was eventually found, but Uncle John's body never was. Elizabeth had to spend days while they searched the desert.

VICTOR *nods*.

He was in a Rumpler biplane.

VICTOR. Why were they in Africa?

EDWARD. Because the air is much lighter.

VICTOR. Oh, yes.

EDWARD. Please don't mention aeroplanes to Elizabeth.

VICTOR (*smiling*). I'm frightened of her already.

EDWARD (*smiling*). Why?

VICTOR. The picture you paint.

EDWARD. She takes one by surprise, quite often.

VICTOR (*as much to himself*). I mustn't mention aeroplanes.

EDWARD *smiles*.

EDWARD. Don't worry about her.

VICTOR. I'm not.

VICTOR *wipes his hands on his trousers*.

EDWARD. What are you doing?

VICTOR *mimes shaking hands*.

VICTOR. Getting ready.

EDWARD *laughs*.

If she's an atheist, why's she at church?

EDWARD. It's where she meets her cronies.

VICTOR. Yet she's all this money?

EDWARD. Aunt Elizabeth doesn't flaunt herself.

EDWARD *mimes hitting a croquet ball*.

VICTOR. Has she any children?

EDWARD (*smiling*). Just me.

VICTOR. I meant of her own?

EDWARD. No. I'm more her child than I am my mother's.

VICTOR. She brought you up, Edward?

EDWARD. Yes. I hardly know my own parents. They're little bits of punctuation in a few letters.

VICTOR. Don't they come back?

EDWARD. Every seven years or so.

VICTOR. Isn't that frightening?

EDWARD. Not when it's what you are used to. And her and my mother hardly see eye to eye.

VICTOR. What about?

EDWARD. About me, and about money. My mother's terribly jealous.

VICTOR. Which of them d'you prefer?

EDWARD. Oh, my aunt.

VICTOR *mimes shaking hands. He laughs.* EDWARD *laughs.*

ELIZABETH *enters. She is wearing her best clothes.*

ELIZABETH (*smiling*). Such jollity.

EDWARD. Aunt, this is –

ELIZABETH. Oh, I don't want to know his name, dear. Names spoil everything.

VICTOR *and* ELIZABETH *walk towards each other.*

VICTOR *wipes his hand on his trousers.*

They shake hands.

VICTOR. Edward was telling me about aeroplanes.

ELIZABETH *laughs. She walks away a few paces. She turns.*

ELIZABETH. And Edward told you not to mention them?

VICTOR (*looking down slightly*). Yes, I'm sorry.

ELIZABETH (*smiling*). It is so lovely to meet his friends.

VICTOR (*shyly*). Thank you for having me for the day.

ELIZABETH. We will have luncheon. And then you shall play the piano.

VICTOR. Yes.

ELIZABETH. And I have some pieces I would like explained. By Schubert.

VICTOR. I'll try.

ELIZABETH. No, dear, you will succeed.

VICTOR *looks at* EDWARD.

VICTOR (*going to* ELIZABETH). Mrs Bradley, I think we've got off on the wrong foot.

ELIZABETH. I will listen to you and see.

VICTOR. Edward didn't tell me you were interested in music.

ELIZABETH. I have an amateur appreciation.

VICTOR. That is all I have.

ELIZABETH. Then why are you at King's?

VICTOR *doesn't know what to say.*

Dear, I do so hate modesty. We will go to lunch.

ELIZABETH *links her arm through* VICTOR's. *They go out followed by* EDWARD.

The lights fade.

Scene Ten

The lights fade up.

The wooded coppice. There is a deckchair.

Three years later. Tuesday, 1 May 1923.

A bright sun is shining.

VICTOR *and* EDWARD *are in shirt sleeves. They are standing on their heads.*

VICTOR. Two hundred and twenty-three.

EDWARD. Two hundred and twenty-four.

VICTOR. Two hundred and twenty-five.

EDWARD. Two hundred and twenty-six.

VICTOR. Two hundred and twenty-seven.

EDWARD. Two hundred and twenty-eight.

EDWARD *topples over.* VICTOR *quickly follows.*

(*Dreamily.*) That was by far the longest.

VICTOR *and* EDWARD *lie back. They are panting slightly. They look at the sky.*

Silence.

What are you thinking about?

Silence.

Aren't we egoists?

Silence.

VICTOR (*dreamily*). You are, Edward.

EDWARD. You, too.

A slight pause.

VICTOR. What were you thinking?

EDWARD. That I hardly knew you.

A slight pause.

If we were queer, we could make love to one another.

VICTOR. I used to think you were.

EDWARD. So did I. I hoped. Wouldn't it have been wonderfully romantic?

A slight pause.

At Eton there were little liaisons in every corridor.

VICTOR *crawls on his elbows closer to* EDWARD.

VICTOR. Did you?

EDWARD. Once or twice.

VICTOR. Who with?

EDWARD. He's in the House of Lords. He was an Oppidan.

A slight pause.

Will I make a writer, Victor?

VICTOR. I don't know.

A slight pause.

I thought you wanted to be a politician.

EDWARD. Both. I can be a socialist and a writer.

VICTOR. No, you can't.

EDWARD *rolls onto his stomach. They are lying in a straight line, looking at one another.*

EDWARD. One must actually write in a socialist way.

VICTOR. How d'you do that?

EDWARD. By understanding people and facing issues.

VICTOR. That's what every artist does.

EDWARD. By facing unpleasant facts.

VICTOR. You're in a privileged position.

EDWARD. Are you going to feel guilty all your life?

A slight pause.

VICTOR. An artist can't have politics. He has to be free.

EDWARD. You're behind the times.

A slight pause.

VICTOR. Maybe.

A slight pause.

All art is arrogance.

EDWARD. All good art.

A slight pause.

VICTOR. I should have told you, Edward, I've applied for a job.

A slight pause.

No, to be honest I've got the job.

EDWARD. Where?

VICTOR. At my old grammar school. Teaching music and maths.

EDWARD. What for?

VICTOR. I've a living to make.

EDWARD. Starve.

VICTOR. You are a romantic. I hadn't realised.

A slight pause.

EDWARD. As a matter of fact, I've done the same.

VICTOR. At Eton?

EDWARD. No, my old preparatory.

VICTOR. Teaching?

EDWARD. Washing up, Victor. (*After a moment's pause*.) Teaching everything.

VICTOR. Why haven't we told each other?

EDWARD. Have you a cigarette?

VICTOR. We smoked the last.

EDWARD. Go to the house for some.

VICTOR. You go. (*After a moment's pause*.) Call Pickles.

A slight pause.

EDWARD. Why do you fight your intellect, Victor? What are you frightened of?

VICTOR. I wish I'd been warned about your charm. And your arrogant self-confidence.

EDWARD. But not self-congratulation. There's a difference.

VICTOR. Is there?

EDWARD. A fine one, admittedly. The difference between genius in confidence and mediocrity in congratulation.

VICTOR. You're too clever for your own good.

EDWARD *rolls onto his back. He looks at the sky.*

EDWARD. A man cannot afford to have doubt. We have to know that socialism is right.

VICTOR. That's just where you're wrong.

EDWARD (*after a moment's pause*). Don't you want the world to change?

VICTOR. You misinterpret everything I say. (*After a moment's pause*.) To be fair, I don't know.

A slight pause.

EDWARD. I was right, you are frightened.

VICTOR (*slightly annoyed*). You say everything from a position of comfort.

EDWARD. I accept that. For the moment. It is largely not my fault. (*Rolling onto his side*.) And actually, I do have doubts.

EDWARD *leans on his elbow*.

I have doubts about my own ability to make sense of what I see.

VICTOR. So do I. That's all I'm saying. The difference between us is one of class. One of assumption. I don't presume, Edward.

EDWARD. I'm sorry, I didn't meant to offend you.

VICTOR. You haven't.

Silence.

You know who I think about most? My mother.

Silence.

The mother who died when my sister was born. I hated her.

EDWARD. Your mother or your sister?

VICTOR. Lucy, my little sister. I was seventeen, taking my exams. I've grown to like her in the hols. Isn't that funny?

EDWARD (*after a moment's pause*). Have you spoken to your father?

VICTOR. I wouldn't ever – not about that.

EDWARD. It's perfectly natural.

VICTOR. Is it?

EDWARD. I've a book by Sigmund Freud.

VICTOR (*annoyed*). Oh shut up, Edward.

ELIZABETH *enters*.

ELIZABETH. Edward, be a dear, and go up the house and collect the tea things.

EDWARD. I can take a hint.

EDWARD *jumps up*.

VICTOR (*picking himself up*). I can go.

ELIZABETH. Edward knows I wish to speak to you on a personal matter.

EDWARD *exits*.

VICTOR (*calling after him*). Bring some cigarettes.

ELIZABETH *is looking at* VICTOR.

VICTOR *takes a cigarette packet from his trouser pocket. He looks inside, it is empty. He puts the packet back in his trouser pocket.*

ELIZABETH *sits in the deckchair.*

What is it, Elizabeth?

ELIZABETH. Edward's a funny boy, don't you think?

VICTOR. Yes, I suppose so.

ELIZABETH. Full, these days, of a peculiar sureness. I would say it was haughty, but I don't think it is. No. That wouldn't quite be the truth. Don't we often express the opposite of what we truly feel, Victor?

VICTOR. Sometimes, yes.

ELIZABETH (*wondering herself*). I wonder why that is? (*Seeing the answer. Brightly.*) Fear, perhaps? The fear of being alone? The fear of – (*Searching for the words.*) standing out.

A slight pause.

No, Edward does have doubt. He needs a little more. He has to find his own way in the world. (*Smiling.*) You, I'm not sure. The world may destroy your talent before it's even born.

VICTOR. I don't understand.

ELIZABETH. Edward is a willow-o'-the-wisp. I think – I think, Victor – that you are not.

VICTOR *looks down slightly.*

Edward has declined my help. I'm sure with good reason. You, I've no doubt, should accept it.

VICTOR *looks up.*

I have no wish for, nor do I expect, your gratitude.

VICTOR *walks a few paces.*

Isn't it funny, Victor, after all this time I still don't feel I know you. Edward is all too obvious. That is why he will never be the great writer. And this socialist nonsense. He knows that, I believe.

VICTOR *opens his mouth to contradict her.*

Saying that has nothing to do with the love that I feel for him.

A slight pause.

I don't know if you will ever truly love anyone, Victor. I don't know what it is. There's something about you. A meanness of spirit.

VICTOR. Will Edward love?

ELIZABETH. Oh, I think so. Quite soon.

VICTOR. You're being very blunt.

ELIZABETH. Yes, I meant to be, as a matter of fact.

VICTOR. What is it that you want?

ELIZABETH. Quite simply, I'd like the honour of helping you.

VICTOR. Would it be an honour?

ELIZABETH (*thinking*). Yes, I don't like you, Victor. Isn't that strange?

VICTOR. Yes, it is.

ELIZABETH. I once told Edward he had to learn to like himself. That's a hard lesson.

A slight pause.

I had in mind a yearly allowance. If we said fifteen hundred to begin with.

VICTOR (*not sure what to say*). That's more than I could ever dream of.

ELIZABETH. I would so like you to dream.

VICTOR. I'd never thought of having a patron.

ELIZABETH. Dreams make our world. How can we dream if we have no money. It will give you a freedom.

VICTOR. Why me, Elizabeth?

ELIZABETH. Yours is a special talent. I want to hear that perfection in your music.

A slight pause.

I don't have to see you. Go abroad. Go anywhere. (*Excited.*) I don't want to see you. We might loathe each other. I want to hear your life in your music. I want to hear your soul.

VICTOR. Have I a soul?

A slight pause.

ELIZABETH. So little faith, Victor.

A slight pause.

You are not perfect, but your music can be.

VICTOR *walks a few paces.*

Compose for me. Please. Please.

VICTOR. I can't, Elizabeth, you know that.

ELIZABETH. I was afraid.

A slight pause.

I'm sorry.

A slight pause.

Sudden blackout.

Scene Eleven

The lights are snapped up.

A lawn beside a road in Cambridge.

There is a postbox on the pavement.

A few days later. Saturday, May 5th.

A bright sun is shining.

DOROTHY *is lying on the grass. She is wearing a summer dress and she is reading a book.*

A pause.

VICTOR *enters. He has a pile of books under his arm, and a letter in his other hand. He walks to the postbox and looks at the collection times.*

VICTOR. Excuse me.

DOROTHY *looks up from her book.*

Has the post been collected yet?

DOROTHY. I haven't noticed.

VICTOR *posts his letter. He exits.*

DOROTHY *goes back to her book.*

A pause.

Sudden blackout.

ACT TWO

Scene One

From the darkness a song. VICTOR *sings the tune,* WILFRED *a harmony.*

A Song

Loud we mourned him aloft we've borne him,
Our young brigadier when we found him,
In the ground we gently laid him,
We beat our drum then we mourned no more,
In his mouth there was music ringing,
At Cerro Rojo with the bullets round him,
Come the Stuka from heaven singing,
Muffle your drum for my love sings no more.

On my bed where I lay weeping
On my bed there is no resting
Many nights now without sleeping
Thoughts of my love go tumbling round.
Dream I see him see him coming
In the clouds I see him standing
Jimmy there in his bloody shroud.

The lights have travelled up during the song.

The platform of a railway station somewhere in the wilds of Spain between Albacete and Villarrubia de Santiago.

Early February, 1937.

Night. A moon is shining.

There is a collection of ENGLISHMEN *on the platform, all are awake but all are trying to catch sleep. They are lying on whatever they can find, and all are wearing the rough 'uniform' of The International Brigade.*

VICTOR ELLISON *and* WILFRED FOX *are side by side.*

ERNEST HURLL *is on his own.*

ERNEST *is* RICHARD's *twin brother and looks identical to him.*

PETER DEAN *is on his own. He is sitting on a bench.* PETER *was born in 1905. He is a thin, wiry, cultured-looking man with receding hair. There is a shyness and gentleness about him, but his voice is neither refined nor soft.*

HEINZ BAYER *is standing on his own. He has just entered. He has listened to the song.*

HEINZ *was born in 1910. He is a German. There is something proud, but not arrogant, about the way he stands and conducts himself. He is blond-haired and clean-faced.*

HEINZ *goes first to* VICTOR *and* WILFRED.

HEINZ. You are English? You have a cigarette for me?

VICTOR. No, sorry. Have you, Wilf?

WILFRED. Smoked 'em.

> HEINZ *goes to* ERNEST.

HEINZ. You are English? You have a cigarette for me?

ERNEST. I don't smoke.

HEINZ. That is rare for an Englishman, comrade.

> HEINZ *goes towards* PETER. PETER *takes a packet of Spanish cigarettes from his pocket. He gives them to* HEINZ.

> HEINZ *opens the packet.*

But it is your last one?

PETER. Then it doesn't matter.

HEINZ. Thank you. You are a friend.

> HEINZ *lights the cigarette with an old lighter.*

PETER. Where are you from?

HEINZ. Of course, from Germany.

PETER. Your English is very good.

HEINZ. Of course, but why not?

PETER. No reason.

HEINZ (*sitting down beside* PETER *on the bench*). I learn my English because I am very clever at school. The top of my class, always. I read your Dickens, and your Thomas Hardy. You speak German, my friend?

PETER. No.

HEINZ. But why is this? This is not good.

PETER (*smiling*). I was always bottom of my class.

HEINZ. This I do not believe. (*Holding the cigarette up*.) This cigarette is proof of generosity.

PETER. I don't understand?

HEINZ. You are here in Spain. You were top of the class. If not then, now.

PETER. Being generous doesn't make you clever.

HEINZ. Oh, but I think so, no? (*To them all*.) *The Mayor of Casterbridge* is a great book.

PETER *looks puzzled*.

You do not read, I can tell. We talk about something else.

PETER *changes position, he gets more comfortable*.

PETER. Whereabouts in Germany are you from?

HEINZ. Berlin. Our greatest city. You know Berlin?

PETER (*shaking his head*). No.

HEINZ. That is a pity, my friend. I love Germany. (*Offering* PETER *the cigarette*.) You wish to inhale?

PETER. No.

HEINZ. Then I steal it all, I do not care. I steal all the time at home in Berlin. It is my life, this begging. (*Holding the cigarette up*.) Where you get this Spanish cigarette?

PETER. A lady put them in my pocket in Albacete.

WILFRED. She gave me a packet.

HEINZ. They are grateful to us, my friends. I get oranges one day. She does not know you do not smoke?

PETER (*smiling*). No. I would have preferred a bottle of wine.

HEINZ. The Manchegan wine it is beautiful here. Like the cheese. The peasants they chill it in the mountain streams. It is the way to be drunk.

PETER. How long have you been in Spain?

HEINZ. I come here to fight, comrade. And you?

PETER. Seven weeks.

HEINZ. At your training camp?

PETER. Yes.

HEINZ. Now you go to the front?

PETER. When our next train arrives.

HEINZ. It is not to be frightened, my friend.

The sound of an aeroplane, high, and in the distance.

The MEN *prick up their ears, they listen.*

VICTOR (*to* WILFRED). Whose is it?

WILFRED. I don't know.

HEINZ. It is a German aeroplane. The enemy. I can tell by his purr. Sadly, we do not see eye to eye.

A slight pause.

He is stupid. He do not know where we are. I am the one with the eyes of a cat.

The aeroplane goes.

Silence.

The MEN *relax.*

PETER. How did you get here?

HEINZ. Of course on a boat from Hamburg. I stow away like Jim in a book called *Treasure Island*. I see the aeroplanes, these weapons. It is dangerous for me. Then when I am here I cross the enemy lines like Jesus, on a donkey.

A moment's pause.

In Berlin I am a prostitute, my friends. My family is very poor. I, the eldest. My father is sick from his work in the glass factory. There are seven children, seven of us and no food. I find the ways and the means. It is dangerous now in Berlin, to be a prostitute. It is dangerous now in Berlin everywhere. The police they raid the Cosy Comer Café. I am a lucky one.

HEINZ *looks between them.*

Of course with other men.

A moment's pause.

One quarter of Berlin is full of boys waiting. Me, I have two.
My rich German banker, my English writer. He, he has poverty, but
I persuade him. My banker is a Jew, with a big house in the country
by a lake. His wife, she does not know. We have to be very
secretive together. My writer is very jealous of this relationship.
I tell him it end, then he empty his pockets for me. I tell him it end,
many times. He always nearly trust me. My writer will be famous
one day. His parents they send him more money.

HEINZ *looks between them.*

But why are you shocked? You have poverty in England? My
brothers they go through school this way.

A slight pause.

I think it is better we speak the truth about ourselves. We are
comrades here. This is the way we should learn. We do not only
fight with a rifle, my friends. In this war we are fighting for the
truth. It is why we are here. The truth is in our souls.

A slight pause.

My fat German banker, he is taken by a jackboot. The interrogation
it leave a scar. He take his family with him when he go. My English
writer also flee this country. My brother, he is fourteen, in his
uniform. He goosestep like a pimpernel. He tell the authorities
about me. You English, you have no imagination. You do not know
about Europe. Only yourselves. Soon, there will be a war. This is
why we must win Spain. Herr Hitler he flex his muscles.

A slight pause.

VICTOR. Yes.

HEINZ. This fascism, it is not inevitable. But difficult. It take strong
    men. And we are strong.

A slight pause.

VICTOR. What is happening to your family?

HEINZ. Herr Hitler he is offering hope, comrade. You, you punish
    Germany too much in 1918. We look for our pride. (*To* PETER.)
    I say to you a moment ago, that generosity make you clever. The

English would have been clever to be generous. (*Looking between them*.) Sadly, not so.

A slight pause.

ERNEST. Mebbe we had our pride an' all like. I lost me dad. Me mam had to bring us up on nothin', yer know.

A slight pause.

We could all go round faulting other folk.

HEINZ (*gently*). I understand, my friend.

ERNEST. Yer have to be responsible for yourself, I reckon.

HEINZ (*looking between them*). Which is why we are here. (*To* ERNEST.) Are you married, comrade?

ERNEST. What's that got to do with owt?

HEINZ. I speak to you as a friend. I am not, as you say, homosexual. My writer, he is very.

ERNEST. Aye, sorry. No, like.

HEINZ (*to* PETER). You?

PETER. No.

HEINZ (*to* VICTOR). You?

VICTOR. Yes. And a girlfriend.

HEINZ (*to* WILFRED). You?

WILFRED. Yes.

HEINZ. A girlfriend also?

WILFRED. I leave that sort of thing up to him.

HEINZ (*looking between them*). And where do you come from?

VICTOR. Guisborough.

WILFRED. Guisborough.

ERNEST. Newcastle.

PETER. Manchester.

HEINZ (*smiling*). I wish I was wiser. My writer, he is from public school. They call it Chatterhouse. Of course, he hate it very much. He teach English in Berlin to the hatted ladies.

HEINZ *blows into his hands.*

It is cold.

HEINZ *changes position, he gets more comfortable.*

PETER. This train doesn't want to come.

HEINZ. It does not, my friend. The trains here they are like a tortoise. (*After a moment's pause.*) May I ask what you do in Manchester?

PETER. I'm an entertainer.

HEINZ. Ah. I see.

PETER. I'm a stage artiste in the variety theatres.

HEINZ. This is something I have not heard. With my writer we go to the opera.

PETER. I've an act which I do.

HEINZ. An act?

> PETER *opens his case. He takes out a boy ventriloquist's doll. It looks very much like him.*

PETER. I work with this thing. He's called Johnnie.

JOHNNIE (*coming to life*). Hello.

HEINZ. Hello, Johnnie. How do you do?

> JOHNNIE *looks at* PETER, *and then back to* HEINZ.

JOHNNIE. I was the trade unionist in a cycle factory.

PETER. A trade unionist in a cycle factory?

JOHNNIE. I was the spokesman.

> JOHNNIE *laughs.*

PETER. Don't be silly. Tell the truth. Johnnie goes to school, don't you?

JOHNNIE. I'm cleverer than him.

PETER. Now don't show off.

JOHNNIE. Why?

PETER. Because it's insulting to be bigheaded.

JOHNNIE. He can't read, you know.

PETER. Stop it, Johnnie.

JOHNNIE. I have to read to him. Don't I?

WILFRED. Where did you learn that?

JOHNNIE (*straining to look*). Did he say something over there?

PETER. Johnnie, come here.

JOHNNIE. I was't learnt, I was conceived, just like you – on a drunken Friday night.

PETER. Ignore him.

WILFRED (*mystified*). I don't know who I'm talking to.

JOHNNIE. Yer talkin' t'me, yer fool. Yer talkin' to a bit of wood.

WILFRED. I'll come over there and saw you in half.

JOHNNIE. Magician, are you?

PETER. Johnnie.

JOHNNIE. What?

PETER. Stop it.

JOHNNIE. He started it.

PETER. Stop it. I –

JOHNNIE. Why?

PETER. Because it's rude.

JOHNNIE. He was rude first.

PETER. That's not the point.

JOHNNIE (*resting his head on* PETER*'s shoulder*). He said he'd saw me in half. I don't want sawing.

PETER (*to* WILFRED). Please say you didn't mean it. He'll never go to bed.

WILFRED (*confused*). I didn't mean it.

PETER (*turning his head to* WILFRED). Thank you.

The doll goes limp.

ERNEST. Where did yer learn that like?

PETER. My father was a vent. Johnnie was one of his dolls.

ERNEST. How long have yer been doing it.

PETER. Since I was twelve.

JOHNNIE (*coming to life*). My age?

PETER. That's right. Go to sleep.

JOHNNIE (*resting his head on* PETER*'s shoulder*). Will I be a vent when I grow up?

PETER. Yes.

JOHNNIE. Can I have a glass of water?

PETER. You'll wet the bed.

JOHNNIE. I won't.

PETER. You will.

JOHNNIE. Won't.

PETER. I'll take you to bits.

JOHNNIE. Wouldn't dare.

> PETER *pulls off one of* JOHNNIE*'s legs.*

> JOHNNIE *looks down to where it used to be. He looks back to* PETER.

> Ow.

PETER. You can have it back in the morning.

JOHNNIE. Is that so I won't come downstairs?

PETER (*taking* JOHNNIE*'s other leg off*). Yes.

JOHNNIE. Ow. What d'you call a man with no legs?

PETER. I don't know. What do you call a man with no legs?

JOHNNIE. A low-down bum.

> JOHNNIE *laughs.*

PETER. Johnnie.

JOHNNIE. What?

PETER. Close your eyes and go to sleep.

> JOHNNIE *rests his head on* PETER*'s shoulder.*

> Better?

JOHNNIE. Yes.

PETER. Sweet dreams.

JOHNNIE. Yes.

A slight pause.

Eh, I haven't had me read, you, read me a story.

The sound of an aeroplane, high, and in the distance.

The MEN *prick up their ears, they look and listen.* JOHNNIE *looks too.*

VICTOR (*to* HEINZ). Whose is that?

HEINZ. Germany again.

A slight pause.

The aeroplane goes.

The MEN *relax.*

JOHNNIE *goes to sleep on* PETER*'s shoulder. Without the doll* PETER *becomes shy again.*

I find this very interesting. He seems to have a life of his own.

PETER. I get tired of him sometimes.

HEINZ. But your hand it work him?

PETER. Yes.

HEINZ. Explain please.

PETER. I'd like him to grow up. He never does. He's always the same.

HEINZ. You could get another doll, no?

PETER. The audience won't let me.

HEINZ. But why?

PETER. An audience likes what it feels comfortable with. I've two acts, I've been doing them for ten years, in the same theatres.

HEINZ *nods.*

VICTOR. Where d'you work?

PETER. Lancashire. The West Riding. Mainly.

HEINZ. You bring him all this way?

PETER. I couldn't leave him at home. (*Smiling*.) We walked across the Pyrenees together. He'll die with me, if we do.

HEINZ. Why do you both come to Spain?

PETER. We're communists. Or I am. He's nothing.

HEINZ. I find you surprising.

PETER. Why?

HEINZ. But I like to be surprised. Karl Marx, he was a German.

PETER. Yes.

HEINZ. He is buried in your London.

PETER. Yes, I know. My father met him.

HEINZ. Your father, he was a communist?

PETER. He didn't know he was. He would be, if he were alive.

VICTOR. Did he?

PETER. Yes.

VICTOR. How?

PETER. He wrote to him. They met in a café.

VICTOR. When?

PETER. Years and years ago. He was a very young man. Marx was frail.

HEINZ. Your father was converted?

PETER. My father was a natural communist. He didn't have an ideology. He didn't give names to things. I do.

HEINZ. My friend, I am not a communist, I have a soul. You understand?

PETER. What d'you mean by the soul?

HEINZ. I mean the mysteries of myself. The things in me that I do not understand. We all have those things. Every day we change a little bit more and it make us think again. Communism, it deny these mysteries. (*Smiling*.) I like to have them. It make me human.

PETER. D'you believe in God?

HEINZ. Comrade, nearly, yes.

PETER. We both believe in human potential, don't we? The church is an instrument of represssion.

HEINZ (*struggling*). You will have to go more slowly. It is hard for me to talk of philosophy in another language.

PETER. I'm sorry.

HEINZ. Please?

PETER (*slowly*). I have sat in churches where the gentry looked down on the peasant.

HEINZ. That for me is not the church. I want a new church.

PETER. No, that is the church.

HEINZ. Then I change it by myself. God is the mystery for me. I like Him.

PETER. The ceremonies of the church deny an individual separate thought.

HEINZ. The ceremony of the church is the human expression of God, no?

PETER (*shaking his head*). No.

HEINZ. But it is.

PETER. No, it's worship.

HEINZ. We are very the same, you and me. I have a different view of God. My view of God will make things right for all people. I am not a communist. I believe in liberty. But I have a soul. It is for my soul that I am here. Jesus, he was a fighter. He overturn the tables of the money lenders.

VICTOR, WILFRED *and* ERNEST *have been listening.*

There is a short silence.

(*Smiling.*) Johnnie he has gone to sleep?

PETER (*smiling*). Yes.

HEINZ. Your father, he is an interesting man?

PETER. Yes.

HEINZ. Johnnie say you cannot read, no? Is that the truth about you?

PETER. Yes.

HEINZ. I thought so. Something tell me.

PETER. I've tried many times. I just can't do it.

HEINZ (*smiling*). I read too much with my English writer.

> PETER *smiles*.

> *A short silence*.

> ERNEST *stands up*.

ERNEST. Are you a Catholic?

HEINZ. Not yet, my friend.

> ERNEST *joins them, he sits down on the bench*.

> But nearly. I look into it. My writer, he is a Catholic. You are from Newcastle?

ERNEST (*getting comfortable*). Yes.

HEINZ. Good, I remember. Comrades, I will tell you why so nearly a Catholic. It is to do with love. If we hate a man and he dies, our hatred dies quickly with him, it is soon forgotten. If we love someone, our love it live on and grow through the years. (*Looking at the sky.*) It is Him up there. He load the dice that way.

ERNEST. I'm a Catholic, yer know.

HEINZ. Then we talk you and me. Catholics are turbulent people.

ERNEST. Isn't prostitution a sin?

HEINZ. We are above that here in Spain. It is for a bigger cause we fight. Jesus, he sat with prostitutes.

ERNEST. Try the Church of England.

HEINZ (*smiling, gripping* ERNEST*'s knee*). My friend, you make me laugh.

ERNEST. I just wanted to know like.

HEINZ. Because, my friend, I am ignorant. I feel somewhere there is a faith, that is all. I try and go towards it.

ERNEST. That's all right like.

HEINZ. Newcastle, Newcastle?

ERNEST. It's the north-east.

HEINZ. That is nowhere near Chatterhouse?

ERNEST. I wouldn't know.

HEINZ. You too walk over the mountains?

ERNEST. Not together like. Not with Peter. I came on me own, without this lot.

VICTOR *stands up*.

HEINZ. You walk too?

VICTOR. Yes.

VICTOR *sits with them on the bench*.

If anyone asks we're in Paris. Beneath the Eiffel Tower. Sipping champagne.

HEINZ. My friend, you joke with me?

VICTOR. Only partly.

ERNEST. It's the way we all got here like, on a weekend trip to Paris.

HEINZ. Yes? (*To* VICTOR.) You also?

VICTOR. Then down through France by train and across the frontier.

HEINZ (*smiling*). We go and borrow a train, no?

HEINZ *blows into his hands*.

It is cold on this station.

WILFRED *stands up*.

You join us too, my friend?

WILFRED *sits with them, on the ground*.

I am glad I came for the cigarette.

WILFRED *takes a packet of cigarettes from his pocket*.

HEINZ *looks at him*.

WILFRED. Yeh, a lied. Sorry.

WILFRED *offers the cigarettes*.

VICTOR *and* HEINZ *take one*. HEINZ *lights them with his lighter*.

They smoke in silence for a moment.

VICTOR. Luxury.

WILFRED. Aye.

HEINZ. I smoke so little, it make me strange.

PETER. Can I have one?

WILFRED *gives him a cigarette.* HEINZ *lights it.* PETER *hasn't smoked before.*

ERNEST. I keep wonderin' what day it is. Or what month even, yer know.

WILFRED. February.

ERNEST. Yer sure?

WILFRED. Aye. Tuesday.

A slight pause.

Or Wednesday. Thursday. One of those.

(*After a moment's pause.*) Monday mebbe. Saturday. (*After a moment's pause.*) Friday.

VICTOR. There's only Sunday left, Wilf.

WILFRED. No, it's definitely not Sunday.

They smile.

ERNEST. Can I have one, please?

WILFRED *gives* ERNEST *a cigarette.*

PETER *gives him his cigarette to light it from.*

They smoke.

PETER. If this train comes.

ERNEST *coughs.*

WILFRED. Give us it 'ere.

ERNEST *gives* WILFRED *the cigarette.*

WILFRED *puts the two cigarettes together between his fingers, he smokes them both.* ERNEST *is still coughing.*

ERNEST (*red in the face*). It's bloody awful.

PETER (*to* VICTOR). D'you want this one?

VICTOR *takes it. He puts it out on the sole of his boot and keeps it.*

They smoke.

ERNEST (*to* WILFRED). I wonder how our lad is?

HEINZ (*not understanding*). What is your lad?

ERNEST. Me brother like, yer know. Me twin, in Newcastle.

WILFRED. All right, I should think, he's got my bike.

ERNEST. I've written to him. Don't know if it'll get there.

WILFRED. It will.

ERNEST. Yer reckon?

WILFRED. Yeh, a certainty.

ERNEST. I don't have your confidence

WILFRED. Why not?

ERNEST (*shrugging*). Don't know. (*After a moment's pause.*) It's a
bloody long way to the north-east.

WILFRED. D'yer miss 'im?

ERNEST. Sometimes, yes. (*After a moment's pause.*) I must have been
mad to set off here.

   ERNEST *smiles.*

   Silence.

   WILFRED *puts the two cigarettes up his nose, one up each nostril.*

   The MEN *smile.*

   WILFRED *takes them out. He smokes.*

   Silence.

WILFRED (*the first time he has said these things*). I don't think I was
mad. I came here for the future. If you can't see a future, what can
yer see? Nothing. It's the possibility of what might be, that makes
your life what it is.

   A slight pause.

   If you can't see anything, what have you? You might as well curl up
   and die.

HEINZ. It is the same for all of us here.

   *The sound of a train. It pulls into the station. Steam from the engine
   billows out.*

   The five MEN *stand up.*

   Sudden blackout.

Scene Two

The lights are snapped up.

'Suicide Hill' on the front line at Jarama.

An open plateau. There are two separate defence shields which have been built very quickly from dry stone: they are little more than mounds, but are roughly in the shape of small shooting-butts. The air in front is smoky, as if the soldiers behind the butts were looking into an infinity.

A few days later. Late afternoon.

PETER *and* HEINZ *are behind one butt,* VICTOR *and* ERNEST, *behind the other. Each has a rifle.*

A loud rifle-fire, and some automatic fire, is ringing out from the enemy a few hundred yards away.

The four soldiers are well down in their butts.

A slight pause.

VICTOR *raises his rifle. He shoots over the butt.* PETER, *in his butt, does the same. When they have let off their shots, they quickly duck down again.* PETER *and* VICTOR *begin to reload.*

A slight pause.

The enemy fire dies to silence.

VICTOR. There's a bastard keeps shooting at me.

PETER. We're out numbered.

VICTOR. How're we meant to move forward?

> *Enemy rifle fire rings out.* ERNEST *and* HEINZ *make a move: it is their turn to shoot.*
>
> Wait till they reload. (*Shouting across to* HEINZ *in the other butt.*) Heinz, wait till they reload.
>
> ERNEST *and* HEINZ *stay down.*

HEINZ (*calling back*). We will not see them then. They will be down like us. We shoot when they shoot.

VICTOR. No. Wait. This way we get the first shots.

HEINZ. They have automatic weapons. (*Holding up his rifle.*) This, this is a hundred years old. It kill me first.

A slight pause.

ERNEST. This is hopeless.

VICTOR. I know.

The enemy fire slowly dies to silence. The silence is almost eerie.

A slight pause.

Right, comrades.

ERNEST, VICTOR *and* PETER *raise their rifles over their respective butts.*

A moment's pause.

All right, Heinz?

HEINZ (*raising his rifle*). Yes, my friend.

VICTOR. Wait until they come up, and you've a clear view. I want them to think we're falling back.

The four soldiers wait, their fingers poised on the triggers of their rifles.

HEINZ. This is the dangerous way, comrades, they get a chance to see us.

PETER. It's better than firing at nothing.

A slight pause.

VICTOR. Where the hell are they?

A slight pause.

HEINZ. Franco, he put them to sleep with his charm.

A slight pause.

I like a joke from Johnnie, at this time.

PETER. I left him in the cookhouse.

HEINZ. I hope he do not eat all our food. These beans and olive oil. It make him go to the toilet all the time, like us, no?

A pause.

ERNEST. Mebbe they've retreated like.

A pause.

HEINZ (*intense*). I have one, comrades. The top of his head. They think we have gone back into the olive groves.

VICTOR. Wait until you can see him more clearly.

HEINZ (*intense*). They will see us if we wait too long.

A slight pause.

Yes, they are beginning to move.

VICTOR. Got them?

PETER. Yes.

ERNEST. Yeh.

A slight pause.

VICTOR. Let them come a bit more, let them come a bit more.

A slight pause.

HEINZ. They are thinking we are cowards. One, he has lit a cigarette.

A slight pause.

Yes, now I see him smoking.

A slight pause.

VICTOR. Wait.

A slight pause.

Wait.

A slight pause.

Wait.

A slight pause.

Wait.

HEINZ *fires first. The other three soldiers follow quickly with their shots. They duck down, behind the butts, immediately.*

PETER. Get him?

HEINZ (*smiling*). I think so, my friend. Where is their answer to that?

HEINZ *raises his head to peer above the butt. A single rifle shot rings out from the enemy.*

HEINZ *is hit in the neck. The force of the shot pushes him away from the butt.*

A massive round of continuous fire rings out from the enemy.

PETER *makes a move to help* HEINZ.

VICTOR (*reloading. Screaming*). Leave him.

The soldiers stay down in their butts, VICTOR *and* ERNEST *still reloading.*

PETER (*screaming*). Heinz. Heinz.

HEINZ (*very slightly raising his head*). I am all right, my friend, it is not bad.

HEINZ *starts to crawl towards* PETER*'s butt.*

Enemy fire is still ringing out.

VICTOR *drops his rifle. He rushes to* HEINZ. *He helps drag him,* HEINZ *trying to stand, to the butt where* PETER *is. They make it. They get down.* HEINZ *has his head on* VICTOR*'s lap.*

Thank you, my friend. Where am I hit?

VICTOR (*looking at him*). In the neck.

Blood is pouring from HEINZ*'s wound.*

HEINZ. The fascists have me, haven't they?

VICTOR (*gently*). No.

HEINZ. My friend, you are a bad liar. It does you credit.

Enemy fire is still ringing out.

In the other butt ERNEST *raises his rifle. He fires the single shot. He ducks own and starts to reload.*

Once, in the slums of Berlin, I see a young boy. He is naked and bleeding from the ruins of his life.

PETER (*gently*). Quiet.

HEINZ. I watch him being clothed, in the false clothes of lies. And as he grows up he becomes proud, the pride of deceit. He is led along this road by inaction and fear. When he is given a bomb, he will drop it wherever he is told. My friends, the bombs will fall on Europe. We are not enough. (*Proudly.*) Though our pride is right. (*Shivering.*) I am cold, so very cold. (*Looking at* VICTOR.) God, he will forgive me, yes?

VICTOR. Yes.

HEINZ. Please, if you would give me absolution from my sins.

VICTOR (*gently*). I don't know how you do that.

HEINZ. A prayer will do, please.

PETER (*gently*). You're not going to die.

HEINZ (*smiling. Blood coming from his mouth*). But of course not.
The prayer is for you, my friends.

PETER *looks at* VICTOR.

VICTOR. O God, the Father of our Lord Jesus Christ, our Only
Saviour, the Prince of Peace: Give us grace seriously to lay to heart
the great dangers we are in by our unhappy divisions. Take away all
hatred and prejudice, and whatsoever else may hinder us from
Godly union and concord:

Enemy fire is still ringing out.

In the other butt ERNEST *raises his rifle. He fires the single shot.
He ducks own and starts to reload.*

that, as there is but one Body, and one Spirit, and one Hope of our
calling, one Lord, one Faith, one Baptism, one God and Father of us
all, so we henceforth be all of one heart, and of one soul, united in
one holy bond of Truth and Peace, of Faith and Charity, and may
with one mind and one mouth glorify Thee today: through Jesus
Christ our Lord. Amen.

HEINZ. That is very good. Only a little bit false.

PETER *looks at* VICTOR.

VICTOR (*shrugging*). My headmaster says it.

WILFRED *enters running, ducking low.*

He has a pistol. He fires. He joins ERNEST.

WILFRED (*shouting*). The command is to pull back beyond the
sunken road. We're heavily outnumbered.

PETER. How many are hit?

WILFRED. Quite a few. It's chaos.

A slight pause.

VICTOR. We'd better prepare to fall back then. Heinz is hit. We need
a stretcher.

HEINZ *has his eyes closed.*

PETER (*looking at him*). He's dead. (*Gently pulling* HEINZ*'s arm.*) Heinz.

VICTOR *looks at* HEINZ.

WILFRED. Is he all right?

VICTOR (*calling back*). No, we think he's dead.

VICTOR *takes off his jacket. His shirt, by his right shoulder, is soaked in blood.*

PETER. When did you get that?

VICTOR (*wincing with pain*). When I helped him.

The enemy fire has stopped: it has ended with one last single shot.

Silence for a moment.

PETER *takes a rag from his pocket, he starts to dab at* VICTOR*'s wound.*

ERNEST (*quite quietly*). What a place, eh?

Silence for a moment.

VICTOR. Help me with my shirt, would you?

PETER *helps* VICTOR *with his shirt, ripping it away from the wound.*

ERNEST. It reminds us of the moors of Northumberland.

Silence for a moment.

I love those moors. They're my wife.

VICTOR *has a large hole in his right shoulder, it is covered in blood.*

WILFRED (*watching them*). How is it?

VICTOR. It doesn't look too good.

PETER *is dabbing at the wound with the torn shirt and the rag.*

WILFRED. You go first then. One by one.

Silence for a few moments.

Right?

VICTOR. Yes.

A slight pause.

VICTOR *moves fast, bending low, towards the sunken road.*

A round of enemy rifle fire rings out.

VICTOR *has gone.*

Silence.

ERNEST. I couldn't ever ask for anything more than those moors like, yer know.

PETER. Or the Pennines, Ernie.

ERNEST *smiles.*

Out on those moors with a paper kite. Made from the *Daily Sketch.* Newspapers flying like air.

PETER *prepares to run.*

WILFRED. You ready, Peter?

PETER. Yes.

A slight pause.

PETER *runs. As he does so: sudden blackout.*

Scene Three

The lights are snapped up.

A ward in a convent hospital on the outskirts of Barcelona.

Two beds. A table and a chair. The table has various hospital records and notes on it.

Wednesday, 3 March. Night.

It is impossible to see who the occupants of the beds are: but they are, in fact, VICTOR *and* EDWARD LONGRESSE.

LUCY ELLISON *is sitting on a chair beside* VICTOR*'s bed.*

SISTER MARY-JOSEPH *is standing beside* EDWARD*'s bed. She has a flashlight in her hand.*

MARY-JOSEPH *was born in 1913. She is a thin, quite tall woman with a brisk, efficient manner. She is wearing the black-and-white habit of the nursing order, and there are rosary beads and a crucifix which hang from the belt on her waist.*

MARY-JOSEPH. Why don't you go and get some sleep?

LUCY (*shaking her head*). No.

  EDWARD *is on a drain, which runs from the bottom of his lungs, to a bottle on the floor. Occasionally, throughout the scene, a reddish-brown liquid drips down the clear pipe.*

  MARY-JOSEPH *picks up the bottle. It is half-full. She looks at it, and then puts it down. She switches the flashlight on, opens* EDWARD's *eyelids, and shines the flashlight in.*

  VICTOR *stirs. He makes a slight grumbling noise.*

  LUCY *stands up.*

  (*Feeling his forehead.*) Victor?

  VICTOR *is still.*

He keeps making little grumbling noises.

MARY-JOSEPH. That's only to be expected.

  MARY-JOSEPH *puts the flashlight on the bed. She moves* EDWARD's *covers, finds his wrist, and takes his pulse. She feels his forehead with her other hand.*

LUCY. How is he?

MARY-JOSEPH. Poorly.

LUCY. Has he been shot?

  MARY-JOSEPH *concentrates on her work for a moment.*

MARY-JOSEPH (*putting his wrist back in the bed*). Yes, in the lung, poor devil.

  MARY-JOSEPH *holds the crucifix before her. She prays silently for a moment.*

  She returns to EDWARD, *straightening his bedcovers.*

LUCY. What were you doing, Sister?

MARY-JOSEPH. Praying.

LUCY. For him?

MARY-JOSEPH. And his soul. I shouldn't use the word devil.

MARY-JOSEPH *picks up the flashlight.*

She goes to VICTOR*'s bed, opens his eyelids, and shines the flashlight in.*

The sound of an aeroplane far overhead.

MARY-JOSEPH *turns the flashlight off and puts it on the bed. She finds* VICTOR*'s wrist and takes his pulse. She returns his wrist to the bedcovers. She picks up the flashlight, walks to the table, and sits down.*

LUCY. Aren't you going to take his blood pressure?

MARY-JOSEPH. I don't think I need to any more.

MARY-JOSEPH *writes up her hospital notes.*

A slight pause.

LUCY *sits down in her chair.*

A slight pause.

(*Without looking up.*) Why don't you bring your chair over here?

A slight pause.

LUCY *picks up her chair. She sits down at the table.*

MARY-JOSEPH *is still writing.*

A slight pause.

LUCY. How old are you, Sister?

MARY-JOSEPH. Twenty-four.

LUCY. You seem so old.

A slight pause.

Am I in your way?

A bomb from the aeroplane explodes in the far distance.

LUCY*'s shoulders rise in instinctive fear.*

What if one of them should hit us?

A bomb explodes in the far distance.

MARY-JOSEPH *has still not looked up from her writing*.

A slight pause.

She looks up.

MARY-JOSEPH. How did you find your brother?

LUCY (*frightened*). I was told he was at Jarama, by brigade headquarters. Then I heard they'd been more or less wiped out. No one knew, so I went round the hospitals.

A bomb explodes in the distance.

They're getting nearer.

MARY-JOSEPH (*gently smiling*). You're a remarkable girl.

LUCY. I don't feel it.

MARY-JOSEPH *writes*.

Is war always like this?

A slight pause.

MARY-JOSEPH (*without looking up*). Sleep at the table. I'll let you know if there's any change.

A bomb explodes in the distance.

LUCY. Is the bombing always at night?

A pause.

MARY-JOSEPH (*looking up briefly. Smiling gently*). Notes. I like to do things properly. Your brother's life may depend on it.

A slight pause.

(*Writing. Not showing her fear.*) It helps me not to think about the bombs.

A bomb explodes in the distance.

They'll go in a minute. This is one raid.

A slight pause.

LUCY. I'm sorry, Sister.

MARY-JOSEPH (*without looking up*). What for?

LUCY. I don't know.

MARY-JOSEPH *leaves her writing. She sits back in her chair.*

Why are you looking at me?

MARY-JOSEPH. What're you doing here?

A bomb explodes in the distance.

LUCY. I came to find my brother.

MARY-JOSEPH *is still looking at her.* LUCY *feels uncomfortable.*

I love him.

A slight pause.

MARY-JOSEPH *goes back to writing her notes.*

MARY-JOSEPH. You must really love him, to come all this way.

LUCY. I do. I had to find out for myself.

MARY-JOSEPH. I'm an only child. There was only me.

LUCY (*after a moment's pause*). Why d'you say these things?

MARY-JOSEPH *sits back.*

MARY-JOSEPH. I had to have the faith of absent brothers and sisters. (*Gently smiling.*) My faith is my love.

LUCY *half-smiles.*

Sometimes I –

LUCY (*after a moment's pause*). What?

MARY-JOSEPH (*she doesn't know if she can explain*). You're just a girl.

A slight pause.

Wonder. Sometimes I wonder. I've counted them. Seventy-eight men have died in this hospital in this war. Those that live, go back.

LUCY. They told me I'd be driving an ambulance.

MARY-JOSEPH *writes her notes.*

I do believe in God, Sister, if that's what you're saying.

MARY-JOSEPH. I'm talking about the foolishness of men.

LUCY. Is that why you pray?

MARY-JOSEPH. He's an atheist. A rude one.

LUCY. Who?

LUCY *looks briefly towards* EDWARD's *bed*

MARY-JOSEPH. I shouldn't talk about the devil, but he makes me. In fun, but he means it.

LUCY (*after a moment's pause*). Where're you from?

MARY-JOSEPH. South London.

LUCY *nods*.

LUCY. I don't know London. I went to the ILP.

MARY-JOSEPH. Haven't you come to fight fascism? That's all they seem to talk about.

LUCY. Err. Yes.

MARY-JOSEPH. I don't believe adventure would bring you here.

A slight pause.

LUCY. Why've you come then?

A slight pause.

Sister?

EDWARD (*calling*). Sister?

MARY-JOSEPH *puts down her pen, she goes to him.*

MARY-JOSEPH (*gently*). What is it?

EDWARD (*difficulty speaking*). My throat's full of blood. Can I sit up?

MARY-JOSEPH. The drain should be doing that.

EDWARD. It doesn't always work.

EDWARD *sits up.* MARY-JOSEPH *helps him. She props up his pillows.*

EDWARD *leans back.*

Thank you, Sister.

MARY-JOSEPH *takes his wrist, she takes his pulse.*

How is it?

MARY-JOSEPH. Ninety to the dozen.

EDWARD. I'm not dead yet then?

MARY-JOSEPH (*gently*). No. Unfortunately.

EDWARD. A pity.

MARY-JOSEPH. Exactly, Mr Longresse.

EDWARD (*coughing*). Sister, has my wife arrived?

MARY-JOSEPH. No, not yet.

EDWARD. She probably can't get through.

MARY-JOSEPH. She will.

> EDWARD *coughs*.

> How ever do I stop you talking?

EDWARD. You can't.

> MARY-JOSEPH *rests his wrist gently on the bed*.

> (*Catching his breath*.) Does she know I've moved hospitals?

MARY-JOSEPH (*gently*). We'll tell her. Stop worrying.

EDWARD (*his hand going to her bottom*). You're a pet.

MARY-JOSEPH (*quickly moving out of the way*). Don't you dare. (*Looking at him*.) Try and sleep.

> MARY-JOSEPH *returns to the table, she sits down*.

EDWARD (*calling*). Are letters getting through to England?

MARY-JOSEPH. I don't know.

EDWARD. I would like to see her. (*After a moment's pause. Modestly*.) I don't want to put anyone out.

> MARY-JOSEPH *is writing*.

> (*More quietly*.) This is a bloody war.

> *A slight pause*.

> Thank you, Sister.

> *A handbell rings in the next ward*.

> MARY-JOSEPH *picks up the flashlight, turns it on, and exits*.

> Excuse me. Could you help me?

> LUCY *goes to* EDWARD.

> I'd like a cigarette. My tobacco's under the mattress.

LUCY *looks where* EDWARD *is showing her. She finds his tobacco, his cigarette papers, and his matches. She gives them to him.*

LUCY. You shouldn't smoke.

EDWARD. Why not?

EDWARD *starts to roll a cigarette. He is well practised.*

VICTOR *stirs very slightly.* LUCY *moves the few feet to his bed, she looks at him.*

VICTOR *is still.*

Where are you from?

LUCY (*moving the few feet back*). Yorkshire.

EDWARD. Oh, yes? I know Yorkshire. My wife and I have tented in the dales.

LUCY. Whereabouts?

EDWARD. At Ripon, I believe.

LUCY. You shouldn't smoke.

EDWARD. This cigarette is between ourselves. It's not for her God-like ears. (*Catching his breath.*) Or nose more precisely. I don't think you're a nurse? You're not behaving like one.

LUCY. No, I came to drive an ambulance.

EDWARD. Good for you. With the ILP?

LUCY. Yes.

EDWARD (*suddenly showing pain*). It's a beastly bloody place, Spain.

LUCY. Can I help?

EDWARD (*covering the pain up*). I miss my wife the most of all.

VICTOR (*stirring slightly. Calling out*). Sister.

LUCY *goes to him.*

LUCY. She's in another ward.

VICTOR. Where am I?

LUCY. Barcelona.

VICTOR *is still and silent.*

A slight pause.

LUCY *moves the few feet back to* EDWARD's *bed.*

He's my brother. He was brought here from the field hospital at Villarejo de Saluanes. So the Sister said.

VICTOR (*smiling gently*). Don't worry.

EDWARD *licks the cigarette paper.*

LUCY. Where were you injured?

EDWARD. Madrid. (*Catching his breath.*) They can't, or won't, get the bloody bullet out. I'd have a go.

EDWARD *has rolled the cigarette.*

MARY-JOSEPH *enters with the flashlight which is still on.*

EDWARD *quietly hides his cigarette and tobacco.*

MARY-JOSEPH *has gone to* VICTOR. *She opens his eyelids and shines the flashlight in.*

LUCY *watches.*

LUCY. Is he all right?

MARY-JOSEPH (*after a moment's pause*). Mmm. Your brother's pulling through.

MARY-JOSEPH *turns the flashlight off and puts it on the bed. She finds* VICTOR's *wrist and starts to take his pulse.*

VICTOR (*quietly*). Where am I?

MARY-JOSEPH. Barcelona.

VICTOR. Have I had the operation?

MARY-JOSEPH. Yes, a few hours ago.

EDWARD. Comrade?

MARY-JOSEPH (*snapping at* EDWARD). Quiet.

VICTOR (*trying to remember*). Where am I?

MARY-JOSEPH. In Barcelona. In a convent hospital. (*Putting her hand on his forehead.*) You're much better here. (*Bending down to him.*) Listen, you must sleep.

VICTOR. I feel sick.

MARY-JOSEPH. That's the anaesthetic. (*Almost whispering.*) You're doing very nicely.

VICTOR. You're beautiful, Sister.

MARY-JOSEPH (*smiling*). Sleep, that's the main thing now.

A slight pause.

MARY-JOSEPH *puts* VICTOR*'s wrist back into the bed.*

He mustn't be woken.

LUCY. Yes, Sister.

MARY-JOSEPH *picks up her flashlight and walks to the table.*

EDWARD (*to* LUCY). She's an ogre, that one.

LUCY (*sitting down*). Talking will do you no good.

EDWARD. It's because I'm an atheist, isn't it?

MARY-JOSEPH. If you wish to meet your maker in that condition.

MARY-JOSEPH *holds the crucifix before her. She prays silently for a moment.*

LUCY *and* EDWARD *watch her.*

MARY-JOSEPH *writes her notes.*

EDWARD (*to* LUCY, *but quite loudly*). She doesn't mean it.

MARY-JOSEPH. Don't I, Mr Longresse?

EDWARD. Sister's faith wanders too.

MARY-JOSEPH. I have never been more serious.

EDWARD (*directly to her*). You're not as committed as you seem, Sister.

EDWARD *coughs. He coughs and coughs.*

MARY-JOSEPH *takes a small metal bowl from a drawer in the table. She takes it to* EDWARD.

LUCY *moves out of the way. She watches.*

MARY-JOSEPH *rubs* EDWARD*'s back, pushing the top of his body gently forward.*

MARY-JOSEPH (*gently*). Careful, careful, careful. Try not to strain the lung.

EDWARD*'s coughing eases.*

That's it.

EDWARD *stops*.

Spit it out.

EDWARD *spits out blood into the bowl*.

VICTOR *stirs very slightly.*

EDWARD. Thank you, Sister.

MARY-JOSEPH. When you feel the coughing starting, try and hold it back.

EDWARD (*catching his breath*). Yes.

MARY-JOSEPH. We want the blood to drain, and not come up.

EDWARD (*catching his breath*). Yes.

MARY-JOSEPH. I'll make sure you see the doctor first in the morning. (*Annoyed with him.*) You do know you're killing yourself, don't you?

EDWARD (*strongly*). No, Sister. I don't care for my own comfort.

A handbell rings.

MARY-JOSEPH *returns to the table with the metal bowl. She picks up the flashlight, turns it on, and exits to another ward the other way.*

A moment's pause.

LUCY. Why d'you provoke her?

EDWARD. She likes it. (*Pointing to the table.*) Go and get a chair.

LUCY. I shouldn't.

A moment's pause.

LUCY *goes to the table. She brings back her chair. She puts it down.*

VICTOR *stirs slightly.*

VICTOR. Have I had the operation?

LUCY (*leaning over him*). A few hours ago.

VICTOR. The surgeon was going to try and take the bullets out.

LUCY. They did.

VICTOR. Where am I?

LUCY. Barcelona.

VICTOR. It's taken weeks to get here.

> EDWARD *has taken his cigarette, tobacco, and matches from beneath the covers. He lights the cigarette.*

LUCY (*turning*). You shouldn't smoke.

VICTOR. Can I have a glass of water?

LUCY. You're not allowed any.

VICTOR. I feel sick.

> EDWARD *is smoking, but very gingerly.*
>
> *He coughs.*

LUCY (*turning*). You shouldn't smoke.

VICTOR (*trying to remember*). Where am I?

LUCY. In a convent hospital, I keep saying.

VICTOR. What day is it?

LUCY. Wednesday.

VICTOR. Lucy?

LUCY. Yes, it's me.

> LUCY *smiles.*
>
> *A slight pause.*
>
> (*Turning.*) He's closed his eyes again.
>
> EDWARD *is holding the cigarette, rather than smoking it.*

EDWARD (*smiling*). Don't worry.

LUCY. I can't help it.

EDWARD. Where was your brother shot?

LUCY. In the shoulder. At Jarama.

EDWARD. You're a brave girl.

LUCY. I don't think I'm here really. I think I'm in a dream.

EDWARD (*smiling*). You're here.

> *A bomb explodes in the far distance.*

The English have been good in this illegal war. The French. The Americans.

LUCY. Why did you come?

EDWARD. To fight fascism.

LUCY. That's what everyone says. Are you a socialist?

EDWARD. I'm a writer.

EDWARD *coughs. He is not smoking the cigarette.*

LUCY. I've never met a writer before.

LUCY *sits in the chair.*

The cigarette has gone out. EDWARD *relights it with a match.*

EDWARD (*the cigarette in his mouth*). I live in Norfolk, in a tiny village.

He puts the spent match back in the box.

(*Taking the cigarette from his mouth.*) My wife and I run the General Stores.

LUCY. Really?

EDWARD (*the cigarette in his hand*). In the mornings, and in the evenings, I do my best to write these terribly bad English novels.

EDWARD *coughs.*

Away from the stink of the London literati. (*Coughing slightly again.*) And the nancy poets.

EDWARD *coughs.*

This bloody lung. (*Giving her the cigarette.*) You'd better put this out for me.

LUCY *takes it. She doesn't know what to do with it.*

On the floor.

LUCY *puts it out with her foot.*

Push the tab under the bed.

LUCY *does so.*

(*His eyes focusing on the future.*) I've written reviews for tuppenny-ha'penny magazines. Defending Kipling. Being attacked by the nancy Left.

EDWARD *looks at* LUCY.

I still want to get my own back on the world.

LUCY (*shyly*). I don't understand.

EDWARD *starts to roll another cigarette.*

EDWARD (*smiling* at LUCY). I'd have liked to have used my hands more. To have been a carpenter, I think. That's why I roll these things. (*A broad smile.*) As well as a great writer.

LUCY *smiles.*

At home we have a smallholding at the back of the Stores. My young son has a pig. I have a goat. My wife, the chickens. I make these little wooden animals, just with a chisel. They're hopelessly inadequate.

EDWARD *smiles.*

I'm sorry, I have the eccentric's habit of always talking about myself.

LUCY (*smiling*). No, I like it.

EDWARD (*smiling*). Why?

LUCY *smiles. She shrugs.*

VICTOR *stirs slightly.*

EDWARD *coughs. The tobacco from the cigarette goes all over the bed.*

Oh, damn.

LUCY *goes to* VICTOR.

VICTOR. What time is it?

LUCY. About two o'clock. It's Lucy.

EDWARD *is trying to pick up the tobacco from the bed and get it back into the paper. He coughs slightly.*

It's Lucy, d'you understand? I'm here.

MARY-JOSEPH *enters. The flashlight is on.*

MARY-JOSEPH. Would you come quickly. I've a patient fallen out of bed.

LUCY. Yes.

MARY-JOSEPH *exits*. LUCY *quickly follows her.*

Silence for a moment.

EDWARD (*talkatively*). Comrade? (*After a moment's pause.*) Comrade?

VICTOR *is still.* EDWARD *lies back with his head on the pillows.*

(*Talking to himself.*) Why am I always next to the sleepy ones?

EDWARD *starts to cough. He coughs and coughs. Little splashes of blood spray out of his mouth.*

After a long while he is still and silent.

(*Gently, quietly.*) Could you help me, Comrade?

A bomb explodes in the far distance. It dies to silence.

Sudden blackout.

Scene Four

The lights are snapped up.

The garden of the convent hospital.

Saturday, 13 March.

The sun is shining.

VICTOR *is sitting in a wheelchair under the boughs of a tree. He is wearing pyjamas and a dressing gown, and there is a blanket over his knees and legs. His right arm is in a sling: in his left hand he is holding a pencil. There is some music manuscript paper on his lap.* VICTOR *is trying to write.*

A slight pause.

MARY-JOSEPH *enters, crossing the lawn.*

VICTOR (*looking up*). Sister.

MARY-JOSEPH. What is it? I'm busy.

VICTOR. If you're busy, then it doesn't matter.

MARY-JOSEPH *stops.*

MARY-JOSEPH. Yes?

VICTOR. I don't suppose you understand music?

MARY-JOSEPH. Very little. (*Going to him.*) A little.

VICTOR. I'm trying to write down a tune. It's impossible with my left hand. I can't write it quick enough. It's so bloody slow.

MARY-JOSEPH *pulls a face.*

I beg your pardon, Sister.

MARY-JOSEPH. Remind me where we're up to?

VICTOR (*smiling*). This isn't good nursing.

MARY-JOSEPH*'s face hardens.*

They are looking at one another.

MARY-JOSEPH (*severely*). Are you special in any way?

VICTOR. No.

A slight pause.

I had the stitches out this morning, Sister.

MARY-JOSEPH (*softening*). What did the doctor say?

VICTOR. Light exercise.

MARY-JOSEPH. Right then, light exercise it is. Why're you using your left hand?

VICTOR (*hesitating*). Erm – I don't know.

MARY-JOSEPH (*gently*). Take your arm out of the sling.

VICTOR. Yes.

VICTOR *does so.*

I know you have a lot of patients.

MARY-JOSEPH (*kneeling down*). I haven't met a man with more excuses for inactivity.

VICTOR. Have you met any men, Sister.

MARY-JOSEPH (*ignoring that. Gently*). Try and write with it.

VICTOR *puts the pencil in his right hand. He tries to write. His hand is like jelly. The pencil goes all over the place. He stops almost immediately.*

I am not going to sit here unless you're going to try.

VICTOR (*angry*). I am trying, you silly woman.

MARY-JOSEPH. Again.

> VICTOR *tries again. The pencil goes all over the place. He looks up.* MARY-JOSEPH *takes his right hand, she helps give strength to* VICTOR*'s wrist.*

> VICTOR *manages to write a few notes.*

> *He looks up at her.*

It's common sense, isn't it?

VICTOR. My arm feels like jelly, that's all.

MARY-JOSEPH. It will for a few weeks, until you've strength back in it.

> MARY-JOSEPH *takes his arm at the elbow and the wrist. By applying pressure, she straightens his arm.*

> *It hurts.* VICTOR *pulls a face.*

Tell me when it really hurts.

VICTOR (*quickly*). It really hurts.

> MARY-JOSEPH *stops applying the pressure.* VICTOR*'s elbow bends.*

> MARY-JOSEPH *applies the pressure, his arm straightens at the elbow.*

(*Pulling a face.*) It really hurts, Sister.

> MARY-JOSEPH *stops.*

MARY-JOSEPH. It was a nasty wound. That's good. I've almost got it straight.

> MARY-JOSEPH *applies the pressure.*

> VICTOR *pulls a face.*

VICTOR (*in real pain*). Go on. Go on.

> MARY-JOSEPH *has his elbow straight.*

MARY-JOSEPH. I'm going to push your arm up now, so we start to straighten the shoulder.

VICTOR (*wincing*). Will it hurt?

MARY-JOSEPH. Mmm, it might do.

MARY-JOSEPH *keeps* VICTOR*'s arm straight. She moves his arm up so that the shoulder is moved.*

VICTOR (*in real agony*). Might do. Bloody hell.

MARY-JOSEPH. All right?

VICTOR (*gasping*). No.

MARY-JOSEPH *relaxes her pressure,* VICTOR*'s elbow bends, and the arm drops at the shoulder. She keeps hold of his wrist and elbow.*

A slight pause.

MARY-JOSEPH (*gently*). Once more?

VICTOR. No.

MARY-JOSEPH. Well, I'm going to do it.

MARY-JOSEPH *straightens his arm. She moves his arm up so that the shoulder is moved.*

VICTOR *is in agony. Tears come into his eyes.*

MARY-JOSEPH *relaxes her pressure.*

She puts his arm on his lap, and her own hands on her own lap.

Silence for a moment.

VICTOR (*wiping away the tears with his left hand*). I'm sorry.

MARY-JOSEPH (*gently*). Try using your right hand.

VICTOR *uses his right hand to wipe away the tears. His arm is like jelly, but he succeeds a little bit.*

VICTOR *is still.*

That's probably enough for an hour or two. We must keep that up.

VICTOR. Why is it so bad?

MARY-JOSEPH. The wound needs time to heal and mend. If we left it without movement, it would just go stiff. You'd lose some mobility in the shoulder.

VICTOR. I haven't to be afraid in other words?

MARY-JOSEPH. That's right.

VICTOR *leans forward, he kisses her on the forehead.* MARY-JOSEPH *pulls her head away.*

I shall pretend you didn't do that. (*After a moment's pause*.) What about this music?

MARY-JOSEPH *takes the manuscript paper and the pencil.*

VICTOR *looks at her.*

VICTOR. Dorian mode, 3-4. Two crochet rests. A above middle C. A low D. E, F, E, D, G. G, A quavers. B. A minim. A crotchet. Low D. E, F, E, D. A group of six quavers. G. F sharp.

MARY-JOSEPH *looks up from her writing.*

It's a passing note. G. A, B, C. A, dotted minim tied to a minim in the next bar.

VICTOR *sings, quite quietly, a snatch of the tune.*

A, B quavers, C dotted crotchet. B, A, G quavers. A. High D. C, B quavers. A, low E, F dotted minim in the next bar. F. G, E quavers. A group of four quavers, D, middle, C, D, E. F, G. C above middle C. B. Low D. E, F quavers. D dotted minim. Double bar nine.

MARY-JOSEPH *finishes. She gives him the manuscript paper and the pencil.*

A little music?

MARY-JOSEPH. I learnt at home. My father was a musician.

VICTOR. Why're you so modest?

MARY-JOSEPH (*starting to stand up*). I should be going, I have work to do.

VICTOR (*putting his hand out to stop her*). Don't go.

MARY-JOSEPH *stays kneeling on her haunches.* VICTOR *takes his hand away.*

MARY-JOSEPH (*embarrassed, she is not sure where to look*). This is most irregular.

VICTOR (*realising*). I'm sorry, Sister, you must go.

A slight pause.

I didn't mean to embarrass you.

MARY-JOSEPH *stands up. She is still.*

MARY-JOSEPH (*suddenly giggling*). The Holy Father would wonder what was going on, being kissed by a man.

VICTOR *smiles*.

VICTOR. I shan't do it again, I promise.

MARY-JOSEPH. My Mother Superior might have a fit. I'm a Sister of Mercy, not a Sister of Love.

MARY-JOSEPH *looks as if she is about to burst into tears. She walks away, back to the wards.*

VICTOR. Sister, come back.

MARY-JOSEPH *stops. She has her back to him.*

VICTOR *steps out of the wheelchair.*

He walks towards her. He stops.

Listen, I'm sorry, I really am.

A slight pause.

Forgive me?

MARY-JOSEPH. Am I such a foolish young girl that you feel you can do what you want?

(*Turning to face him.*) Sit in your wheelchair, please.

VICTOR (*after a moment's pause*). All right.

VICTOR *walks back to the wheelchair.*

MARY-JOSEPH. Sitting, not standing.

VICTOR *sits in the wheelchair.*

Sudden blackout.

Scene Five

The lights are snapped up.

A small river about two kilometres from the hospital. The river is in a gully which is wooded on either side. A wooden jetty stretches out from the river bank.

Saturday, 3 April.

The sun is shining brightly through the trees.

MARY-JOSEPH *is sitting on the end of the jetty, her feet are above the water. She has taken off her shoes and stockings and they are beside her.*

VICTOR *is standing at the other end of the jetty, by the bank. He has just entered. He is wearing civilian clothes and he is using his arm almost normally.*

VICTOR *is looking at her.* MARY-JOSEPH *is looking at the river, she looks deep in thought.*

A pause.

VICTOR. Mary-Joseph.

MARY-JOSEPH (*without turning*). Sister Mary-Joseph. (*Turning to look at him.*) How long've you been there?

VICTOR. Not very long. (*Walking forward.*) They told me at the hospital you'd come along here.

MARY-JOSEPH (*covering her legs*). I'm naked, practically.

> VICTOR *sits down beside her. He kisses her on the forehead.* MARY-JOSEPH *kisses his forehead.*

Where've you been these last few days?

VICTOR. Helping Lucy with the ambulance.

MARY-JOSEPH. More casualties?

VICTOR. Yes.

MARY-JOSEPH. It's a real war, isn't it? I thought it would all be over in a few weeks.

VICTOR. I'm going back to the front. I wanted you to be the first to know.

MARY-JOSEPH. Why?

VICTOR. To help us try and win.

MARY-JOSEPH. No, why did you want me to be the first to know?

VICTOR (*smiling*). Because you're my friend.

MARY-JOSEPH. That sounds so simple.

VICTOR. It is.

> MARY-JOSEPH *smiles*.

> What's the matter?

MARY-JOSEPH. I've had a telling off.

VICTOR. Oh, dear.

MARY-JOSEPH. From the Mother Superior. She was furious. (*Smiling*.) Far worse than my Mother Superior in England, and she could be terrifying.

VICTOR. What about?

MARY-JOSEPH. Don't be silly, Victor. Isn't it obvious to you?

VICTOR. No.

MARY-JOSEPH (*smiling*). It is to her.

VICTOR (*smiling*). Have tongues wagged?

MARY-JOSEPH. Somebody's has.

VICTOR. I'll go and see her. It's not fair that you should have this.

MARY-JOSEPH. You can't just go and see her.

VICTOR. Why not?

MARY-JOSEPH. Well, you can try.

VICTOR. Let me tell her about our friendship. I don't want you in hot water. I like you too much for that.

> MARY-JOSEPH *smiles*.

MARY-JOSEPH. It will do no good. They live in worlds of their own, these people. Who knows what they believe, or why.

VICTOR (*gulping*). Goodness.

MARY-JOSEPH. What have I said?

VICTOR. I don't know, Sister. An awful lot, suddenly.

VICTOR *quickly starts to take his shoes off. He uses his right arm carefully.* MARY-JOSEPH *watches him for a moment.*

MARY-JOSEPH. You're still being careful with that right arm, aren't you?

VICTOR. A little bit.

MARY-JOSEPH. You shouldn't be by now.

VICTOR *rolls his trouser legs up. He jumps off the jetty. He walks out across the shallow water. He stops some distance away.*

VICTOR. What's your real name, Mary-Joseph?

MARY-JOSEPH. That's not a question you ask. Bernadette.

VICTOR. After Bernadette of Lourdes?

MARY-JOSEPH. Yes.

VICTOR. Bernadette what?

MARY-JOSEPH. Bernadette Cook.

VICTOR. Well, Bernadette Cook, what do I say to the Mother Superior?

A slight pause.

MARY-JOSEPH. Don't, Victor, please.

A slight pause.

VICTOR. I'm sorry. (*After a moment's pause.*) I'm finding it hard not to feel the way I do.

MARY-JOSEPH. Is that my fault?

VICTOR (*after a moment's pause*). No.

MARY-JOSEPH (*looking at him*). I love you.

A slight pause.

VICTOR. That's both of us in love then.

MARY-JOSEPH (*after a moment's pause*). I'm trying not to.

A slight pause.

Doesn't my faith matter to you?

VICTOR. Yes, it does.

VICTOR *walks back. He climbs onto the jetty. He sits beside her.*
Yes, it does.

MARY-JOSEPH. How much does it matter?

VICTOR. A lot. I can't say. I don't want to see you hurt.

MARY-JOSEPH. I didn't deny it to the Mother Superior.

VICTOR (*brightly*). Mary-Joseph.

A pause.

MARY-JOSEPH. I know what she'll do.

VICTOR. What?

MARY-JOSEPH. Send me somewhere else. Like they sent me here to Spain.

VICTOR *is looking at her.*

I was foolish enough in England to tell the Mother Superior, that I didn't love God as much as I thought I could.

A slight pause.

Isn't that a terrible admission?

VICTOR (*gently*). For you, yes.

MARY-JOSEPH. You know why she sent me?

VICTOR. To defend the church against the Republic.

MARY-JOSEPH. She thought if I saw the churches being burnt –

A slight pause.

I'd think –

A slight pause.

It worked until the war began, and I saw the wounded.

A slight pause.

I still do hate the desecration. But somehow it doesn't seem to matter any more. Because the Church here has nothing to do with the people. (*Almost smiling.*) My Mother Superior would have me in Hell.

A slight pause.

It must be hard for you to understand what I'm saying?

VICTOR. Perhaps, yes.

MARY-JOSEPH. What a sin it is?

A slight pause.

Can you understand?

VICTOR (*carefully*). I think I know what it's like to have a faith, and believe.

MARY-JOSEPH. Honestly?

VICTOR. I didn't, I haven't. You're a part of that understanding. And the war is, too.

MARY-JOSEPH (*smiling*). We're alike.

VICTOR. Mmm.

A slight pause.

MARY-JOSEPH. This doesn't help me decide.

VICTOR. I can't be a part of that decision.

MARY-JOSEPH. That's the most stupid thing you've said.

VICTOR. My life's far too complicated for you.

A slight pause.

MARY-JOSEPH. I wonder if God meant it this way? The simple things are the most truthful.

VICTOR. Have you asked God?

MARY-JOSEPH. Yes.

VICTOR. What did He say?

A slight pause.

MARY-JOSEPH (*looking at him*). I think God can only guide those who are certain.

VICTOR *is looking at her. He looks away.*

If Christ had truly entered my heart

VICTOR (*after a moment's pause. Still looking down*). Then what?

MARY-JOSEPH. I couldn't love you.

A slight pause.

I am certain. I think finally God has spoken.

A slight pause.

I've no sin in my heart.

VICTOR (*sliding off the jetty, walking away*). You don't know what you're saying.

VICTOR *turns, he looks at her.*

MARY-JOSEPH. God forgives you, Victor.

VICTOR (*shaking his head slightly*). No. No, he doesn't.

MARY-JOSEPH. Yes, he does.

VICTOR. I can't love you. (*Looking at* MARY-JOSEPH.) She was right.

MARY-JOSEPH. Who?

VICTOR (*after a moment's pause*). Elizabeth's aunt – Edward's aunt.

MARY-JOSEPH. Who was she?

A slight pause.

VICTOR. It's something that haunts me.

A slight pause.

MARY-JOSEPH. Tell me?

VICTOR (*after a moment's pause*). She said I'd no soul. That I didn't care.

A slight pause.

That I'd no passion. That I'd never cry.

A slight pause.

I did love Edward, in my own way. I think she knew that.

A slight pause.

(*To himself.*) I think so. I think she did know that.

A slight pause.

(*To* MARY-JOSEPH.) I don't know where he is now. I've not seen him for fourteen years.

MARY-JOSEPH. Who?

VICTOR. Edward. He writes novels. He's successful. I'm a bit jealous.

MARY-JOSEPH. Why don't you find him? If he was your friend.

VICTOR. I think I will. (*After a moment's pause.*) He might not want to see me.

MARY-JOSEPH. Why not?

VICTOR (*shrugging*). I don't know.

A slight pause.

(*Shaking.*) I could get in touch with his publisher, maybe. (*Hardly able to get the words out.*) Write to him and explain.

MARY-JOSEPH *slips off the jetty. She goes to him, and stops a short distance away.*

MARY-JOSEPH. You're shaking. Why?

VICTOR (*his whole body shaking*). I don't know.

MARY-JOSEPH. What's the matter?

VICTOR (*the words hardly coming out*). I'm frightened.

MARY-JOSEPH. What of?

VICTOR (*trying to stop it, but he can't*). Letting go.

MARY-JOSEPH. Stop it, Victor.

VICTOR. I can't.

His whole body is shaking.

I can't.

MARY-JOSEPH. What are you frightened of?

VICTOR. I don't know. (*The words hardly coming out.*) Loving you, I think. I'm afraid.

MARY-JOSEPH. Why're you afraid?

VICTOR. I've been running.

MARY-JOSEPH (*puzzled*). Who from?

VICTOR *is still shaking violently.*

VICTOR. I'm sorry.

MARY-JOSEPH. Don't worry.

A slight pause.

Don't worry.

VICTOR *begins slowly, to control himself.*

A pause.

VICTOR *is almost still.*

Is that better?

VICTOR (*the shaking starting again*). This has never happened before.

VICTOR *controls it. He is still.*

A slight pause.

MARY-JOSEPH. I'd like to kiss you, very much.

They move to kiss. Their noses bump.

Whoops.

Sudden blackout.

Scene Six

The lights are snapped up.

The river. The jetty.

A few days later.

The sun is shining brightly through the trees.

The three soldiers are on leave, they are with LUCY. LUCY *is sitting, with her shoes and stockings next to her, on the jetty.*

WILFRED *is sitting close by, he too has his shoes and socks off. They are both writing letters.*

PETER *and* ERNEST *are paddling, some distance apart, in the shallow water. They are still.* PETER *is bending over, looking at something.*

A pause.

ERNEST *walks to* PETER, *he bends over to look.*

PETER. Lots of little fishes.

A pause.

PETER *walks to the jetty. He climbs up. He sits.*

ERNEST *paddles through the water to somewhere else. He bends down, he looks.*

ERNEST. There's a few here as well.

A pause.

Sudden blackout.

Scene Seven

The lights are snapped up.

Guisborough, High Cliff.

Wednesday, 26 May.

Early evening. A red sky which is beginning to darken. A few twinkling lights, from the town down below, can just be seen.

THOMAS ELLISON *is sitting on the grass. He is wearing a shirt and an unbuttoned waistcoat.*

PEGGY SMITH *is standing some distance away. She is wearing a summer coat.*

THOMAS *turns.*

THOMAS. Peggy.

He stands up. PEGGY *walks towards him.*

Have you come to say goodbye?

PEGGY. Yes.

THOMAS *kisses her on the cheek.*

They hesitate for a moment and then both sit on the grass.

(*Smiling.*) I hope I'm all packed and ready.

THOMAS (*starting to take it off*). Here, sit on my waistcoat.

PEGGY. No.

THOMAS (*keeping it on*). Are you sure?

They smile at one another.

What time are you leaving?

PEGGY. We'd like to make as early a start as is possible. Daddy's loading the Riley now.

THOMAS *nods.*

THOMAS. I'm not very good at goodbyes.

CONSTABLE WILLIAM PRICE *enters from the surrounding woods. He is not wearing his uniform, but civilian clothes: trousers, waistcoat and jacket.*

Willy.

PRICE *joins them. He squats down.*

PRICE. I heard someone'd seen a pine marten in the woods. Yer've not seen it by any chance?

THOMAS. No.

PRICE. There's supposed to be a family of 'em. There was a male and female years ago, but they disappeared.

PEGGY. Why was that, Mr Price?

PRICE. I reckon they don't like people much. There's a few rabbits up here. Yer'd've thought they might stay.

PRICE *starts to stand up.*

THOMAS. Yer all right, Willy.

PRICE (*sitting*). I really wanted to see 'em. (*After a moment's pause.*) Yer off tomorrow then?

PEGGY. Yes.

PRICE. Yer still goin' to be doctoring where yer goin?

PEGGY. Yes. I think it's time I let my father get on with his own work, unhindered.

PRICE. Isn't he upset?

PEGGY. He understands why. It's been difficult, at times, living under his shadow.

THOMAS. Wouldn't you do the same, Willy?

PRICE. I'm not that clever.

PRICE *stands up*.

My supper will be on the table.

PEGGY (*looking up at him*). I thought you were treated very shoddily.

PRICE. A few folk've said that.

PEGGY. I'm sorry.

PRICE. It's one of those things. All the best.

PEGGY *stands up*.

See yer, Thomas.

THOMAS. No doubt.

PRICE *exits the way he came*.

PEGGY. He was treated very shabbily. Wasn't he?

THOMAS. I don't know. Yes, probably.

PEGGY *sits*.

I don't feel sorry for him. He should have done something about it. It wasn't just generosity. He wanted a quiet life. He was bound to be sacked sooner or later. The world is changing.

PEGGY *smiles*.

Shouldn't you be seeing Dorothy?

PEGGY. Yes, at eight o'clock. Is that why you came up here?

THOMAS (*smiling*). I said I hate goodbyes. (*After a moment's pause*.) She's upset.

PEGGY. I'm not sure how to handle her?

THOMAS. I wouldn't. Be yourself. She'll get over it. (*After a moment's pause*.) I know she's been grateful to you.

PEGGY. It's mutual. I've enjoyed her company.

THOMAS. I don't know if she knows why you have to go.

PEGGY *looks down*.

PEGGY (*looking back up*). Do you?

THOMAS. I think so, Peggy.

PEGGY. When did you find out?

THOMAS. A second ago. I've had my doubts for months.

A slight pause.

I shan't ever tell her. I don't know what will become of Victor. It almost seems irrelevant, in a way.

PEGGY. I'm guilty of breaking their marriage.

THOMAS. Perhaps.

PEGGY. I loved him, you know.

A slight pause.

THOMAS. Thank you.

PEGGY (*doesn't understand*). Why?

THOMAS. Because there is nothing to be gained from saying anything else. Dorothy will give her own thanks.

A slight pause.

It's a long way, isn't it?

PEGGY (*firmly*). Yes.

THOMAS. If you ever come back, come and see us.

PEGGY. Who can say?

An aeroplane circles far overhead.

I would be happier, if you didn't tell Dorothy.

THOMAS. I've said I shan't.

PEGGY. Were you hiding up here?

THOMAS. No. If I saw you I would have to say something.

A slight pause.

I didn't want to upset you. I was hiding. But for the right reasons.

A slight pause.

PEGGY. I hope I'm doing the right thing. I told my father. He was furious. I felt I owed him an explanation.

A slight pause.

I would be happier if Dorothy didn't know.

THOMAS. Stop yourself from saying anything, Peggy.

PEGGY. I will, I'll try.

THOMAS (*after a moment's pause*). The truth is often right. In this case, it isn't.

The aeroplane goes.

In any case, it's not that far.

PEGGY. Where?

THOMAS. To Canada. We'll come and see you.

PEGGY *smiles, half-laughs.*

It won't be that far in a few years' time. The world is getting smaller.

PEGGY. It seems a long way to me.

THOMAS. Why did you love him, Peggy?

PEGGY. Didn't you?

THOMAS. Yes, I did.

PEGGY. Then you know why.

THOMAS. No, I don't.

A slight pause.

He's one of the most selfish people I've ever met.

A slight pause.

The world is changing, isn't it?

A slight pause.

It's not me. Or even Victor. Or you. It's something in the air. (*After a moment's pause.*) War, perhaps. It's almost as if we're getting ready. The world will turn again. Thank God, I'll be too old this time.

THOMAS *smiles.*

PEGGY. What're you smiling for?

THOMAS. Because I'm helpless. (*Stands up quickly.*) Perhaps I do understand why Victor went to Spain.

PEGGY *flinches for a split second, feeling for a moment that* THOMAS *might hit her.*

Ask Dorothy to show you Lucy's letter.

PEGGY. How is Lucy?

THOMAS. Her letters are full of her brother. He's back at the front, apparently. Or will be by now, fighting. She's a Spanish boyfriend.

PEGGY. I'd rather not see it. I've tried not to show any interest.

A slight pause.

THOMAS. You sail from Southampton?

PEGGY. Yes. On Saturday morning.

(*After a moment's pause.*) My father's still taking me.

A slight pause.

Do you think I'm doing the right thing?

THOMAS. I hope so, Peggy, for your sake

PEGGY. My father didn't want me to go. Now, he can't wait. Isn't that awful?

THOMAS. No.

PEGGY. Is being in love such a sin?

THOMAS (*after a moment's pause*). Yes.

A slight pause.

We're all going to have to change. Aren't we?

PEGGY (*running her hands through her hair*). I'm sorry, I feel faint.

PEGGY *sits with her head between her knees.*

THOMAS. Don't worry.

A slight pause.

PEGGY (*sitting up*). That's better. It's gone.

PEGGY *smiles.*

THOMAS. What time does your boat sail on Saturday morning?

PEGGY. Eight o'clock.

Sudden blackout.

Scene Eight

The lights are snapped up.

The wooded coppice at ELIZABETH BRADLEY*'s house by the river Thames in Twickenham.*

The summer of 1946.

A bright sunlight is filtering through the apple trees.

There is a lawnmower, turned upside-down, on the grass. The green hopper is elsewhere on the lawn.

ELIZABETH *is kneeling beside the lawnmower. She is wearing trousers and a cardigan. There is a hammer and a small oilcan beside her: she is tampering, very unpractically, at the lawnmower with a wooden-handled screwdriver.*

VICTOR, *wearing trousers and a short-sleeved jumper, is standing some distance away. He has just entered.*

A slight pause.

VICTOR. Elizabeth.

ELIZABETH *turns her head.*

There is a slight pause while she works out who it is.

ELIZABETH (*as if he had never been away. Standing up*). Victor, my dear, how lovely to see you.

ELIZABETH *has the screwdriver in her hand. They are looking at one another.*

VICTOR. It's been a long time.

ELIZABETH. Oh, surely not that long. (*Kicking the lawnmower.*) Now then, dear, whilst you are here, would you fix this thing for me?

VICTOR (*walking forward*). What's the matter with it?

ELIZABETH. Oh, it doesn't work, the usual story. (*Holding up the screwdriver.*) This might not be the right tool.

VICTOR *takes the screwdriver, he bends down, he looks at the lawnmower.*

The things that go round have stopped going round. It's a most nuisant thing.

VICTOR. I'm not very practical.

ELIZABETH. Dear, none of us are. We're all making do.

> ELIZABETH *bends down to show him.*

I think it might be somewhere in these little screws.

> ELIZABETH *picks up the hammer.*

VICTOR. I wouldn't bash it.

> ELIZABETH *kneels down. She bashes at the lawnmower with the hammer.*

ELIZABETH. Is that doing it?

VICTOR (*trying to turn the blades, they still won't move*). No.

> ELIZABETH *bashes again.*

> (*The screwdriver stuck in the blades.*) No.

> ELIZABETH *sits back.*

The house is full of children?

ELIZABETH. Yes, dear. They all paint and sing. (*Standing up, walking away.*) They're all mentally retarded, so they do it very badly. (*Turning to face him.*) I laugh. Quite a lot.

VICTOR (*standing up*). Whose idea was that?

ELIZABETH. Oh, they needed somewhere to express themselves.

VICTOR. It was a shock.

ELIZABETH. Dear, you're so normal.

VICTOR. How many are there?

ELIZABETH. Fifteen. We put on a concert last year. I laughed – (*Turning, walking away a pace.*) No, it was something we did in the war, when the bombs were falling. (*Turning to face him.*) How mean the world has become, Victor.

VICTOR (*after a moment's pause*). I came to say various things.

ELIZABETH (*turning, walking away*). I saw Edward the other day. He said you'd met.

VICTOR (*surprised*). Really?

> ELIZABETH *is standing with her back to him.*

I thought Edward had died in the Spanish Civil War.

ELIZABETH (*turning*). No, dear, you've got it quite wrong. When I saw your name in my newspaper the other day, I said to Mrs Wellbeloved, that at last you were both successful. Of course Edward has a brilliant streak, dear.

VICTOR (*after a moment's pause*). I'm sorry, Elizabeth. We were in the same hospital. I never knew.

ELIZABETH (*turning, walking away*). He has that touch of genius that you'll always lack.

ELIZABETH *stands with her back to him.*

VICTOR. I came to ask if you'd like to come?

ELIZABETH. No, dear, the children are enough.

A slight pause.

I wondered if I'd upset you that day. The day I offered you money.

VICTOR. No.

A slight pause.

ELIZABETH. I'd hate your music if it wasn't perfect. Has it your soul in it, Victor?

VICTOR. I don't know.

ELIZABETH. Is it mean?

VICTOR. I hope not.

ELIZABETH (*turning to face him*). Don't you find the world so bloody mean these days? No passion? No commitment? No imagination.

BERNADETTE COOK (SISTER MARY-JOSEPH) *enters. She is wearing a summer dress.*

It's all so bloody small-minded.

BERNADETTE *walks to* VICTOR.

And what do you do, dear?

BERNADETTE. I'm a nurse.

VICTOR *takes her hand.*

One of the children is asking for you.

ELIZABETH. Isn't there a teacher with them?

BERNADETTE. Yes.

ELIZABETH. I'm just the gardener.

VICTOR (*after a moment's pause*). Bernadette nursed Edward.

ELIZABETH (*turning her back on them*). I don't want to know.

   VICTOR *and* BERNADETTE *look at one another.* VICTOR *shrugs.*

   ELIZABETH *turns to them.*

He died fighting for what he believed in?

VICTOR. Don't you know that already, Elizabeth?

   A slight pause.

ELIZABETH. I forget, the war has changed everything. Good, I'm
   glad.

   A slight pause.

How long has it been, Victor?

VICTOR. Twenty-three years. Won't you come to the concert? I thought
   you might be pleased.

ELIZABETH. I am, dear, I am. No, I saw your name in my newspaper.
   (*Walking to the lawnmower.*) The world today is full of such
   horrible things, I only ever read the nice.

   ELIZABETH *kneels down. She picks up the can of oil and starts to
   oil the lawnmower. She bashes at it with the hammer.*

   The lights fade.

   Darkness.

   The company sing the opening song.

   It is symphonic in tone. It is VICTOR*'s.*

   As they sing the light grows in intensity.

   The End.

MUSIC FOR THE PLAY

OPENING SONG: THE SLEEPERS

Hard fac-es of an-ger and white eyes of doubt —,

She with her palm on the hip of her spouse, The

bo-dies on the battle-field, the in-sane in their rooms, and so the

new-born e-merge from the gates of the old.

CAROL: 'WHILE SHEPHERDS WATCHED'

398

THE SLEEPERS: FINAL CHORUS

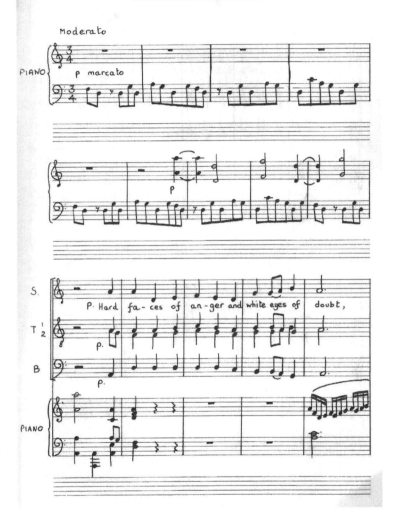

400

(Child) pau-sing and ga-zing and ben-ding con-fused,

(Child) And so the new-born e - merge from the gates of the old.

He with his hands on the hip of his spouse.

Swift-ly from si-ght is borne the brave corpse, and so the

THE OVERGROWN PATH

The Overgrown Path was first performed at the Royal Court Theatre, London, on 31 May 1985, with the following cast:

DANIEL HOWARTH	Peter Vaughan
MIMIKO	Christopher Karallis
NICHOLAS MARKS	Stuart Wilson
SARAH JEFFS	Deborah Findlay
BETH HOWARTH	Doreen Mantle
CLARE	Martha Parsey
CHILDREN	Saya Akiba
	Suzanne Fenelon
	Tomoya Hanai
	Ayako Kimura
	Ken Kotake
	Haigi Okada
	Sayuri Okada
	Nami Sekata
Director	Les Waters

Characters

DANIEL HOWARTH, *seventy-three*
MIMIKO, *sixteen*
NICHOLAS MARKS, *thirty-eight*
SARAH JEFFS, *thirty-six*
BETH HOWARTH, *sixty-nine*
CLARE, *twelve*
CHILDREN

Setting

ACT ONE
Scene One: A school stage.
Scene Two: The house.
Scene Three: The house.
Scene Four: A hillside.

ACT TWO
Scene One: A hillside.
Scene Two: A hillside.
Scene Three: The beach.
Scene Four: The beach.

ACT ONE

Scene One

The small stage of a primary school in modern-day Nagasaki.

A black drape hangs at the back. A low wooden bench is set to one side. A long blue ribbon is lying on the wooden floor.

A group of nine Japanese CHILDREN, *all ten years old, are about to present their play. Eight of the* CHILDREN *now enter, one after the other, through the drape. The* CHILDREN *are smartly dressed in their school uniforms. One of the* GIRLS *walks to the front. Two of the* BOYS *go to either end of the ribbon where they kneel down. The rest of the* CHILDREN *sit on the bench.*

The girl at the front, her name is SUZUKO, *waits for the* CHILDREN *to settle, and then she bows to the audience.*

SUZUKO. Mrs Oogushi's class welcome you to their play. (*She narrates the story.*) It is a hot, August morning. The sky has been cloudless for several weeks, and the citizens of Nagasaki grumble as they go about their business.

The CHILDREN *on the bench make the 'sounds' of grumbling. One of the* BOYS *takes a bird-whistle from his pocket and blows it.*

The birds sing. Only the children are happy in this heat.

The BOYS, *kneeling, raise the blue ribbon.*

Imagine the Urakami River on that sultry day in 1945. Nature has formed a small pool here. The river flows gently.

The BOYS *flutter the ribbon.*

It was to this pool that five children came, whenever they could sneak away, to play their game called Find the Bell.

The five CHILDREN *on the bench, three* GIRLS *and two* BOYS, *stand up. As they go to the riverbank, the narrator continues.*

The game was simple.

The five CHILDREN *mime getting undressed.*

One of the children, Etsuko, had a small gilded bell. When they were wearing nothing but their pants, Etsuko would throw the bell into the pool.

The girl playing ETSUKO *mimes throwing the bell.*

The children would dive in after it.

The five children dive in. They look very happy as they swim and dive searching for the bell. The boys with the ribbon quicken their fluttering.

It was great fun. Whoever should find the bell first was the winner. But, on this particular morning, the river was cloudy.

The five CHILDREN *climb out onto the riverbank. One of the boys, his name is* KOICHI, *speaks first.*

KOICHI. Etsuko, I can't find it.

YASUKO. Nor I.

KEIKO. Nor I, Etsuko.

ETSUKO *pulls a long face. The narrator continues.*

SUZUKO. Etsuko was worried. She had taken the bell from her sister's workbox without her permission. It had to be found. Etsuko well knew the wrath of her angry sister.

ETSUKO *dives into the river. The* BOYS *flutter the ribbon.*

So, once again, she dived into the Urakami River, and was gone for thirty seconds.

ETSUKO *disappears beneath the ribbon.*

A BOY *enters through the drape. He is padded-up to be grotesquely fat, his suit is the colour of metallic black. He is* FAT MAN, *the atomic bomb.*

The BOYS *flutter the ribbon as if there were a violent storm.*

(*Shielding her eyes.*) There was a blinding white flash like lightning, and the next moment Bang! Crack! as thunder rang out. It was Fat Man, the atomic bomb.

The boy playing FAT MAN *rushes about. As he touches the* CHILDREN *playing the divers, they fall over. Then the boy playing* FAT MAN *disappears the way he came, back through the drape.*

There is silence for a moment before the girl playing ETSUKO
appears from beneath the ribbon.

Etsuko surfaced, having not found the bell, to find everything
different. Gone was her primary school. Gone, too, was the College
Hospital where, under a protest of screams, Etsuko had been taken
by her mother to have her injection. The Mitsubishi Steelworks had
disappeared. Etsuko climbed from the river.

ETSUKO *mimes climbing out.*

Her friends were gone, too. Was this a new game they were
playing? Had they found the bell and not told her? If that was so,
it wasn't fair. Suddenly it began to snow on Nagasaki.

The two BOYS *holding the ribbon put it down. They stand up. They
have white confetti in their pockets which they throw over*
ETSUKO.

White snowflakes fell over the whole city.

ETSUKO *hugs herself.*

Etsuko, thinking it was already winter because everything looked so
dark and desolate, hugged herself to keep warm. She cried out:
'Mummy.'

ETSUKO *mimes calling.*

'Mummy, where are you?' But her cry must have been in silence for
her mother never appeared.

ETSUKO *catches a single piece of the confetti.*

And when she touched the snow it didn't melt, but crumbled in her
fingers.

The two BOYS *stop throwing the confetti.*

That is the end of our story, except to say that Etsuko never did find
her friends, but grew up and is the name of our teacher, Mrs
Oogushi. We hope you liked out play with the happy ending.

The CHILDREN *stand up.* FAT MAN *comes through the drape.
They hold hands, and bow.*

Scene Two

Thursday 10 May. Two o'clock in the afternoon.

The frontage of a house at the village of Panormos on the Greek island of Tinos.

The front of the house has two doors. One is the main entrance and leads into the house through the kitchen. The other is to a small, spare bedroom. This door is painted pale blue. The kitchen door is open, coloured strips of plastic hang over the entrance. Beside the entrance is a small, cross-paned kitchen window which is painted the same pale blue. The wall of the house is whitewashed, as are the irregular-shaped flagstones which pave the ground in front. A small Judas tree, set to the right, is growing out of these flagstones and has cracked and bevelled the areas surrounding it. The base of the tree's thin, twisty trunk has been painted pale blue.

An old wooden table stands on the flagstones. Two old bentwood chairs are pushed into it, and there is a third by the kitchen entrance. Elsewhere, there are two larger, heavier, cane wickerwork, easy chairs. One is by the tree, and the other beside the table.

The front of the house has a used feel to it. The tables and chairs have been bumped and scraped. In odd places the whitewash has weathered and come away. But nothing is decrepit or dirty.

The sun is high and is powering down. It is very, very hot. A shadow is being cast by the Judas tree across the kitchen entrance.

Sitting asleep, on the bentwood chair, in this shadow, is DANIEL HOWARTH. DANIEL *is so precariously balanced that it looks like he might tumble off the chair at any moment.*

Above his head is a washing line. It runs from the tree to a hook above the bedroom door. Two squid are hanging on the line, drying in the sun.

DANIEL *is seventy-three. He is a big, stocky man with broad shoulders. He has big feet and hands, soft deep-set eyes, and thick dark hair. He is wearing a baggy black suit with a white shirt. He has sandals on has feet.*

The sound of a bus arriving and coming to a halt, nearby. After a moment its engine stops.

DANIEL *snorts in his sleep.*

MIMIKO *enters. He is carrying a large canvas holdall.*

MIMIKO *is a Greek boy of sixteen. He is small and thin and wiry. He has jet-black hair and his ears stick out. He is dressed roughly in shoes, trousers, coloured shirt, and jacket. He is overdressed and his clothes are ill-fitting.*

MIMIKO *hurriedly puts down the holdall and calls back the way he came.*

MIMIKO. This way. This way.

After a moment NICHOLAS MARKS *enters.*

NICHOLAS *is thirty-eight. He is tall and distinguished with intelligent eyes. He has an alert, almost boyish face. He is well-dressed in white plimsolls, brown cord trousers, and a checked shirt.*

NICHOLAS *stops by his holdall.* MIMIKO *has walked towards* DANIEL.

Asleep see. He is an old man. Old men sleep all day, then wake at night. (*Going to wake* DANIEL.) I wake him for you. It do him good.

NICHOLAS. No, don't.

MIMIKO. He is an old fool. (*Bending down.*) I tickle his chin.

MIMIKO *tickles* DANIEL'*s chin.*

NICHOLAS. I'd rather you left him. I'm happy to wait.

DANIEL *snorts.*

MIMIKO. In a moment he shout out his dreams. (*Looking up, his face close to* DANIEL'*s.*) Big clown, big nit, daft idiot. Big Koko. (*To* NICHOLAS.) He likes me to be rude. He enjoy a game. I slap him for you now.

NICHOLAS. Don't do that.

MIMIKO *stands up, he looks dejected.*

Thank you for carrying my bag for me.

MIMIKO. This man is famous in England.

NICHOLAS. Yes.

MIMIKO. You?

NICHOLAS. No. I'm not famous at all in England.

MIMIKO. You must like our island?

NICHOLAS. What I've seen of it so far, very much.

MIMIKO (*going to him*). I like England. We are friends.

He offers his hand. NICHOLAS *shakes it.*

For carrying your case I receive money. Daniel would give me, but he is asleep.

NICHOLAS (*delving into his pocket*). Yes, of course.

MIMIKO. I cannot take coin. I have my pride.

NICHOLAS *puts the coins back. He takes his leather wallet from his back pocket.*

Are you always mean when it comes to money?

NICHOLAS. I'm sorry?

MIMIKO. I not take anything now. You have hurt me. We are not friends. Goodbye.

MIMIKO *goes off, looking deliberately forlorn.*

NICHOLAS, *a note in his hand, looks perplexed.*

A slight pause.

DANIEL *snorts.*

NICHOLAS *looks at* DANIEL *for a moment. He walks to the edge of the flagstones and looks at the view. He puts the note in the wallet and the wallet back in his pocket.*

A bird, a bee-eater, calls nearby.

DANIEL *gives a loud snort.*

NICHOLAS *looks at him.*

DANIEL *wakes as if he had never been asleep.*

DANIEL. Ah, you've arrived. (*Getting up, going to him.*) Daniel Howarth. You've come to ask about my work on the hydrogen bomb.

NICHOLAS. I'm sorry if I woke you.

DANIEL. No, no, I wasn't asleep, just dozing. You must be Richard. Nice of you to come.

NICHOLAS (*shaking his hand*). Nicholas, not Richard. Nicholas Marks.

DANIEL. Let's not get ourselves confused.

Their hands part.

Nicholas. Now then, you'd like a drink.

He goes through the plastic strips into the kitchen.

NICHOLAS *walks to the edge of the flagstones, he looks down over the village once again.*

A slight pause.

The bee-eater calls.

A slight pause.

DANIEL *returns, he is carrying a tray. On it are two glasses of water; two smaller, empty glasses; and a bottle of ouzo.*

(*Going to the table.*) Why did I think you were a Richard.

He puts the tray down.

NICHOLAS. You live in a beautiful part of the world, Professor Howarth.

DANIEL (*picking up the bottle of ouzo*). D'you drink this stuff?

NICHOLAS. Thank you very much.

DANIEL. It's aniseedy. The British, I believe, feed aniseed to cattle.

He pours ouzo into the two small glasses.

NICHOLAS. I think that's silage.

DANIEL. The two are not the same. We shouldn't take too much notice of it – the British will feed anything to anything.

NICHOLAS. I spent part of my childhood on a farm.

DANIEL. Really? Tell me what you like and we'll get it in. Shyness will make your stay miserable.

He picks up the glasses of ouzo.

There is water on the table.

NICHOLAS (*taking his glass from* DANIEL). Thank you.

They walk to the edge of the flagstones.

DANIEL. Good journey?

NICHOLAS. Not too bad.

DANIEL. The Greeks are terribly unreliable.

They sip their drinks.

NICHOLAS. I was thinking how beautiful the island is.

DANIEL. Have you been to Greece before, Nicholas?

NICHOLAS. No.

DANIEL. Most things have a beauty. The truth comes with time.

NICHOLAS. I noticed so many small churches on the way.

DANIEL. There are a few. No, Tinos is a Greek island, if that makes
sense to you. We get very few European tourists. The town of Tinos
has a shrine. A holy icon of the Virgin Mary was found in 1823 by
St Pelagia. The islands became a place of pilgrimage for the Greeks,
like Lourdes for the French. The island is sacred. It holds miracles.
Has magic.

NICHOLAS. Is that why you chose it?

DANIEL (*smiling*). I wonder, do you?

NICHOLAS (*shrugging*). I don't know.

DANIEL. It has a peace which we like. Especially here, away from the
main town. The English are arrogant abroad – don't you find?

NICHOLAS. Sometimes, yes.

DANIEL. I expect it's because we're arrogant at home. We have tiny
minds. I say that with regret.

NICHOLAS. When did you first come here?

DANIEL. Now you ask a question. Would it be 1975? (*Incredulously.*)
I believe it was, you know.

NICHOLAS (*smiling*). You obviously like it.

DANIEL. Oh, I think so, don't you?

NICHOLAS. Yes.

DANIEL. I see no reason to move.

   DANIEL *indicates the chairs at the table.*

Let me say from the outset that we can't put you up. (*Walking to a bentwood chair*.) Much as we'd like to. Unfortunately my daughter is staying with us.

NICHOLAS (*following him*). I didn't expect you to.

DANIEL (*sitting down*). How odd. I thought we'd put in a letter that we would.

NICHOLAS (*sitting in the other bentwood chair*) You did, but it doesn't matter.

DANIEL. You're being kind. It's of no consequence, she's here and that's that. I've arranged a room for you.

NICHOLAS. Thank you.

DANIEL. There's no hotel. She's a widow – you'll be having her son's room. I've left the financial arrangements up to you. She won't charge you much – they're very generous. She'll allow you your privacy, that's the main thing, isn't it? I'll take you to her, later.

NICHOLAS. I hope I'm not putting her son out?

DANIEL. No, no, she's used to guests. You'll find she doesn't speak English.

NICHOLAS. My Greek isn't very good. We'll manage.

DANIEL. Tonight you'll eat with us. After that, it's entirely up to you. There are two tavernas in the village. Both are nice. You are welcome here whenever you feel like it.

NICHOLAS. Thank you.

DANIEL *sits back, his glass of ouzo in his hand. He is drinking very little.*

DANIEL. You work in a sweet shop, Nicholas?

NICHOLAS. Yes.

DANIEL. I found that interesting.

NICHOLAS. I don't know that it is really.

DANIEL (*excited*). Why, tell me why that is?

NICHOLAS. It's routine, for the most part. The hours are long if you open as we do.

DANIEL. And you were brought up on a farm?

NICHOLAS. I used to go to the farm for my holidays.

DANIEL. I see.

NICHOLAS. I know the shop like my hand.

DANIEL. How fascinating.

NICHOLAS. It's in Yorkshire – Cleveland.

DANIEL. D'you sell pineapple chunks?

NICHOLAS. Yes. And cigarettes. And kiddies' toys. Birthday and anniversary cards. Daily Papers. You can imagine the sort of shop.

DANIEL (*nodding*). Mmm.

NICHOLAS. I have a manageress – Mrs Robson – which is why I'm able to get away.

DANIEL (*pondering*). Mmm.

NICHOLAS. There's a similar shop in every high street.

DANIEL. Mmm.

NICHOLAS. It's good of you to see me, Professor Howarth.

DANIEL. Is it? I'm not sure that it is.

NICHOLAS. I was told you don't see many people.

DANIEL. I believe, not many people want to see me. It flatters my ego if they do.

DANIEL stretches forward and picks up the bottle of ouzo, he unscrews the top. He offers some to NICHOLAS.

NICHOLAS. A little, please.

He pours some into NICHOLAS*'s glass.*

Thank you, that's plenty.

DANIEL doesn't have any himself.

DANIEL (*putting the bottle down*). I'll show you the island whilst you're here. We might enjoy that together. The miracles I mean. And tell you curious stories that will seem far-fetched to begin with.

NICHOLAS. I hope I won't intrude on your privacy.

DANIEL. No, no.

DANIEL takes a packet of plain Senior Service cigarettes from his jacket pocket. He lights one with a match.

(*Putting the cigarettes and matches away.*) Tell me, Richard, d'you like stories?

NICHOLAS. Nicholas.

DANIEL. Nicholas. I love stories. They have in them the richness of our lives.

DANIEL *stands up.*

NICHOLAS. I don't know quite what you mean? Please explain.

DANIEL (*the cigarette in his mouth, taking off his jacket*). I supposeI mean myths. Legends. Parables.

NICHOLAS. I read all sorts of stories as a kid. Fairytales.

DANIEL. I did too.

DANIEL *puts the jacket over the bentwood chair. His shirt sleeves are rolled up; he is wearing two watches, one on each wrist. He takes the cigarette from his mouth.*

(*Walking to the tree.*) You're young still. I don't expect stories are important to you yet.

NICHOLAS. D'you mean stories help to explain our lives?

DANIEL *sits on the cane chair in the shade of the tree.*

DANIEL. It may be an age thing. Are you married?

NICHOLAS. No. No, I'm not.

DANIEL. If Beth should fuss you, ignore her. Women are like that.

NICHOLAS. Beth is your wife.

DANIEL (*drawing on his cigarette*). My second wife. What were we talking about, Richard?

NICHOLAS. I think you get my name wrong on purpose.

DANIEL (*chortling slightly*). Do I? Do I? It's Nicholas, isn't it? (*Leaning forward.*) I may tell you stories because I hate facts. The world today is far too factual, don't you find? The pleasure of a story is in its interpretation. It has a philosophy. A fact has nothing. Like a name. (*Sitting back.*) I may call you Richard, if that's all right?

He puffs on his cigarette.

A slight pause.

NICHOLAS stands up with his glass of ouzo, he walks to the edge of the flagstones and looks at the view.

I'm sorry I didn't meet you off the bus. I had meant to.

NICHOLAS (*turning to him*). I haven't really any specific questions.

DANIEL. Good.

NICHOLAS. I was worried you'd think that was lazy.

DANIEL. No, no.

NICHOLAS. It might take me a few days to get my bearings.

DANIEL. I'm sure.

A slight pause.

NICHOLAS. And not having done anything academic for so long – well, that's my problem, not yours.

DANIEL. No, no.

NICHOLAS. I want you to know that I'm not here to make judgements.

DANIEL. We liked your letters. We found them honest.

NICHOLAS (*suddenly with shyness*). Thank you.

A slight pause.

I think I told you I'd had enough of the shop.

Cigarette ash falls onto DANIEL's trousers. He brushes it off. He uses the ashtray which is beside him on the flagstones.

DANIEL. I don't know why, but never mind. Beth and I found it so intriguing.

NICHOLAS (*smiling*). People do.

A slight pause.

When did you marry Beth, Professor Howarth?

DANIEL (*brightly*). Would it be 1962? I believe it was, you know. The grass was full of white snowdrops.

A bus horn honks several times, nearby.

You worked in London?

NICHOLAS. Yes, for a while, after university.

DANIEL. Beth has your letters. (*After drawing on his cigarette.*) We were married in a London February. What a mantle of depression London had then – didn't you find?

NICHOLAS. Sometimes.

DANIEL. It has one colour – that of meanness. I learnt to loathe the bloody place.

NICHOLAS *smiles.*

I tried not to be there as much as I could.

The bus horn honks again.

(*Standing up.*) There's your bus about to go back.

NICHOLAS. Am I disturbing you?

DANIEL (*joining* NICHOLAS *at the edge of the flagstones*). No, no.

NICHOLAS. Perhaps for our talks we should arrange a timetable?

DANIEL. As you wish.

SARAH JEFFS *enters, running. She is carrying a small, brightly coloured beach bag.*

SARAH *is thirty-six. She is small and thin with a boyish frame and face. Her blonde hair is short. She is wearing a pair of off-white long shorts, a red T-shirt and flip-flops.*

SARAH (*dashing to the spare bedroom door*). I want to catch the bus before he goes.

She opens the door and hurries in.

DANIEL (*calling after her*). There's no bus back, pet. Not today. You'll be stuck in Tinos.

SARAH (*from inside*). No, I know. (*Reappearing without her bag. Carrying an envelope.*) I want him to post a letter for me.

DANIEL. This is Nicholas, pet.

SARAH. Hello.

NICHOLAS. Hello.

SARAH. I'll see you later.

SARAH *dashes off.*

The bus engine turns over. After a few rickety attempts, it starts.

NICHOLAS *and* DANIEL *watch*.

NICHOLAS. How often is the bus?

DANIEL. There's two a day – one in the morning, one in the afternoon. They drive like bloody madmen.

NICHOLAS *smiles*.

That's Yanni. They think they're like cats with nine lives. (*Turning, walking to the tree*.) Yanni's used three of his while I've been on the bus.

DANIEL *stands above the ashtray. He flicks his cigarette, ash swirls down towards it. He looks at* NICHOLAS.

You're from Skelton – is that right?

NICHOLAS. Yes.

DANIEL. Tell me about it

NICHOLAS. It's a small market town in the Cleveland Hills, in what was once Yorkshire.

DANIEL. I'm Lancashire, of course. (*Chortling slightly*.) We're sworn enemies. Manchester – where it rains. Soddin' awful place. I think I'd kick the bucket if I had to go there now.

NICHOLAS. I went and looked for your house.

DANIEL. Did you indeed? That was thorough.

NICHOLAS. It's – er – not there.

DANIEL. I know. (*Puffing on his cigarette*.) It was pulled down with my mother inside it. The old fool wouldn't budge. (*Bending down*.) She was one of those.

The bus horn honks. The bus pulls away into the distance.

DANIEL *stubs out his cigarette*.

NICHOLAS. I met your old science teacher.

DANIEL (*straightening up*). Good God. Is he still alive? (*Thinking*.) Wait a minute, wait a minute – I used to go and visit him.

NICHOLAS. Mr Cuthbertson.

DANIEL (*smiling*). That's it.

NICHOLAS. He's ninety-six. He asked me to give you his regards.

DANIEL. How wonderful.

A slight pause.

(*A grunt of pleasure.*) Arr. How did you find him?

NICHOLAS. I went to the school.

DANIEL (*stumbling with pleasure*). He, he, he, like all good teachers, made you think you were learning something for the first time – that your knowledge was unique. Then he broadened the context, and showed you the avenues. That's made my day. Fancy him still being alive. After all these years.

NICHOLAS *smiles.*

NICHOLAS. He told me you were a scholarship boy?

DANIEL. Oh, I expect I was. (*A glazed look behind his eyes.*) Manchester Grammar School. Mr Cuthbertson. Thank you, Nicholas.

NICHOLAS. He remembers giving your mother some money to buy you shoes.

DANIEL. There's nothing in class, you know. I'm aware your generation thinks there is.

NICHOLAS. It was a well-heeled school.

DANIEL. Still is, I believe.

NICHOLAS. How much of an outsider did you feel?

DANIEL. Good God. Not a bit. I had a mind, I used it.

MIMIKO *enters. He has his hands in his pockets, he is sulking.*

Ah, Mimiko.

MIMIKO *goes to* DANIEL.

I want you to meet an English friend of mine.

DANIEL *turns* MIMIKO *round to face* NICHOLAS, *he puts his hands on his shoulders.*

This is Nicholas.

MIMIKO *sticks his tongue out.*

You'll be seeing a lot of Mimiko.

NICHOLAS. Hello.

MIMIKO. This man is rubbish. I carry his case. He is the rudest man in Greece.

DANIEL. Oh dear.

MIMIKO *walks from* DANIEL*'s hands. He goes to* DANIEL*'s jacket on the bentwood chair.*

Mimiko is easily upset. Aren't you, Mimiko?

MIMIKO *has found the cigarettes and matches in* DANIEL*'s jacket.*

MIMIKO. Daniel, a cigarette? (*Taking one from the packet.*) Beth she go off, early this morning, where she go to?

DANIEL. Pyrgos.

MIMIKO. Who for?

MIMIKO *lights the cigarette.*

DANIEL (*sitting down in the cane chair*). There is an outbreak of measles in the village, amongst the children.

MIMIKO (*putting the cigarettes and matches back in the pocket*). The spots have come again. (*To* NICHOLAS.) You are a friend of Beth too?

NICHOLAS. No. This is my first visit.

MIMIKO (*sitting in the bentwood chair*). Who he stay with?

DANIEL. Mrs Melianos.

MIMIKO. She is a good woman. She look after you. (*Turning to* DANIEL.) This morning I see a funny thing. A white bird. The pink eyes of a god. He is flying along. I think he is a sparrow. Another bird, a bigger bird, I think a jackdaw, swoop from the sky and attack him.

DANIEL. The sparrow was an albino.

MIMIKO. This I know. (*Miming with his hand.*) The bigger bird chase him like a race.

NICHOLAS *sips his ouzo.*

DANIEL. Did the jackdaw kill the sparrow?

MIMIKO. This I did not see. From the way it was going, I think so. (*To* NICHOLAS.) These birds attack what they do not understand.

(*To* DANIEL.) They cause a nuisance in the sky.

DANIEL *smiles*.

(*To* NICHOLAS.) In return for cigarettes, I explain to Daniel.

DANIEL. Whenever Mimiko wants a cigarette, he has a story to tell.

MIMIKO. I smoke too much. It is the way I get a fag. You smoke, Nicholas?

NICHOLAS. No, I used to. I gave it up.

He walks towards the other bentwood chair.

MIMIKO (*incredulous*). You have no stories now?

NICHOLAS *sits*.

Some days we smoke like a big chimney. At the end of the day we are demolished like an old chimney. We have told a hundred stories.

DANIEL *smiles*.

(*Pushing it under* NICHOLAS*'s nose*.) This is an English cigarette.

NICHOLAS *moves his head*.

Senior Service. The best. Daniel only puff English.

DANIEL. Sarah sends, or brings me them.

MIMIKO. It is the only thing about England Daniel miss. Senior Service.

DANIEL *chortles*.

I make him laugh, the old fool. Greek cigarettes are mud to him. I think it is rude. But we ignore it. He is like a Greek when he tries. Nicholas is a new friend?

DANIEL. Yes.

MIMIKO. Ah, I see. You do not know Sarah?

NICHOLAS. No.

MIMIKO. Sarah, she is special. His daughter. Or Beth?

NICHOLAS. No.

MIMIKO. Beth, she is an American, she is not like Daniel.

DANIEL. That's enough, Mimiko.

MIMIKO. Beth, she is a doctor. I have watched her, she is a clever woman. The spots they go like a magic trick.

DANIEL. Enough.

MIMIKO. He likes it when I am rude. He is a clown. Big Koko.

DANIEL. That's your name. You're the clown.

MIMIKO. He give us all names. What name he give you?

NICHOLAS. Er – Richard.

MIMIKO (*twisting his finger away from the side of his head*). It is so his mind can wander in a fantasy about us.

DANIEL. Thank you, Mimiko.

MIMIKO (*turning to* DANIEL). You tell me this many times. (*To* NICHOLAS.) He like to make things up.

SARAH *enters. She is carrying another envelope.*

What name he give you, Sarah?

SARAH. I don't think he dare.

DANIEL. Did you catch Yanni, pet?

SARAH. Yes. There's a letter for Beth.

DANIEL. Where from?

SARAH. Athens. (*Putting the envelope on the table.*) From the hospital.

SARAH *sits on the table.*

Aren't you hot?

MIMIKO. The heat is nothing.

SARAH. I don't know how you do it.

MIMIKO. I think of winter.

DANIEL. You didn't notice her in the village?

SARAH. No. Where did she go this morning?

DANIEL (*standing up*). Pyrgos.

MIMIKO. The spots are back.

DANIEL (*walking to the edge of the flagstones*). One of the teenagers came down. She's usually back before now. I wish she wouldn't take so much on. Have a word with her, will you? She listens to you.

SARAH (*jumping off the table, going to him*). Don't be silly. I'm sure she's fine.

SARAH *kisses* DANIEL *on the forehead*.

DANIEL. This evening. Tell her off for me. Shout at her and things. Make a fuss.

SARAH. Come on, come for a swim.

DANIEL. No. You go.

MIMIKO. I race you, Sarah. *Bame. Dtrechomme*.

SARAH. What does that mean?

MIMIKO (*getting up, running off*). Go. Run.

MIMIKO *goes*.

SARAH. Come on.

DANIEL. You go, love.

SARAH *hesitates*.

If he beats you, we'll never hear the last of it.

SARAH *dashes into the spare bedroom. She returns a second later with her beach bag*.

SARAH. You coming?

NICHOLAS. I'll stay here, thanks.

SARAH *goes*.

DANIEL. If you would like some more, help yourself.

NICHOLAS *pours a drop of ouzo into his empty glass*.

We're none of us great drinkers now, but don't let it stop you.

NICHOLAS *stands up. He joins* DANIEL *at the flagstones*.

I hope you won't take Mimiko too seriously.

NICHOLAS. His knowledge of English is remarkable.

DANIEL. Yes, it is.

The bee-eater calls.

The little bugger knows he can be charming.

NICHOLAS. How old is he?

DANIEL. Sixteen.

NICHOLAS *pulls a face.*

The bee-eater calls.

DANIEL *looks as if he is about to say something.*

(*Changing his mind.*) No, no, you're not married, are you.

DANIEL *walks to the cane chair. For the moment he seems in a world of his own. He sits down.*

NICHOLAS. Maybe I should go and find my room?

DANIEL. We'll give her a few more minutes, let siesta be over.

A slight pause.

Forgive my pacing about. I will find time to relax with you. It's so bloody hot today.

A slight pause.

DANIEL *chortles.*

Mr Cuthbertson. Well I wonder what he's doing now? D'you play that game?

NICHOLAS *looks perplexed.*

No, no, it's nothing, you'll think me daft.

NICHOLAS. Which game is that?

The bee-eater calls.

DANIEL. Oh, it's just a silly thing Mimiko and I play – he leads me on in his inimitable way. We think of someone, and we imagine what they might be doing at the moment we're talking about them. We have the fantasy game. The realistic game. Sometimes we imagine characters from another century. I need little encouragement, Nicholas.

NICHOLAS *smiles.*

It's fantastic fun with people you don't much like. So watch it. (*Chortling.*) We put them on the lavatory. Or in other despicable situations.

BETH HOWARTH *enters. She is pushing an old, black bicycle. Her doctor's bag is on the back.*

BETH *is sixty-nine. She is a strong-looking woman with a homely, gentle face. Her greying hair is tied in a bun. She has greater cares than her appearance and is wearing a flowered, short-sleeved, cotton dress. She has sandals on her feet. Her voice is soft and has barely a trace of an American accent.*

BETH *is tired, and has been for several months, but you would hardly know it. She wheels her bicycle towards the spare bedroom door.*

BETH. What on earth are you two talking about?

DANIEL (*standing up*). Here you are. Beth, this is Nicholas.

BETH (*resting her bicycle against the wall*). I can see that. (*Smiling.*) Hello. You managed to find us.

NICHOLAS. Yes, thank you.

BETH. Hopefully Daniel's not been bullying you too much?

NICHOLAS. Not at all, Dr Howarth. Quite the opposite.

BETH *has the bicycle settled. She looks at* NICHOLAS.

BETH. He is the most terrible tyrant. (*Offering her hand.*) We've been waiting to meet you.

NICHOLAS. And you.

They shake hands.

DANIEL. Was it measles?

BETH. Yes, that's why I've been so long. (*Breathing deeply.*) One little girl – (*To* DANIEL.) Soula, remember her? – has got it quite badly, that's why I've been so long.

DANIEL *is walking to the bicycle.*

Her temperature's way, way up.

BETH *leans against the table.*

DANIEL (*at the bicycle*). D'you want your bag, love?

BETH. Yes, please.

DANIEL *unclips the bag from the back of the bicycle.*

DANIEL (*taking it to the table*). Have you cycled from Pyrgos?

BETH. It's downhill most of the way. There's just that bit in the middle.

DANIEL *puts the bag on the table*.

DANIEL (*going back to the bike*). Sarah's going to tell you off this evening.

DANIEL *wheels the bicycle into the spare bedroom*.

BETH (*her breathing getting easier*). Has Daniel explained that their own doctor is away?

NICHOLAS. No.

BETH. I help out. It can be a slog.

DANIEL (*from inside*). There's a letter for you.

BETH (*calling back*). I noticed. I sent a blood sample for analysis.

DANIEL *comes out*.

Does Sarah mind the bike in there?

DANIEL. I shouldn't think so.

BETH. Have you asked her?

DANIEL. Should I have done? She'd have said, wouldn't she?

BETH. It's not very comfortable, sleeping with a bike. Have you explained to Nicholas?

DANIEL (*standing beside her*). Stop interfering, woman.

BETH. It could go in the kitchen.

DANIEL. Not on your nelly. I'd be tripping over it every other second.

BETH. I saw Mrs Melianos. She's up.

DANIEL. Oh, right.

BETH. She was asking. I wasn't sure if Nicholas had made it.

DANIEL. He was brought up on a farm.

BETH. Oh, were you?

NICHOLAS. Er – no.

The bee-eater calls.

It was my aunt and uncle's farm. I spent my summers there.

DANIEL. He's an expert on silage.

NICHOLAS (*shaking his head slightly*). No. I'm not.

BETH. Stop it, you old goat.

DANIEL. Did they keep pigs?

DANIEL *chortles, boyishly.*

BETH (*more quietly*). Daniel.

DANIEL (*perching beside* BETH *on the table*). No, I used to love pigs. I could watch them for hours. Didn't we?

BETH *takes* DANIEL*'s hand.*

(*To* NICHOLAS.) In the fields between Cambridge and Bedford. In those corrugated huts. When they first arrived they stopped the traffic. We'd have liked to have been farmers.

BETH (*squeezing* DANIEL*'s hand*). Why don't you take Nicholas up.

DANIEL. We went round one, didn't we? (*To* NICHOLAS.) It was like a small factory. D'you know, he bred over six thousand pigs a year. Milled his own wheat. Added the fishmeal. Cubed it into pellets with molasses. And dropped the pellets into the field in a hopper behind the tractor. We stayed in Cambridge because of those pigs.

BETH. Take him up. Don't keep her waiting.

DANIEL (*going to his jacket*). I loathed Cambridge. (*Taking his jacket off the chair.*) Hated academics.

BETH. Daniel exaggerates.

DANIEL (*putting his jacket on*). Beth likes to keep things smooth.

NICHOLAS *smiles.*

Farms are for growing up on. I envy you.

NICHOLAS. Which way do we go?

DANIEL (*walking to* NICHOLAS*'s holdall*). It's just up the hill a little. Nicholas was asking when we were married, I couldn't remember.

BETH. 1962.

DANIEL (*picking up the holdall*). Oh, I did remember. I said something with a two in it.

NICHOLAS. I'll take that.

DANIEL. No, no.

DANIEL *walks off with the holdall.*

NICHOLAS. I'll see you later. Thank you, Dr Howarth.

BETH (*smiling*). It's a pleasure.

> NICHOLAS *goes, following* DANIEL. BETH *watches them go.*
>
> *A slight pause.*
>
> *The bee-eater calls.*
>
> BETH *picks up the letter, opens it, and starts to read.*
>
> *The bright sunlight fades to blackout.*

Scene Three

Early the following morning. Friday, 11 May. Five o'clock.

The house.

*There is a clear, starlit sky which can be seen above the house.
A bright, semicircular moon is shining amongst them.*

The squid have gone from the washing line.

The sound of insects.

BETH *is standing, alone. Her hair, now hanging in a long plait, is
dishevelled from sleep. She is wearing a white nightdress. She has the
letter in her hand, she is reading.*

A pause.

DANIEL *enters through the open kitchen door. He is wearing striped
pyjamas – the sort that tie at the waist with a cord.*

He goes to her. They embrace. DANIEL *kisses her and then pulls back
slightly. He looks into her eyes.*

DANIEL. Won't you tell me?

BETH. Tell you what, you old goat.

DANIEL. Oh I don't know – anything, something – as long as it's
the truth.

> BETH *puts the letter in the envelope.*

It's no good putting that away, I'm going to read it.

BETH *puts the letter behind her back.*

I shall count to four.

He doesn't.

A slight pause.

BETH. I sent a blood sample to Athens. Mine, my blood.

DANIEL. And?

BETH. It was positive. (*Taking his hand.*) I've not been well, Daniel, you know that.

DANIEL. Hiding like a bloody cowering mouse.

BETH. That isn't quite fair.

DANIEL. Why, Beth?

BETH. Because it's serious. I wanted to be certain.

DANIEL. Aren't we here to share for f'God's sake?

BETH. It's leukaemia.

DANIEL. Oh, fuck.

BETH (*tightly holding his hand*). Quite acute, I guess. But not desperate yet.

DANIEL. Shit. How advanced? How long?

BETH. Four or five months, perhaps six maybe. Maybe even a year. Two. It has been known, Daniel.

DANIEL (*squeezing her hand*). Oh, Beth.

A pause.

They embrace.

Tears come into BETH*'s eyes.*

BETH. I'm not unhappy about it. Don't you be, love. I love you.

A pause.

DANIEL. What's the treatment, pet.

BETH (*shaking her head slightly*). I don't want it.

They pull back from the embrace.

It's chemotherapy. It's dreadful, it's worse than the disease. I've seen patients go through it.

DANIEL (*wiping* BETH*'s tears away with his thumb*). You're crying.

   A slight pause.

   (*Taking both her hands*.) I love you too, you know.

BETH. What a pair of silly donkeys we are.

DANIEL (*flapping her arms. Brightly*). Why?

BETH. When I was a girl I longed to love a man forever. Now I've my chance. Do you forgive me?

DANIEL. Oh, Beth.

BETH. For not telling you before?

DANIEL. When did it start?

BETH. I first noticed it before Christmas, I guess. I kept feeling tired, really tired.

DANIEL. I know.

BETH. Then an ulcer arrived in my mouth. And my throat was sore – really like sandpaper.

DANIEL. I don't think I will forgive you, you know.

BETH. If I hadn't been a doctor, I'd have told you. I knew what it was from the start – somehow. I saw the the symptoms too often in Japan. The anaemia, the breathlessness.

DANIEL. Yes.

   A slight pause.

BETH. I want to go back.

   DANIEL *looks at her.*

   To Japan.

DANIEL. We'll go.

BETH. I'd like to try and find Etsuko. I'd really like to know if she's alive or dead.

DANIEL. Yes.

BETH. I've kept wondering if I was just being silly.

DANIEL. She may be dead, you know that?

BETH. I know.

DANIEL. You always said you wanted to think of her as being alive.

BETH. I guess I have to know for sure.

They are looking into each other's eyes. They kiss.

A shooting star chases across the sky behind them.

They pull back from the embrace.

What time is it?

DANIEL. Five o'clock, half-past five.

BETH *smiles.*

They hold hands.

Who's going to tell Sarah?

BETH. Can't we leave it for a while. I don't want a fuss, Daniel.

DANIEL. That's not very fair on her.

BETH. Let me decide. Please.

DANIEL. Of course, love. I don't want you to do anything you don't want.

BETH. And no secret words – promise?

DANIEL (*jokingly humming and hawing*). Mm-mm-mm-mm-mm-mm. Promise.

BETH. You old goat.

DANIEL *smiles. He starts to chortle.*

What're you laughing at?

DANIEL (*he has stopped*). I shouldn't be. Nicholas. He's come all this way. We're not going to be here.

BETH. I liked him.

DANIEL (*half-surprised*). Did you?

BETH. Yes, I thought he was very genuine.

The very first faint sunlight of dawn can be seen.

DANIEL. No, I liked him too. He's none of the aggression of an academic. It's what you thought.

BETH. Does he want to go back to Cambridge?

DANIEL. I presume so. He's odd. He's just like a sweet shop, don't you think?

BETH. What's a sweet shop?

DANIEL. He is.

BETH. Don't be obtuse. Don't play him a merry dance, will you?

DANIEL. Why, have I done? Am I such an old cunt?

BETH. He's shy.

DANIEL. I know. And pompous, like all would-be academics. You see, I bet.

BETH *puts her hand to the side of her face*.

What's the matter?

BETH. That ulcer. I've still got it, I can't shift it. (*Hiding her pain*.) It's right on the inside of the gum.

DANIEL. Oh, Beth.

BETH (*brightly*). Don't you worry.

DANIEL *takes both her hands*. BETH *smiles*.

DANIEL. It's at times like this I feel so selfish.

A single tear rolls down DANIEL*'s cheek*. BETH *frees one of her hands and wipes it away with her fingers*.

BETH. No tears, my love.

DANIEL*'s eyes flood with tears*.

DANIEL. I used to dream of feeling like this. Like crying.

BETH *takes him in her arms*.

BETH. It's all right, love, it's all right.

DANIEL. For years I had no feelings.

BETH. You did. It just feels that way now. No one is all wrong in what they do.

DANIEL. I do so love you.

BETH. I know.

DANIEL. I still have the feeling I could have stopped work sooner than I did. At least helped a little when I did walk away.

BETH. You helped, don't be silly.

DANIEL. That's my arrogance, I expect.

A slight pause.

I'm not sure I can face Etsuko.

BETH. I know, I know. *(after a moment's pause.)* You will.

A slight pause.

We both need to, Daniel.

DANIEL. Why didn't we go years and years ago?

BETH. Because I was afraid.

A slight pause.

DANIEL. How odd we all are. How little we understand of ourselves.
But we stumble on, refusing to be pricked by anything.

A slight pause.

That is why I like Greece, you know – they've been pricked and
pricked and pricked.

A cockerel crows, nearby.

The dawn sunlight is still coming up. The stars have almost gone.

DANIEL *has a few remaining tears*, BETH *brushes them away with
her thumb. She still has the letter.*

You didn't let me read the letter.

BETH *takes her thumb away.*

I will try and change.

BETH. Don't be an old goat.

The dawn light fades to blackout.

Scene Four

Four days later. Tuesday, 15 May. Three o'clock in the afternoon.

A hillside overlooking the town of Panormos and its small harbour.

The ground rises in a steady, even incline from the bottom to the top. At the top of the hill are two lemon trees. Standing in between them is a beehive. The beehive is brightly painted in horizontal lines (using up paint) in blue, yellow, orange, red and green. The ground is hard and baked. What grass there is is scorched and brown.

The sun, at its highest point in the sky, is burning down. The hillside is bathed in sunlight.

SARAH *is lying at the bottom of the hill reading a hardback copy of an Evelyn Waugh novel. Her bag is beside her. She is wearing her long shorts and a yellow T-shirt. Her shoes are on the grass.*

NICHOLAS *appears at the top of the slope beside one of the lemon trees. He is wearing jeans, a white T-shirt, and plimsolls.*

He walks down towards her. SARAH *looks up.*

NICHOLAS. Your father brought me here on Saturday. He said it was one of your favourite places.

He stops near her.

How long d'you think they'll be gone?

SARAH. Five years, four years, three years.

NICHOLAS. He said he thought a week. I was wondering whether to stay or not?

SARAH *reads her book.* NICHOLAS *sits down.*

It's bloody inconvenient.

SARAH. Have you got a worm in your mouth?

NICHOLAS. What?

SARAH. Nothing.

NICHOLAS. What?

SARAH. It sounds like there's something wriggling about.

NICHOLAS. D'you mind talking about him, Sarah?

SARAH. Yes, I do mind.

She reads her book.

Have a holiday.

NICHOLAS. What was he like as a father?

SARAH. Are you sure you've not got a worm in your mouth?

NICHOLAS. If I knew what you meant, I'd tell you.

A slight pause.

I don't think you know.

SARAH. Go and get a book.

NICHOLAS. I don't feel like reading.

SARAH. Sulk then.

NICHOLAS. Sorry.

A slight pause.

He's rather like a child, isn't he?

SARAH. Who, you?

NICHOLAS. Daniel.

SARAH (*still reading*). Have you always been the centre of everyone's attention?

NICHOLAS. As far as I'm aware it's very much the opposite.

SARAH. Oh dear.

NICHOLAS. Why?

SARAH. I love being the centre of attention.

NICHOLAS. He said he would tell me stories. I haven't heard one yet.

SARAH. Then you've not been listening.

NICHOLAS. What should I have listened for?

SARAH (*looking up*). Mmm?

NICHOLAS. He's hard work.

SARAH *reads her book.*

NICHOLAS *stands up, he starts to walk back up the slope.*

SARAH (*putting her book aside*). It isn't you. He's like that.

NICHOLAS *stops and turns*.

And he won't thank me for gossiping. So I'm not going to.

NICHOLAS. We've walked miles together these last few days – all he's had me do is talk about myself.

SARAH. I'd stay. When they get back, I'd talk to Beth.

SARAH *picks up her book, she reads*. NICHOLAS *is still*.

You do a good impression of a statue.

NICHOLAS. I feel I'm disturbing everybody.

SARAH. You are.

NICHOLAS. Even Mrs Melianos, she wants me out of the house.

NICHOLAS *walks back to* SARAH.

SARAH (*putting her book to one side*). He is a child. All academics are children. They're so obsessed with themselves that they never grow up. Like you.

NICHOLAS. Is that right?

SARAH. That's what I remember.

NICHOLAS. Were you born in Cambridge?

SARAH. Yes.

NICHOLAS. I think they're obsessed with their work. I'm not an academic. Not yet.

SARAH *lies back, she looks at the sky.*

You're very like him, Sarah.

NICHOLAS *sits down*.

SARAH. I try to be.

MIMIKO *enters*.

Hello, Mimiko.

MIMIKO *sticks his tongue out at* NICHOLAS. *He walks up the hill and sits down in the shade beneath one of the lemon trees*.

NICHOLAS. Why have they gone to Japan?

SARAH. Didn't he tell you?

NICHOLAS. He didn't really.

MIMIKO *takes a small lizard from his jacket pocket. He plays with it. He lets it walk away a few inches before catching it again.*

He mumbled something about Beth being part of the American Red Cross team.

SARAH *sits up.*

SARAH. After the war when the Americans went into Japan, Beth was one of them. I don't know if it was the Red Cross – it was some sort of medical relief team. In Nagasaki she found a young girl. As far as I understand it, the girl was saved because she was diving and under water the second the bomb fell.

NICHOLAS. Really?

SARAH. She escaped the major force of the blast because she was playing a game and diving for a bell.

NICHOLAS. Go on.

MIMIKO. This girl, she took a shine to Beth. Followed her everywhere like a mascot. These two, they became friends.

NICHOLAS. How old was she?

MIMIKO. Little, little. Ten or nine, I think. This girl, she is one of many in the orphanage.

NICHOLAS. What happened to her?

MIMIKO. Beth, she wants to find her again at the end of her life.

NICHOLAS. They don't know if she's alive?

MIMIKO. That is Etsuko's story.

MIMIKO *goes back to playing with the lizard.*

NICHOLAS. When did Beth come to England?

SARAH. Shortly after that.

NICHOLAS. Because of Nagasaki, and this little girl?

SARAH. Presumably.

MIMIKO *(catching the lizard).* Beth, she hated the Americans for doing that. Her country.

NICHOLAS. When did she meet your father?

SARAH. I don't know. Nineteen-fifty something. (*Lying back, looking at the sky.*) They met at a bus stop in Belsize Park in London.

NICHOLAS. And your father's never been to Nagasaki?

SARAH. No.

MIMIKO (*holding up the lizard*). See my lizard? He is called Daniel Howarth.

SARAH (*tilting her head back*). Very nice, Mimiko. Where did you find it?

MIMIKO. Under a stone. Shortly I let him go.

NICHOLAS. He loves her, doesn't he?

SARAH. You're extraordinary, Nicholas Marks.

NICHOLAS. Sorry.

SARAH. Extraordinarily rude. (*Lying on her elbow, looking at him.*) Are paper shops always inquisitive?

NICHOLAS. Afraid so.

SARAH. I think I'll ravage you. Why don't you take all your clothes off?

NICHOLAS. Stop being silly.

SARAH. I'm perfectly serious.

NICHOLAS. I know.

SARAH. Spoilsport. (*Seductively.*) Oh, please.

NICHOLAS (*his voice rising*). No.

SARAH. I'll just have to imagine you then.

NICHOLAS (*embarrassed*). Stop it.

SARAH. Too late. I already have.

   NICHOLAS *looks embarrassed.*

   Prude.

NICHOLAS. All right, I'm a prude. I'm not, of course.

SARAH. Sensitive little flower, aren't we?

NICHOLAS. Yes, I am, if you must know.

SARAH. Are paper shops sensitive, too?

NICHOLAS. Can we talk about your father, please?

SARAH. No, show me your willy.

NICHOLAS. Which bus stop? I know Belsize Park.

SARAH *lies back, she looks at the sky.*

SARAH. What did you read at Cambridge?

NICHOLAS. Modern History.

SARAH. Why the paper shop then?

NICHOLAS. It fell my way.

SARAH. From the sky?

NICHOLAS. No, I thought it might buy me time.

SARAH. Did it?

NICHOLAS. Yes.

SARAH. What's it like?

NICHOLAS. It's like a million newsagents.

SARAH. Papers?

NICHOLAS. Papers and sweets. Toys. Videos.

SARAH. What did you want the time for?

NICHOLAS. To make decisions.

SARAH. What about?

NICHOLAS. Many important decisions are made too quickly.

SARAH. Who said?

NICHOLAS. It's only an observation.

SARAH. Were you clever at school?

NICHOLAS. No.

SARAH. I bet you were.

NICHOLAS. I worked hard, yes.

SARAH. Now you're doing a doctorate.

NICHOLAS. I hope to.

SARAH. It's brave.

NICHOLAS. Is it?

SARAH. Are you going to publish your thesis?

NICHOLAS. Your father made me promise I wouldn't.

SARAH. A promise never stopped a clever boy at school.

NICHOLAS. I'll see.

SARAH. Arrogant bastard.

A slight pause.

Have you made those important decisions?

NICHOLAS. I think so.

SARAH. You're covered in worms, Nicholas Marks.

A slight pause.

NICHOLAS. My old college had always asked me to go back.
I had an open invitation. I didn't want to go before I'd thought
things out. It's taken me a long time.

SARAH *sits up slightly. She leans on her elbows.*

SARAH. Why does Daniel interest you?

NICHOLAS (*thinking*). I think academics can find themselves on the
one path, that it's then hard to get off.

SARAH. Is that why you waited?

NICHOLAS. I witnessed that at Cambridge. The thuggery of
academics. The morality of any research becomes unimportant.

SARAH. My father wasn't a thug.

NICHOLAS. I'm sure he wasn't.

SARAH. Did you expect him to be?

NICHOLAS (*thinking*). Erm – no.

SARAH. He was always rather gentle.

NICHOLAS. Go on.

SARAH. But cut off. As if someone had wrapped him in paper. Like
you.

NICHOLAS. Am I like that?

SARAH. A bit.

NICHOLAS. Did you tease your father?

SARAH. I learnt how to. He was also the most moral of men.

A slight pause.

NICHOLAS. I felt wobbly after Cambridge. I had a year in London working for a publishers, and then I opened the shop.

SARAH. Where?

NICHOLAS. I went home. In Skelton.

SARAH. Who's looking after it now?

NICHOLAS. Mrs Robson, my assistant. (*Smiling.*) I had to put all this in my letters.

SARAH. He always wants to know more about the other person.

NICHOLAS. Have there been many like me?

SARAH. No. I don't know what's changed his mind.

A slight pause.

NICHOLAS. Beth changed his life, didn't she?

SARAH. Yes.

MIMIKO *stands up.*

MIMIKO. I take my Daniel Howarth back to his stone. Tomorrow, I catch him again.

MIMIKO *exits the way he came.*

NICHOLAS. Mimiko's like a puppy.

SARAH *stands up, she walks up the slope.*

Where are you going?

SARAH. Up here, to sit in the shade for a while.

SARAH *sits back against one of the lemon trees, leaning on it.*

(*Pointing*). There's a flying carpet, look.

NICHOLAS. What's a flying carpet?

SARAH. A bumblebee. He's called Axminster. He was here yesterday.

NICHOLAS *stands, he walks up the slope. He sits and leans against the other lemon tree.*

Are you gay, Nicholas.

NICHOLAS. Why d'you ask that?

SARAH. Just my intuition. (*Pointing.*) There's Shagpile coming out, off on a flight.

A slight pause.

I wouldn't mind if you were.

NICHOLAS. Is it important?

SARAH. Not especially.

A slight pause.

NICHOLAS. Where d'you live?

SARAH. London. Highgate. Near the cemetery.

NICHOLAS. Are you married?

SARAH. I used to be.

NICHOLAS. Who to?

SARAH. A man.

A slight pause.

Ask a silly question.

A slight pause.

I live with a painter.

NICHOLAS. An artist?

SARAH. Yes.

NICHOLAS. What's his name?

SARAH. Stuart Craig.

A slight pause.

He's an old man.

A slight pause.

He's sixty-six. (*Closing her eyes.*) Stuart's the sort of person who never gets up. He spends the entire day in his dressing gown.

(*Opening her eyes.*) Before you think he's eccentric, his paintings sell for a small fortune.

NICHOLAS. How did you meet?

SARAH. He stopped me in the street and asked me to change a light bulb. He's frightened of electricity.

NICHOLAS. Was he in his dressing gown?

SARAH. Yes. His voice has never broken.

NICHOLAS. Why?

SARAH. He's resisted adulthood.

A slight pause.

(*Closing her eyes.*) He doesn't walk, he shuffles.

A slight pause.

His passion is for porcelain dogs. He's hundreds of them.

A slight pause.

NICHOLAS. What does he paint?

SARAH. Dogs.

SARAH *opens her eyes.*

At the moment he's painting pictures of his childhood. In Polperro. Of the fishermen he remembers, with their rowing boats. On the beach sorting fish. But they're not completely real – there's elements of fantasy. In one of them they're picking gulls from the nets, and the fish are flying. They're so, so beautiful.

A slight pause.

He teaches at The Slade.

NICHOLAS. How much do they sell for?

SARAH. Thousands now.

A slight pause.

I think I love him because he's like Daniel. He loves me because I accept him for what he is. I don't criticise.

A slight pause.

He was brought up as a girl, by his burly father.

NICHOLAS. Really?

SARAH. In the house, yes.

NICHOLAS. What did his mother do?

SARAH. Acquiesce.

A slight pause.

When Stuart paints himself, it's as a girl. There's always a girl and a dog in most pictures. I'm in one or two.

SARAH *closes her eyes.*

He used to have a spaniel called Joey. Joey was gay.

A slight pause.

NICHOLAS. Sarah.

A slight pause.

Sarah?

NICHOLAS *stands up. He takes off his T-shirt. He holds it. He walks down the slope to* SARAH's *bag. He puts the T-shirt on the ground and picks up the book. A photograph tumbles out.* NICHOLAS *looks at it. He puts it back between the pages.*

SARAH *opens her eyes.*

D'you read Evelyn Waugh?

SARAH. Yes.

NICHOLAS *puts the book on the grass. He walks a few paces. He stands looking at the view.*

What're you looking at?

NICHOLAS. Just the village. There's not a flicker.

SARAH. I always think you can hear silence.

Silence.

The burning sunlight fades to blackout.

ACT TWO

Scene One

A week later. Tuesday, 22 May. Two o'clock in the afternoon.

The hillside.

The sun is high and bright. It is powering down once again.

SARAH *enters, running. She is wearing a red bikini, and is wet from swimming. She is carrying* NICHOLAS*'s clothes, and his swimming trunks, in a bundle under her arm. She is laughing.*

SARAH *stops.*

NICHOLAS *enters. He, too, is wet from swimming. He is naked.*

NICHOLAS. This is not funny.

SARAH. Of course it is.

NICHOLAS (*taking a step forward*). Can I have them, please.

SARAH *takes a step back, keeping her distance.* NICHOLAS *stops.* SARAH *stops.*

(*Appealingly.*) Oh, look.

SARAH *shakes her head.*

(*Shouting.*) Give me them now.

SARAH. Naughty, naughty. Ask nicely.

NICHOLAS. I've fucking well asked nicely. Where's it got me?

SARAH *walks to one of the lemon trees. She throws the swimming trunks right to the top.*

SARAH. There you are.

NICHOLAS. What the bloody hell's the point of that?

SARAH *laughs.* NICHOLAS *rushes towards her.* SARAH *dashes away. They stop. They are still again.*

SARAH. Let me count your pubic hairs. Go on. Stuart's got two thousand and seven, and his're dropping out cos he's an old man.

NICHOLAS. I'm not going to ask again, Sarah.

SARAH (*walking back to the tree*). You've ever such a dinky bottom. (*A sing-song voice.*) Underpant time.

SARAH *makes as if to throw his pants into the tree.*

NICHOLAS (*his voice rising*). Oh, don't.

Instead she throws them to him.

Thank you for nothing.

NICHOLAS *picks up his pants and puts them on.* SARAH *throws him his green T-shirt.* NICHOLAS *puts that on.* SARAH *is left holding his jeans.*

She puts them on, they are far too big for her.

SARAH. If you want these, you know where they are.

SARAH *sits down.* NICHOLAS *goes to her. He bends down, he unfastens the jeans and takes them off her. He puts them on. He sits down beside her.*

Liar. Cheat. Fibber. Runt. Imposter.

SARAH *takes her hand to his head. She gently runs her fingers through his hair.*

When I said last week I wouldn't mind if you were gay, what I meant was I would mind, rather a lot.

A slight pause.

I must've been making your life hell.

NICHOLAS. I must've made yours.

A slight pause.

SARAH. Have you a boyfriend?

NICHOLAS. Yes.

SARAH. Is he sexy? I bet he is.

NICHOLAS. He's quite sexy.

NICHOLAS *smiles.*

SARAH. On a scale of nought to ten, how sexy?

NICHOLAS. Eleven.

SARAH. He sounds like he's worth at least fifteen.

NICHOLAS *pulls a face*.

SARAH *puts her hand on his shoulders*.

Don't look like that. What's the matter?

NICHOLAS. I don't know.

SARAH. Have you broken up?

NICHOLAS. No. I don't know. He messes me about – trouble is I'm bloody well infatuated. It's one of those. I love him but he doesn't love me.

SARAH. Smack his bottom for him.

NICHOLAS *smiles*.

Where did you meet?

NICHOLAS. You'll laugh – I'm not telling you. He was a customer in the shop.

SARAH *massages his neck*.

He's young, too young really. I'm getting old, Sarah.

SARAH. You don't mean that.

NICHOLAS. No, I do.

SARAH. How old is he?

NICHOLAS. Only eighteen. There's another guy he sees. He's bright, I enjoy his company.

SARAH. I shall ravage you in a minute.

SARAH *takes her hands away*.

NICHOLAS. I was enjoying you doing that.

MIMIKO *enters. He looks forlorn*.

MIMIKO (*walking up the slope*). I have lost him.

SARAH. Lost who, Mimiko?

MIMIKO. My Daniel Howarth. My lizard. (*Sitting down beneath a lemon tree*.) He is not by his stone.

SARAH. I'm sure he'll come back.

MIMIKO *stretches out, he lies on his elbow*.

What are you going to do after your PhD?

NICHOLAS (*stretching out, lying on his elbow*). You keep asking me that.

SARAH. It's one of the many questions to which I never get an answer.

NICHOLAS. I'd like to be a don. Teach. Lecture. Write.

SARAH. At Cambridge?

NICHOLAS. Not necessarily. I'll go where the job is. Anywhere that will have me.

SARAH. It's taken you all these years to decide? Like your sexuality.

NICHOLAS. Something like that.

MIMIKO *stands up. He walks towards them.*

MIMIKO. Now Nicholas will tell us his story of the farm.

NICHOLAS. Oh God.

MIMIKO *sits down.*

It's too hot.

SARAH (*gently kicking* NICHOLAS). Don't miss out the grisly bits.

MIMIKO. Grisly bits.

NICHOLAS. There isn't any story. I wasn't brought up on a farm. Your father seems to have found great delight in telling everyone I was. Even Mrs Melianos tried to ask. The phrase book wasn't bloody adequate.

SARAH (*kicking him*). Get on with it.

NICHOLAS (*quickly*). Bl- bl- bl- bl- bl- bl- bl- bl- bl- bl- bl- bl- bl- bl- bl- bl- bl- bl- bl- bl- bl- (*Getting quicker.*) bl- bl- bl- bl- bl- bl- bl- bl- bl- bl- bl- bl- bl- bl- bl-

MIMIKO. It is because he has not a cigarette.

MIMIKO *takes a packet of Greek cigarettes from his jacket pocket.*

NICHOLAS. I told you it yesterday.

MIMIKO *puts a cigarette in* NICHOLAS's *mouth. He lights it with a match.*

SARAH. Not that one. Another one.

NICHOLAS. I don't know any more stories.

MIMIKO. Tell us about you this time.

NICHOLAS. Oh, look.

MIMIKO. Yes, yes, you must.

NICHOLAS. About me? This isn't fair.

NICHOLAS *sits up*.

MIMIKO. Nicholas's story.

NICHOLAS. My aunt and uncle had the farm. At a village called Castleton, near Skelton, which was where I was brought up an where my home is now.

A cloud passes in front of the sun. The sun goes in.

It was a hill farm. Quite poor and not at all grand. I used to spend my summers there.

MIMIKO. This we got yesterday.

SARAH *kicks* NICHOLAS.

NICHOLAS. I didn't very much like the farm because I was an only child, and had no one to play with. Sob, sob.

MIMIKO. What is this sob sob?

SARAH *kicks* NICHOLAS.

NICHOLAS. My aunt and uncle were very old-fashioned where children were concerned. But I went because my mother wanted me to.

MIMIKO *nods*.

My mother was old-fashioned. Very, very. More than my aunt and uncle. I'm what's known as a bastard, Mimiko.

MIMIKO (*nodding*). Bastard.

NICHOLAS. But not the swear-word kind. A bastard in the sense that I don't know who my father is. I've never been able to find him. (*To* SARAH.) When my mother died I looked through her papers, but there was nothing. All I know is that my mother never worked, but we always had money. Some money. Not a lot. But enough. (*To* MIMIKO.) If my mother were being truthful, I think she'd say she never wanted a child. Don't get me wrong, she wasn't unkind. It was just that she didn't know how to talk to a small boy.

NICHOLAS *drags on the cigarette*.

We lived a life of flowered wallpaper, heavy curtains, and silences by the coal fire. Me with my homework on my knee. At the grammar school. Working for all I was worth.

MIMIKO. This is the best so far.

NICHOLAS. When she died I discovered fifteen thousand pounds in a bank account. With that, I bought the shop.

MIMIKO. I prefer this story of a bastard.

NICHOLAS *offers* MIMIKO *the cigarette*.

You keep it, it is a present for you. Smoke it, and you find your father.

NICHOLAS. I don't want to. It's not a story about longing.

MIMIKO. You see. One day he will come through the mist. He will say to you, 'Son, I have found you.' Everyone will be happy.

NICHOLAS. You're an optimist, Mimiko.

MIMIKO. What else is there to be in this life? I ask you? Pessimism is only for those who congratulate themselves on their own pessimism. Pessimism is for those who only love themselves.

NICHOLAS *drags on the cigarette*.

We must have hope. Without hope, what are we? We are a people revelling in misery. I am young, I have told you. (*Pointing*.) You see the highest hill on our island?

NICHOLAS *looks*.

There is your father. Go to him.

NICHOLAS *looks back to* MIMIKO.

I, too, have no father. I have no mother. I live like a dog on the edge of things. But that is best. I tell you my story and not smoke cigarette. My health is better.

NICHOLAS *and* SARAH *smile*.

We Greeks have many stories. I tell good?

SARAH. Yes.

MIMIKO. You think also?

NICHOLAS. Yes.

MIMIKO. Then I am pleased. I am a storyteller like old Lekas.

NICHOLAS. Who's he?

MIMIKO. Old Lekas is the best storyteller on our island.

The cloud goes. The sun comes out.

Old Lekas is very old. One hundred and fifty at least. (*Pointing*.) He live beyond the hill of your father. Old Lekas, he is an informer in this war, when the Germans are here. Our fathers, my father, they cut his tongue out for this. Daniel, he call him his guru.

MIMIKO *waves his hands through the air.*

Like this they tell stories. I have seen.

SARAH. They've invented a sign language.

MIMIKO. It is so. They talk in silence, these two. This man is a sage. He has no tongue. I have seen them.

NICHOLAS. Why didn't you tell me?

SARAH. Daniel keeps him to himself. Mimiko hasn't met him, either.

MIMIKO. Yes, yes, you woman. I sneak behind Daniel one day on his walk. See where he go. (*Pointing*.) We go over the hill. A long walk. I sneak for half a day. They sit outside his hut, and smoke. All the time, smoking. This going on.

MIMIKO *demonstrates the sign language more accurately. His face becomes very expressive, like a clown, as he touches it with his fingers, very quickly, in various different places.*

It make me want to laugh. I laugh so much I scare up the birds. They see me. I am drawn to them. Old Lekas, he fetch wine. We drink like three fuck fishes. This man he is a thousand years old, for his wisdom. This man, he is the history of our country.

NICHOLAS. Is this true?

MIMIKO. You think I am a liar?

NICHOLAS. No. What do they talk about?

MIMIKO. It is about this big exploding bomb which Daniel make. It go bang many times.

He demonstrates the bomb going off with his voice and hands.

Bang. Bang. Bang. A big firework for the world. This bomb, it is so big it create new stars in the sky. It is as powerful as the very sun. Daniel, says to Lekas, he is not a strong man now. The making of the sun has weakened him. Old Lekas, he is the one who understand this new universe. He is history. He forgive Daniel. That is why he and Daniel talk.

A slight pause.

These two traitors only see each other. When he die, I take his place. I become like the land of Greece. My blood become soil. My heart a mountain. I sit at the top, a wise man. At the moment I am young. I wait for the wisdom of the history of my country.

A slight pause.

When I have my lizard, I hear you say, you study history?

NICHOLAS. Yes.

MIMIKO. Daniel, he say history is not the study of facts. It is the study of ourselves. Of our stories. The stories we tell each other. When we understand our stories, then we are in a position to look at the facts. This is how we learn the whys and wherefores. From Daniel, I begin to see this. It is only the genius who understands and does not lie.

NICHOLAS. Yes.

MIMIKO. You lie?

NICHOLAS. Sometimes.

MIMIKO. But of course, the truth is savage. Real truth, make real changes in our lives. Daniel, he strive to be a man.

A slight pause.

Is this why you work in the paper shop? To find the truth?

NICHOLAS *smiles*.

And now you leave your Mrs Robson? It is a good thing. You give her the shop. That act of generosity make her think about I her life.

MIMIKO *stands up. He walks up the slope to one of the lemon trees. He sits down.*

A slight pause.

NICHOLAS. Have you been to school, Mimiko?

MIMIKO. What are schools? They are useless.

SARAH (*lying on her side, on her elbow*). Yes, you have.

MIMIKO. I go for a few years. Like Daniel, I prefer stories. Schools, they do not listen. Too much teaching.

NICHOLAS *lies on his side, on his elbow.* MIMIKO *leans back against the tree.*

The sun goes in.

The weather, it is sticky today.

SARAH *lies on her back, she looks at the sky.*

SARAH. Is it going to rain?

MIMIKO. Later, maybe. This is why my lizard is not by his stone. He go underground.

NICHOLAS *lies on his back. The three of them are still.*

A pause.

A light change: the overcast summer sunlight slowly fades. A darker light is left from a rain-filled sky.

Time has passed. Two hours later.

A pause.

A bee-eater calls from one of the lemon trees.

MIMIKO *stands up, he goes to the other tree. He looks into it, searching with his eyes.*

The bee-eater calls.

MIMIKO *whistles, imitating the bird's call. He stretches out the flat of his hand.*

NICHOLAS *stands up.*

MIMIKO *whistles.* NICHOLAS *walks towards him.*

Move slowly, please.

NICHOLAS *walks carefully. He joins* MIMIKO.

This is my friend the bee-eater. See?

NICHOLAS (*quietly*). Yes.

MIMIKO. Sometimes he will land on my palm. Not today. It is because of the storm. (*Suddenly moving his hand, following the flight of the bird.*) There he go, look. I follow him. It will rain soon.

MIMIKO *follows the bee-eater. He exits.*

NICHOLAS *watches him go. He takes his wristwatch from his pocket and puts it on.*

SARAH *still hasn't moved.*

NICHOLAS *walks to the beehive. He looks at it.*

SARAH. It's empty.

NICHOLAS. I wondered why we hadn't been stung to death.

SARAH *rolls onto her stomach, so that she can see him.*

SARAH. He's extraordinary.

NICHOLAS. Mimiko?

SARAH. Yes. I was a teacher.

NICHOLAS *smiles.*

What're you smiling at?

NICHOLAS. What did you teach?

SARAH. Infants.

NICHOLAS. Have you a child, Sarah?

SARAH. Worms, worms, and more worms.

NICHOLAS. A photograph fell out of your book.

SARAH *jumps up. She walks towards him.*

SARAH. Lie down, please.

NICHOLAS, *warily, lies down.* SARAH *sits astride him.*

NICHOLAS. You'll crush my ribcage.

SARAH *pushes up his T-shirt. She 'hoovers' his navel – the sound with her voice, the actions with her hand.*

What you doing?

SARAH. Hoovering your belly button.

She stops. She pulls his T-shirt down.

Yes. She lives with her father. I was the one who walked out.

NICHOLAS. For Stuart?

SARAH. Did you ever imagine a light bulb could change your life?

NICHOLAS. No.

SARAH. I tried with Philip.

NICHOLAS. Stop pretending.

SARAH. No, I did – I tried really hard. Meals on the table. Slippers by the fire. Not quite, but almost. Philip's remarried. She's a terrific home. (*Smiling*.) I still hate him.

NICHOLAS *smiles*.

No, Philip's very conventional. I discovered I wasn't, that's all.

NICHOLAS. How often d'you see her?

SARAH. Half of each school holiday. One weekend in two. They live in Bristol – so not as often as I'd wish. People said how could I walk out and leave a child.

NICHOLAS. It hurts you, doesn't it?

SARAH. D'you like to think of people being hurt?

NICHOLAS. Don't be silly.

A slight pause.

SARAH. As a matter of fact, it is hell. Fucking hell, Nicholas.

NICHOLAS. I'm sorry.

SARAH *jumps up, she runs away down the slope. She stops.* NICHOLAS *stands up. He walks to her. He comes up behind her and puts his hands on her shoulders.*

SARAH. I came here to talk to my dad. He's so brick-wallish now, it's impossible. If only he'd talk to me – tell me what's wrong.

NICHOLAS. I know.

SARAH. Do you? No, you don't. I came here to talk about Stuart.

NICHOLAS *puts his arm around her waist.*

I'd been overseeing an exhibition. I came back and he was lying on the floor in his studio. He was sort of crumpled. A dreary stroke.

NICHOLAS. How long had you been together?

SARAH. Five and a half years. He died just as I got him to the hospital. Six weeks ago. The house is a tip. It's odd, because I've been finding things ever since. Things I didn't know about. I found a pile of uncashed cheques under a carpet I pulled up. Hundreds of old letters. And letters from your mother in Skelton. About you.

NICHOLAS *looks down.*

About how you were doing at school. About how she needed more money for pencils. It's a big house, he kept everything.

NICHOLAS *walks away a pace. He looks at her.*

NICHOLAS. Why, Sarah?

SARAH. Why what?

NICHOLAS. These games? This frivolousness. It's not fair.

SARAH. No. Mimiko was right.

NICHOLAS. How? It's silly, like you.

SARAH. I don't know how.

NICHOLAS. How could they have met? Tell me, paint the picture for me.

SARAH. I can't do that.

NICHOLAS. It's preposterous.

SARAH. It's not.

A slight pause.

NICHOLAS. Completely and absolutely ridiculous. It's not so.

SARAH. I'll show you the letters. In London.

NICHOLAS. Tell me how they could possibly have met?

SARAH. I don't know that.

A slight pause.

It suddenly hit me.

NICHOLAS. When?

SARAH. Just now, when you told Mimiko. I know your mother's name.

NICHOLAS. Telling stories is one thing. (*Shaking his head.*) No, Sarah.

SARAH. It's the truth.

NICHOLAS. Oh, I don't know. What the hell do I know about anything.

A slight pause.

Tell me her name?

SARAH. Joyce. I know it's right.

  NICHOLAS *looks down.*

  I found all sorts of paintings I didn't know about.

NICHOLAS. Is it true, what you said about him?

SARAH. Yes.

NICHOLAS. His being brought up as a girl.

SARAH. Yes.

NICHOLAS. Well, we'll never know, will we?

SARAH. No.

  NICHOLAS *walks up the slope. He stops and turns.*

  Was your mother's name Joyce?

NICHOLAS. Yes.

  SARAH *walks to him. They embrace. They sway from side to side.*

SARAH. I'm sorry.

NICHOLAS. What for? I'm sorry for you. Losing someone that you loved. That's nice. You're nice and warm.

SARAH. You've been terrific this last week.

NICHOLAS. Have I?

SARAH. Letting me abuse you.

NICHOLAS. I got used to it. I suppose technically we might be related.

SARAH. We were never married. Stuart wouldn't. He had a thing about it. He wouldn't have children, either. Because of what his father did.

NICHOLAS. It all makes sense, in a way.

SARAH. Stories do.

  DANIEL *and* BETH *enter.*

  DANIEL *is wearing his suit with his white shirt.* BETH *is wearing a dark purple tweed skirt and a white blouse. They have sandals on their feet.*

  DANIEL *and* BETH *look well and refreshed.*

NICHOLAS *sees them. He and* SARAH *part.*

We weren't expecting you for ages. When did you get back?

DANIEL. Half an hour ago, didn't we?

BETH *smiles.*

SARAH. Have you had a good time?

BETH. Wonderful.

DANIEL (*walking forward a pace*). We'll tell you, pet.

BETH. Some sadness – to be among the people of the city and know what they lived through.

DANIEL. The Peace Memorial itself is not very nice. Is it?

BETH. No, it's rather ugly. A huge bronze Buddha. His right hand is held to the sky from where the bomb fell, and his left to the ground, holding back the forces of evil.

DANIEL. His eyes are closed in prayer.

BETH. We spent a morning there, talking.

SARAH. So you're glad you went?

DANIEL. I'm glad, pet, yes.

BETH (*walking to* DANIEL). It's been the journey of my life. I think you got more from it than me, didn't you?

DANIEL. Are you going to tell them?

DANIEL *and* BETH *look at one another.*

BETH. I wish you both could have seen her. (*Taking* DANIEL*'s hand.*) Wasn't she lovely?

SARAH. Come on then.

BETH. I might even have recognised her, Sarah.

DANIEL. She saw Beth straight away.

BETH. There she was. Standing there. In her school corridor.

DANIEL. Etsuko nearly had a heart attack.

SARAH. You did find her?

DANIEL. We thought it might take us weeks and weeks.

BETH. We found her on the first afternoon.

SARAH. What's she like?

DANIEL. We'll tell you.

BETH. She's alive and well. She's married – called Mrs Oogushi.

DANIEL. She's a teacher in a primary school.

It starts to rain. It rains hard. The sound echoes off the baked earth.

Let's shelter under the trees.

BETH *and* DANIEL *go to one tree.*

SARAH *and* NICHOLAS *to the other. The sky is darkening. They talk over the rain.*

BETH. She's two children of her own. We took them all out to dinner.

DANIEL. Tell them the best bit.

BETH. I was saving that.

DANIEL. Tell them.

SARAH. What?

DANIEL. Tell them, or I will.

BETH. On our last afternoon there, she invited us back to the school. Her children performed a play for us.

DANIEL. It was beautiful, Sarah.

NICHOLAS *is looking at the sky. It is now very dark. Almost black.*

BETH. About her life. They'd been performing it the week before, for parents. They did it again especially for us.

A bright flash of lightning.

This is immediately followed by an enormous clap of thunder. It rumbles and shakes the ground.

It rains harder. The sound echoes loudly off the baked earth. They have to shout.

DANIEL (*taking* BETH *with him away from the tree*). It's an electric storm. Come out. It's dangerous under there.

SARAH. What?

DANIEL. Don't stand under the trees.

NICHOLAS (*walking from the tree*). Your father's right.

DANIEL (*pointing to the sky*). It's right overhead.

NICHOLAS. Sarah.

DANIEL (*beckoning her*). Come out, love.

SARAH. We'll get wet.

A flash of lightning. It strikes above SARAH's *head.*

The lemon tree splits in half, but doesn't fall completely.

SARAH *is still, rigid.*

A thunderclap echoes and rumbles.

NICHOLAS (*shouting*). Sarah.

SARAH *falls back a few inches. She is left propped up, standing, against the broken tree.*

NICHOLAS *rushes towards her.*

DANIEL (*rushing himself*). Don't touch her, Nicholas. (*Joining him.*) Leave it a second.

They wait a second.

DANIEL *picks her up. He carries her in his arms away from the tree. A flash of lightning.* DANIEL *puts her down.*

NICHOLAS *kneels.* BETH *kneels. She takes* SARAH's *pulse.*

A thunderclap echoes.

BETH (*calmly, to* NICHOLAS). Push on her chest when I say.

BETH *takes a deep breath, she holds* SARAH's *nose and breathes into her mouth.*

Now.

NICHOLAS *pushes on* SARAH's *chest.*

They repeat this. Occasionally BETH *takes* SARAH's *pulse.* DANIEL *watches.*

BETH *takes* SARAH's *pulse.* BETH *changes position. With her hands she hammers into* SARAH's *body above her heart.* SARAH *jumps under the weight of the blows.*

The rain is beginning to quieten a little. BETH *takes* SARAH's *pulse.*

DANIEL. Is there anything I can do, love?

BETH. I don't think so.

> BETH *hammers again. Her hair is falling out of place. She is beginning to breathe deeply, having to catch her breath.*

> *The rain is quietening.*

NICHOLAS. What if I breathe into her mouth?

BETH. Yes.

> NICHOLAS *breathes into* SARAH's *mouth.* BETH *continues with her hammering.*

> *A bright ray of sunlight slants down through a hole in the clouds.*

> *The rain is quietening.* BETH *takes* SARAH's *pulse.*

She's dead, I'm afraid.

> DANIEL *puts his hands on* BETH's *shoulders.*

I don't know what else I can do.

> *The rain stops.*

> *Silence.*

NICHOLAS. She can't just be dead.

> *Silence.*

> *The bright ray of sunlight slowly fades to blackout.*

Scene Two

Four days later. Saturday, 26 May. Ten o'clock in the morning.

The hillside.

The sky is clear. A dazzlingly bright sunlight is burning down.
CLARE *enters, running by one of the lemon trees. She runs down the slope and stops.*

CLARE *is twelve and, if anything, looks slightly young for her age. With her short blonde hair, and slight thin frame, she is the spitting image of* SARAH. *She is wearing sandals, knee-length white socks, and a white, short-sleeved dress. A pause.*

BETH *enters by the tree, slightly breathless. She is wearing her flowered dress.*

BETH. You chased ahead of me.

　　CLARE *turns to* BETH.

CLARE. Is this the place, Gran?

BETH (*walking down*). Yes, love.

　　CLARE *looks about.*

CLARE. Was that the tree?

BETH. Yes.

CLARE. It will be a sad tree forever, won't it, Gran?

BETH. Unfortunately, love, it will.

　　BETH *takes* CLARE*'s hand.*

CLARE. D'you know how many letters Mummy sent me from Greece?

BETH. No?

CLARE. Three. I gave the stamps to a boy at my school.

BETH. Did you?

CLARE. Is the funeral tomorrow?

BETH. Yes, love.

CLARE. When I was eight my guinea pig died.

BETH. Did he?

CLARE. He was a her.

BETH. That's right, I remember now. Sally, wasn't it?

CLARE nods.

CLARE. We buried Sally in the garden.

BETH. Mummy will be buried here, won't she?

CLARE nods.

CLARE. I've got gerbils now.

A slight pause.

BETH. You just wanted to have a quick look, didn't you? Shall we go back?

CLARE. Gran?

BETH. Yes, love?

CLARE. Why did Mummy die, Gran?

BETH thinks for a moment.

BETH. Mummy was unlucky, wasn't she?

CLARE nods.

Mummy lives in our memories of her, Clare.

CLARE nods.

You're being a brave girl.

CLARE. Daddy wasn't sure if I should come. I wanted to.

BETH. It was a long way, wasn't it, on your own?

CLARE nods.

D'you want to find Grandpa? And Nicholas? Or d'you want to spend more time here.

CLARE nods.

Which?

CLARE. Find Grandpa and Nicholas.

They walk towards the beach. CLARE stops. She turns and looks at the hillside. BETH turns.

CLARE. Grandpa told me when Mummy was my age – you know what she did?

BETH. No?

CLARE. Well, you know how you put a book above the door? And when the person comes in it lands on their head? Mummy put a pound of flour, eggs, some butter, some sugar, and some cherries. Grandpa came in. By the time it hit the floor it was a cherry cake.

They walk towards the beach.

BETH. I think your Grandpa's teasing you, Clare.

CLARE. I'm going to tease him when I think of something.

CLARE *skips off.* BETH *follows her.*

The bright sunlight fades to blackout.

Scene Three

Saturday, 26 May. A few seconds later.

The beach at Panormos.

The sand rises in a steady, even incline from the sea at the bottom to the high-tide line at the top. There are a few pieces of sea debris on this line. The sand is almost white. To one side a whitish rock rises from the sand. Painted on it in white, so that it is barely readable, is 'No Nude Sunbathing'.

The same dazzlingly bright sun is burning down.

Spread out on the sand at the top of the slope, close to the rock, is a large bath towel. DANIEL's clothes are lying in a heap beside it.

NICHOLAS *is standing at the bottom of the slope beside the sea. He is wearing his cord trousers and his checked shirt. His shoes and socks are beside him on the sand. He is looking out to sea.*

MIMIKO *enters along the high-tide line. He walks towards* NICHOLAS.

MIMIKO. Beth is with Clare. They go to the place where it happened. I do not like to go with them.

He stands beside NICHOLAS.

Her body, it is in a coffin now, in the cool of our church. My people, we pay our respects, too. It is good that she be buried here.

MIMIKO *is looking at the sea*.

How is he today?

NICHOLAS. He seems better. I think Clare being here has helped.

MIMIKO. He blame himself for everything, this man.

NICHOLAS. I know.

MIMIKO. We have to tell him, the storm, it is not his fault. Look how he swim like the fish, despite his age.

A slight pause.

We first meet when I am seven years old, Nicholas.

NICHOLAS *smiles*.

You stay for the funeral?

NICHOLAS. Yes. I'm going on Monday.

MIMIKO. To write your thesis?

NICHOLAS. I shall try.

MIMIKO. On Daniel?

NICHOLAS. No. On chance. How chance has shaped history.

MIMIKO. Is this a change for you?

NICHOLAS. It was always part of my thinking. But, yes.

MIMIKO. I understand chance.

NICHOLAS. Do you?

MIMIKO. It is every day around us. It involve us all.

NICHOLAS *smiles*.

I speak the obvious thing sometimes.

NICHOLAS. Will you ever come to England?

MIMIKO *shrugs*.

MIMIKO. It is in the future. Who can tell?

NICHOLAS. If you do, write to me, let me know.

MIMIKO. I will. What is your one thought of our island.

NICHOLAS (*after thinking for a second*). It has a freedom.

DANIEL *enters from the sea. He is wearing a pair of baggy, old-fashioned swimming trunks. He shuffles to his towel.*

DANIEL. You should have gone in, Nicholas.

DANIEL *picks up the towel and starts to dry himself.*

MIMIKO (*looking at the sea*). Petros is out there, Daniel.

DANIEL. Yes, I saw him. He's still rowing back.

MIMIKO (*to* NICHOLAS). Petros is one of our fishermen, in his boat. He is slowest. Daniel, he likes the slowest.

DANIEL. Petros is a wise man, Mimiko.

MIMIKO. It is the wise man who move slowly, eh, Daniel?

DANIEL. Yes.

MIMIKO (*to* NICHOLAS). He have time to understand.

MIMIKO *screws his finger into his temple.*

Petros want a motor. Then he get his breakfast.

DANIEL. Push off. *Egho thelo milo Nicholas.*

MIMIKO. You wish to talk together.

MIMIKO *walks up the slope, to the high-tide line.*

Before I go, Daniel – may I take Clare fishing one evening? I have my rods.

DANIEL. I'm sure she'd love that. Speak to Beth.

MIMIKO. Thank you.

DANIEL. *Efharisto.*

MIMIKO *goes the way he came.*

(*Holding the towel.*) Yes, I like an early-morning dip. Sarah was a brave swimmer.

He continues to dry himself.

I get jealous of Mimiko. His youth, his time. When he was little we used to make things up together. Oh, silly things.

He is still. He holds the towel.

I hope I've not hurt him. Or spoiled him in any way.

NICHOLAS. No, you've done a good job.

DANIEL. I never found the space for my own students. Pity. Will you?

NICHOLAS. I'd hope to.

DANIEL. Mmm.

NICHOLAS. What?

DANIEL. Oh, your hope may not be enough. Those cloisters have their own power to mislead. Perhaps I'm telling you what you already know?

NICHOLAS. A bit.

DANIEL. It never hurts us, does it?

NICHOLAS. What?

DANIEL. Being told we're right.

NICHOLAS. No.

DANIEL. If I get self-indulgent, please stop me.

He spreads his towel on the sand.

No, I've never asked to be liked for what I've done. I don't think it's admirable. Mmm? Do you?

NICHOLAS. Yes, I do think it's admirable. I'm sorry to surprise you. What is not, is the pity and disgust.

DANIEL. No, no.

NICHOLAS. It's an arrogance that allows you to take the blame.

DANIEL. Of course you're right.

NICHOLAS. Then stop.

DANIEL. I have tried to change. I've just never been very successful.

A slight pause.

No, there is no whole or absolute truth. Not in what I say.

A slight pause.

I am the same person, Nicholas, that I was thirty years ago. I could build those bombs again. The 'I' is important. I led the programme.

There were others who have some comfort. You see, if I don't take the blame, all I begin to do is justify. Because, by God, they were exciting times.

A slight pause.

Forgive me. Already I'm justifying.

He puts his finger to his laps.

Sssh. Mmm?

NICHOLAS. Is that why you've remained silent?

A slight pause.

Why did you agree to see me?

DANIEL. I hoped you might understand my paradoxes.

NICHOLAS. Would you – now – work on the programme?

DANIEL. No, of course I wouldn't. What I'm saying, is that I still have the desire for that excitement. I realise, intellectually, how appalling that is, or must seem – emotionally, I'm not sure. Because that's what I want. No, I am sure, it's equally appalling.

A slight pause.

What is history, Nicholas?

NICHOLAS. I'm begining to feel it's nothing but a series of random chances.

DANIEL. I'm not a historian, but it seems to me we look at history in the wrong way. We have to look at ourselves first. At our own stories. When we stop repeating our own failings, and take responsibility for our actions, maybe we have a chance.

A slight pause.

I have tried to take responsibility for mine.

A slight pause.

I repeat, I'm not asking to be liked for what I've done. If that is self-pitying, so be it.

NICHOLAS *walks up the sand to the high-tide line.*

NICHOLAS. What about your own history?

DANIEL (*picking up his jacket*). My father was a docker. A unionist, an agitator.

He takes a packet of cigarettes and a box of matches from the pocket. He puts the jacket down.

When they sacked him I must have been in my early teens. You were right, we did go without shoes for a while.

DANIEL *lights a cigarette.*

My father was a stoic. A great educationalist. He read the Co-op library from cover to cover. When he died there were over a thousand people at his funeral. There's a school named after him in Manchester. The William Howarth School.

He throws the cigarette packet and the box of matches onto his jacket.

He taught us that learning meant dignity. He was wrong, of course. How I wish I'd been a plumber, or an electrician.

NICHOLAS. Do you feel you've abused that?

DANIEL. What?

NICHOLAS. That dignity.

DANIEL. Oh, I think I have, don't you?

He puffs on his cigarette.

When I left Manchester Grammar School I worked for a company which specialised in making laboratory equipment. I was nineteen, twenty, twenty-two. Eventually, kindly, they saw me through Cambridge. Can you imagine how exciting those years were? Mingling with the best, beating them.

He puffs on his cigarette.

To use your analogy, the path of atomic physics seemed clear. I just walked along it. No, strode arrogantly. I envy you your intelligence.

NICHOLAS. How much of an idea had you of what the research might mean?

DANIEL. We knew it was important. Obviously, we did. How much d'you ever know the consequences of something which isn't yet finished? The pattern comes later. We were aware it had implications, yes we were. And we knew research of a very similar kind was going on all over Europe. And America.

DANIEL*'s hand is shaking slightly. He puffs on his cigarette.*

I was a junior then, don't forget. It wasn't until the war – the war escalated the whole bloody damn thing. When the government finally realised what had been going on – well, that was it, it was out of our hands. Correspondence with Europe stopped. The Americans moved into Los Alamos.

DANIEL*'s hand is shaking.*

In 1945 we were frightened that Hitler would get there first.

DANIEL *puffs on his cigarette.*

And after the war, well – for the same reasons we'd been frightened of Germany, we were now scared stiff of the Russians. For all we knew, Russia already had an atom bomb.

A slight pause.

So I went on working, Nicholas.

A slight pause.

Most of my real work was done on the hydrogen bomb in the fifties. Though that's not important. It was too late by then. As you should know, knowledge has its own momentum. It's unstoppable. That's what my father didn't understand.

NICHOLAS. I have read somewhere that you thought you were philosophers.

DANIEL. If philosophy is the study of the ultimate nature of existence. Then we were meddling with something at the very heart of that – the atom. The atom had been the one certain law of the universe. To split it, split all laws.

DANIEL *picks up the packet of cigarettes.*

I think there is still one law I still respect. One truth.

He lights a second cigarette from the first.

You see, Nicholas – unlike the atom – knowledge can never be destroyed. That's what hurts me.

He stubs out the first cigarette.

What I've left behind, the world has to find a way of coping with. And that's fine if you think about it for a few weeks, or a few months, or a few years. But think about it for centuries.

A slight pause.

NICHOLAS. I'm sorry.

DANIEL *walks to the edge of the sea.*

DANIEL. Oh, I don't blame you.

NICHOLAS *walks down the sand to the sea. They are standing some distance apart.*

You have to remember we were dealing with the unknown. Daily. Day in, day out. I think now the word philosophy implies that one does some good. We didn't.

He puffs on his cigarette.

I led the programme throughout the fifties.

NICHOLAS. And you left because of Beth?

DANIEL. That's right.

He puffs on his cigarette.

To say I fell in love, sounds simplistic – but it's the truth.

A slight pause.

I fell in love with her story. Of her, a young woman in that desolate city. And a girl.

DANIEL*'s hand is shaking again. He puffs on his cigarette.*

Stories change our lives, if only we'd listen to them.

DANIEL *walks up the sand to the high-tide line. He turns and looks at the sea.*

I stood in front of Etsuko and all I could do was apologise.

DANIEL*'s eyes fill with tears.* NICHOLAS *goes to him. He puts his hands on* DANIEL*'s shoulders.*

NICHOLAS. It was the wrong time to ask a lot of questions.

DANIEL. No, no.

They fall into a hug.

And now Sarah. What appalling self-pity.

NICHOLAS. It's honest.

A pause.

You feeling better?

They break the hug. NICHOLAS *takes a handkerchief from his pocket.*

DANIEL. Is it clean?

DANIEL *takes it. He dries his eyes with it.*

NICHOLAS. It isn't brilliantly clean. I only brought the one.

DANIEL. It's a hanky.

A slight pause.

DANIEL *stands with the handkerchief in his hand.*

You are staying for Sarah's funeral?

NICHOLAS. Yes, of course I am.

DANIEL (*holding up the hanky*). D'you want it back?

NICHOLAS. Keep it.

A slight pause.

DANIEL*'s eyes fill with tears again. They hug.*

Eh.

A pause.

Eh.

A slight pause.

Eh.

They break the hug.

DANIEL. Oh dear.

DANIEL *dries his eyes on the handkerchief.* NICHOLAS *wipes away a tear, with his thumb, from his own eye.*

Have I got you at it?

DANIEL *bends down, he stubs out the cigarette.*

What are you going to do?

NICHOLAS. Go home. Think.

DANIEL *walks down the sand.*

They are both looking at the sea.

DANIEL. If I can find the courage – I may go back myself, Nicholas.

NICHOLAS. You should.

DANIEL. D'you think? Is it worth the chance?

NICHOLAS. Yes.

DANIEL. D'you know what I most regret – is the loss of innocence.

NICHOLAS *walks down the sand to the sea.*

If you look at the sea. Oh, I don't know. Every drop of it contains some sort of story. Is open to influence. If only from the wind. The tide comes in and out. Every drop of it's been somewhere.

He looks at the sea.

What every story has is a threat hanging around it.

A slight pause.

I don't know if we'll ever put that right.

The bright sunlight fades to blackout.

Scene Four

Three days later. Monday, 29 May. Nine o'clock in the evening.

The beach.

The sky is bright and starless. Only a full moon can be seen, casting a shadow from the rock. It lights the beach with a rich glow.

At the base of the rock are the dying embers of a small fire. Above the fire is a metal grate which has been used for grilling fish.

BETH *enters from the village, walking by the sea. She is wearing her flowered dress and a cardigan.*

DANIEL *enters behind her. He is wearing his suit and his white shirt.*

BETH *stops and turns.* DANIEL *holds out his hand.* BETH *takes it.*

DANIEL. The village were wonderful, don't you think?

BETH. Marvellous. I hadn't quite realised how much they'd taken Sarah to their hearts.

DANIEL *brushes his finger along her cheek.*

DANIEL. How is it?

BETH. Not too bad. So far, so good.

DANIEL. You will say, won't you, if you want anything?

BETH. I want nothing.

DANIEL. I know, but you should.

MIMIKO *enters from along the beach. He is carrying two small fish, one in each hand.*

MIMIKO (*going to the fire*). Clare says you are to have these. We've had ours.

MIMIKO *puts the fish on the metal grate.*

BETH. How many have you caught?

MIMIKO. Clare's caught twenty-seven. I've caught six.

DANIEL. That's well done.

MIMIKO. I don't know how she does it. (*Walking back the way he came.*) Don't forget, you are to turn them over in seven minutes.

BETH. Tell Clare it's nearly her bedtime.

MIMIKO. She says not to be silly, it's not nearly her bedtime.

MIMIKO *goes.*

DANIEL. That told you.

BETH. I'm sure it won't hurt her, for once.

DANIEL. I don't know how she does it, either.

BETH. It's easier for children. Clare is what she is.

DANIEL. Yes.

BETH. She had a good cry with me this morning.

DANIEL *puts his arm around her waist.*

DANIEL. When did we meet?

BETH. Don't be an old goat.

DANIEL. I felt lucky that day.

A slight pause.

It doesn't seem that long ago. Does it to you?

BETH. Not really.

DANIEL. It's twenty-five years, you know.

BETH. It isn't. (*After thinking for a moment.*) Yes, it is, isn't it?

DANIEL. We forget. What are we going to do?

BETH. About what?

DANIEL. You.

    BETH *walks up the sand to the high-tide line. She sits down.*

    DANIEL *follows her. He sits down.*

    I wish you'd go to the hospital. And at least see them. Give yourself a chance to decline the treatment.

BETH. No, my love.

DANIEL. I don't know. What am I to do with you? Stubborn as a mule.

    MIMIKO *enters. He stops.*

MIMIKO. Clare says, I have to come and tell you, she won't be happy until you come and fish with us.

BETH. It is really way past her bedtime.

MIMIKO. She says it's only nine o'clock. Silly billy.

BETH. We've got to get her to Athens and on a plane tomorrow.

MIMIKO. You will keep putting her in bed an hour before her time. Even her dad doesn't do that.

DANIEL. It's because we're old.

MIMIKO. I'll tell Clare you're coming. Don't forget about the fish.

    MIMIKO *goes.*

BETH. You go. I'm going to sit up here. You know what Mimiko's like, he'll be there all night.

DANIEL. Let them, it doesn't matter.

BETH). Go on, go. You don't need me there.

DANIEL. In a minute.

    A pause.

    Will you be all right?

BETH. I'm fine, Pet.

A slight pause.

DANIEL *stands up.*

DANIEL. The old bones are creaking a bit.

He looks at BETH.

BETH. Go on, for goodness' sake.

DANIEL *goes towards* MIMIKO *and* CLARE.

BETH *is looking at the sea. She stands up, walks to the fire, and turns the fish over.*

The moonlight fades to blackout.

'A great published script makes you understand what the play is, at its heart' *Slate Magazine*

Enjoyed this book? Choose from hundreds more classic and contemporary plays from Nick Hern Books, the UK's leading independent theatre publisher.

Our full range is available to browse online now, including:

Award-winning plays from leading contemporary dramatists, including *King Charles III* by Mike Bartlett, *Anne Boleyn* by Howard Brenton, *Jerusalem* by Jez Butterworth, *A Breakfast of Eels* by Robert Holman, *Chimerica* by Lucy Kirkwood, *The Night Alive* by Conor McPherson, *The James Plays* by Rona Munro, *Nell Gwynn* by Jessica Swale, and many more…

Ground-breaking drama from the most exciting up-and-coming playwrights, including Vivienne Franzmann, James Fritz, Ella Hickson, Anna Jordan, Jack Thorne, Phoebe Waller-Bridge, Tom Wells, and many more…

Twentieth-century classics, including *Cloud Nine* by Caryl Churchill, *Death and the Maiden* by Ariel Dorfman, *Pentecost* by David Edgar, *Angels in America* by Tony Kushner, *Long Day's Journey into Night* by Eugene O'Neill, *The Deep Blue Sea* by Terence Rattigan, *Machinal* by Sophie Treadwell, and many more…

Timeless masterpieces from playwrights throughout the ages, including Anton Chekhov, Euripides, Henrik Ibsen, Federico García Lorca, Christopher Marlowe, Molière, William Shakespeare, Richard Brinsley Sheridan, Oscar Wilde, and many more…

Every playscript is a world waiting to be explored. Find yours at **www.nickhernbooks.co.uk** – you'll receive a 20% discount, plus free UK postage & packaging for orders over £30.

'Publishing plays gives permanent form to an evanescent art, and allows many more people to have some kind of experience of a play than could ever see it in the theatre' *Nick Hern, publisher*

www.nickhernbooks.co.uk

www.nickhernbooks.co.uk

facebook.com/nickhernbooks

twitter.com/nickhernbooks